The Science and Business of Drug Discovery

Edward D. Zanders

The Science and Business of Drug Discovery

Demystifying the Jargon

 Springer

Edward D. Zanders, Ph.D.
PharmaGuide Ltd
Herts, UK
ed.zanders@pharmaguide.co.uk

ISBN 978-1-4419-9901-6   e-ISBN 978-1-4419-9902-3
DOI 10.1007/978-1-4419-9902-3
Springer New York Dordrecht Heidelberg London

Library of Congress Control Number: 2011931534

Printed on acid-free paper

Springer is part of Springer Science+Business Media (www.springer.com)

To Rosie

Preface

Jargon, according to the *Concise Oxford Dictionary*, can either mean unintelligible words, or gibberish, barbarous or debased language, or else a mode of speech only familiar to a group or profession. Anyone trying to approach the drug discovery industry from the outside might have some sympathy with all of these definitions, particularly if required to deal with industry insiders on a professional basis. The language may indeed seem barbarous or gibberish, but mostly of course, it is the mode of speech familiar to the scientists, clinicians and business people who are responsible for discovering and developing new medicines. All the different professional groups that deal with the pharmaceutical industry will be exposed to the jargon at some point, because the business is highly technical. It is true that a non-scientist, for example, in a technology transfer office, will not be expected to have a detailed knowledge of a product or service being offered to a pharmaceutical company because that is normally left to technical colleagues. On the other hand, he or she should at least be able to recognize where these offerings fit into the bigger picture of drug discovery and why their clients might be interested in taking discussions to another level. In some ways, listening to scientists talking in a business meeting is the same as listening to conversations in a foreign language; just having a sense of the meaning rather than the full detail is enough to avoid feeling excluded. These general principles apply to other professions as well, such as recruiters and translators who, of course, have their own specific issues with jargon. So the need for a guide to the drug discovery industry for non-specialists is clear enough, but what form should it take?

One possibility is a training program like the *How the Drug Discovery Industry Works* course that I run in Cambridge, England. Although it is quite possible to cover the main points about the biopharmaceutical industry in a single day, only a limited amount of information about such a vast subject can be conveyed to delegates without all concerned feeling that they had just finished the New York marathon. My thoughts turned to producing something that could be hosted online. This not only has obvious attractions in terms of distribution and reach, but also runs the risk of being submerged in the vast oceans of information available in cyberspace. Since there is something quite comforting about reading the printed word on paper (or e-Reader), I resisted the temptations of the new and decided to write a book instead. The aim is to provide a thorough review of the technical and business aspects of drug discovery in a way that can be understood by a reader with little scientific knowledge while still retaining the jargon and terminology that is actually used in the pharmaceutical industry. This jargon and terminology can be daunting even to a trained scientist, so in keeping with the second part of the title *Demystifying the Jargon*, the meanings behind the key terms and phrases are explained in simple terms and placed in the relevant context.

There is no single source of information about all the activities occurring within the pharmaceutical industry, as the sheer number and variety of different processes make this impossible. These activities include such disparate topics as the biology of an infectious microbe, or the leakage of contaminating chemicals from bottle stoppers. Reference material about drug discovery and development is, of course, readily available on the Internet and elsewhere, but this is both a curse and a blessing. When approaching the subject for the first time, it is very difficult to put the information in context, to find authoritative sources and to discriminate between what is important and what is not. On the other hand, once the path through the maze of information has been mapped out, the available resources are incredibly powerful and can provide detail on almost any topic. This book focuses on the most important elements of drug development by laying out a smorgasbord of the topics that underpin discovery, clinical trials, marketing and the pharmaceuticals business, without going into excessive detail about specific points. The vast subject of biochemistry, for example, is covered in fewer than two pages, but the information given is sufficient to give the reader a sense of the essence of the subject, so they are in a position to make an informed (rather than random) search of outside sources.

In writing this book, I have drawn upon experiences gained while working in the pharmaceutical and biotechnology industries for over 20 years since leaving academia. I discuss the technical aspects of chemical and biological research from the perspective of a lab scientist and cover more commercial and strategic issues from a research management background. The great challenge is to convey this knowledge in a way that is intelligible to non-scientists and PhD level scientists alike. I hope that I have been able to achieve this by offering a choice of material that can be used or bypassed according to the reader's experience. Chapter 3, for example, covers the chemistry of small and large molecules in a very basic way and will probably be glossed over by anyone with a science background. However, even in a chapter like this, there will be material that is tailored specifically for some aspect of drug discovery and its jargon, so it will still be useful to those with a more advanced knowledge of chemistry.

Science and business move at such a rapid pace that it is sometimes difficult to keep up with events. Despite this, every effort has been made to keep this book as up to date as possible on both the technical and commercial aspects of drug development. New technical areas (or rebranded old ones), such as systems biology, translational medicine and chemical genomics, are covered in various chapters, as well as the full range of molecular entities that have pharmaceutical potential, including nucleic acids and stem cells. Attention is also given to the major structural upheavals underway in research-based pharmaceutical companies and how these create both opportunities and barriers to those who deal with the industry.

Finally, to make the demystifying process less arduous, this book intersperses factual information with lighter comments and asides gained from personal observations of the pharmaceutical industry and the behaviour of the participants in this fascinating and important world.

A Brief Note About Terminology

The names used to describe the drug discovery industry and the companies that form it are used interchangeably according to context:

Drug discovery industry/company
Pharmaceutical industry/company
Pharma industry/company
Biotechnology industry/company
Biotech industry/company
Biopharmaceutical industry/company
Big pharma
Research and development organization
R&D organization

The context should be obvious in most cases. For example, a big pharma company like Pfizer is clearly not the same as a small biotechnology company, although it does use the same technologies. The term "biopharmaceutical company" is a useful term for companies of all sizes that research and develop new medicines, so this term will be used from now on as a generic name for a drug discovery organization. Clearly, a Research and Development organization (or R&D organization) is not restricted to pharmaceuticals, but the term is still used in practice.

Herts, UK   Edward D. Zanders

Acknowledgments

I should firstly like to acknowledge my former employers and colleagues in the biopharmaceutical industry who gave me the opportunity to learn about drug discovery both as a lab scientist and as a manager. In particular, I would like to thank Dr Alan Williamson for opening the doors of large pharma to me and Drs David Bailey and Philip Dean for doing the same with the biotech world.

This book grew out of my drug discovery training courses and it would not have been possible to write it in its present form without helpful discussions and feedback from my delegates, in particular Dr Graham Wagner from Medical Research Council Technology in London. He is an enthusiastic supporter of the approaches I use to explain the complexities of drug development and I am very grateful to him for his encouragement.

I am grateful to Springer Science + Business Media, LLC for agreeing to publish this book and appreciate the editorial assistance of Renata Hutter at their New York office.

I have also had very useful discussions with pharmaceutical translators, who keep me on my toes by picking me up on my use of English. I very much appreciate the assistance of a number of pharmaceutical translators who have helped me with the courses in general and specifically Chap. 20 of the book. They are: Christine Kirkham, Maria Wyborn, Rebekah Fowler, Barbara Patel, also Shelley Nix and some members of her ITI Pharmaceuticals Special Interest Group.

I have been greatly helped by Drs Wendy Snowden and Eddie Blair, who have provided helpful comments and additions to the chapters on clinical trials and diagnostics.

A number of individuals and publishers have kindly supplied figures and data; these include Drs Francesco Falciani, Andrew Filer and Dagmar Scheel-Toellner from the University of Birmingham, Dr Philip Dean from Cambridge, Michael Eckstut from Archstone Consulting and David Campbell from IMS Health in London.

Lastly and by no means least, I am grateful as always to my wife Rosie for her support and encouragement, particularly as she has been experiencing the same ups and downs while writing her own book as I have with mine.

Contents

Part V   Professional Interactions with the Drug Discovery Industry

Chapter 1
Introduction

Most people reading this book will be doing so because they want to know how medicines are discovered and developed by the biopharmaceutical industry. They will already know that success and failure in drug development cost money and that there is currently no political or economic will among governments for all the burden of medicines development to be funded by the taxpayer. This means that private drug companies are here to stay for the foreseeable future, despite the less than flattering image that some of them may have acquired over recent years. Whatever the rights and wrongs of the many viewpoints expressed about the pharmaceutical industry, the fact remains that millions of people have first-hand evidence of the power of modern medicines to improve and even save their lives. It is beyond the scope of this book to discuss the different viewpoints in any detail. Having worked in both a major pharmaceutical company and smaller biotechnology start-ups, I can only offer the perspective of a scientist with first-hand experience of what actually goes on inside these organizations and the motivations of the people who work for them. These employees display the range of human personalities found in all walks of life, from the well adjusted, to the perhaps not quite so well adjusted. All of these people have one thing in common: they are enthusiastic about their work and the fact that they might be able to make a positive contribution to human welfare. Sometimes, this last feeling is reinforced when patients write to the company to express their appreciation for a particular medicine used to treat their illness. Despite these fundamentally positive aspects, the challenges facing the biopharmaceutical industry in image and substance are very real. These challenges, and the industry's responses, are discussed further in Chap. 17.

1.1 The Benefits of Medicines

Is it possible to measure how much use the biopharmaceutical industry has been to society? One way is to look at the increase in life expectancy at birth that has occurred over the twentieth century. Statistical data from England and Wales combined serve

E.D. Zanders, *The Science and Business of Drug Discovery: Demystifying the Jargon,*
DOI 10.1007/978-1-4419-9902-3_1, © Springer Science+Business Media, LLC 2011

as a representative example of the "developed world" (defined as Europe, North America, Japan, Australia, New Zealand and the former Russian states) (Hicks and Allen 1999). A boy born in 1901 could expect to live for 45 years and a girl for 49 years. By the end of the century, these figures are now 78 and 83 years for boys and girls respectively. Equally striking is the decrease in infant mortality, falling from 140 per thousand live births in 1900 to fewer than 10 at the end of the twentieth century.

How much of this is attributable to better medical intervention? Despite the view held by prominent medical scientists and others that medicines have made the greatest contribution to increased lifespan and decreased mortality, there is considerable debate among historians as to exactly how much of this is due to new medicines and how much is a result of improved nutrition and hygiene. There can be no doubt that the introduction of new medicines in the form of vaccines and antibiotics has contributed to a decline in mortality by controlling infectious diseases. There is, however, a clear distinction between longevity alone and quality of life. There is not much point in extending the lifespan in old age if that means having to put up with chronic disability and suffering. Without wishing to go too much further into this complex subject, it is interesting to note the work of epidemiologists who have studied the contribution of medical intervention to health outcomes. Bunker and colleagues, for example, have made an attempt to quantify these issues, although they recognize that these estimates are based on incomplete data (Bunker 2001). To summarize their results, clinical services, i.e. preventive services and therapeutic interventions, accounted for approximately 17% of the 30-year increase in life expectancy from 1900 to 1950. For the period from 1950 to the turn of the twenty-first century, they estimate that these interventions have contributed to 50% of the 7-year increase in life expectancy. As much as half of this increased medical benefit (post-1950) has been due to the reduction in deaths from heart disease or stroke (cardiovascular diseases); this has been achieved by both antihypertensive (anti-high blood pressure) drugs and cardiac surgery. The remaining 50% increase is due to improved treatments for many other conditions, none of which has individually made such an impact upon life expectancy.

> Everything in life that's any fun, as somebody wisely observed, is either immoral, illegal or fattening.

These words from the humourist P.G. Wodehouse (Wodehouse 1970) have a certain ring of truth to them; leaving out the immoral and illegal bit, this summarizes the dilemma of those with an affluent Western lifestyle who pay for it with a high incidence of chronic disease, such as obesity and diabetes. Major causes of death have changed markedly between 1880 and 1997, most noteworthy being the increase in cancer and cardiovascular disease and the significant reduction in infectious diseases. Respiratory diseases have also been reduced significantly; tuberculosis, for example, killed about 80,000 people in 1880 in England and Wales, but only 440 in 1997 (Hicks and Allen 1999). From a biopharmaceutical industry perspective, there will always be a demand for drugs to treat acute infection, but it is through managing chronic illnesses that the drug discovery industry has the greatest potential to make a positive impact upon human health and wellbeing. This has already been

Table 1.1 A list of conditions and drug types used to treat them. This is a personalized illustration of the health benefits of modern medicines

Medicinal product	Benefit
Anesthetic	General anesthesia for operations (tonsillectomy, dental abscess) local anesthesia – dentistry
Antibiotics	Control of numerous infections, including bronchitis and pleurisy
Vaccines	Freedom from polio, smallpox, diphtheria, tetanus, etc.
Antipyretics	Aspirin, paracetamol for fever and acute pain relief
NSAIDs	Anti-inflammatories for muscle strains and gout
Allopurinol	Freedom from gout
ACE inhibitors	Normalized high blood pressure
Opiates	Pain relief for slipped disk
Inhaled steroids	Control of seasonal rhinitis

Abbreviations: *NSAIDs* non-steroidal anti-inflammatory drugs, *ACE inhibitors* angiotensin-converting enzyme inhibitors

illustrated in the case of cardiovascular disease (primarily stroke), where the death rate in USA has fallen threefold between 1950 and 1996.

These statistical data, although informative, are also rather impersonal. Another way of assessing the benefit of medicines is simply to look at one's own life and ask whether it would be significantly different if the treatments were not available. I have been fortunate enough to have enjoyed reasonable health from childhood to middle age without (so far) any serious chronic illness, so the different medical treatments I have required over the years are not very remarkable (Table 1.1).

It is hard to avoid the conclusion that my chances of reaching my present age would have been slim without the vaccines and antibiotics. Furthermore, the control of blood pressure by ACE inhibitors has made it more likely that I can postpone a heart attack or stroke (still the biggest killers) for a few more years at least. Other medicines have enhanced the quality of my life rather than saved it. The anti-inflammatory and analgesic medicines have made it more bearable, as anyone who has suffered an acute attack of gout will understand, and the allopurinol has effectively eliminated this disease, and the accompanying risk of kidney stones, for as long as I take the tablets.

This, of course, is one person's luck of the draw; all of us have lost friends or relatives to cancer, and as we get older, we become more aware of the scourge of dementia. This should focus the mind on what the biopharmaceutical industry is ultimately in business for. The technical and commercial challenges are enormous, but ultimately surmountable, if past experience is anything to go by.

1.2 Economic Health

What about the contribution of the biopharmaceutical industry to economic wellbeing? The industry is mainly comprised of individual businesses that have to trade at a profit in order to support their existence through innovation and by attracting investment from the financial markets. Although its primary role should be to improve human (and animal) health,[1] the economic contribution by pharmaceutical and biotech companies to countries, organizations and individuals can be substantial. One economic indicator is a strong balance of trade in pharmaceutical products. Switzerland, for example, made over $20 billion profit in exported pharmaceuticals during 2007 (Association of the British Pharmaceutical Industry (ABPI) 2010). Other indicators are tax revenues and job creation. The following headline figures for the US economy in 2006 have been published by Archstone Consulting LLC and Professor Lawton Burns of the Wharton School, University of Pennsylvania (Archstone Consulting and Burns L 2009), and are reproduced with the kind permission of Archstone Consulting, a division of The Hackett Group, Inc.

- Jobs
  686,442 direct jobs and 3.2 million jobs
- Ripple effect
  Each direct job in the biopharmaceutical sector supported 3.7 other jobs
- Wages
  Average annual wages of $88,929
- Tax revenues
  Average of $21,858 in federal taxes compared to an average of $7,384 for employees in the rest of the economy
- Macroeconomic Impact
  $88.5 billion direct contribution to GDP, triple the average contribution from sectors in the rest of the economy. On a per-employee basis, the sector's direct contribution to GDP was 71% more than the average contribution from sectors in the rest of the economy. For every dollar that biopharmaceutical companies contributed to GDP in 2006, the ripple effect of that activity supported another $2.33 in contribution to GDP from other sectors
- Investment in R&D
  US biopharmaceutical companies invested $56.1 billion in research and development. This estimate represents an investment in US research of $65,381 per direct employee, approximately eight times the published estimates of R&D spending per employee in all manufacturing industries between 2000 and 2004

Although the US (and global) economy has undergone some major changes since 2006, the strong economic influence of the biopharmaceutical sector is still being felt. There is a feeling in scientific circles that the twenty-first century is the century of biology, just as the twentieth century was dominated by physics. This has caught the attention of governments worldwide, who consider investment in the life sciences to be critical for the future economic wellbeing of their countries.

---

[1] This book does not cover veterinary medicine and drugs, but the scientific principles are the same for humans and animals.

1.3   Third World No Longer

The Westernized "developed" economies are, by a very large margin, the largest markets for prescription medicines. It is, therefore, inevitable that any coverage of the biopharmaceutical industry will assume that its research and development activities are directed almost exclusively at these affluent nations. The problem for millions of people in the developing world is that treatments for tropical diseases such as malaria are not economical to develop and that medicines for "Western" diseases are too expensive. This situation is now changing because of economic, political and social factors, including the rise of "venture philanthropy" and new pricing models. Perhaps most significantly, rapidly growing economies (China, India and Brazil, for example) are sustaining a large number of people with Western lifestyles and the diseases to match. This may be one reason for an increased willingness on the part of multinational pharmaceutical companies to invest heavily in R&D in these countries and to offer generous pricing models for drugs that treat infectious diseases such as malaria. The area of pharmaceutical markets and commercial trends will be covered in Chaps. 16 and 17.

1.4   Why Can We Put a Man on the Moon but Still Not Cure Cancer?

The answer to this question is fundamental to understanding the technical challenges that are particular to drug discovery and the life sciences. Put simply, we do not have enough understanding of how living things operate to make precise predictions of what would happen if we perturb them with a drug. Darwinian evolution goes a long way in its explanation of biological phenomena at the population and molecular levels, but this does not really help the pharmaceutical scientist to be more predictive. In fact, evolution throws up a number of obstacles, drug resistance, for example. Physics, in contrast, is underpinned by well-established laws backed up by precise measurements that are often accurate to many decimal places. I have heard a famous physicist state that the subject is actually quite simple. I wouldn't personally go that far (think of quantum theory), but she has a point if a comparison is made with biology. If we look at how physical laws are applied, in electronics for example, the basic idea of digital information being represented by the presence or absence of electrical charge is easy enough to grasp. Combining this with materials science, we get solid state electronics combined with miniaturized power supplies to design computers, mobile phones and the like. The laws of physics create an upper limit to how far these devices can be improved, but it is still possible to say that the limits of present technology have not yet been reached and that better devices will come onto the market. We can almost guarantee that a new electronic device will operate as specified, but we simply cannot do the same for a medicine designed to treat a complex disease. A useful analogy comes in the form of two US initiatives from the second half of the twentieth century: the Apollo moon landings and the War on Cancer. President Kennedy delivered an address to Congress in 1961 that included the sentence "I believe that this nation should commit itself to achieving the goal, before this decade is out, of landing a man on the moon and returning him safely to the earth". As we know, this was achieved in 1969, through an impressive display of technical skill, project management and bravery on the part of the astronauts. The point here is that the technology was in place to be able to turn a highly ambitious proposal into an achievable objective within a relatively short period of time. Again, the laws of physics were understood and properly exploited. In signing the National Cancer Act in 1971, President Nixon expanded the remit of the National Cancer Institute and enshrined cancer research and prevention into federal law, effectively declaring a "war on cancer". Although it was then understood that the elimination of the disease would take longer to achieve than landing astronauts on the moon, it is now obvious to anyone that 40 years later, despite huge advances in cancer medicine, we are still a long way off the original goal. The blame does not lie with the skilful scientists who have made huge strides in understanding the cellular and molecular biology of cancer and the clinicians who deliver treatments based on drugs, surgery and radiation. Instead, it must lie with the sheer complexity of the disease, with its widespread genetic abnormalities and poorly understood interactions between cancer cells and the cellular environment in the rest of the body.

James Watson is in a good position to comment on the progress in understanding the basic science of cancer since he is co-discoverer of the structure of the DNA molecule. He has written a provocative, but thoughtful, article in the New York Times (Watson 2009) where he recognizes that the 1971 war on cancer has stalled despite the impressive progress that has been made in understanding the molecular details of cancer biology over the last few decades.[2] He also understands that despite the increased number of promising new drug targets for cancer, the drug development process is technically complex, very costly and should be supported in part by government agencies (such as the National Cancer Institute) and the biopharmaceutical industry.

This last sentence neatly encapsulates the themes to be covered in subsequent chapters, namely the technical complexity of drug discovery and the business models that are evolving in industry and academia to support the discovery, development and marketing of these drugs.

---

[2] Later chapters will cover the technologies (e.g. genetic engineering, DNA sequencing, cell biology and immunology) that have contributed to this knowledge.

References

Archstone Consulting and Burns L (2009) The Biopharmaceutical Sector's Impact on the U.S. Economy: Analysis at the National, State, and Local Levels. http://www.archstoneconsulting.com/biopharma.aspx. Accessed 29 Oct 2010

Association of the British Pharmaceutical Industry (ABPI) (2010). http://www.abpi.org.uk/. Accessed 29 Oct 2010

Bunker JP (2001) The role of medical care in contributing to health improvements within societies. Int J Epidemiol 30:1260–1263

Hicks J, Allen J (1999) A Century of Change: Trends in UK statistics since 1900 (2010). http://www.parliament.uk/commons/lib/research/rp99/rp99-111.pdf. Accessed 29 Oct 2010

Watson JD (2009) To fight cancer, know the enemy. New York Times (2009). http://www.nytimes.com/2009/08/06/opinion/06watson.html. Accessed 29 Oct 2009

Wodehouse PG (1970) The woman in blue. Hutchinson, London

Part I
Background to Drug Discovery and Development

Chapter 2
Introduction to Drugs and Drug Targets

Abstract This chapter lays out some formal definitions of a drug or medicine and introduces the concept of a drug target. It then describes the wide range of drug types that are being produced by the biopharmaceutical industry. These include orally available drugs, proteins, nucleic acids, vaccines and stem cells. Some background on all of these different types of molecule is provided to create a foundation for the remainder of the book.

2.1 Introduction

The main focus of this book is the discovery and development of prescription-only medicines (POMS),[1] with some description of the diagnostics being developed to support their use in the clinic. Medical devices, such as metered dose inhalers and osmotic pumps, which are important for delivering drugs to the right places in the body, are only briefly mentioned.

The terms drug and medicine are used interchangeably, although the word "drug" has the connotation of an illegal substance, such as cocaine or heroin (controlled drugs in the UK). The American Food and Drug Administration (FDA) (http://www.fda.gov/Drugs/InformationOnDrugs/ucm079436.htm#D, Accessed 31 Oct 2010) defines a drug as follows:

- A substance recognised by an official pharmacopoeia or formulary
- A substance intended for use in the diagnosis, cure, mitigation, treatment or prevention of disease
- A substance (other than food) intended to affect the structure or any function of the body
- A substance intended for use as a component of a medicine

---

[1]Once drugs have been approved for use without prescription, they become over-the-counter medicines (OTCs).

E.D. Zanders, *The Science and Business of Drug Discovery: Demystifying the Jargon*, DOI 10.1007/978-1-4419-9902-3_2, © Springer Science+Business Media, LLC 2011

Fig. 2.1 The dart board analogy of drugs binding to their target. The drugs that bind strongly and selectively to their biological targets are analogous to a dart that sticks firmly to a dart board in a high scoring position. Many drugs bind weakly to a number of targets, giving rise to both desirable and non-desirable side effects

A more scientific definition might be as follows:

A drug is an agent which modifies a drug target in order to bring about a change in the functionality of that target. Drugs may reduce or accelerate target activity.

A drug target can be thought of as a dart board, where the drug molecules are the darts (Fig. 2.1). Strong, accurate binding of a drug to its target is important for successful activity; by analogy, hitting a high scoring section of the dart board (like the bull's eye in the middle) helps to win the game. The real nature of drug targets and how they are discovered will be covered in the following chapters.

2.1.1 Different Types of Medicines

Many people think of drugs as medicines that are swallowed in the form of pills or capsules. I generally get this answer when I ask my course delegates what comes to their minds when they hear the word drug (leaving aside illegal products). The biopharmaceutical industry was built upon the discovery of orally active medicines and this is still the preferred outcome for any drug development programme. The medicines can be self-administered in a regular way (once or twice daily), with consistent dosing and high patient compliance. Other routes of administration, such as injection, inhalation or topical application, are used to ensure that certain drugs have a chance to enter the circulation without being broken down in the stomach or liver, but these are simply not as straightforward as oral delivery. While working on drug discovery programmes for asthma, I was told that the ideal drug for a world-wide market would be delivered orally, partly as the result of cultural issues in some countries regarding the use of inhalers. Inhaled drugs are actually very effective in treating asthma, but the point was made that we should always try to develop a pill for this disease if at all possible; indeed this was the desired objective for all our research programmes.

Although orally active small molecules are preferred for new medicines, they are far from the only products being developed by the biopharmaceutical industry, as will become clear in this chapter.

2.1.1.1 Small Molecules

These drugs are usually taken by mouth, although other routes of administration may be required. The chemical definition of a small molecule will be covered in Chap. 3, but drugs of this type are small enough to cross the alimentary canal (stomach and duodenum) after being swallowed. They can then enter the bloodstream and pass into the liver. They are then distributed throughout the body via the circulatory system (Fig. 2.2). The target for the drug is associated with the cells that make up the organs and tissues of the body.

The oral (bio)availability of small molecules that cross the stomach into the liver can be reduced dramatically by a metabolism, which can cause their rapid break-down and excretion from the body; in addition, drugs can strongly bind to proteins in the blood, thereby reducing the amount available to interact with the drug target. Both metabolism and protein binding contribute to the pharmacokinetic properties of a drug, an important area that is covered in detail in Chap. 11.

If small-molecule drugs are adversely affected by this first-pass metabolism, alternative routes of administration ensure that the drug passes directly into the general circulation. Apart from injection, drugs can be delivered transdermally or subcutaneously (i.e. through, or under the skin respectively). Sometimes drugs are administered rectally in the form of suppositories, particularly if the intended target is associated with gastrointestinal disease. Another route of administration is under the tongue (sublingually), where the drug can reach its target without first passing through the liver. An example of this is the sublingual delivery of nitroglycerine, an important heart medicine in addition to being a high explosive.

2.1.1.2 Proteins

The word protein was first used in 1838 by the Dutch chemist Gerhard Mulder as a result of his studies on biological products such as silk, blood, egg white and gelatin (Vickery 1950). Although not aware of the exact chemical nature of these materials, he reasoned that each source harboured a common "radical" in combination with phosphorus and sulphur. Mulder named this radical "pro-tein" after the Greek word *proteios* meaning "of the first rank or position".

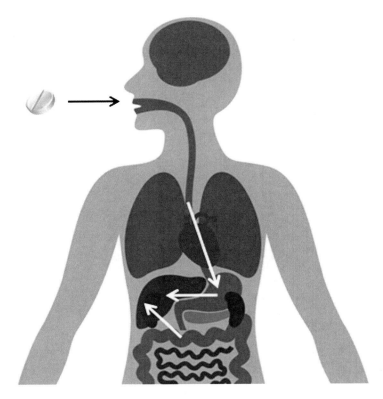

Fig. 2.2 Passage of orally available drugs into the body. After swallowing a tablet or capsule, the drug is dissolved in the stomach fluids and is passed through the intestines where it is absorbed by the blood vessels entering the liver (hepatic portal system). After the drug has been exposed to metabolic systems in the liver, it passes into the general circulation. Once it reaches the areas where the drug target is expressed, it binds to it and exerts its biological effect

This seems entirely appropriate, as it reflects the central importance of these large molecules in the function of living organisms. From a pharmaceutical perspective, these molecules are both targets for drugs and drugs in their own right. The chemical nature of proteins and their function as drug targets will be extensively covered later in this book.

The first protein drug to be injected into a patient (if we discount vaccines), was insulin. This was purified in 1922 by Banting and Best in Canada who used it to treat a 12-year-old boy with diabetes. After overcoming some initial problems with severe irritation caused by impure samples, the scientists managed to treat the diabetes successfully for several years until the premature death of the patient in a motorcycle accident (Sneader 2005) The success of this, and subsequent trials, led to the introduction of pure forms of porcine insulin (from pigs) and subsequently, human insulin produced using recombinant DNA technology.

Insulin itself is part of a group of biological molecules called peptide hormones, small proteins that are secreted into the circulation by specialised organs such as the pancreas or pituitary gland. Because these hormones are small and relatively easy to produce in natural or synthetic form, they have been investigated extensively by the biopharmaceutical industry. Examples include somatotropin (growth hormone) for stunted growth in children and gonadotrophin used to induce ovulation.

Although these peptide and protein drugs have been marketed for many years, there was, until recently, little incentive to develop a protein if a small molecule could be found to do the same thing. However, the explosion of information about drug targets brought about by advances in cell and molecular biology in the 1990s led to the realisation that not all of them could be influenced by small molecules. Some very significant targets in major diseases such as cancer and arthritis can only be affected with large protein molecules, so the biopharmaceutical industry has been forced to take them seriously as drugs. Modern protein drugs fall into the following categories:

- Hormone-like molecules, including those that stimulate the growth of blood cells after cancer therapy
- Protein decoys that mimic the drug target to prevent the natural protein from binding to the target, or that neutralised the drug target by removing it from the circulation
- Antibodies, normally produced by the immune system to fight infection, but which are instead directed against specific drug targets

The size range of protein drugs is quite wide: insulin, for example is 25 times smaller than a full-size antibody. What they have in common, however, is a lack of oral availability, since they are both too large to pass through the stomach and are broken down by the digestive system. This means that they must be delivered into the circulation by injection or other means. Currently, over 12 billion injections are made annually, a figure that is likely to increase substantially as new drugs based on proteins and other large molecules are introduced to the marketplace. Much effort is being expended by the medical devices industry to find effective means of delivery that can be performed without either physical or psychological discomfort to the patient. Devices such as autoinjectors have made subcutaneous injection (*sub cut*) a fairly straightforward procedure for self injection, but attention is currently being focused on needle-free devices. These use high pressures to drive the protein through the skin; although this can cause more bruising than with using needles, the technology to improve this situation is being advanced all the time (Aroroa et al. 2007). Other delivery methods for proteins are being investigated, including transdermal patches, implants, intraocular administration, inhalation and even oral delivery, if the protein is small enough, using special carrier molecules.

2.1.1.3   Nucleic Acids

Genes lie at the heart of biology in both health and disease. Through a digital code based on four "letters" used in groups of three, each gene specifies a protein with a distinct function in the cell, or in biological fluids such as blood. The path to identifying the chemical nature of the gene has been a long one, starting in 1869 with Miescher's isolation of nuclein from the pus in the bandages of soldiers fighting in the Crimean War. The name nuclein was later changed to nucleic acid and less than 100 years later, the double helix structure of deoxyribonucleic acid, or DNA, was announced by Watson and Crick in Cambridge. I regularly pass through the unassuming site where they did this work and look at the blue commemorative plaque on the Eagle pub where Francis Crick announced to the (apparently underwhelmed) drinkers that they had "discovered the secret of life". The structure led to an immediate realisation of how genetic information could be passed from cell to cell through the generations, an essential prerequisite for a living organism.

DNA is one member of the family of nucleic acids, large molecules with structures that can pair with each other in a highly specific manner. This phenomenon, called hybridization, is essential for the natural function of nucleic acids, and it can also be exploited in a wide variety of laboratory investigations. Furthermore, hybridization can be exploited to target the activity of specific genes and, therefore, has potential use in drug development. For example, if a gene carried by a virus is silenced by a drug, the virus may be unable to survive in the cell that it has infected and will, therefore, die. Alternatively, a cancer cell that is growing uncontrollably because a gene is permanently stuck in the "on" position could be stopped by arresting its expression in a similar way. Drugs of this type are at an early stage of development and are based on ribonucleic acid (RNA). This versatile molecule is essential for transferring the genetic code from DNA and translating it into a specific protein. From more recent work, it appears that RNA is also closely involved in the regulation of genes, i.e. the process of switching them on or off at defined times and locations within the living cell. This has implications for diseases such as cancer, where many genes are deregulated, leading to uncontrolled cell growth.

Figure 2.3 gives a simple illustration of the relationship between DNA, RNA and protein and shows the point where RNA-based drugs stop the production of specific proteins by silencing the expression of the gene coding for that protein.

Some terminology

The four letters ACGT that make up DNA (in RNA, T is replaced by U) are small molecules from the nucleotide family. These can be added together in the laboratory to form chains of different lengths. Short chains are oligonucleotides (*oligo*, few) and longer ones are polynucleotides (*poly*, many). The length of the chain of any nucleic acid is measured in bases or base pairs (Bps) depending on whether the chains are single or paired (single stranded or double stranded). The order of letters in any of these chains is called the sequence.

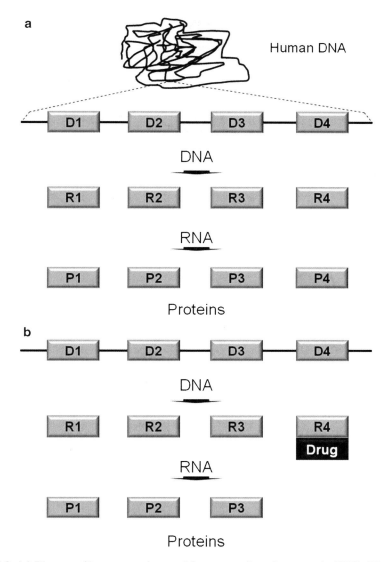

Fig. 2.3 (**a**) Diagram of human genetic material represented as a long strand of DNA. The strand (in fact, a double helix) contains thousands of stretches of DNA encoding the genes that are passed from parents to offspring. Four genes D1–D4 are shown plus the messenger RNA (mRNA) copies (R1–R4) of those genes. The mRNA is translated into proteins (P1–P4), which are the building materials of human cells, allowing them to function. (**b**) The same array of DNA, RNA and protein as in (**a**), but with the addition of a nucleic acid drug that binds to a specific mRNA (R4) and stops the production of protein P4 while leaving the remainder untouched

What follows is a brief summary of the main types of nucleic acid drugs with pharmaceutical potential.

Antisense DNA

This technology was developed in the 1980s as a tool to silence genes in cells isolated in the laboratory. Antisense molecules are modified oligonucleotides (about 25 bases) that bind to a specific gene sequence copied in the form of an RNA molecule. Once bound, this sequence signals the cell to break down the RNA at that point and thus stop the production of the protein specified by that gene. Alternatively,

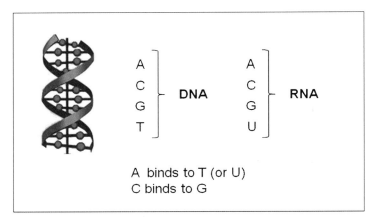

Natural double-stranded DNA

Sense	-ACGTTTTAACGTGCA-
Antisense	-TGCAAAATTGCACGT-

RNA with synthetic antisense oligonucleotide

Sense	-ACGUUUUAACGUGCA-
Antisense	-TGCAAAATTGCACGT-

Fig. 2.4 Sense and antisense in DNA sequences. Nucleic acids (DNA and RNA) are large molecules built up from four chemical building blocks (nucleotides) written as A, C, G and T (or U in RNA). Each strand of a DNA double helix is a linear string of nucleotides written out as in the figure. The sequence of the "sense" strand is retained in the mRNA used to code for protein, while the "antisense" strand is complementary to the sense strand. This is because A only hybridises to T (or U) and C only to G. An antisense drug molecule is based on a specific antisense sequence as it will select its complementary sense sequence out of millions of others

the cellular process of creating protein from the mRNA is physically blocked by the antisense/mRNA hybrid structure. Antisense molecules are illustrated in Fig. 2.4.

Antisense DNA has had a checkered history for technical reasons, and like all nucleic acid-based therapeutics, has to be introduced into living cells via the parenteral route. There are, however, some promising clinical candidates based on this technology. Most research has been directed towards virus infections and oncology, with the Isis Pharmaceuticals product fomivirsen actually in the clinic for CMV retinitis. This, however, is a highly specialised case in which the drug is injected directly into the eye in order to inhibit the replication of the CMV that provokes eye inflammation. Another Isis Pharmaceuticals product is the antisense molecule mipomersen; this lowers cholesterol in patients by reducing the levels of a key protein involved in the production of the so-called bad cholesterol (Akdim et al. 2010). Late stage clinical trials with patients who do not respond to standard cholesterol-lowering drugs have shown very promising results, to the extent that Genzyme Corporation has licenced the product from its inventor for further development and marketing.

Peptide nucleic acids (PNA) are antisense molecules which are part protein and part nucleic acid. This combination gives them the same gene-targeting effects as antisense nucleic acids, but makes them much more resistant to breakdown in the blood. They also have the unique ability to interact directly with DNA, unlike the other nucleic acid drugs which only interact with RNA. Despite these attractive properties, interest in PNAs appears to be because of their diagnostic potential rather than their use as therapeutic drugs.

Small Interfering RNA

Despite the advances with antisense drugs described above, it has proven very difficult to find molecules that will consistently target the gene of interest. A newer technology, "small interfering RNA" (siRNA), has emerged recently that appears to be more consistent and reliable than antisense. The phenomenon of RNA interference was demonstrated by Fire and Mello in animal cells in the late 1990s and led to its rapid adoption by the biomedical research community. In fact, the two scientists received the Nobel Prize for Physiology or Medicine in 2006, which is a remarkably short time after their initial discoveries. siRNA is used in the same way as antisense and there are similarities between the two. For example, both types of nucleic acid force the breakdown of RNA specific for the gene of interest, have to be chemically modified to improve resistance to metabolism and must be introduced parenterally. The difference lies in the fact that siRNA is introduced as a double-stranded, rather than single-stranded oligonucleotide and is processed by the cell in a different way to that of antisense molecules. As a result of these differences, siRNA is more efficient in targeting specific genes and is being used worldwide in basic research and drug development. The biotech company Alnylam (in partnership with Cubist) has conducted early proof of principle trials with an inhaled siRNA drug designed to inhibit the RSV that infects patients who have received lung transplants. The results, although preliminary, are promising enough to support further clinical development of this novel type of drug (Zamora et al. 2010).

Micro RNAs

siRNAs either occur naturally in the viruses that infect cells, or are produced in the laboratory as research tools or drugs. By contrast, another class of small RNAs is produced by the cells themselves. These microRNAs (miRNAs) were discovered only in 2001, but have caught the attention of scientists because of their ability to regulate the expression of a large variety of genes in the body and through being implicated in a number of diseases, including cancer and infection. For example, when the hepatitis C virus enters the liver, miRNA 122 is produced by the infected cells and stimulates the production of more viruses. An inhibitor of this miRNA, itself a modified RNA molecule, has been shown to suppress the growth of the virus, so it could offer a new way of treating patients infected with hepatitis C (Lanford et al. 2010). It is sobering to reflect upon all the years that scientists, including myself, have concentrated on the larger RNA involved in producing proteins and in the process have literally thrown these smaller molecules down the sink without realising their importance.

Ribozymes

Although all the RNA-based drugs covered so far have their individual characteristics, they have in common the ability to bind to target RNA molecules to create a double-stranded RNA. This process then triggers the cell to break down the RNA into fragments using enzymes.[2] Ribozymes are also made of RNA, but they are unique in that they themselves are enzymes and can be tailored to destroy specific genes or repair gene sequences that are defective. A small number of early clinical programmes have been instigated using ribozymes for cancer or viral infection, but these appear to have stalled, possibly for drug delivery reasons or the increasing attractions of siRNA.

Aptamers

So far we have considered nucleic acid-based drugs that bind to other nucleic acids such as RNA. Aptamers (Latin, *aptus*, to fit) are different in that they are designed to bind to protein targets just like small-molecule and protein drugs. The particular chemical nature of nucleic acids makes them ideally suited for this purpose. Aptamers are produced in the laboratory as a mixture of trillions of different molecules, only a few of which will strongly bind to the drug target and prevent it from working. There are a number of aptamer drugs in clinical development, including one on the market for treating age-related macular degeneration (Centerwatch FDA approved drugs 2011). This drug pegaptanib, marketed as Macugen® by Pfizer,

---

[2]Most enzymes are proteins that enhance biochemical reactions in the body. These will be discussed later in the book.

works by binding to VEGF, a protein responsible for the abnormal growth of blood vessels in the eye; it is the first of possibly many aptamer drugs that may find clinical use in the future.

Zinc-Finger Nucleases

These are molecules that are designed to recognise specific DNA sequences in double-stranded DNA and to then change the DNA to enhance the activity of a gene, inhibit it, or change it through mutation. The zinc-finger nuclease (ZFN) is part protein and part polynucleotide. The "zinc finger" is a finger-like structure adopted by the protein component when modified by the addition of zinc atoms. ZFNs are being developed by the Californian company Sangamo Biosciences Inc for a number of diseases; a treatment for diabetic neuropathy based on this technology is currently undergoing clinical trials (Sangamo 2010).

Off-Target Effects

All the above drugs are designed to bind to and inhibit the expression of specific genes, either at the level of RNA or directly on the DNA itself. The nature of the nucleic acid molecule, and the way it binds (hybridises) to its target sequence, means that sometimes the binding may occur to other regions, thereby giving rise to the so-called off-target effects. These can be reduced by careful design of the drug, as can another problem, immunogenicity. This term relates to the ability of a molecule to stimulate the immune system, a clearly undesirable feature of a drug that is going to be administered to humans. The main problem with nucleic acid-based drugs, however, is their delivery into target tissues, something that is of concern to many biopharmaceutical companies.

2.1.1.4 Gene Therapy

The nucleic acid-based drugs in the previous section are all designed to inhibit the function of genes involved in diseases such as cancer or AIDS. Gene therapy, on the contrary, involves the replacement of faulty genes with normal copies in people who have inherited particular conditions, such as haemophilia or cystic fibrosis. These are distressing genetic diseases that result from mutations (Latin *mutare*, to change) in a single gene. The number of people suffering from single gene defects, although significant, is much smaller than the number with major chronic diseases such as neurodegeneration or cancer. Therefore, in order to make gene therapy a mainstream objective of the biopharmaceutical industry, the technology must be applied to a broader range of diseases. One example is type I diabetes, where insulin-producing cells have been destroyed by the patient's own immune system. Gene therapy using a gene coding for insulin would allow the patient to make the protein *in situ* and, therefore, cure the diabetes. This approach works in animals, but trials in humans will be some way off.

The challenges for gene therapy are considerable, but the potential rewards are great enough for companies to persevere with its development. The DNA used for gene therapy is a synthetic molecule that can be designed to encode any desired protein; this is relatively straightforward, but problems arise when attempting to efficiently deliver DNA into the body. If not enough DNA gets into the cells, there will not be enough protein expressed to compensate for the faulty version produced by the patient. Even if the DNA is effective upon first injection, if it is cleared too rapidly, it will not be possible to maintain levels of the new gene to keep the disease at bay. This problem has proven to be the bane of a number of gene therapy trials.

To make gene therapy work, the DNA has to be transported in a "vector" (Latin, one who conveys or carries). This is itself a DNA molecule, often based on the DNA found in viruses. This is because viruses have to infect human (or other) cells to make proteins from their own genes because they do not have the machinery to do this independently. The components of the virus that are used to infect cells can be purified in the laboratory and reassembled into a new virus containing the gene therapy DNA. This virus is then introduced into patients. In the process of creating the modified virus, any elements that might cause disease are removed. Sometimes, for example the components of the HIV are used, which is testimony to the confidence that scientists have in applying this technology to human subjects. Despite the efficiency of viral vectors, it has not been possible to completely eliminate their ability to provoke an immune response in the patient. This response may be a mild inflammation, or a fatal reaction (in a small number of cases), which has cast a shadow over the whole field of gene therapy. Another major problem arises when the viral nucleic acid literally integrates with the DNA in the patient's own cells and causes cancer. This happens because the new DNA switches on genes that are normally silenced in order to avoid inappropriate cell division. These problems have prompted research into alternatives to delivery vectors based on viruses, with a number of promising avenues being explored by academic and industrial researchers.

To summarise the current state of gene therapy, several clinical trials have demonstrated that the technology works where other treatments fail or are non-existent. For example, several children with immune deficiency caused by a single gene defect have been cured using gene therapy. Direct administration of genes into the eye has been shown to partially restore sight in patients with a particular form of congenital blindness. There are now over 1,000 clinical trials for gene therapy listed by the FDA, and many of these are being applied to cancer and other chronic diseases, rather than just rare conditions. This means that confidence in gene therapy is growing, although it will be some time (if ever) before it becomes a truly mainstream pharmaceutical product.

2.1.1.5 Vaccines

Although vaccination has been performed for hundreds of years, it only came to the world's attention in 1796 after Jenner's pioneering work on smallpox. He coined the word "vaccine" (Latin *vacca*, for cow), because of the cowpox virus he used to immunise his subjects. Since then, vaccination has, along with better hygiene and sanitation, become arguably the single most effective public health measure in human history. Recent experiences with HIV, SARS and new strains of the influenza virus have brought home the fact that infectious diseases are still capable of catching us off guard, and sadly, we are also living with the threat of bioterrorism. Of course, it must not be forgotten that the developing world still has to live with the scourge of tuberculosis, leprosy, malaria and other tropical diseases.

Like other medicinal products, vaccines are produced by the biopharmaceutical industry and have to meet the same standards of safety and efficacy as any other drug. All medicines carry some risk, which has to be balanced against the benefits provided. There are particular issues with vaccines however, since most are designed to provide protection against future infections (prophylactic vaccination) and are, therefore, administered to healthy people who have to take the risk (admittedly small) of unwanted side effects due to immune system activation. This, along with the relatively low financial returns of vaccines, has discouraged the biopharmaceutical industry from working in this area of drug development. When I joined the industry in the 1980s, working in an immunology department, there was absolutely no interest in developing vaccines. Ironically, I had previously worked in a tumour immunology unit whose long-term aim was to discover how the body uses the immune system to fight cancer. Armed with this knowledge, it might then be possible to vaccinate against the disease. Indeed a cancer vaccine has recently been introduced for the human papilloma virus (HPV) that causes cervical cancer and is helping to revive industry enthusiasm for vaccines in general. However, this vaccine is still based on the conventional principle of immunising healthy individuals prophylactically to prevent possible infection by the virus in the future. The point of the tumour immunology approach is that it should be possible to develop a therapeutic vaccine to treat the disease itself once it has become established. Attempts at producing true cancer vaccines along these lines have been made for many years now, and the work is slowly producing encouraging results. Vaccines are also being developed for other chronic diseases such as Alzheimer's, which, like many cancers, has no obvious association with infection.

These developments, along with new sources of funding for research into infectious diseases, have brought vaccines back into mainstream research into biological therapies. From a commercial perspective, the old mantra, which has already been well demonstrated with protein-based drugs, still applies: "nothing succeeds like success".

How Vaccines Work

The immune system has evolved to provide protection against invading organisms and is divided into two main areas: innate and adaptive. The innate system is the first line of defence against attack by bacteria and viruses, but it has no memory of the encounter with these agents. The adaptive system is brought into play after the initial infection and reinforces the attack that, if successful, will clear the infection from the body. This is where antibodies and white blood cells called lymphocytes appear on the scene. The adaptive system retains a memory of the encounter so that a further infection will be cleared rapidly and efficiently, possibly some decades later. Until quite recently, the two arms of the immune system were seen to be separate entities; from an immunology researcher's point of view, the adaptive system was the most challenging and interesting and the innate system was frankly considered a bit boring. Times have changed, and the field has been energised with new discoveries about how the innate system recognises patterns of molecules on invading bacteria and viruses and how closely it is integrated with the adaptive system. This is highly relevant to vaccine research, since the adaptive arm is responsible for creating an "immunological memory" to be activated upon later encounter with the infectious agent. Vaccines are made up of two components: an antigen combined with an adjuvant. Antigen is a general term for the agent that provokes an immune response. The adjuvant literally acts as a helper to enhance that response. This is particularly useful when then antigen alone may not be very immunogenic (i.e. does not provoke a strong immune response) and it also means that the amount of antigen per dose of vaccine can be kept to a minimum. Adjuvants work in part through stimulating the innate immune system, which in turn enhances the adaptive arm. This means that new findings about this aspect of immunology are being translated into a new generation of adjuvants with superior performance to existing molecules.

Types of Vaccine

When microorganisms, such as a bacteria or viruses, infect the body, antibodies and lymphocyte responses are produced naturally to allow clearance of the invader. Vaccines fool the body into thinking that it is being invaded because they mimic the ability of the microorganism to stimulate an immune response, but without causing disease at the same time. In practice, the vaccine may be anything from a live attenuated virus, to fragments of viral or bacterial DNA.

- Live attenuated virus
  This vaccine uses the organism that it is designed to protect against to create immunity without triggering disease. This means that the organism in the vaccine is diluted or attenuated. Recipients of these vaccines are inoculated, rather than immunised. Examples include measles and chickenpox vaccines

- Inactivated vaccines
  These are whole organisms that have been rendered uninfectious by treatment with heat or chemicals. The term "inactivated" applies to vaccines derived from viruses, while those from bacteria are known as "killed". Because these products are less potent than live vaccines, more has to be administered in each dose. Polio and hepatitis A vaccines are commonly used examples of this type, where the virus has been inactivated by formalin (formaldehyde) treatment

- Toxoid vaccines
  Certain bacteria, such as tetanus, diphtheria and cholera bacteria, produce proteins called toxins that are responsible for the characteristic symptoms of these diseases.

These proteins are purified from bacteria grown in culture and converted by formalin treatment into "toxoids" that are devoid of harmful activity. These toxoids are used as vaccines in combination with adjuvants

- Subunit vaccines
  Bacteria and viruses are very different in appearance and life cycle, yet both are covered with proteins that assist in gaining entry into human cells. Influenza viruses are a good example of this as they express two proteins, haemagglutinin (H) and neuraminidase (N), which can be purified and used in combination as a vaccine. Antibodies generated against each of these proteins prevent the virus from entering the cells of the respiratory tract. Subunit vaccines can be purified from whole viruses or bacteria, or else produced in cell cultures using recombinant DNA technology. Some bacterial vaccines are based on surface carbohydrates (sugar-like molecules) instead of proteins

- DNA vaccines
  Whether the vaccine is based on whole organisms or subunits, the cost of manufacture and safety testing can be considerable. Stability of the product where there is no refrigeration can also be a problem. DNA vaccines offer a possible solution to this because they are relatively simple to produce and are quite stable. The idea for this approach to immunisation came from gene therapy, where it was noticed that DNA could provoke an immune response, which could be exploited in vaccination, rather than just be dismissed as a side effect. DNA vaccination requires the same kind of vector as that used for gene therapy and is introduced into the body by injection or the lungs by aerosol. If the DNA is designed to code for a protein normally found in a subunit vaccine, it will produce it directly in the human tissues and provoke an immune response. DNA vaccines are being evaluated in early clinical trials for, amongst other things, influenza H5N1 (Smith et al. 2010) and cancer.

2.1.1.6 Cell Therapy

It may seem surprising that whole cells are being considered as pharmaceutical products to be sold in the same way as small molecules. This is because of the excitement generated over stem cells and the possibility of repairing damaged tissue by injecting these cells into patients (regenerative medicine). The human body contains roughly 200 different cell types (see Chap. 5) and yet originates from only one cell, i.e. the fertilised egg (ovum). This means that there must be some process operating during development of the embryo (and later the adult) that generates these different cell types. This process relies on pluripotent stem cells in the embryo which turn into different cell types, such as nerve, muscle and blood, during the course of development. Adult stem cells replenish mature cells that have a limited lifespan, such as blood and skin cells, and are present throughout life. Since many Western diseases can result in permanent tissue damage, any therapeutic approach that reverses or repairs the damage is going to be of interest to the biopharmaceutical industry, hence their involvement in stem cell research. In fact, stem cell therapy is not new; bone marrow transplantation to restore normal blood has been performed for decades. In the case of leukaemia, for example, blood stem cells are purified from the blood or bone marrow of the patient (autologous), or a normal donor (allogeneic), and can be stored outside the body, during which time radio- and chemotherapy are used to remove all blood cells, including the leukaemia. The non-cancerous stem cells are then reintroduced into the body, where they divide and repopulate the blood. Although these procedures are hazardous and often used as a last resort, they do open up the possibility of using gene therapy to introduce specific genes into the blood of patients by modifying the stem cells used in transplantation. Clinical trials are underway that use this approach for a number of blood diseases, including AIDS.

The transplantation described above uses adult stem cells, but the dream of restoring damaged tissue such as heart, muscle or brain will require stem cells derived from embryos, or adult cells produced by complex manipulation in the laboratory. Pfizer has embarked upon a collaboration aimed at using stem cells to repair the damage to eyes caused by macular degeneration, a major cause of blindness in the elderly people and a large market for drug therapy (see also aptamers, this chapter). Other companies will be watching with interest how a major player like Pfizer can develop a business model for selling this type of medicine.

Summary of Key Points

Drugs are agents that bind to a target to increase or slow down the activity of the latter.

Most drugs are small molecules that can be taken by mouth, but many other products are being introduced to the clinic. These are as follows:

Proteins
Nucleic acids
Gene therapy vectors
Vaccines
Stem cells

References

Akdim F et al (2010) Effect of mipomersen, an apolipoprotein B synthesis inhibitor, on low-density lipoprotein cholesterol in patients with familial hypercholesterolemia. Am J Cardiol 105:1413–1419

Aroroa A et al (2007) Needle-free delivery of macromolecules across the skin by nanoliter-volume pulsed microjets. Proc Nat Acad Sci USA 104:4255–4260

Centerwatch FDA approved drugs (2011). http://www.centerwatch.com/drug-information/fda-approvals/drug-details.aspx?DrugID=872. Accessed 11 Jan 2011

Lanford RE et al (2010) Therapeutic silencing of microRNA-122 in primates with chronic hepatitis C virus infection. Science 327:198–201

Sangamo (2010). http://www.sangamo.com. Accessed 31 Oct 2010

Smith LR et al (2010) Phase 1 clinical trials of the safety and immunogenicity of adjuvanted plasmid DNA vaccines encoding influenza A virus H5 hemagglutinin. Vaccine 28:2565–2572

Sneader W (2005) Drug discovery a history. Wiley, Chichester

Vickery HB (1950) The origin of the word protein. Yale J Biol Med 22:387–393

Zamora MR et al (2010) RNA interference therapy in lung transplant patients infected with respiratory syncytial virus. Am J Respir Crit Care Med. doi:10.1164/rccm.201003-0422OC

Chapter 3
Background to Chemistry of Small and Large Molecules

Abstract What are small and large drug molecules exactly? How do they physically interact with their protein targets to activate or inhibit them? How are drugs named?

The answers to these questions could take up several books and degree level courses in chemistry and biochemistry. Fortunately, the points that a non-specialist really needs to know can be simplified without losing their essential meaning. The aim of this chapter is to give readers a guide to the fundamental chemistry of drugs and their targets. Those who are familiar with elementary chemistry will be tempted to skip this chapter altogether. Although this is understandable, they need to be aware that some of the material on drug size and nomenclature may not have been covered in school or college chemistry.

3.1 Introduction

"Better Living through Chemistry". This slogan, based on a DuPont Corporation strap line, was sometimes seen on T-shirts in the latter part of the twentieth century. It can, of course, be taken either at face value or as a piece of irony, if you feel that chemicals have done more harm to humanity than good. Since this is a book on drug discovery, it can be safely assumed that the author believes that on balance, chemistry has proven to be a benefit to humanity rather than the opposite.[1]

Chemistry is defined as "the science of substances: their structure, their properties, and the reactions that change them into other substances". This 1947 definition by the double Nobel Laureate Linus Pauling is a useful starting point. Experimental chemistry has been performed for thousands of years and was developed in the Arab world (the word chemist is of Arabic origin) before being adopted in Europe and developed into a highly sophisticated branch of science.

---

[1] The United Nations has declared 2011 to be the International Year of Chemistry.

E.D. Zanders, *The Science and Business of Drug Discovery: Demystifying the Jargon*, DOI 10.1007/978-1-4419-9902-3_3, © Springer Science+Business Media, LLC 2011

3.1.1 Elements, Atoms, Molecules and Compounds

> Hydrogen is a colorless odorless gas that given enough time turns into people

This quote by the late cosmologist Edward Harrison (Wiley 1995) sums up the situation quite well. Hydrogen is the simplest element that formed soon after the "Big Bang" that brought the universe into existence 13.7 billion years ago. An element is a pure chemical substance made up of one kind of atom. During the evolution of the universe, hydrogen was converted in the process of nuclear fusion to another element, helium. Further nuclear reactions created all of the elements that exist in stable forms on earth, for example iron, carbon and oxygen. These elements were originally blown out of stars in giant supernova explosions, thereby producing clouds of material that ultimately coalesced into planets. Since we too are made up of these elements, this means, rather romantically, that we are ultimately derived from stardust.

There are 94 stable elements found on earth and another 24 produced artificially under extreme conditions, such as those created by nuclear reactions. Of all these, only a few are used by living organisms (and by drug discovery chemists).

The famous Periodic Table of the Elements was compiled in 1869 by the Russian chemist Dimitri Mendeleev as a means of classifying the elements into groups with shared properties (Fig. 3.1). The names of the elements are abbreviated to one or two letters. For example, hydrogen is H and beryllium is Be. Many abbreviations betray the original name of the substance in antiquity. Potassium, for example is written as K for *kalium* and sodium, Na for *natrium*.

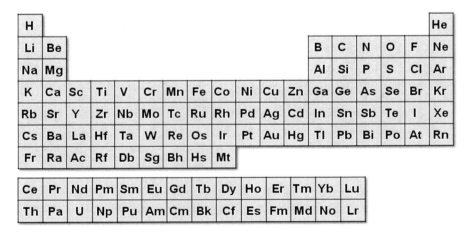

Fig. 3.1 The Periodic table of the elements. A simplified representation of the famous table compiled by Mendeleev which shows just the abbreviation used for each element. Elements are grouped together in the table according to their chemical properties. The section below the main table represents the so-called lanthanide and actinide group of elements, none of which are naturally occurring in living organisms

3.1.1.1 Atoms and Molecules

Each element is made up of the basic building block of matter, the atom. There are a number of ways of envisaging what an atom really is, depending on the depth of understanding required for a particular scientific problem. For the purposes of this very basic introduction, we can think of the atom as a billiard ball without any internal structure.

Molecules are combinations of atoms ranging from two, to almost any number. The atoms may be part of the same element, or exist as combinations of different elements. Examples of elements that exist as atoms or molecules are shown in Fig. 3.2.

3.1.1.2 Compounds

Compounds consist of atoms of two or more different elements bound together. They have properties that are different from their component elements. Figure 3.3 shows the example of the simple compound water, made up of the elements hydrogen and oxygen. Water is a liquid at room temperature and its properties are clearly different from that of the gases hydrogen and oxygen.

The number of compounds that can theoretically be produced by the combination of the main elements found in nature (carbon, oxygen, etc.) is almost infinite (see Chap. 7). In drug discovery, the word "compound" is often used to describe a small molecule drug, for example

this compound is effective for treating diabetes.

Alternatively, the word "molecule" is used, to give

this molecule is effective for treating diabetes.

Strictly speaking, a molecule could be an element and not a compound (e.g. nitrogen in Fig. 3.2), but this is unlikely to be the case with drug compounds as they are almost always built from at least three different elements.

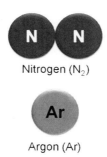

Nitrogen (N_2)

Argon (Ar)

Fig. 3.2 Simple representation of elements as atoms or molecules (association of more than one atom). Two elements nitrogen and argon are shown here. Under the conditions of atmospheric pressure and temperature found on earth, nitrogen is a molecule N_2 consisting of two atoms, with argon being just a single atom

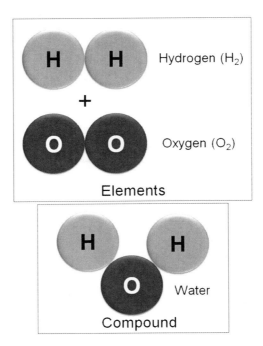

Fig. 3.3 Elements combine in chemical reactions to produce compounds with quite different physical and chemical properties. This example is an illustration of water being produced by the reaction of hydrogen with oxygen. Note that since both hydrogen and oxygen are made up of two atoms, the numbers here do not add up; the chemical reaction is really $2H_2 + O_2 = 2H_2O$. More detail about basic chemical reactions can be found in any chemistry textbook or online educational resource

3.1.1.3   Simple Compounds and Molecular Weights

The "small" in small molecules (and "large" in large ones) refers to their "molecular weights". This is explained as follows: a simple molecule such as ethanol (ethyl alcohol, or just alcohol) is a compound made up of two carbons, six hydrogens and a single oxygen atom. Each element, from hydrogen (the lightest) onwards, has a value called the atomic weight, which is normally written underneath the symbol as it appears in the Periodic Table. The weights are based on a system in which hydrogen has a value of 1, carbon 12, oxygen 16 and so on. The atomic weights can be added together to produce the molecular weight. In the case of ethanol, the molecular weight (MW) is 46 (Fig. 3.4).

Molecular weights are often abbreviated as MW and are expressed as units called daltons, after the English chemist who devised the system in the early 1800s.

Even though ethanol has drug-like properties, its molecular weight is quite modest. Most small molecule drugs range from 200 to about 500 Da. If the value is too small, the compound will not have enough variety (chemical diversity) to ensure strong and selective binding to a target. If the value is much greater than 500, it will be too large to be orally active (see Chap. 2).

Fig. 3.4 Calculating the molecular weight of a compound. The example shown is the small molecule ethanol with a molecular weight of 46 produced by adding up the atomic weights of 2× carbon, 6× hydrogen and 1× oxygen atoms. Molecular weights of natural and synthetic molecules range from tens to millions

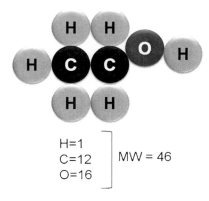

$$H=1$$
$$C=12 \quad \Big\} \quad MW = 46$$
$$O=16$$

Notes

1. The true weight of an atom is so small that it would be inconvenient to use these values. A carbon atom, for example weighs approximately 2×10^{-23} grams!
2. In reality, each element is a mixture of isotopes with slightly different atomic weights, so the values are not exact multiples of 1. Isotopes are important in several branches of chemistry and are powerful tools for labelling molecules to investigate biological processes.
3. Molecules are physically very small. From the example above, 46 g of ethanol (about a large whisky) contains approximately 6×10^{23} molecules.

3.1.2 Organic Chemistry

Life is based on carbon (C) and a number of other elements including hydrogen, oxygen, nitrogen, sulphur and various metals. This is because carbon has the ability to combine readily with itself and other elements in a wide range of configurations such as chains and rings. This versatility has been exploited by nature and by human beings for many different applications, such as polymers, dyestuffs and, of course, drugs. The study of carbon compounds is known as organic chemistry. As a brief aside, the composition of an adult human in terms of the percentages of the different elements is shown in Table 3.1. Oxygen is very abundant, since about 70% of the human body is made up of water. Although the percentage of calcium is quite small, this figure still represents a weight of about 1 kg per person, much of which is in the skeleton, although this metal is also vital for cell function.

Table 3.1 Percentage of
elements in an adult human

Name	Abbreviation	Percentage
Oxygen	O	61
Carbon	C	23
Hydrogen	H	10
Nitrogen	N	2.6
Calcium	Ca	1.4
Phosphorus	P	1.1
Potassium	K	0.2
Sulphur	S	0.2
Sodium	Na	0.14
Chlorine	Cl	0.12
Magnesium	Mg	0.027
Iron	Fe	0.006
Copper	Cu	Trace
Molybdenum	Mo	–
Zinc	Zn	–
Iodine	I	–

Data taken from Emsley (2001) with the kind permission
of Oxford University Press

3.1.2.1 Writing Down Structures

Simple two-dimensional (2D) representations of molecules have their uses and are
easy to write down on paper. However, these diagrams do not readily convey one
of the essential properties of molecules, which is shape. Drug molecules and their
targets have complex three-dimensional (3D) shapes that must be compatible if
they are to interact selectively with each other. Different combinations of atoms in
compounds have well-defined shapes formed by the links (bonds) that hold them
together. Carbon, for example is often found as a tetrahedron in association with
hydrogen or certain other elements. The compound methane is illustrated below in
the simple 2D representation and in a 3D computer-generated model showing the
bonds between the atoms as tubes (Fig. 3.5).

   It is obviously impractical to write down chemical structures on paper using
either of the above illustrations, so the next section describes how to think like a
chemist and interpret the 2D structures that these scientists use on a routine basis.
It is possible to make an analogy between chemists and musicians in the following
way: a number of great musicians have delivered a perfect performance on their
chosen instruments without ever having played the piece before; they learned
everything they needed to know just by reading the score. The score is a 2D representation of musical notes that follows a series of accepted rules so that the trained
musician knows exactly how the piece will sound. The same principle applies in
chemistry. The trained chemist will look at a molecular structure written on
paper and be able to identify many of the key properties of the molecule in question.
He or she will also be able to name the compound using an internationally accepted

Fig. 3.5 (**a**) A simple organic
molecule (methane) based
on a carbon atom surrounded
by four hydrogen atoms.
(**b**) Three-dimensional representation of the same molecule
using a computer-generated
"ball and stick" model.
The shape corresponds
to a tetrahedron

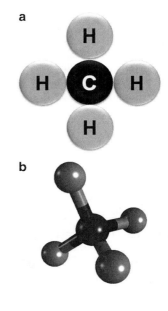

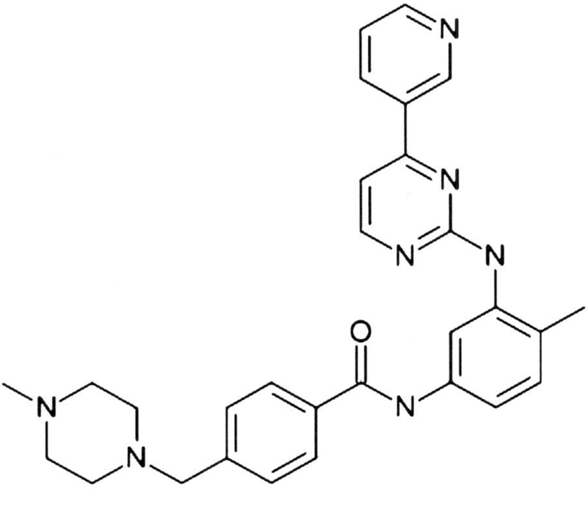

Fig. 3.6 Two-dimensional
structure of a small molecule
drug imatinib used to treat
cancer. This illustrates the
standard format used by
chemists to write down
structures

set of rules for chemical nomenclature. The following section gives a simple
introduction to chemical formulae and nomenclature of the organic molecules that
make up most drugs.

The structure of the anti-cancer drug imatinib (trade name Gleevec®) may look
quite fearsome to the uninitiated (Fig. 3.6). It can, however, be better understood by
learning some simple rules about how carbon and other elements join together in

Fig. 3.7 Illustration of single, double and triple bonds in simple carbon compounds and their three-dimensional display

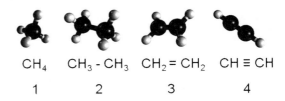

CH_4 $CH_3 - CH_3$ $CH_2 = CH_2$ $CH \equiv CH$

1   2   3   4

fixed proportions and how complex organic molecules are made up of smaller "functional groups".

Where are the Carbon Atoms?

It is much easier to draw structures without having to place every carbon and hydrogen atom in the molecule. The above diagram has rings and lines joining them, so where there is no letter specified (unlike the Ns for nitrogen, for example), it is assumed that a carbon atom is present.

Why are There Two Lines in Places and No Hydrogen Atoms Displayed?

As with the carbon atoms, hydrogens are left out to avoid cluttering the picture. The number of hydrogens at each position will vary because of the maximum number of bonds that each carbon atom can make. This introduces the concept of "valency" developed in the nineteenth century. The valency of an element is literally its combining power with other elements. For example carbon has a valency of 4, nitrogen 3, oxygen 2 and hydrogen 1; this means that one carbon atom can combine with a maximum of four hydrogen atoms. Some simple examples are shown in Fig. 3.7. Every carbon atom uses four bonds, even if there are not four recipient atoms. This is illustrated in examples 3 and 4 where a double or triple bond forms to make up the valency of 4.

The above two points are reinforced in Fig. 3.8, where imatinib is now displayed with all of the carbon and hydrogen atoms. The positions of single and double bonds determine how many hydrogen atoms are attached to each carbon atom, so they can convey where these atoms are situated in the molecule without creating a cluttered diagram like this example.

3.1.2.2   Working Out the Shape of a Molecule

Shape is an important factor governing the precise interaction between a drug and its target, and in many cases, a substantial part of this shape is formed by rings of atoms. There are two general types of ring: alicyclic and aromatic, which are exemplified in the compounds cyclohexane and benzene shown in Fig. 3.9. The original

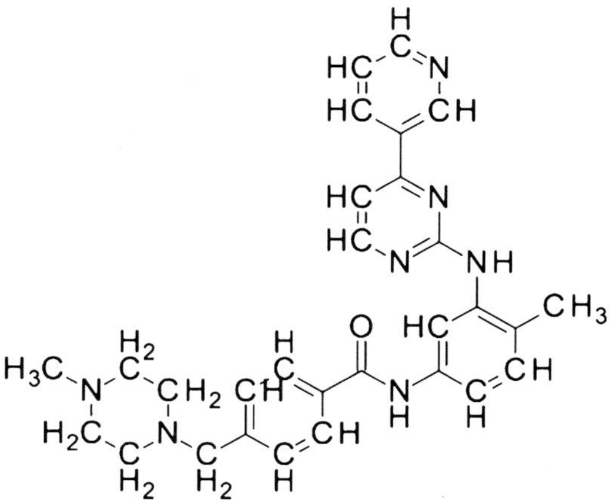

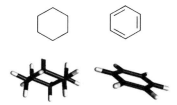

Fig. 3.8 Structure of imatinib molecule showing all the hydrogen atoms. Compare this with Fig. 3.6, which is the preferred representation of an organic molecule

Fig. 3.9 Molecular structures of cyclohexane (*left*) and benzene (*right*). The alternating single and double bonds in benzene force the ring into a flat shape shown using the stick display produced by the computer graphics. The disposition of double bonds in a ring indicates to the chemist whether the ring is flat (planar) or bent (puckered). These shapes are important features in drug molecules and their target proteins because they help to determine binding strength and selectivity

characteristic of aromatic compounds was their odour, hence the name. According to modern chemical theory, aromatic compounds are defined by the configuration of alternating single and double bonds that force the ring into a flat shape. Alicyclic compounds may have some double bonds, but they do not alternate in the same way and the rings are bent or "puckered". This particular "conformation" of the molecule is apparent to the chemist just by looking at the disposition of single and double bonds on the structure drawing.

3.1.2.3 Rings and Other Functional Groups

Many organic compounds and drugs contain rings of different shapes and sizes. The ring backbone may be constructed entirely out of carbon, or else be mixed in with other elements such as nitrogen, oxygen or sulphur, in which case they are called heterocycles. Some examples are shown in Fig. 3.10.

Fig. 3.10 Examples of
heterocycles used in organic
molecules, including drugs

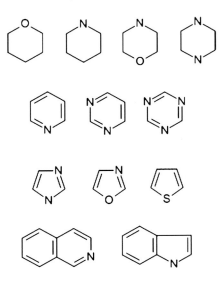

These structures (and many other groups of atoms that are not necessarily ring
shaped) are "functional groups" linked together in more complex molecules. These
groups are rather like modules or building bricks that can be taken "off the shelf"
and assembled in different ways to create a huge variety of different structures.
A knowledge of these groups allows the medicinal chemist to create new molecules
(or modify existing ones) in order to produce drug compounds that interact strongly
with their target (see Chap. 7). The names of certain atoms specifically associated
with functional groups follow certain rules; for example thio means sulphur; aza,
nitrogen; oxo, oxygen and chloro, chlorine. A knowledge of the names of these
groups helps to explain how complex molecules such as drugs are named.

3.1.3 Drug Nomenclature

Naming conventions in science are often hit and miss because most objects are
named by the discoverer, hence the efforts of international bodies to create an
agreed nomenclature that is linguistically consistent. Organic chemistry has been in
existence for roughly 200 years and many hundreds of compounds have been
named, often based on their appearance or the material from which they were first
extracted, for example piperidine from pepper. Small molecule drugs are named at
three levels: their formal chemical name, generic name and brand or trade name.[2]
The formal chemical name follows a set of rules laid down by the International

---

[2]The Anatomical Therapeutic Chemical (ATC) classification system for drugs based on the target
organ or body system is covered in Chap. 19.

Union of Pure and Applied Chemistry (IUPAC) (International Union of Pure and Applied Chemistry (IUPAC) 2010). Every functional group of a compound is named and its position identified by a numbering system. In many ways, it is like compound nouns in the German language. These can be made up of a string of individual small words to form an impressively long one. My favourite, vaguely remembered from school years, is "schnellzugzusatzschein" or "express train supplementary ticket".

The IUPAC name for imatinib is 4-[(4-methylpiperazin-1-yl) methyl]-N-[4-methyl-3-[(4-pyridin-3-ylpyrimidin-2-yl) amino] phenyl]benzamide. This is not a very good starting point for the uninitiated, so the following compound (a common painkiller) will be used as an example of the different levels of drug nomenclature.

3.1.3.1 IUPAC Name: *N*-(4-Hydroxyphenyl) Acetamide

This molecule is made up of three groups: hydroxyl and phenyl groups which are linked to acetamide (Fig. 3.11). The hydroxyl group is joined to the phenyl group at position 4. The acetamide is linked to the resulting hydroxyphenyl group via the nitrogen N. Note that one of the hydrogen atoms on acetamide is lost after it has been joined to the H at position 1.

3.1.3.2 Generic Name

Since the IUPAC nomenclature is too unwieldy for general use, there are international organizations that agree on a manageable name that is not proprietary. This may be the International Nonproprietary Name (INN) (WHO guidelines for INN 2011) or the United States Adopted Name (USAN) (United States Adopted Names Council 2011), the former being under the auspices of the World Health Organization. The INN for *N*-(4-hydroxyphenyl) acetamide is "paracetamol" and the USAN is "acetaminophen".

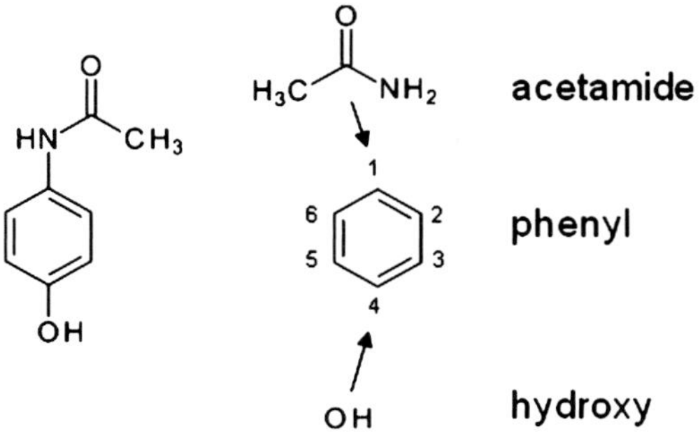

Fig. 3.11 Layout of functional groups (acetamide, phenyl and hydroxyl) and numbering system for *N*-(4-hydroxyphenyl) acetamide (*left*)

3.1.3.3 Proprietary or Trade Name

Here we leave the world of science and medicine and enter the world of creative media. These names are proprietary to the company that sells the product and are generated in the same way as that for any other consumer product. There are many trade names for paracetamol, including Calpol, Panadol and Tylenol.

3.1.4 Hydrates and Salts

Drug compounds are often named in two parts, for example amoxicillin hydrate, ranitidine hydrochloride, sildenafil citrate and imatinib mesylate. The first word is the drug itself and the second, its hydrate or salt form. Hydrates are compounds that are associated with one or more molecules of water which may help to stabilise the compounds in a crystalline form. If the water is removed, they become anhydrous compounds or anhydrates.

Salt forms are often used in small molecule drug development as they can improve the stability of the parent compound in the different chemical environments of the body. They are also important for manufacturing, so the selection of appropriate salt forms is a key part of the formulation process (covered in Chap. 10). There may also be a strong financial incentive to investigate the development of alternative salt forms as these can extend the patent life of a drug.

Salts are formed by the chemical reaction of an acid and a base to form a neutral compound. Although a detailed explanation of this phenomenon is outside the scope of this book, mention will be made of the term "pH", which is a measure of the degree of acidity or alkalinity (basicity) of a substance. The pH scale ranges from 0 to 14, where 0 is very acidic and 14 is very basic. Strong hydrochloric acid is very acidic and ammonia is very basic. A neutral substance (water, for example) has a pH of 7. Since the pH scale is logarithmic, each number represents ten times more than the other, so a solution at pH 0 is one million times more acidic than the one at pH 6.

Drugs can be basic in character and neutralised with an acid (termed acid addition salts), or vice versa. Some of the acids used to neutralise the drug are inorganic, i.e. not primarily based on carbon atoms. The majority of these are hydrochlorides, sulphates and phosphates based on hydrochloric, sulphuric and phosphoric acid respectively. Alternatively, organic acids (such as acetic acid) are used. Examples of acids commonly used to produce salt forms of drugs are shown in Fig. 3.12. The functional group in common is the carboxyl group COOH (except for the SOO in the mesylate) which provides the acidity. Where a base has been used to neutralise an acidic drug, most of the resulting salts contain a metallic element such as sodium, calcium or potassium.

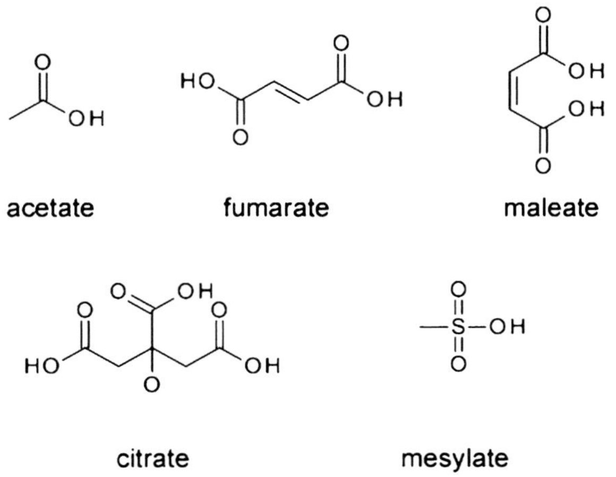

Fig. 3.12 Structures of the acids that are commonly used to produce salt forms of drugs (hydrochloric acid is also used but not shown here)

acetate   fumarate   maleate

citrate   mesylate

3.1.5 The Chemistry of Proteins

Proteins have already been introduced in Chap. 2 as injectable drugs, but they are also central to small molecule drug discovery as they form the physical basis of drug targets. This section introduces the chemistry of proteins and describes the properties that make them central to life processes and drug discovery.

Unlike small molecules of around 500 Da molecular weight, proteins are classed as macromolecules, with sizes ranging from about 6,000 to over 1,000,000 Da. Proteins are biological polymers that can be produced in an almost infinite number of chemical forms, so in order to understand why this is the case, it is helpful to first look at polymers in general.

Everyone is familiar with polymers in the form of plastics, the word polymer being derived from the Greek for "many things". A simple polymer like polythene consists of a chain of identical chemical units or monomers. In this case, the monomer is ethylene, hence the name polyethylene, otherwise shortened to polythene. Nylon, on the contrary, is made up of two different monomers linked together in a chain. This chemical linkage is created via the amide functional group; hence nylon is sometimes known as a polyamide. Proteins are naturally occurring polymers made from about 20 monomers called amino acids. Unlike synthetic plastics, the chain length is precisely defined and the order of amino acids can be varied in any permutation.

This is summarised in Fig. 3.13 where the amino acids are indicated as numbers for simplicity.

The 20 amino acids that occur naturally in most proteins are, of course, more than numbers. They are small molecules with molecular weights around 100–200,

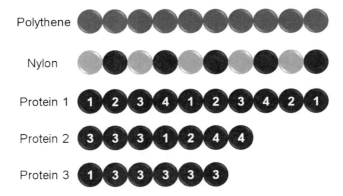

Fig. 3.13 Schematic example of different polymers. Chemically unique monomers are shown as different coloured discs. Synthetic plastics such as polyethylene (polythene) and nylon are made up from one and two different monomers respectively. Proteins are built up from around 20 different monomers called amino acids. The three proteins here use amino acids 1, 2, 3 or 4 in different permutations. In reality, the protein chain will be much longer and the amino acids given specific names (see below)

with two functional groups that allow them to join together in a chain. These are the amino and carboxylic (a type of acid) groups that give this class of compounds its name. When this linkage occurs in a protein, it is called a peptide bond. When a chain consists of two or more amino acids, up to about 40, it is known as a peptide, although the exact upper limit is rather imprecise. After that, it is more correct to call it a polypeptide or protein.

Although the names of the amino acids all end in the letters "ine", individual compounds are named in the same haphazard way as other organic compounds. Asparagine, for example was so named because it was first isolated from asparagus. Incidentally, this amino acid is responsible for the particular smell of urine passed after eating this vegetable.

Each amino acid is given a three letter or single letter abbreviation according to use. The latter is used in protein databases where the sequence[3] is written in the single letter code for clarity and for reading by computers (see bioinformatics, Chap. 6).

Table 3.2 lists the common amino acids by name and abbreviation.

Despite having amino and carboxyl functional groups in common, each amino acid is chemically quite unique; this means that the proteins formed from their joining up (polymerization) show great diversity in their chemical structure and, therefore, their biological function. Figure 3.14 shows the structure of a heptapeptide, i.e., a peptide made up of seven amino acids.[4] Notice the different rings and

---

[3] The use of the words "sequence" and "sequencing" is the same for proteins as it is for nucleic acids, but in the latter case the units are nucleotides and not amino acids.

[4] The length of small peptides is indicated by the Greek number prefix i.e.: di, tri, tetra, penta, hexa, hepta, octa, nona, and decapeptide for 2–10 amino acids.

Table 3.2 List of 19 common amino acids and their three letter and single letter codes. These codes are used to illustrate protein sequences in the same way as A, C, G and T are used for nucleic acids. Amino acids not shown include cystine (two cysteines linked together) and hydroxyproline, which is present in connective tissue proteins

Name			Name		
Alanine	Ala	A	Lysine	Lys	K
Aspartic acid	Asp	D	Methionine	Met	M
Asparagine	Asn	N	Phenylalanine	Phe	F
Cysteine	Cys	C	Proline	Pro	P
Glycine	Gly	G	Serine	Ser	S
Glutamic acid	Glu	E	Threonine	Thr	T
Glutamine	Gln	Q	Tryptophan	Trp	W
Histidine	His	H	Tyrosine	Tyr	Y
Isoleucine	Ileu	I	Valine	Val	V
Leucine	Leu	L			

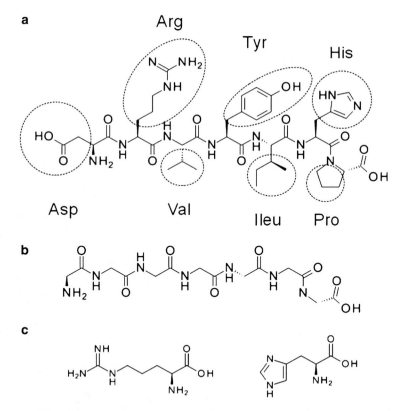

Fig. 3.14 Structure of the heptapeptide Asp Arg Val Tyr Ileu His Pro (DRVYIHP in single letter code). (**a**) Structure with side chains of the individual amino acids highlighted. (**b**) Same diagram as (**a**) but minus the side chains to show the peptide structure that is common to all peptides and proteins. (**c**) Examples of unlinked amino acids, arginine and histidine

chains that grow off the string of atoms that is formed by peptide bonds. It is the side chains that impart different structures to the peptides and proteins formed when the amino acids are linked together.

3.1.5.1   Molecular Origami

Chains of amino acids are known as the primary sequence of a protein and can be written down as a string of letters, for example (single letter code) "GHISSTWLSTVVN". The structures formed when the protein chain folds up according to the chemical structures of the constituent amino acids are called the secondary and tertiary structures. The quaternary structure relates to the association of more than one polypeptide chain. The example of the heptapeptide in Fig. 3.14 introduces the idea of complex structures in protein chains. This is one of the most important areas in biochemistry, as it determines how proteins function in living cells and whether they are suitable drug targets for small molecules or other proteins. Once the protein chain is formed in cells, it folds into a precisely defined conformation, although it is still unknown how this happens as there are literally trillions of possible structures. Proteins are either globular or fibrous according to their overall shape. Globular proteins perform catalytic functions within cells (see enzymes, Chap. 6) and many other roles. They tend not be structural, however, so fibrous proteins are instead employed in tissues such as hair, nails and skin where their greater mechanical strength is required. Structures for both types are shown in Fig. 3.15.

Fig. 3.15 Three-dimensional structures of collagen (*left*) and pepsin (*right*). Computer-generated wire frame models showing extended fibrous nature of collagen and globular nature of the enzyme pepsin. Amino acid side chains can be seen protruding from the collagen structure, which is a triple helix made up of three protein chains

More details about proteins and their functions in drug discovery will be presented in later chapters. Meanwhile, this chapter will continue with a description of large molecules other than proteins and conclude with a section on the way in which drugs bind to their targets, focusing on the interactions between small molecules and proteins.

3.1.6 Large Molecules Other than Proteins

3.1.6.1 Nucleic Acids

Deoxyribonucleic acid and ribonucleic acid (DNA and RNA) have already been introduced in Chap. 2. So far, the nucleotide building blocks that make up these molecules have just been given the letters A, C, G, T and U, but the full names of the four nucleotides used to build a DNA molecule are deoxyadenosine triphosphate (dATP), deoxythymidine triphosphate (dTTP), deoxyguanosine triphosphate (dGTP) and deoxycytosine triphosphate (dCTP). These are small molecules consisting of a nucleobase linked to deoxyribose linked to triphosphate (Fig. 3.16). This is why DNA is called deoxyribonucleic acid (the acid part is provided by the phosphate group). RNA is made up of ATP, CTP, GTP and uridine triphosphate (UTP) instead of TTP. In RNA, the deoxyribose is replaced by ribose, hence ribonucleic acid.

The structure in Fig. 3.17 shows the four nucleotides of DNA joined together in a chain. The principle is similar to that of the peptide chain being built up from amino acids, although the phosphate–deoxyribose linkage is chemically different. The nucleobases protruding from the DNA chain allow two chains to link together to form a double helix. The figure shows the 3D structure of part of a double helix where bases from each strand of DNA are aligned together and form weak hydrogen bonds (see later in chapter). From the earlier section on ring structures, it will be noticed that the rings in the nucleobases are completely flat because of the disposition of single and double bonds.

The synthesis and manipulation of nucleic acids are fundamental to biotechnology and modern drug discovery, so this important class of large molecules will be revisited in later chapters.

3.1.6.2 Lipids

The lipid family is extensive and diverse and is not as readily categorised as proteins and nucleic acids. Nevertheless, the basic principles of lipid structure are straightforward; the molecules consist of an extensive water-insoluble portion which dissolves readily in an organic solvent like gasoline, but not in water (unless it is a natural detergent-like molecule). Lipid molecules, along with specialised proteins, form the membranes which enclose cells and are also important signalling molecules that allow communication between cells. Lipids are important for drug

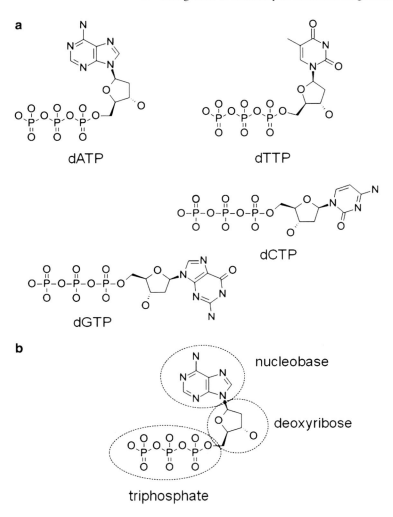

Fig. 3.16 (**a**) Structures of the nucleotides used to produce DNA with hydrogen atoms omitted. The deoxyribose and phosphate groups are the same for each compound, the difference being the nucleobases whose initials A, C, G and T are used when writing down a DNA sequence. (**b**) The nomenclature of the different chemical groups that make up DNA

development for a number of reasons: cholesterol, for example is a lipid that has been implicated in coronary heart disease, so drugs that reduce its level in the blood are considered to be of great importance. Other lipids have been used for the delivery of drugs into cells, or modified to be drugs in their own right. Some of these points are covered in later chapters. Representative examples of different lipids are shown in Fig. 3.18. Note that their molecular size is modest compared with that of proteins and nucleic acids, but they can associate with each other to form much larger "complexes", as for example in the cell membrane.

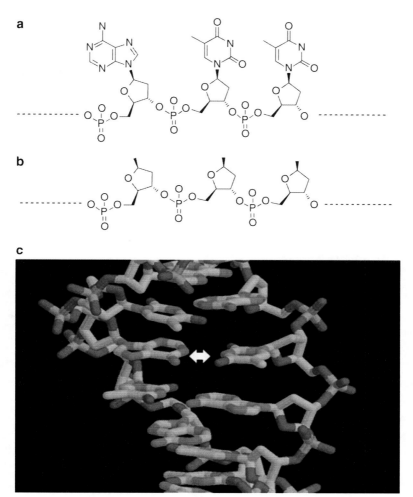

Fig. 3.17 (**a**) Linkage of three nucleotides (dATP, dTTP and dTTP) to illustrate the way DNA strands are built up. (**b**) Backbone of DNA strand which is common to the whole molecule. (**c**) Three-dimensional structure of part of DNA double helix showing the nucleobases stacked in the same plane. The *arrow* points to a nucleobase from each strand linking together in space to hold the structure together. This reversible linkage forms the basis of hybridization of nucleic acid strands to each other and is critical for normal gene function as well as biotechnology

3.1.6.3 Carbohydrates

Like lipids, carbohydrates are varied and complex molecules with a wide range of molecular weights. They are built up from units called saccharides, which are commonly known as sugars. Glucose consists of one saccharide molecule, while sucrose has two, so these compounds are known as monosaccharides and disaccharides

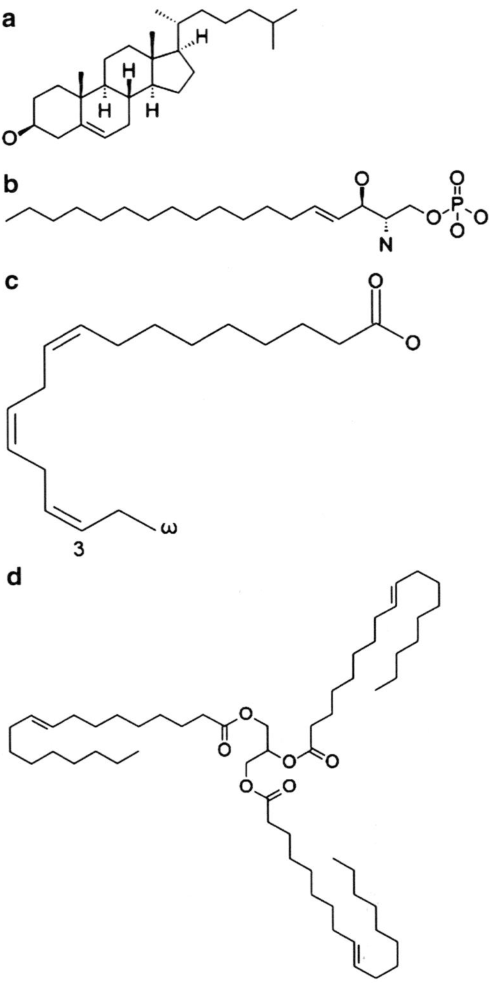

Fig. 3.18 Examples of different lipid molecules with most
of the hydrogen atoms omitted. (**a**) Cholesterol; note the
predominance of carbon
atoms that confers solubility
in organic solvents. The
complex ring structures are
formed from open chains that
curve round on each other.
(**b**) Sphingosine-1 phosphate;
a complex lipid involved
in signalling between cells.
(**c**) α-Linolenic acid; a dietary
lipid member of the omega-3
fatty acid family promoted
as a supplement for improved
cardiac health. The naming
derives from the double
(unsaturated) bond 3 carbon
atoms away from the omega
(ω) carbon atom at the end
of the chain. (**d**) A triglycer-
ide; this is a lipid formed
between three fatty acid
chains (hence "tri") and a
smaller glycerol molecule.
These large water insoluble
structures are commonly
known as fats

respectively. Large molecule carbohydrates, such as cellulose, are polysaccharides,
by analogy with polypeptides and polynucleotides. Carbohydrates not only provide
the fuel that feeds the energy-producing systems in cells, but also combine with
proteins to provide structural elements in the body, such as cartilage and connective
tissue. These protein–carbohydrate associations (glycoproteins) are expressed
on the surfaces of cells to create adhesive surfaces that allow cells to interact
physically with each other in biological tissues. This is important in terms of drug
discovery for a number of reasons. Firstly, cell interactions via glycoproteins are
the hallmark of inflammation and viral infection, so compounds that inhibit the
interactions between carbohydrates on different cells (or between a virus and a cell)
may be useful drugs for these conditions. Secondly, carbohydrate molecules are
sometimes necessary for optimal activity of protein drugs produced using recombinant DNA technology. This is covered later in Chap. 8.

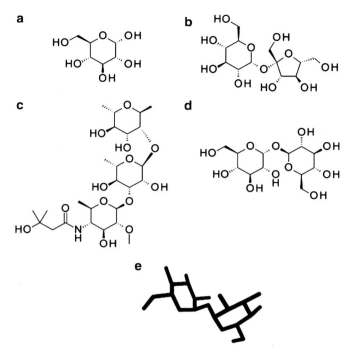

Fig. 3.19 Examples of carbohydrates (**a**) Glucose, a monosaccharide; (**b**) Sucrose, a disaccharide; notice the joining of a six-membered and five-membered ring via an oxygen atom. (**c**) A complex carbohydrate of the type found attached to proteins on the cell surface. (**d**) The disaccharide trehalose and (**e**) the three-dimensional structure of (**d**)

The nomenclature of carbohydrates is quite involved, particularly the terms used to describe their 3D configuration in space. Glucose, for example is also called α-D-glucopyranose, the α-D referring to the 3D configuration of the molecule in space, a property known as "chirality" (see Chap. 7). The word pyranose refers to the size of the ring (six membered) as opposed to the five-membered furanose ring found in other sugars such as sucrose and is the reason why sugars are also classified as pentoses and hexoses. Further details can be found in any textbook of organic chemistry or biochemistry, or online educational resources. Some examples of carbohydrates are shown in Fig. 3.19.

3.1.7 Drug–Protein Interactions

3.1.7.1 Visualising Interactions in the Computer

The visualisation of drug–protein interactions has been transformed by computer-generated 3D images of proteins and small molecules. Several examples have already been presented in the figures using the ball and stick, or stick representations of atoms and bonds, but there others which are useful, particularly where the images are complex. These include wireframe, spacefill and ribbon displays. Examples are given using the binding of the small molecule imatinib to its target protein which is activated in certain cancers. The drug works by locking the target protein in a fixed position, thereby preventing its normal function as a signalling molecule (Fig. 3.20).

The imatinib structure fits into a pocket inside the protein formed by the folded amino acid side chains. The shape and configuration of the compound will ensure that it is able to access the pocket neatly, but these features are not sufficient for the drug to have an effect on the protein. It must also bind into the protein pocket with enough strength to hold it in position, but not so strongly that it is impossible to remove it.[5] This is where other features of the molecules come into play.

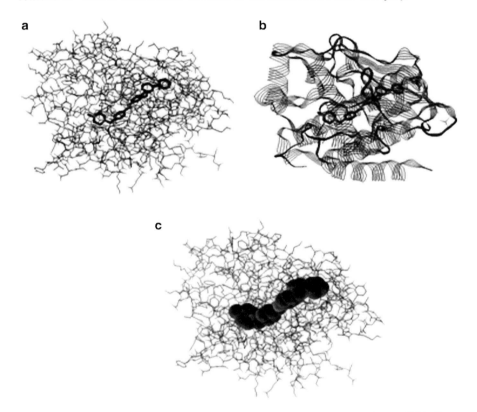

Fig. 3.20 Computer-generated models of the small molecule drug imatinib (Gleevec®) binding to its drug target protein. (**a**) Protein displayed as wire frame with imatinib buried within its surface and visualised as a stick model. (**b**) Protein rendered as a ribbon diagram that shows the way this particular polypeptide chain forms a helix. (**c**) Drug molecule displayed as a surface model with each atom denoted by a sphere. With no pun intended, these are "spheres of influence" that define the limits of interaction between the drug and the protein side chains

---

[5]This is not true for all drugs; some work by permanently blocking an active site on the target and are called irreversible (as oppose to reversible) inhibitors.

3.1.7.2 Electricity and Fat

These may seem strange subjects to introduce, but in fact they are related to chemical bonding. This topic is part of the basic chemistry of atoms and molecules, but has not been mentioned up to now so as to avoid unnecessary complication. Unfortunately, it is impossible to understand drug binding without at least a basic idea of how molecules interact with each other. These interactions involve electrical charges and attractions to fatty molecules.

3.1.7.3 Atoms are More than Just Billiard Balls

Our understanding of atomic structure has come a long way since Dalton's time in the early 1800s. Instead of just being seen as billiard balls, modern quantum theory describes atoms as collections of subatomic particles whose exact position can never be observed directly. The subatomic particles created in the first moments after the Universe was born later joined together to form hydrogen, the first element. Modern particle accelerators (atom smashers) like the Large Hadron Collider at CERN are designed to reverse the process to recreate these early particles. While all of this is fascinating from a scientific point of view, the simple notion of atoms as combinations of two charged particles, protons and electrons, is sufficient for a basic understanding of chemical bonding.[6] Protons carry a positive charge and electrons a negative one. Since like charges repel and unlike charges attract (same with magnetic poles), atoms with different charges will attract or repel each other accordingly. Figure 3.21 shows an atom with eight protons shown with + symbols surrounded by electrons (– symbol). The atomic diagrams are, of course, highly schematic. The interior (the nucleus) is so small relative to the total size of the atom that the physicist Ernest Rutherford

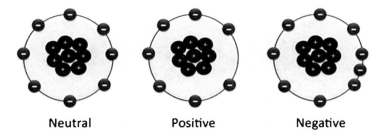

Neutral   **Positive**   **Negative**

Fig. 3.21 Simple diagram of atom showing protons in the nucleus (+ sign) orbited by electrons (– sign). A neutral atom has an equal number of protons and electrons; when one electron is missing, the atom is positively charged, and if an electron has been gained, it is negatively charged. This charge is fundamental to the way in which atoms join together

---

[6] Actually recent findings about chemical bonding means that we understand far less about it than was originally thought; luckily this does not negate the explanations given in the main text.

described it as the "fly in the cathedral". The electrically neutral atom in this example has eight electrons to balance the charge. The positively charged atom has lost one electron and the negative atom has gained one. Without this free movement of electrons in and out of atoms, we would not have electricity, which of course in our world is unthinkable.

Covalent and Ionic Bonds

The strength of the bond between different atoms in a molecule varies according to the disposition of electrons. Most of the bonds that make up a drug molecule are strong covalent bonds where the atoms link closely by sharing electrons. These bonds can be so strong that they require high temperatures or reactive chemicals to break them. Ionic bonds are formed when a positively charged atom links with a negatively charged one by electrical attraction. Ionic bonding is so named because charged atoms are called ions. Bonds of this type are found in salts such as sodium chloride, where positive sodium ions interact with negative chloride ions. Figure 3.22 shows a diagram of covalent and ionic bonding.

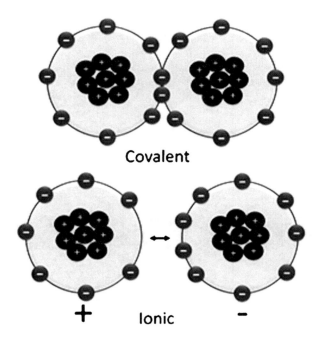

Fig. 3.22 Illustration of two main types of strong electrical bonding between atoms. Covalent bonding involves the sharing of electrons between the two atoms to produce a very strong bond. All of the compounds and large molecules illustrated in this chapter contain covalent bonds between their constituent atoms. Ionic bonding is a strong interaction between a positively charged and a negatively charged atom. These bonds are more easily broken and are used to create the salt forms and hydrates of drugs along with some interactions between drug molecules and their protein targets

Hydrogen Bonding

Hydrogen bonding occurs between hydrogen and a negatively charged atom such as oxygen or nitrogen. Because less energy is required to break hydrogen bonds compared with covalent or ionic bonds, they are useful for holding molecular structures in particular conformations without locking them too tightly. The two helices of DNA are held together by hydrogen bonds, as are protein chains and many other molecules, including water. Most interactions between a drug and its target occur through the formation of hydrogen bonds between amino acids in the protein-binding pocket and atoms within the drug itself.

Hydrophobic Interactions

This is where the fat comes in. Many organic molecules like the hydrocarbons found in oil do not dissolve in water. Water is a polar solvent, a substance bearing an electrical charge, but oil has no charge and, therefore, cannot interact with other molecules through ionic binding. Oily molecules are classed as hydrophobic (literally "water hating"), whilst salts and many other compounds are hydrophilic ("water loving"). The opposite terminology is often used in drug discovery: oily compounds are lipophilic (fat loving) and possess the property of lipophilicity. Oily molecules prefer to associate with each other through hydrophobic interactions, which are part of a more general group known as van der Waals forces. Named after a Dutch scientist, these forces are weaker than covalent, ionic or hydrogen bonds and operate at very close distances between atoms. Despite this weak binding activity, they are highly important for holding molecular structures together.

Drug molecules consist of a mixture of hydrophobic and hydrophilic groups, the proportion of which determines the overall amount of charge or polarity of each molecule. The hydrophobic groups interact with hydrophobic amino acids in the binding pocket of the target protein to complement the hydrogen bonding elsewhere in the molecule. The lipophilicity and polarity of compounds are vitally important for drug development as they determine the solubility of the drug in the blood and how it is dealt with in the body after administration.

The final figure (Fig. 3.23) in this chapter shows computer-generated images of a small molecule bound to a target protein, in which the areas of hydrogen and hydrophobic bonding are marked with coloured spheres. This figure represents the fundamental essence of what drug discovery is all about, namely the search for molecules that strongly and (usually) reversibly bind to a target protein with exquisite selectivity in order to change the function of that target and treat disease.

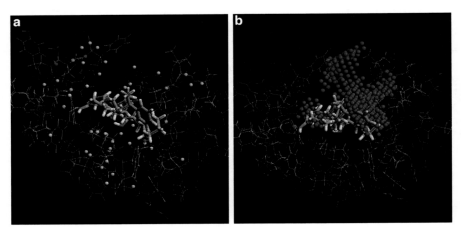

Fig. 3.23 A small drug molecule (*green stick model*) interacting with a protein target (wire frame) (**a**) Points in space where hydrogen bonding can occur between the drug and protein marked with yellow, *white* and *purple* spheres. (**b**) Same interaction, but with points of hydrophobic bonding marked with *red* spheres. As well as illustrating how drugs can bind to their target, this information is useful for computer-aided drug design, Chap. (7). Images courtesy of Dr Philip Dean, Cambridge, UK

Summary of Key Points

All matter is based on elements that exist in the form of atoms or molecules.

Two or more elements bind together to form compounds.

The chemistry of life (and drugs) is based on the element carbon.

Molecular weights are based on a value of 1 for the lightest element, hydrogen. Small molecule drugs have molecular weights from 200 to 500.

Proteins and other macromolecules are large molecules with molecular weights from thousands to millions.

Organic compounds are built from smaller functional groups with defined 3D shapes.

Drugs are named at three levels:

Organic compounds (IUPAC rules)
Generic names (INN/USAN rules)
Proprietary/trade names

Hydrates and salts of drug compounds can improve their medicinal properties.

Salts are neutral combinations of acids and bases. Degrees of acidity and basicity are measured using the pH scale.

(continued)

> **Summary of Key Points** (continued)
>
> Proteins are polymers built from around 20 amino acids and fold into defined 3D shapes that are globular or fibrous.
>
> Proteins have defined functions in life processes and are the targets for most drugs, as well as being drugs themselves.
>
> Lipids and carbohydrates are important classes of organic molecules which are used in different aspects of drug development, including targets, drugs and delivery agents.
>
> Atoms are bound together by chemical bonds with different strengths:
>
> Covalent > Ionic > Hydrogen bonding > Hydrophobic interactions

References

Emsley J (2001) Nature's building blocks an A–Z guide to the elements. Oxford University Press, Oxford

International Union of Pure and Applied Chemistry (IUPAC) (2010). http://www.iupac.org/. Accessed 7 Dec 2010

United States Adopted Names Council (2011). http://www.ama-assn.org/ama/pub/physician-resources/medical-science/united-states-adopted-names-council/adopted-names.shtml. Accessed 7 Jan 2011

WHO guidelines for INN (2011). http://apps.who.int/medicinedocs/en/d/Jh1806e/1.html. Accessed 7 Jan 2011

Wiley JP (1995) Smithsonian magazine. http://www.smithsonianmag.com/science-nature/phenom_dec95.html. Accessed 1 Nov 2010

Chapter 4
Laying the Foundations: Drug Discovery from Antiquity to the Twenty-First Century

Abstract This chapter gives a brief overview of the history of drug discovery from antiquity up to the early decades of the twentieth century, and then describes the "golden age" of drug discovery when most of the medicines in current use were developed. This latter era saw the introduction of pharmacology as a distinct discipline of biological science, along with major advances in synthetic chemistry. The basic concepts and terminology of pharmacology are explained and examples given of how the discipline has been used to develop medicines to treat diseases, such as asthma and duodenal ulcers. New biological technologies began to make an impact on mainstream pharmaceutical research in the 1990s, foreseeing the wider use of large molecules as medicines. The transition from traditional pharmacology to the modern era of drug discovery is also discussed.

4.1 Introduction

"You have to know the past to understand the present". This quote from the astronomer, Carl Sagan, was never as true as with the science of drug discovery. The "present", as much of this book shows, is the technology-driven push towards making drug discovery as efficient a process as possible. The "past" is the accumulated knowledge of medicine, biology and chemistry that has underpinned pharmaceutical research over the years. Science, although rigorously objective in outlook, is subject to trends and fashion because it is conducted by human beings. This means that "what goes around comes around again" just like clothing or music styles. Old ways of looking at chemistry or biology are reviewed in the light of new ideas and technologies. Alternatively, new uses are found for old drugs to the benefit of both the patient and the manufacturer.

E.D. Zanders, *The Science and Business of Drug Discovery: Demystifying the Jargon*, DOI 10.1007/978-1-4419-9902-3_4, © Springer Science+Business Media, LLC 2011

4.1.1   Medicines from Antiquity

We often view the past from the perspective of the present, and this is also true when considering the use of medicines. It is difficult for those of us with a modern way of thinking to avoid at least a hint of bemused condescension when learning about the bizarre rituals and often disgusting materials administered to sick people in ancient times and even up to the present day. However, the inner voice of reason tells us that something good must have come out of literally thousands of years of trial and error with materials derived from plants and animals. The numbers may be low, but the products, like alcohol and pain-killing opiates, continue to have a major impact upon human society.

4.1.1.1   Greek and Arabian Influences

The Ancient Greeks were the first to approach medical practice and drug therapy in a rational way. Aristotle sought reasoned explanations for the physical phenomena, although he never troubled himself with experiments to see if the theory stood up to reality. It was left to major figures, like Hippocrates (around 400 BC) and Galen (around 150 AD), to turn speculation into experiment by making systematic observations of the effects of medicinal extracts on their patients. Later generations who followed these prominent teachers had an enormous influence on drug discovery right up to the nineteenth century. Unfortunately, the medical theories of the Ancient Greeks were based on false premises. Their idea that diseases arose due to imbalances in the four humours of the body, while at least providing a hypothesis to explore, excluded the notion that diseases could be due to external causes. Another obstacle was the idea that a disease is specific to each individual patient so that the required therapy has to be prepared to order. This holistic approach to medicine makes it impossible to evaluate treatments in a truly objective way using controlled trials on a statistically significant number of subjects. There is also the issue of polypharmacy, in which more than one medicine has to be administered in order to have an effect. This means that it is impossible to identify a single agent that can be administered in a standardized form with the confidence that it will work in most patients. Although these ideas were superseded by the discoveries of single agents that could treat large numbers of patients, they foreshadowed some important issues in modern drug discovery. For example, not all patients with a particular disease will respond to the same medicine; understanding and dealing with this fact is now possible through the science of pharmacogenetics, where the genetic make-up of patients influences their responses to medicines (covered in Chap. 14). Another example is the use of combination therapies to treat particular illnesses. These therapies consist of more than one purified medicine administered at the same time in single or multiple tablets. A good example of combination therapies are the drugs used to control AIDS; these consist of as many as three separate compounds which simultaneously attack individual targets in the HIV virus.

These are modern developments on an ancient theme, perhaps echoing Carl Sagan's quote at the beginning of this chapter.

The first millennium AD saw the centre of gravity of medical and pharmaceutical study move towards the Arab world. Abu Bakr Al-Razi was a major figure in Baghdad who suggested that medicines should be tested on animals before administration to humans. Later figures, such as al-Zahrawi (936–1013 AD), produced comprehensive texts that laid out systematic procedures for extracting, storing and using medicinal preparations from a large variety of plant and animal sources. This knowledge, along with the Greek approach to understanding disease, was carried from the Arab world to Europe via Salerno in the eleventh century. Due to religious and other factors, pharmaceutical thinking remained fairly static for hundreds of years and was confined to the teachings of Galen and the Arab physicians. Some progress was made, nonetheless. The preparation of medicinal products became the responsibility of specialists called apothecaries (now pharmacists), who devised a series of weights and measures for quantifying very small quantities of medicines. The term "apothecary" is derived from *apotheca*, a storage place for wine, spices and herbs.

4.1.1.2 Asian Medicine

Records of ancient Indian medicine (Ayurvedia) are contained in one of the Vedas that constitute the written basis of Hinduism. The basic concepts behind Indian medicine and that of Galen are similar in that the disease is caused by an imbalance between "humours" in the body. Therapy is directed towards correcting the imbalance by compensating for a loss of humour (no pun intended) or antagonizing an overactive humour.

Chinese herbal medicine is very much in evidence today, although it has its origins in the first millennium AD. As with medicines from other civilizations, it relies upon correcting an imbalance of humours, in this case, the well-known balance of *yin* and *yang*. Chinese herbal remedies have received a great deal of attention from modern pharmaceutical scientists because there is a spirit of cooperation between them and the herbalists who treat diseases in modern western settings. This does not, of course, mean that the scientist is not exasperated by the fact that the exact composition of herbal mixture is changed for each patient or that some of the treatments might be presented in an apparently bizarre way. However, most scientists in biopharmaceutical companies realize that it is foolish to dismiss Chinese herbal medicine out of hand. I have had personal experience with herbal medicines used to treat skin inflammation in children. These were concocted by a practitioner of Chinese medicine in London and used with apparent success by a major children's hospital using western criteria for measuring clinical outcomes. As I was working on inflammation biology at the time, this seemed promising enough to investigate further with the aim of extracting the active ingredient in purified form. We, therefore, dispatched a member of the project team to Chinese stores in Soho, London, to collect samples according to the various recipes given by the herbalist. Rather than trying to use individual mixtures according to Chinese practice, we just pooled everything and extracted the material with solvents to produce an uncharacterized mixture of chemicals to be tested against various inflammation targets. There appeared to be some anti-inflammatory activity, so each individual herb was extracted and tested in turn.[1] One of these produced the effect we were seeing with the whole mixture, and the active compound was subsequently purified and identified. It turned out to be a known anti-inflammatory compound, although one that had fairly modest activity. We decided to terminate the project based on the conclusion that this compound was not interesting enough to be pursued further. There was still the possibility that more than one herb contained active compounds that, administered in combination, would give a greater benefit than each one in isolation. This is called an additive effect, when the total activity is the sum of the activities of each individual compound. If the total effect is greater than the sum, it is known as a synergistic effect. Nevertheless, the prospect of testing and purifying many combinations of herb extracts was just too daunting. Even if there were a series of novel compounds that had to be used together, the obstacles to developing them as a combination therapy would have been far too great. Although this outcome was not positive, there is a great deal of research in Chinese medicine by conventional scientists, including those at Chinese companies and universities. The rapid expansion of the Chinese biopharmaceutical industry will no doubt ensure that this research continues apace.

4.1.2 The Dawn of Rational Drug Discovery

For centuries after the fall of the ancient empires, doctors still relied almost exclusively upon crude medicines isolated from naturally occurring sources, plants in particular. Some genuinely effective treatments were discovered, including cinchona bark brought to Europe from South America in the early seventeenth century. Extracts of the bark were seen to be effective in controlling fever, but it was not until the early nineteenth century that the active principle, quinine, was isolated and used as a pure compound for malaria. Despite the successes with herbal extracts, the theoretical foundations of drug discovery were still based to a large extent upon the old ideas of correcting imbalances in the body. Slowly, however, these gave way to new theories based on the application of the scientific method. This method is summed up as follows: perform experiments to produce data upon which to form a hypothesis and then repeat the process by performing further experiments to confirm, reject or modify the hypothesis and so on. The scientist has to be as objective as possible by interpreting the experiments in the light of observations rather than preconceived prejudices – the experiments do not lie (usually).

---

[1] Details of how these types of experiments are performed will be given in later chapters, as they are central to modern drug screening.

One of the first examples of this approach was the first controlled clinical trial undertaken in 1747 by the British naval surgeon, James Lind. He wanted to find agents to treat scurvy, a disease that was rife in the British navy. Twelve patients were assigned an identical diet along with selected agents, such as sea water, dilute sulphuric acid (!) and citrus fruit. The sailors who had eaten oranges and lemons were rapidly cured while the others were unchanged. Although this was a dramatic example of the application of the scientific method, it was not until 50 years later that the British Admiralty made the supply of lemons or limes mandatory on its ships.

4.1.2.1 The Move Towards Pure Drugs

A major figure in the history of drug discovery was the Swiss physician, Paracelsus (1493–1541). He was one of the first to advocate the use of pure chemical compounds as medicines rather than the herbal mixtures used for centuries previously. Although his ideas of diseases were wildly off the mark, his philosophy of the quintessence of nature led him to administer drugs singly rather than in combination. This was a significant turning point towards modern practice. Since Paracelsus and his followers were operating long before the era of organic and natural product chemistry, they used a number of *inorganic* compounds, mainly minerals containing specific metals (mercury, for example, was used to treat syphilis). The use of arsenic, another toxic metal, has a long history going back perhaps 5,000 years in Chinese medicine. Paracelsus recognized it as a treatment for cancer, and in fact the compound arsenic trioxide, a component of traditional Chinese medicine, has been approved for the treatment of leukaemia. The detailed mechanism of action of this compound has only just been unravelled, but it is interesting to note that historical treatments, like this example, can be put on a firm scientific foundation.

4.1.2.2 Natural Products

As the name suggests, these are compounds that have been isolated from natural sources, i.e. plant, animal or microbial. Approximately 50% of the current medicines have their origins as natural products, so they are of intense interest to the biopharmaceutical industry. It is worth stating at the outset that natural products are no different in chemical terms from those made purely synthetically in the laboratory. In the early years of chemistry, it was thought that natural products had a special property (vitalism) just because they were found in living things (shades of this today?). This was disproved in 1828 by Wöhler, who showed that urea excreted by animals could also be synthesized in the laboratory to produce a compound that was identical to the naturally occurring substance.

Natural product chemistry advanced through the development of techniques to extract substances from plants or other materials and identify the chemical structures of the biologically active molecules. Solvent extraction was introduced (and is still used today) as a means of dissolving compounds in liquids that could be later

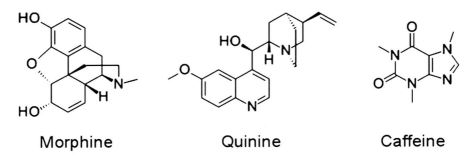

Morphine   **Quinine**   **Caffeine**

Fig. 4.1 Structures of common alkaloids. These heterocyclic compounds are natural products from poppies, cinchona bark and coffee, respectively. They are extracted from plant materials using alkaline solutions, hence the name

evaporated to reveal crystalline substances. The act of making a cup of tea is not dissimilar to the first stage: add the plant material to boiling water, infuse for a while to extract the active substances and then filter out the insoluble material using a tea strainer or the paper of a tea bag. By using a variety of solvents (e.g. acids, alkalis and alcohols), chemists were able to identify many different plant substances, one of the first of which was morphine. This was extracted from poppies and appeared to be alkaline in nature as opposed to the many acidic substances that had been isolated from plants up to that point. Later, the term alkaloid was applied to natural products of this type, which are of fundamental importance in small-molecule drug development. Many of the heterocycles that make-up drug molecules (described in Chap. 3) were first identified in alkaloids. Other important chemical features of natural products are discussed in the chapter on medicinal chemistry (Chap. 7). These discoveries advanced drug discovery enormously, but many natural products are too complex to make in the laboratory, so drug developers have to rely upon an abundant source of the biological starting materials. Morphine, for example, is a complex compound with a difficult synthesis that was achieved only in 1950. Figure 4.1 shows the structure of morphine and some other common alkaloids.

4.1.3 Nineteenth Century Synthetic Chemistry

Despite the rapid progress in drug discovery in the nineteenth century brought about by natural product chemistry, the problems of production at scale meant that ways would have to be found to produce purely synthetic drugs. The opportunity came in the form of an ugly waste product of the gas industry, coal tar. This material provided a wealth of organic compounds, including aniline, which was used to make synthetic dyes, the first, mauveine, being invented by William Perkin in 1856. I recall seeing an example of nineteenth-century mauve clothing exhibited in the main reception area of the pharmaceutical company I was working for, presumably displayed to remind visitors about the origins of the business in synthetic chemistry.

The discovery of a whole range of synthetic dyes based on aniline and other coal-derived compounds helped to fuel the massive growth of the chemical industry, particularly in Germany. The advances in organic chemistry that accompanied this industrial activity allowed chemists to make a wide variety of compounds, not necessarily dyes, which could be tested for medicinal activity. A classic example is the development of aspirin by F. Bayer and Company. This has its origins in the extracts of willow bark known to have antipyretic (fever-reducing) properties. The active compounds were called salicylates based on *Salix*, the botanical name for willow. These compounds are based on phenol which was purified from coal tar and later converted to salicylic acid. This acid has antipyretic properties, but is corrosive and, therefore, irritating to the stomach when swallowed. Felix Hoffmann was involved with attempts to reduce the irritant effects by masking the phenol group. His compound, acetylsalicylic acid, was tested in 1897 and found to be well tolerated with antipyretic (fever-reducing) and analgesic (pain-killing) properties. It was marketed as Aspirin® and turned out to be a remarkably successful drug for fever and inflammation, as well as for heart disease due to its activity on blood platelets. Despite this success, it is sobering to think that aspirin would not be approved as a drug in our current regulatory environment. The compound blocks the production of small-molecule prostaglandins in the digestive system, which act to protect against stomach and duodenal ulcers. Long-term administration of high doses of aspirin to patients leads to a high incidence of ulcers, which can lead to fatal internal bleeding. This has led to the development of safer aspirin analogues (such as diclofenac) that have a reduced side effect profile of this type.

4.1.4   Interactions Between Synthetic Compounds and Biological Tissues

The staining of biological materials with dyes has been observed for over 200 years and is employed with clinical samples on a daily basis for diagnosis in hospital laboratories. The German scientist, Paul Ehrlich, recognized the connection between the chemical composition of different dyes and the types of animal tissue to which they bound. He developed the method of "vital staining", in which live animals were injected with dyes and then sacrificed before examining their different tissues under the microscope. In 1885, he showed that one of these dyes, methylene blue, stained nerve cells whilst leaving most other tissues unaffected. Two consequences followed from these investigations, one being that the dyes could be used as medicines in their own right. The results from the methylene blue staining implied that the compound could act as a pain killer because it could bind to nerve cells. Ehrlich did indeed find that this was the case when tested on patients, although the dye was too toxic on the kidneys (nephrotoxic) to be clinically useful. The other important point was that small molecules could bind selectively to biological structures; the era of identifying drug targets had begun.

4.1.4.1 Introducing Pharmacology

Pharmacology[2] (Greek *pharmakon*, drug) is a scientific discipline concerned with the study of how drugs and other chemicals interact with the body. Although pharmacology has been undertaken in one form or the other for many hundreds of years, the first department of that name was established in 1847 in Estonia by Rudolf Bucheim. His former student, Oswald Schmiedeberg, moved to Strasbourg to set up an Institute of Pharmacology that was to prove highly influential in training generations of drug discovery scientists. The technical background to pharmacology is now described in some detail, since many of its concepts are used in modern drug discovery.

Ligands and Receptors

Receptors (Latin *receptor*, receiver or harbourer) are the central focus of pharmacology, as they constitute the physical entities to which drugs bind in the body. A ligand (Latin *ligare*, to bind) is the generic name for agents that bind to receptors, so ligand–receptor interactions are very significant. The terms low-molecular-weight ligand or high-molecular-weight ligand are sometimes used to refer to small and large molecules (e.g. proteins) that bind to their receptors.

The receptor is the drug target, which in most cases, is a protein. Not all drug targets are receptors in the strict definition of the word; enzymes, for example, are part of a separate target class of proteins that catalyze biochemical reactions; these targets have been used to develop an impressive range of drugs to treat AIDS, high blood pressure and many other conditions. This chapter concentrates more on receptors, with other target classes being covered in due course.

Physiology and Cellular Communication

This chapter now moves towards the biology of health and disease in order to explain how pharmacology works in practice. The whole point of drug discovery, of course, is to offer the medical and veterinary professions the tools to cure a disease (or at least to alleviate its symptoms). In order to understand disease, we have to understand physiology, the healthy background from which pathology arises, either through infection or internal changes in the body. Physiology is the science of how the body functions by regulating fundamental processes, such as respiration, nervous transmission, excretion and digestion. In mammals, these work together in homeostasis, where changes in the body are automatically brought back to a normal state, for example, in response to external heat in which the skin is cooled by the evaporation of sweat.

---

[2] Pharmacology is not the same as pharmacy, which is concerned with the preparation and administration of medicines.

These processes are controlled through feedback mechanisms which operate in a similar way to the thermostat on a central heating boiler that maintains a constant temperature at home. In biology, feedback regulation occurs through the actions of both large and small molecules to regulate cell function, so this area is of great interest to cell biologists as well as physiologists. Scientists in each discipline find it easier to envisage these regulatory pathways as comprised of familiar objects from engineering, such as wires, switches, wheels and pulleys. In reality, they are made up of highly sophisticated self-organizing machines, despite the tissue they reside in having the appearance of a wet gooey mass. Even the simplest organisms have an awesome complexity, something I briefly reflect upon as I swat yet another fly in the kitchen.

Disease occurs when these regulatory systems are disrupted in some way and cause an imbalance. This is a modern take on the ancient doctrine of humours, where a disease was thought to be caused by imbalances in phlegm, yellow bile, black bile and blood that were associated with phlegmatic, choleric, melancholic and sanguine temperaments, respectively. In modern terms, a viral or bacterial infection provokes an immune response in the body which is orchestrated by a large number of cells and chemicals that were previously at low levels in the healthy person. The end result is (hopefully) the clearance of the infection, but unfortunately, the symptoms of fever and muscle pain are part of the cure. Disease may also arise through defects caused by genetic mutation, for example, in conditions where proteins involved in the clotting of blood are inactivated, thus leading to haemophilia or uncontrolled bleeding.

The body is organized at different anatomical levels, with organs being the largest, followed by tissues, cells and then subcellular components. As a generalization, pharmacology has traditionally been concerned with whole organs and tissues while the more recent disciplines of cell and molecular biology operates at the level of cells and the molecules that comprise them.

4.1.4.2 Chemical Signals in the Body

Communication between different parts of the body occurs through both the transmission of chemical signals in the blood or other body fluids and electrical signals conducted through cells, like current through a wire. The molecules that drive these chemical and electrical signals are used by pharmacologists as starting points in the design of small molecules that will interact with the drug target. The different classes of chemical signals are as follows:

Hormones

This large family of compounds is comprised of small molecules, peptides and proteins that circulate in the blood to communicate with target organs. They are produced by specialized organs, such as the pancreas (insulin), adrenal glands (adrenaline) and the testes (testosterone). These compounds have multiple effects on the body through their interaction with receptors on different cells within the target organ. Adrenaline (epinephrine in US terminology), for example, is a small-molecule hormone that is secreted into the bloodstream by small glands situated above the kidneys. It is well known as the "fight or flight" hormone that prepares the body for dealing with stress. This is achieved through the enhancement of brain, lung and circulatory system functions that result from the hormone binding to receptors on some of these target organs. Hormones are also implicated in cancers; for example, some prostate and breast cancers grow in response to the male and female sex hormones, respectively.

Cytokines

While the study of hormones has a long history, the identification and characterization of cytokines really started only in the 1970s. Cytokines are proteins that are produced by many different cell types, in contrast to the specialized endocrine cells that secrete hormones. They can operate over very short ranges to allow cooperation between cells that cluster together or even activate the same cells that produced them. The immune system operates through cytokine communication; the feeling of malaise that accompanies a cold is caused by cytokines binding to receptors in the brain to switch on fever mechanisms or to act on muscles to induce fatigue. Extreme cases of immune system activation through cytokines occur in septic shock caused by bacterial infection. The resulting "cytokine storm" leads to a series of extreme reactions, including a lowering of blood pressure that can prove fatal.

Cytokines are not restricted to the immune system, but are present throughout the body to stimulate the growth of many different cell types in a controlled manner.[3] However, cancer can arise if the cell growth becomes independent of cytokines as a result of mutations, since the cell is no longer controlled but just keeps on dividing. A new generation of anti-cancer drugs, which target the mechanisms of cell growth normally controlled by cytokines, are being developed by several major biopharmaceutical companies; for this and other reasons, there is a great deal of interest in the biology of these important molecules and their potential use in drug development.

Neurotransmitters

In contrast to hormones and cytokines, neurotransmitters operate through a physically wired network of nerve cells that can produce extended structures up to a metre long. Electrical impulses are transmitted down the nerve cells or neurons linked together in a chain. The linkage is not complete, however, since there is a

---

[3]Cell growth in this context really means cell division to produce daughter cells.

gap of about a 20 millionth of a millimetre between them (called a synapse after the Greek for "holding together"). Some synapses transmit the nerve impulse via an electrical signal, but others employ small molecules called neurotransmitters. Acetylcholine was the first such molecule to be discovered and was found to transmit signals between nerve cells and muscle. Once acetylcholine has performed its task in transmitting a signal, it is rapidly broken down by the enzyme acetyl-cholinesterase to terminate the signal. Some nerve gases inhibit this enzyme leading to enhanced nerve activity in the muscle with resulting spasms and death. More subtle inhibition can, however, be used to compensate for the loss of neurotrans-mission in diseases, such as Alzheimer's, where nerve cells have been destroyed. This is the basis for the current treatments of this disease (revisited in Chap. 15). There are other neurotransmitters based on amino acids (glutamate) or hormones (adrenaline/epinephrine, noradrenaline/norepinephrine). Electrical communica-tion in the body occurs through the movement of charged elements, such as potas-sium and calcium through ion channels in many cell types, including nerves. Ion channels are covered later in Chap. 6. Research into both neurotransmitters and ion channels is important in understanding the central nervous system (CNS) diseases as well as the mechanisms of sensing pain, both of which are extremely active areas of drug discovery. The above categories of signalling molecule are summarised in Fig. 4.2.

4.1.4.3 Experimental or Classical Pharmacology

This is a venerable discipline going back to the early years of the twentieth century, hence the slightly pejorative term "steam pharmacology" given to it by biologists caught up with modern cell and molecular biology. However, classical pharmacolo-gists can rightly point to the many important drugs which have been discovered using the techniques of experimental pharmacology. These techniques involve the following actions:

1. Identify the human or animal tissues that provide a model for the disease of interest.
2. Identify a physical response of the organ or tissue and devise a way of measuring it in a reproducible manner.
3. Identify hormones or neurotransmitters involved in the response and use natural products or synthetic compounds to either enhance or suppress the response.[4]
4. Select compounds with the highest activity and selectivity for the natural mole-cules, and then test them in whole animals (and ultimately humans) to assess their potential as drugs.

---

[4]Note that cytokines did not have much impact on classical pharmacology because little was known about them and also because they are proteins and not small molecules.

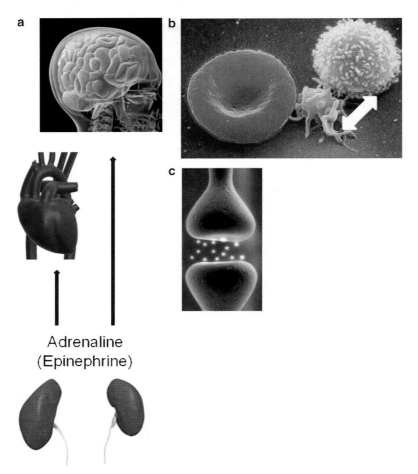

Fig. 4.2 Modes of communication between organs, tissues and cells in the human body. (**a**) Hormones produced by specialised endocrine organs, such as the adrenal glands situated above the kidneys. Adrenaline/epinephrine released into the blood and acting on the heart and (indirectly) on the brain to increases the responsiveness to external threats. (**b**) Communication between two white blood cells by means of protein molecules called cytokines. (**c**) Neurotransmitters passing across a synapse between two nerve cells to propagate a signal

Example: Small-Molecule Drugs for Treating Asthma

This classical pharmacology approach is now illustrated using the above procedures to discover drugs to treat the respiratory disease, asthma.

Disease Model, Selection of Tissue and Test System

Asthma is characterised by an inflammation of the airways in the lungs brought about by allergic reactions to pollen and other environmental stimuli. The main symptom is the shortage of breath caused by the narrowing of the bronchial tubes, thereby reducing the supply of air to the lungs. A drug that counteracts the narrowing will, therefore, relieve the symptoms (although it would not provide a cure). This focuses the attention onto the bronchial tubes, since these tissues could be used to test potential drugs. The tubes are made up of smooth muscle tissue that contracts and relaxes in the similar way to the skeletal muscle that moves the limbs. This contraction (and relaxation) can be measured in the laboratory using a tissue bath and recording equipment (Fig. 4.3). Once this is set up, it is then possible to introduce experimental compounds into the apparatus and look for those that relax the bronchial tissue.

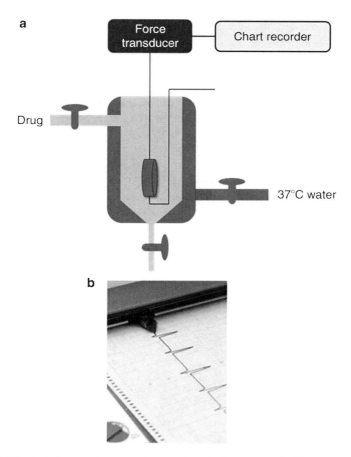

Fig. 4.3 (**a**) Typical pharmacology experiment using the tissue suspended in an organ bath. The apparatus consists of a sealed outer chamber filled with circulating water to keep the tissue at body temperature (37°C). The inner chamber is filled with nutrient solution to keep the tissue (*dark grey* cylinder) in the same state as in the live animal. Drugs or test compounds are introduced through a valve and the force of contraction of the muscle tissue measured using a force transducer that sends a signal to a chart recorder. (**b**) A chart recorder showing peaks drawn by a pen over a regular period of time. The height of the peak and the frequency with which they occur provide numbers that can be used to further analyze the effects of the drug in a quantitative way

Identify Molecules that Relax the Bronchial Tissue (Bronchodilators)

It was known for many years that adrenaline (epinephrine) caused bronchial smooth muscle to relax. This hormone is actually used as a drug to counteract the anaphylactic shock brought about by severe allergic reactions. Unfortunately, it is unsuitable for use as a bronchodilator because of its undesirable side effects (raising blood pressure and causing insomnia, for example) consistent with its role as a "fight or flight" hormone. Adrenaline also has a short half-life[5] because it is rapidly broken down in the body, so symptomatic relief of asthma would be only short-lived. This is where pharmacologists use analogues or derivatives of the natural hormone to see if they have improved properties. A range of such analogues was produced during the first half of the twentieth century, the most relevant one here being isoprenaline, first synthesized in the late 1930s and used as a bronchodilator for many years. Isoprenaline was an improvement on adrenaline, as it did not cause as much elevation of blood pressure through constriction of the blood vessels, but it was rapidly broken down in the body. The problem of the short half-life was solved by altering the parts of the molecule that caused it to be broken down by the body's metabolism (Chap. 11). In addition, compounds were identified (using the tissue bath experiments and other techniques) that had limited effects on the heart tissue; in other words, they exhibited greater selectivity for bronchial smooth muscle over the heart tissue. One of the most successful of these compounds was salbutamol, discovered by David Jack and others in the 1960s at Allen & Hanbury's, a division of Glaxo (now GlaxoSmithKline). This was marketed as an inhaled bronchodilator with the trade name, Ventolin®, and gave symptomatic relief for 4 h (Fig. 4.4).

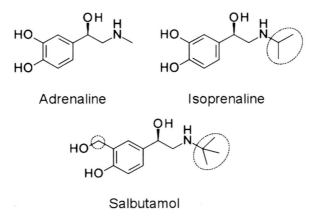

Fig. 4.4 Modification of a natural hormone adrenaline to produce drugs that relax muscle in the airways. Note the small modification (addition of isopropyl group to adrenaline) in isoprenaline. The ring with two OH groups is a catechol group that is rapidly broken down by the body. A simple modification of one of the OHs in salbutamol slows down the breakdown and makes the drug effective for several hours while the substitution of a *t*-butyl group (*circled right hand side*) results in greater selectivity for lung tissue

---

[5] The half-life is the time taken for 50% of the compound to disappear.

Until recently, drug discovery scientists would taste the compounds they produced, testing for sweetness or other sensations. This certainly helped in making discoveries, but had an obvious downside. David Jack was a discovery scientist in this heroic mould, but one night he had to phone his doctor because of a massive increase in his heart rate brought on by tasting some adrenaline analogues; luckily, he survived to become a research director, but they certainly do not make them like that anymore.

The above example highlighted some important facets of experimental pharmacology and the power of medicinal chemistry to provide compounds that resist metabolism and bind to receptors on biological tissues in a highly selective manner. By implication, this means that there must be separate receptors for adrenaline on different tissues, in other words, receptor subtypes. This is a fundamental aspect of drug discovery that is examined later in this chapter.

4.1.4.4 Agonists and Antagonists

The two main categories of receptor-binding drugs are agonists and antagonists.

When a natural ligand (hormone, neurotransmitter, etc.) binds to its receptor, the latter is activated to switch on whatever function is associated with it. In the case of adrenaline, this is the relaxation of smooth muscle. The agonist is a molecule that binds to a receptor in the same way as the hormone and triggers the response, but it may have a very different chemical composition. This is illustrated in the Fig. 4.5, where the normal house key fits into the lock, but the agonist is in the form of a hairpin that is used to pick the lock. An antagonist is a molecule that blocks the binding of the natural ligand to the receptor, thereby preventing its activation. This is illustrated in the figure by the attempt to put the key into the lock having previously jammed it with a twig by mistake (perhaps while under the influence of one of the oldest drugs?). The names agonist and antagonist are derived from the Greek *agonistes* "contestant" and *antagonistes* "opponent", respectively. This is quite appropriate since the agonist competes for its place on the receptor with the natural ligand and displaces it because it binds more tightly. The antagonist must also bind more tightly than the natural ligand, but in doing so opposes its action. There are further pharmacological terms, such as partial agonist or inverse agonist, that are explained in any basic pharmacology resource; and to avoid further complication, these are not discussed here any further.

4.1.4.5 Measuring Drug Efficacy and Selectivity

Pharmacology is not just a qualitative (descriptive) discipline; it is also quantitative because the action of drugs on their targets can be described in mathematical terms. The simple weights and measures used in drug discovery are introduced in this section, along with the concepts of affinity and efficacy.

Fig. 4.5 Agonist and antagonist drugs illustrated by analogy to a key in a lock. The natural hormone, cytokine or neurotransmitter is the key; the agonist is a hairpin with the correct shape to allow the lock to be picked, yet, without the overall appearance of the key; the antagonist is a twig jammed in the lock to prevent the key from getting inside it

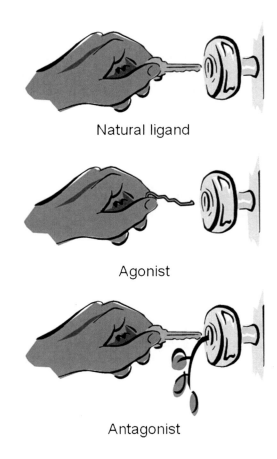

Natural ligand

Agonist

Antagonist

Weights, Concentrations and Molarities

Consider the fact that many small-molecule drugs are administered in doses as small as 10 mg to a person weighing 70 kg. This represents one seven-millionth of the weight of an average-sized person, so the drug must clearly be very potent. Drugs are often used in very low concentrations in laboratory experiments, and this is reflected in the terminology for weights and measures. Table 4.1 shows some examples of weights defined as fractions of a gram.[6]

---

[6] As an aside, the world reference kilogram weight made of platinum–iridium alloy is stored near Paris; it is no longer its original weight because it is losing too many atoms, so physicists are trying to find a more accurate alternative.

Table 4.1 Units of measurement used in drug discovery. Because drug molecules are highly potent, the quantities used for experiments are small fractions of a gram

Name	Abbreviation	Numerical value
Milligram	mg	1 thousandth gram
Microgram	μg	1 millionth gram
Nanogram	ng	1 billionth gram
Picogram	pg	1 trillionth gram
Femtogram	fg	1 thousand trillionth gram

The table above is applicable to volumes as well, so the word "gram" is substituted with "liter" (note "litre" used in UK English).

There are two ways of expressing the concentrations of a drug: the weight per unit of volume and the molarity. In the first case, a solution of drug made up in water (solid compound dissolved in water) might have a concentration of 10 mg per millilitre. Laboratory scientists would normally write this as 10 mg/ml and pronounce it "migs per mill" (μg/ml is pronounced "micrograms per mill", not "mikes per mill"). Sometimes, the concentration is expressed as mgL^{-1} which is the same as milligrams per litre. The different usage of symbols for weights and measures can be confusing, particularly for technical translators who have to work with formal regulatory documents. Guidelines do exist for publication in academic journals as well as for regulatory submissions, examples of which can be found in the following references (Proceedings of the National Academy of Sciences (USA) 2010; ICH M5 EWG Units and Measurements Controlled Vocabulary 2010).

The other way of expressing concentrations is through the term molarity. This is the concentration of a compound expressed as a function of its molecular weight. An experiment might be designed to compare the activity of two drugs, for example, a small molecule and an antibody with molecular weights of 500 and 150,000 Da, respectively. The antibody has 300 times less "activity" than the small molecule on a weight-for-weight basis, so it is impossible to make a comparison on the basis of weight alone.[7] The solution to this problem is to use a system of measurement that combines the molecular weight and the weight of a compound. The terms, mol and molar (M), are introduced in Fig. 4.6 using the molecular weight of ethanol as an example.

Going back to the comparison between the small molecule and antibody, 1 mol of each would weight 500 and 150,000 g (150 kg), respectively. In practice, the amounts used in laboratory experiments are reduced by factors of a thousand or more. Many experimental compounds, for example, are dissolved at millimolar concentrations and still have activity when diluted 1,000 times to micromolar (μM) or even 1,000,000 times for nanomolar (nM). Drug discovery scientists like compounds that are active in the low-micromolar or nanomolar range, and some drugs, like steroids, are still active at picomolar (pM) concentrations.

---

[7] The terms, weight and mass, are often used interchangeably. These are only the same when considering the force of gravity on Earth; the weight of a compound with a given mass will be greater on our planet compared with, for example, the Moon.

Fig. 4.6 Mol, molarity and molar. In this example, the molecular weight of ethanol is 46, so 1 mol of ethanol weighs 46 g. A 1-molar (1 M) solution of ethanol in water contains 46 g of ethanol dissolved in 1 L of water

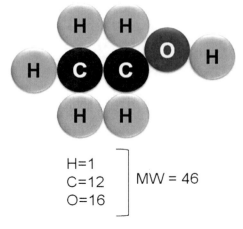

$$H = 1$$
$$C = 12$$
$$O = 16$$

$$MW = 46$$

1 mol ethanol = 46 grams

1 molar (M) ethanol = 46 grams/liter

Ligand Binding to Receptors

The only way to make meaningful comparisons between natural ligands and synthetic drugs is to express the strength of their binding to receptors as a number. This number, called the affinity, is calculated using an equation that requires knowledge of the concentrations of free ligand and receptor as well as the concentration of bound ligand. Drug binding, of course, is not an end in itself; it must lead to a biological response, such as muscle contraction. The degree to which a drug promotes such a response is called the efficacy. It is possible for a drug to bind to only a small fraction of receptors present in a tissue and yet to display a high degree of efficacy. These concepts arise from experiments in classical pharmacology, in which compounds are used to provoke a response in isolated tissues or organs that can be measured in the lab. Pharmacology experiments can be set up in different ways, for example, to see if the tissue response increases in proportion to the amount of drug added; alternatively, the time taken to reach a maximum drug response might be measured. These measurements help to determine the rate of association of a drug to its receptor. Ligands do not remain bound to their receptors, but rapidly become detached from them (dissociate) and exist in a balance (equilibrium) between the bound and unbound states. These measurements of rates of association and dissociation are known as the binding kinetics of a ligand to its receptor. The various measurements described here provide information about the number of receptors present on each tissue and their biological properties. Very importantly, the presence of more than one type of receptor for the same ligand can be inferred from these experiments, something that is relevant to the adrenaline agonist (salbutamol) described previously and the histamine antagonists to follow later.

Drug Potency: The EC_{50} and IC_{50}

The EC_{50} of a drug literally means "effective concentration 50%". In a typical pharmacology experiment to test the activity of a drug, there will be a point at which adding more and more of the drug will make no difference to the activity; in other words, the latter will have reached its maximum. The EC_{50} is the amount of added compound (measured in weight or molarity) that gives 50% of the maximum activity.

If the drug is inhibiting the binding of a ligand to its receptor (i.e. is an antagonist), the term IC_{50} is used, meaning inhibitory concentration 50%. The actual way in which the binding is measured is covered later in this chapter, but in the meantime, the basic concept is illustrated in Fig. 4.7.

The EC_{50} and IC_{50} values are referred to in various ways; for example, "compound Z inhibited the binding of adrenaline to its receptor with an IC_{50} of 20 nM". Alternatively, the following phrase might be used when comparing the action of two drugs: "Compound X had an EC_{50} of 30 μM on bronchial smooth muscle relaxation compared with compound Y which had an EC_{50} of 30 nM". Note that the EC_{50} values in the example can be used to evaluate the comparative efficacy of compound X over compound Y and its selectivity for the target receptor on the bronchial tissue.

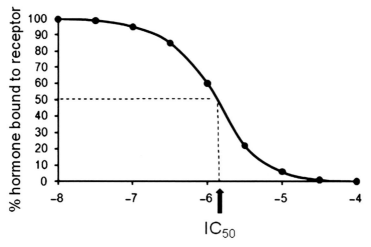

Amount of competitor drug added (M)

Fig. 4.7 Estimating the IC_{50} for a drug binding to a receptor. Example of a hormone binding to its receptor on a tissue; the amount bound is expressed as a percentage, so 100% is the maximum amount that can be bound. An antagonist drug is added to push the hormone off the tissue (displace it). As the amount of antagonist added is increased, the level of hormone binding drops off until eventually it is all removed (at the 0% point on the graph). The amount of added competitor drug is expressed in molar units using the shorthand −8, −7, −6, etc., which is another way of expressing 10^{-8}, 10^{-7} and 10^{-6}. To clarify further, 10^{-6} M is one millionth or 1 μM. The IC_{50} is read off the graph as indicated. In this case, the value is roughly 2×10^{-6} M or 2 μM

In this example, compound X has to be used at a 1,000 times higher concentration to give the same effect as compound Y (30 µM is 1,000 times greater than 30 nM). In drug discovery terminology, compound Y has 1,000-fold selectivity over compound X.

4.1.4.6   Receptor Subtypes and the First Blockbuster Drugs

The earlier section on the development of adrenaline agonists to treat the symptoms of asthma highlighted the fact that adrenaline itself acts on different organs of the body, including the lungs and blood vessels. However, agonist drugs, like salbutamol, are mostly active on the lung. This means that the same ligand (adrenaline) must bind to different subtypes of the receptor and generate responses according to where each subtype is expressed in the body. This idea was first exploited by James Black, who developed adrenaline antagonists in the 1960s (beta blockers) to treat high blood pressure. Later, at Smith Kline and French in the UK, he developed antiulcer drugs based on antagonists of histamine, a natural hormone that had been isolated in the early years of the twentieth century. The discovery and development of the histamine antagonists is an example of how pharmacology became the most successful drug discovery technology in the years leading up to the modern era of biotechnology (see later).

Histamine Receptors

Histamine (derived from the amino acid histidine) is a small molecule which contributes to the symptoms of allergic reactions, such as skin reddening (erythema), running eyes and nasal congestion. These unwanted symptoms are treated with histamine-binding antagonists, the so-called antihistamines, which are commonly prescribed in the hay fever season. In addition to its role in allergic diseases, histamine promotes the secretion of gastric acid in the stomach. This is a concentrated solution of hydrochloric acid that contributes to the breaking down of protein chains during the initial stages of digestion. Despite the corrosive potential of this acid, the stomach is normally protected from damage; however, this protection sometimes breaks down, leading to peptic ulcer disease, in which the stomach lining and duodenum are perforated leading to potentially life-threatening consequences. It has been known since the late 1940s that certain histamine analogues promote acid secretion, and by the early 1970s, it was clear that there were two histamine receptors, named H1 and H2 (for the receptors linked to allergy and acid secretion, respectively).[8] This meant that if compounds could be developed to selectively block H2, they would reduce the amount of acid secreted into the stomach, and thereby give enough time for the peptic ulcers to heal. James Black and his colleagues took up the challenge, the first task being to establish a suitable biological

---

[8] In later years, the number of receptors was increased to four by the discovery of the H3 and H4 receptors, neither of which are connected with acid secretion.

test system. There is a general terminology for these tests depending upon the level of tissue being examined. The assay is conducted *in vivo* if a whole animal is being used to test an experimental compound. If a piece of tissue has been taken out of the animal and is still viable, then it is an *ex vivo* assay. If the tissue and cells are ground up into fragments and assayed in a test tube (or modern equivalent), this is an *in vitro* assay as the old biochemistry joke goes: *in vitro veritas*.

Black and his co-worker set up a low-throughput *in vivo* assay that measured the secretion of acid into the stomachs of anaesthetized rats. The chemists then synthesized over 200 analogues of histamine to try and find one that would inhibit acid production in the assay. It was 4 years after the start of this work in 1964 that one of their compounds, guanylhistamine, was shown to have some modest antagonist activity; however, it also stimulated some acid release on its own, a phenomenon known as partial agonism. To eliminate this undesirable effect (sometimes called breeding out the effect), the medicinal chemists identified the part of the molecule responsible for inducing acid secretion and replaced it with a different chemical group (a thiourea). In 1970, the new compound, burimamide, was also found to block acid secretion, albeit with low activity. Again the compound structure was reviewed and a new analogue, metiamide, with a tenfold higher activity than burimamide, was produced and tested on 700 patients. A few of these developed a blood disorder, which fortunately was reversible, but which meant that the drug could not be developed further. The thiourea group was shown to be responsible for the toxicity, so metiamide was modified to produce a new compound cimetidine. This was launched as Tagamet® in 1972, creating revenues of millions of dollars for Smith Kline French and becoming the first blockbuster drug in the process. It had taken 8 years to produce a compound (cimetidine) with the required activity and features (like oral bioavailability and minimal toxicity) that would make it a good medicine. Despite this, it took a further 4 years before cimetidine reached the marketplace. The work of James Black on histamine antagonists, along with his earlier work on beta blockers, helped to earn him a Nobel Prize in 1988.

The phrase "nothing succeeds like success", to reiterate the point made earlier, is very applicable to marketing drugs; the commercial success of Tagamet® ensured that other companies would attempt to develop their own H2 blockers and occupy some of the by-now lucrative market for anti-ulcerant drugs. The Glaxo scientists, Roy Brittain and David Jack (of salbutamol fame), were aware of burimamide and its lack of oral bioavailability. They, therefore, produced their own analogues with improved activity, until they had a compound with the same thiourea group as the one found in metiamide. Glaxo scientists then replaced the offending group with a non-toxic substitute to produce ranitidine. This was more potent than cimetidine and did not have the side effects of that drug. Ranitidine was developed and marketed as Zantac®, becoming the best-selling drug in the world for several years. For Glaxo employees at that time, it really was a golden age of drug discovery (Fig. 4.8).

A number of important points arise from the histamine antagonist programme:

1. Some understanding of the disease is necessary for identifying a molecular target that can be affected by a small-molecule drug. In the previous example,

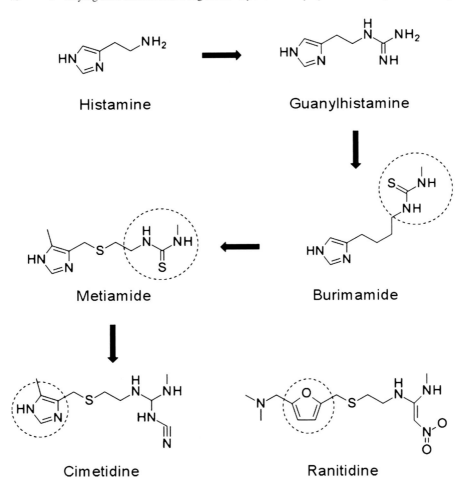

Fig. 4.8 Creation of H2 receptor antagonist drugs based on naturally occurring histamine molecule. Chemical modifications of histamine leading to cimetidine marketed as Tagamet®. The thiourea group that caused toxicity is *circled* in burimamide and metiamide. A rival H2 antagonist ranitidine (marketed as Zantac®) is shown for comparison with cimetidine. In this molecule, the original histamine structure has all, but disappeared, with the basic ring structure completely replaced (technically, an imidazole group by a furan, *circled*)

peptic ulcer disease was known to arise as a result of excess secretion of acid in the stomach driven by the action of histamine (although in fact, other mechanisms operate as well). Classical pharmacology experiments led to the identification of histamine H2 receptors as suitable targets for antagonist drugs.

2. A test system has to be put in place to measure the activity of experimental compounds. In the above example, a simple *in vivo* test was used. The rate limiting step in this programme was not the assay itself, but the several years taken to synthesize compounds, test them and then modify active molecules

in the laboratory. Although the basic principles of synthesis and testing are the same today, the test (assay) would now be performed on purified cell fractions or even the receptors themselves. Furthermore, thousands of compounds would be submitted for testing rather than just a few hundred.

3. A thorough knowledge of organic chemistry is required to modify drug molecules and predict the biological consequences of these modifications. The histamine work was a *tour de force* of medicinal chemistry, where functional groups were chosen to impart good solubility in water, reduced brain penetration and greater binding to the histamine receptor. The scientists also learnt by hard clinical experience that the thiourea group was toxic and had to be avoided in future programmes. There are now in fact chemical databases of so-called toxic groups that are routinely searched when designing new molecules.

4. It is possible for competitors to produce their own compounds that act on the same target to treat the same disease. Some areas of drug discovery are so competitive that there may be as many as six different compounds under development for the same target. This is commercially viable only if each company has secure patent protection on its inventions. In the case of histamine H2 antagonists, cimetidine and ranitidine were protected by composition of matter patents because the two compounds are sufficiently unrelated in chemical terms. Patents, of course, have a limited lifetime, so both drugs have lost patent protection and Zantac® is now sold over the counter.

The phrase "me-too drugs" has entered the vocabulary of drug discovery, although it often bears negative connotations. "Me-too" implies that each company is marketing a drug to gain profit, despite the fact that it may not offer any advantage to a patient over an existing product that works by the same mechanism. It is certainly true that many drug discovery projects have been (and still are) modelled on those being undertaken by rival companies and that marketing campaigns attempt to exploit even the slightest difference between competing products. In the case of the H2 antagonists, however, ranitidine was shown to have eight times more activity than cimetidine and display fewer side effects (Konturek et al. 1980). The physician has the choice of a number of medicines, even if these work on the same target. In real-world clinical practice, these medicines have different effects on different people (a fact to which I can testify personally). The reasons are not always clear, but the responses (or side effects) may be influenced by the patient's genetic background. This area of pharmacogenetics is covered in Chap. 14.

4.1.5 Pharmacology Revisited

In the period leading up to the late 1960s, drug discovery was undertaken almost exclusively with live animals, whole organs or isolated tissues. The cells that make-up these structures all express receptors that are targets for thousands of different ligands found in the human body. Many of these will have no relevance to drug discovery at all, either now or in the future, but natural scientific curiosity, if nothing else, demands that their biochemical properties be fully understood. This can only be achieved if receptors are characterized as real molecules rather than as figures on a graph.

4.1.5.1 Radioactive Ligands

It may seem surprising that up until the 1960s, no one had really succeeded in doing the obvious experiment of directly measuring the binding of ligands to their receptors. The problem lies with having to measure the physically minute amounts of ligand that binds to equally minute amounts of receptor. The numbers involved are so small that there is no question of being able to see the material and weigh it on a balance. The weight of the adrenaline receptor (adrenoceptor) in 1 g of lung tissue is approximately 1 ng (one thousand millionth of a gram); therefore, in order to obtain enough pure receptor to see by eye (as a dried deposit on a tube), at least 5 kg of lung tissue would be required. The situation with the ligand is even worse, as it weighs roughly 100 times less than the receptor. This scenario is almost universal in drug discovery science; the main players, be they chemical or biological, operate at levels that are far below the limits of human vision. Nevertheless, they can be detected and measured with great accuracy using the technology developed for physics, chemistry and biology.

One of the most common ways of measuring binding is to physically attach a label to the ligand to make it easily detectable, even at very low concentrations. Radioactive atoms fulfil this role perfectly, as the radiation they emit can be accurately measured using suitable instruments. The ligand is then used as a radioactive probe for receptors. Mention the word "radioactivity" to most people and they will think of atomic weapons or nuclear reactors producing radioisotopes, such as uranium and plutonium. These emit high levels of harmful radiation that must be contained in highly specialized laboratories under conditions of tight security. Medical isotopes, by contrast, although still dangerous if mishandled, are routinely used in hospitals, universities and biopharmaceutical companies. Some isotopes, like ^{60}Co (60 is the total number of protons and neutrons in these atoms: 27 plus 33, respectively), are used to irradiate cancer cells to drive them into a cell suicide programme. It is also used to irradiate white blood cells for immunology research; I recall standing outside the huge concrete doors of the irradiation room to control the system that opened the ^{60}Co source. A brief sound of moving machinery and that was it; the radiation is silent and undetectable, except with a Geiger counter. Radioisotopes, like ^{60}Co, emit powerful gamma rays and are not suitable for measuring ligand binding to receptors. Historically, a range of isotopes were discovered that only emitted weak radiation, so they could even be used in human subjects. The Nobel Prize winning Hungarian scientist, George de Hevesy, was a pioneer in this field of biological tracers. He started early because while living in a boarding house as a young man, he placed a small amount of radioactivity in the remains of his dinner to prove that the landlady was serving the leftovers in the following evening's meal.

Since their introduction to laboratories in the 1940s, the following radioactive elements have been used to label a vast range of compounds for both basic and applied research. These are ^{3}H (tritium), ^{14}C (carbon 14), ^{35}S (sulphur 35), ^{32}P (phosphorus 32) and ^{125}I (iodine 125). All of these elements are present in organic molecules in a stable non-radioactive form, so one or more of the natural atoms can be substituted with radioactive ones produced in small reactors. Specialized radiochemical companies have been set up to supply the research community with customized or "off-the-shelf" radiochemicals, including a number of ligands for pharmacological receptors. It is also possible to produce radiolabelled proteins and nucleic acids in the laboratory by purchasing prelabelled amino acids and nucleotides which are then incorporated into the larger molecules.

The isotopes mentioned above emit different types of radiation, namely, beta (^{3}H, ^{14}C, ^{35}S and ^{32}P) and gamma (^{32}P and ^{125}I). The weaker beta radiation can be measured using a scintillation counter which detects and measures the tiny flashes of light produced when radiation hits a specially formulated liquid, known as scintillation fluid. Samples of radioactive materials are added to this strong-smelling organic liquid in glass or plastic vials which are then capped and placed in racks before being read in a machine. Although this technique has made a fundamental contribution to biomedical research, the filling and capping hundreds of vials, plus the hours of waiting before seeing all the results, has to be one of the most tedious procedures undertaken in any laboratory.

4.1.5.2 Binding Assays

Once a ligand has been produced in radioactive form, it is possible to use it in binding assays that measure how much of it binds to its receptor. The word assay originates from the French *essayer*, to try, and originally referred to the determination of the purity of metals. The word is frequently used in biological and pharmaceutical research in the form of the binding assays mentioned already and others, such as screening assays, inhibition assays and competition assays, all of which are described in this book at some point.

Early ligand–receptor binding assays involved overlaying thin sections of whole tissues with radioactive ligand to allow receptor binding. The unbound ligand was then washed away and the tissue section exposed to X-ray film of the type routinely used in hospitals. Because the radiation source was tritium and therefore very weak, the film had to be exposed in the dark for many days or even weeks to generate a visible darkening, where the ligand had bound in the tissue. This autoradiography procedure is still used to locate ligand binding in tissue sections, particularly for visualizing the distribution of experimental drugs in the tissues of whole animals. Unfortunately, the procedure is time-consuming and of low throughput; in other words, only a small number of samples can be analyzed at any one time. Autoradiography may help to locate the site of binding, but it does not give a figure for how much ligand is bound. This is where "grind and bind" comes in. In this procedure, whole tissues are ground up in a blender (similar to the type used in the kitchen) to produce an extract containing fragments derived from damaged cells. Included in these fragments are the cell membranes that bear receptor proteins, so it is normal practice to purify these membranes prior to mixing them together with radioactive ligands to allow binding. This incubation process is carried out in a filtration device that permits the removal of unbound ligand in a simple washing step. Ligand that is specifically bound to receptor on the cell membrane is radioactive, so the amount bound can be determined by simply measuring the radioactivity of the membrane preparation in a scintillation counter. The results are expressed as either disintegrations per minute (dpm) or counts per minute (cpm). This powerful technique is used in competition assays to compare the binding strengths of different drug candidates to a particular receptor. They are called competition assays because unlabelled compounds are used to displace the radioactive ligand by competing for sites on the receptor. If an unlabelled compound binds to the receptor with a higher affinity than that of the radioactive ligand, the amount of bound radioactivity will be reduced in proportion to the amount of unlabelled compound added to the assay (Fig. 4.9).

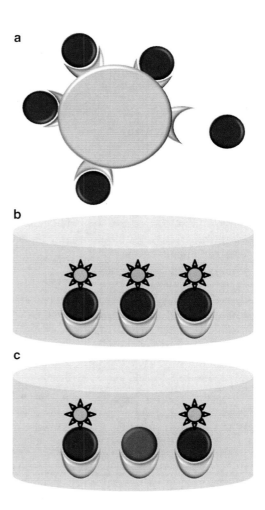

Fig. 4.9 Schematic diagram of membrane-binding competition assay. (**a**) A cell (*large circle*) with receptor proteins on the surface. Each receptor binds a natural ligand, such as a hormone (*blue disc*) (**b**) The cells are broken up and the membranes bearing the receptor placed in a tube along with the hormone that has been tagged with a radioactive isotope, like tritium (^{3}H). The receptor is now occupied by the labelled molecules. (**c**) A drug (*red disc*) that competes with the hormone for a place on the receptor is added to the tube; the radioactive hormone is displaced and washed away, so the radioactivity is reduced. This reduction can be measured and used to work out the percentage of hormone left on the receptor, and hence the IC_{50} of the drug

This is the information used to construct the IC_{50} graph shown in Fig. 4.7, and it is also used in other calculations to work out the affinity of a drug for its receptor.

These experiments to test the binding of compounds to membrane preparations are now undertaken as a matter of routine. However, problems with non-specific binding can arise, where minute amounts of compounds bind to equally minute amounts of receptors in the presence of much larger amounts of cell membranes and other biological materials. Small ligands can stick to this extra material to produce a high background signal on tissues that do not express the receptor. This problem of non-specific binding is almost universal in biomedical research and gives rise to its own terminology, including the phrase "promiscuous binders", which should be self-explanatory. One way round this problem is to purify receptor proteins away from other cellular materials or to produce them in recombinant form by using genetic engineering (see later chapters). Unfortunately, membrane proteins are difficult to produce in a "native form", i.e. in a form that is folded correctly to allow it to bind a ligand (in contrast to the 90% of cellular proteins that are not membrane-associated). In practice, genetic engineering is used to introduce (transfect) the receptor protein into a cell, where it is normally absent; it is then possible to compare the degree of ligand binding to cells bearing the receptor and exactly the same cells without it. Pharmacology has, in a sense, moved from a classical phase (tissue baths) to a "post-modernist" phase (genetically engineered receptors) by joining forces with cell and molecular biology to understand receptor (and therefore drug target) action in unprecedented detail. To understand how this transition occurred from the late 1980s onwards, it is necessary to review the development of biotechnology.

4.1.6   Introduction to Biotechnology

At the same time that pharmacology was delivering novel drugs based on receptor-binding small molecules, the early seeds of a biotechnology revolution were being sown in labs around the world. The revolution had really begun in the 1940s with research on antibiotics, but this would move on to transform the biopharmaceutical industry through the development of genetic engineering. Biotechnology is not new, of course; it has been used for thousands of years to create useful products (like baked bread or alcohol) from living organisms, such as yeast.[9] In the twentieth century, the principles of biochemistry and microbiology were applied to the industrial-scale production of vitamins and other important chemicals from living organisms. These products were not only small molecules, but also bacterial proteins, like the enzymes used in "biological" washing powders. Since microbiology is such an important part of biotechnology, the next section gives an overview of this important scientific discipline.

---

[9] The importance of yeast in the early study of biochemistry is illustrated by the fact that the word enzyme literally means "in yeast", since proteins extracted from this fungus had the ability to ferment sugar into alcohol in the absence of cells.

4.1.6.1 Microbiology

This is the study of single-celled organisms that include bacteria, fungi and protozoa, but exclude, for example, mammals and higher plants. Viruses are absent from this list as they really come under the discipline of virology. This is because viruses are unable to survive independently, but must infect cells in order to grow and reproduce. It is actually this property that makes viruses such useful tools for modern biotechnological processes, such as genetic engineering and gene therapy (Chap. 2).

Microbiology is important for the biopharmaceutical industry for many reasons. Firstly, microbes (or micro-organisms) are responsible for infectious diseases, so they are the targets for drugs (sometimes called anti-infectives). More specifically, bacteria are targeted by antibiotics (or antibacterials), viruses by antivirals, fungi by antifungals and protozoa by antiprotozoals. Secondly, microbes use the process of fermentation to produce small-molecule drugs or nutritional supplements that could not otherwise be synthesized in the laboratory. These molecules may be produced completely from scratch, or else from an existing precursor that is fed to the microbe and converted to the final product in a process called biotransformation. Finally, microbiology is at the heart of genetic engineering and the production of recombinant protein drugs.

Some Background and Terminology

Micro-organisms (excluding viruses) are classified as belonging to one of the following three evolutionary domains: archaea, prokaryotes (bacteria) and eukaryotes (fungi, protozoa). Archaea and prokaryotes have DNA but no cell nucleus, a structure present in eukaryotes that contains DNA packaged into chromosomes. Plants and animals are eukaryotes, but are made up of many cells (multicellular) opposed to yeast, for example, which is single-celled (unicellular).

The systematic names of microbes are written as two italicized words, for example, *Escherichia coli*, for the common bacterium, and *Saccharomyces cerevisiae*, for baker's yeast (it is not hard to guess the use to which *Saccharomyces carlsbergensis* is put). Sometimes, the first word is shortened to the first letter, so the bacterium becomes *E.coli*.

Microbes/micro-organisms are grown in culture or are cultured. A culture medium is a watery (aqueous) solution containing sugars, salts, amino acids and other nutrients that support microbial growth. Very often, it is convenient to grow microbes on a solid medium in culture dishes known as agar plates (the round plastic plates called Petri dishes are often used for this). Agar is a gelatinous material derived from seaweed that behaves like gelatin in cookery. It is dissolved in boiling water, along with the nutrients normally present in liquid cultures, and then allowed to set by cooling. Samples of microbes are literally spread onto the surface of the agar with a glass rod and the plates incubated in a temperature-controlled box for a number of hours, after which

---

(continued)

> **Some Background and Terminology** (continued)
>
> colonies of bacteria or fungi appear dotted over the agar. These are picked off the plate using a toothpick and used to inoculate a liquid culture that generates large numbers of organisms within a few hours. Bacteria, like *E.coli* for example, will double their numbers every 20 min and yeast every 45 min. This means that the numbers can reach astronomical proportions after a relatively small number of generations (doublings). I have always been impressed by the (untestable) story about placing a grain of rice onto the first square of a chessboard and then adding double the number for each subsequent square. By the time the 64th square is reached, the amount of rice used would supposedly be enough to cover the whole of India to a depth of 9 ft!

4.1.6.2   Antibiotics

Life Hinders Life

So wrote the great French scientist, Louis Pasteur, in 1877 based on his observations that one type of microbe could inhibit the growth of another when cultured together in the same vessel. There was a surprising amount of insight into this process of "antibiosis" well before Alexander Fleming's discovery of penicillin in 1928, and tantalizing accounts of the antibacterial activity of *Penicillium* moulds were written as early as the nineteenth century. However, it was not until Fleming directly observed the killing of Staphylococci bacteria on an agar plate by *Penicillium notatum* fungus that antibiotic research really began to take off. This plate was later preserved in formaldehyde and is now in the British Museum in London. The agent produced by the *Penicillium* fungus then had to be isolated as a pure compound and tested against bacteria in animals and eventually patients. Howard Florey and Ernst Chain took on this problem in Oxford, where they determined the structure of penicillin and showed that it had antibacterial activity in human subjects. Soon, the pharmaceutical industry in the USA showed an interest, and a consortium of companies was established to produce large amounts of the antibiotic in deep fermentation tanks. This level of cooperation and intensity of effort was possible because of the military need for antibiotics in the closing years of World War II.

The story of the discovery and development of penicillin is far more detailed than outlined in this brief summary and in some ways, given the series of coincidences that led Fleming to his original observation, is barely credible. The technical challenges of producing penicillin in large quantities required new experimental techniques. For example, mutant strains of the *Penicillium* fungus were generated by irradiation with X-rays and selected for their enhanced synthetic capacity. The outstanding success of penicillin as a medicinal product and the clear recognition that microbes were a source of anti-infective compounds meant that biotechnology rapidly became a mainstream pharmaceutical activity in the post-war years. Despite this, pharmaceutical companies remained the traditional providers of small-molecule drugs, whether they came from chemistry laboratories or from fermentation tanks. The research organization of these companies included a biotechnology department whose remit was to produce anti-infectives or other natural products from microbes. However, it was not until the first independent biotechnology companies came onto the scene that the modern biopharmaceutical industry really began to take shape.

4.1.6.3   Loosening Up

The social revolution of the 1960s and 1970s had an impact upon the management styles and the formalities of dress and behaviour that had previously existed in large pharmaceutical companies. Until quite recently, industry scientists were considered to be very conservative by comparison with their counterparts in academia. All this changed with the emergence of stand-alone biotechnology companies in the State of California.[10] This state produced more than the Beach Boys, as it was (and is) home to some of the greatest research universities in the world. It was here in 1972 that Herbert Boyer (UCSF) and Stanley Cohen (Stanford) developed the recombinant DNA technology that allowed, for the first time, the recombining in the laboratory of DNA from one organism with that of another (actually, it happens naturally all the time with viruses). The DNA to be recombined might code for a particular protein in a human cell, for example; so if it is transferred to a recipient organism, such as a fast-growing bacterium like *E.coli*, it is then possible to produce far larger amounts of (recombinant) proteins than would be possible with normal human tissue. Protein drugs like insulin can, therefore, be made in huge quantity by bacterial fermentation rather than through extraction of the natural protein from the pancreatic tissue of pigs. Furthermore, it is far preferable to treat diabetes with human, and not pig (porcine) insulin, because this reduces the risk of provoking an immune response to the protein in the patient.

The details of recombinant DNA technology are covered in a later chapter, but ironically, the tools needed for this new biotechnology revolution were provided by traditional microbiology. These tools include the antibiotics that are added to agar plates to ensure that only bacteria-containing recombinant DNA can grow; the vast majority of bacteria added to the plate are killed off because they lack a resistance gene that is transferred along with the human DNA.

The world's first biotechnology company was founded in 1976 by Herbert Boyer and the venture capitalist, Robert Swanson. The company, Genentech Inc., still thrives and is based at 1 DNA Way, South San Francisco. It created a new model for a drug discovery business, one that did not carry the organizational and historical baggage of a large pharmaceutical company. Equally, however, it did not (at least in the early days)

---

[10] I always enjoy the New Yorker cartoon of a road sign in California that reads "you are now leaving California, please resume normal behaviour".

have the latter's financial resources, so its first drug, recombinant human insulin, was marketed through Eli Lilly and Company (in 1982). Many biotechnology companies have been formed (and dissolved) since the mid 1970s; some of these have been "spun out" from university departments, so in some cases, the academic ethos has been preserved in an industrial setting. The emergence of the biotechnology company as a separate part of the drug discover industry means that large pharmaceutical companies are now exposed to competition from "leaner and meaner" research organizations; on the other side of the fence, the universities have been exposed to the realities of drug discovery, sometimes the hard way. Modern biotechnology is now fully integrated into mainstream drug discovery within the large pharmaceutical companies; this has been achieved by internal investment in the technology as well as through the acquisition of small biotech companies.

4.1.7 The Present

Research and development in the biopharmaceutical industry has come a very long way since the early days of drug discovery. This is exemplified by the list of medicines produced during what could reasonably be called a "golden age" of drug discovery in the twentieth century (Table 4.2). The targets for these drugs vary from receptors for small molecules to enzymes and (in the case of cancer) DNA itself.

Table 4.2 Examples of drugs developed during the twentieth century for a variety of medical conditions. The list is far from exhaustive, but does give an idea of the drug development projects considered worthwhile by the biopharmaceutical industry at that time

Condition	Medicine
Bacterial infection	Antibiotics
Inflammation	Corticosteroids, NSAIDs
Hypertension	Beta blockers, ACE inhibitors, diuretics
Blocked arteries	Statins
Thrombosis	Anticoagulants (e.g. warfarin)
Cancer	Cisplatin, fluorouracil, vinblastine
Allergies	Antihistamines
Asthma	Beta agonists
Ulcers	H2 blockers, proton pump inhibitors
Diabetes	Insulin, metformin
Psychosis	Chlorpromazine
Depression	Fluoxetine
Anxiety	Diazepams
Transplant rejection	Immunosuppressants – cyclosporine, FK506
HIV infection	Reverse transcriptase and protease inhibitors
Pregnancy	Oral contraceptives
Anaesthesia	Halothane, benzocaine
Parkinson's	L-DOPA

This chapter has attempted to provide a historical timeline of drug discovery, starting with the uncharacterized medicines of antiquity and ending with the synthetic compounds and biotechnology drugs of the present day. Despite the undoubted successes achieved by the modern drug discovery industry, the returns on a significant investment in research and development are not as great as they should be; the number of novel medicines entering the clinic each year is low compared with that in the past (see Chap. 17). Biopharmaceutical companies are trying to solve this problem by adapting older scientific disciplines to make them compatible with present day thinking. The transformation of experimental pharmacology into the new discipline of systems biology is one example of this. Pharmacology has a proven track record in drug discovery, as has been described several times in this chapter. It does, however, suffer from the limitation of using organs or intact tissues to measure drug responses; unfortunately, organs and tissues are like a "black box", an engineering concept where it is possible to measure inputs and outputs (ligand-binding and muscle contraction, for example) without having any idea of what happens inside the box (tissue). Systems biology (a combination of cell and molecular biology with mathematics and engineering) is an attempt to shine some light into the black box by studying the individual cells and molecules in the tissue and determining in a holistic way how they interact with each other. One objective of systems biology is to provide a detailed description of how a given drug target operates within a complex biological system; this information may then be used to guide the selection of a drug which has very high selectivity for that target. Alternatively, this information may be used to produce a drug that affects more than one target simultaneously. This multiple activity may enhance the drug's activity against a disease, or else produce unwanted side effects. Actually, both situations occur in many of the drugs in the market; the trick is to be able to predict the outcome at the earliest stage, well before the drug enters the clinic.

4.1.7.1 Chance and Design

This historical overview concludes with a brief commentary about the role of serendipity in drug discovery. It can be dispiriting for a drug discovery scientist to reflect on the fact that many ground-breaking medicines were discovered by accident rather than through a purely logical process. In his informative book on the chemistry of drug molecules (Sneader 2005), Walter Sneader describes a number of examples of accidental discoveries (this book also provides an in-depth coverage of the history of drug discovery). One of the most famous accidental discoveries was that of penicillin, which has already been mentioned here. Less famous is the story of the platinum-based anti-cancer compound, cisplatin; this life-saving drug was discovered under what can only be described as slightly bizarre circumstances. Barnett Rosenberg and colleagues at Michigan State University were examining the effects of an electrical field on the growth of *E.coli* bacteria. The experiment consisted of two platinum electrodes inserted into a nutrient solution containing the bacteria. They found, to their surprise, that when a voltage was applied to the electrodes, the bacteria did not divide by normal cell division but grew to over 300 times their normal length (Rosenberg et al. 1965). At first sight, it would appear that the electrical current was responsible for the effect; after further investigation, however, it became clear that the platinum in the electrode had reacted with the salt solution to produce compounds that arrested cell division. The active platinum compound was eventually identified as cisplatin and shown to be a potent inhibitor of cell division in both bacteria and animal cells. Since uncontrolled cell division is a hallmark of cancer, cisplatin was tested on tumours and found to arrest their growth (Rosenberg et al. 1969). The platinum compound and later derivatives are now used routinely to treat solid tumours and are partly responsible for the extremely high cure rate of testicular cancer.

This story adds further support to Pasteur's dictum that "chance favours only the prepared mind". There is no doubt that more drug discoveries will arise from unexpected directions in the future; this supports the case for preserving the "curiosity-driven research" undertaken by individuals who are not necessarily interested in applications, but who simply want to know how the world works.

Summary of Key Points

The use of naturally occurring medicines in plants and animals goes back to antiquity.

The modern era of pharmaceutical research began in the nineteenth century with the development of organic chemistry and the receptor theory of drug action.

Pharmacology is the study of drugs and their effects on the body. Experimental pharmacology uses organs and tissues to identify small-molecule drugs that act on a variety of receptor subtypes.

Biotechnology grew out of research into antibiotics and other important small molecules, but became synonymous with the recombinant DNA technology from the 1970s onwards.

The mid-twentieth century onwards saw a "golden age" of drug discovery that used pharmacology and molecular approaches to develop many of the drugs which are still in use today.

Many drugs have been discovered by accident.

References

ICH M5 EWG Units and Measurements Controlled Vocabulary (2010). http://www.ema.europa.eu/docs/en_GB/document_library/Scientific_guideline/2009/09/WC500002731.pdf. Accessed 6 June 2011

Konturek SJ et al (1980) Comparison of ranitidine and cimetidine in the inhibition of histamine, sham-feeding, and meal induced gastric secretion in duodenal ulcer patients. Gut 21:181–186

Proceedings of the National Academy of Sciences (USA) Usage of symbols (2010). http://www.pnas.org/site/misc/iforc.shtml#abbreviations. Accessed 6 June 2011

Rosenberg B, VanCamp L, Krigas T (1965) Inhibition of cell division in Escherichia coli by electrolysis products from a platinum electrode. Nature 205:698–699

Rosenberg B et al (1969) Platinum compounds: a new class of potent antitumour agents. Nature 222:385–386

Sneader S (2005) Drug discovery: a history. Wiley, Chichester

Part II
The Drug Development Pipeline: Discovery to Testing in Humans

Chapter 5
Drug Discovery Pipeline Overview

Abstract The highly complex process of discovering and developing new medicines requires the application of many different skill sets over a time frame of years. The whole process is best visualised as a pipeline, with an input at one end and an exit at the other. This short chapter provides a brief overview of the drug development pipeline, enabling the reader to get a "helicopter view" before obtaining more detailed information in subsequent chapters.

5.1 Introduction

Figure 5.1 shows a diagram of the drug discovery pipeline, starting at the discovery phase on the left and finishing at phase IV, i.e. when the drug is in the market.

5.1.1 Discovery

- Selection of the disease to be treated
- Identification of a drug target
- Creation of small molecules and/or biologicals in the laboratory
- Screening against the target to identify leads for further development
- (Leads are compounds/antibodies, etc. that are selective for the target and have high levels of potency)
- Testing leads in disease models (test tube experiments *in vitro* or animals *in vivo*)

5.1.1.1 Outcome

The selection of a small molecule or a large biological molecule for detailed assessment as a potential drug candidate

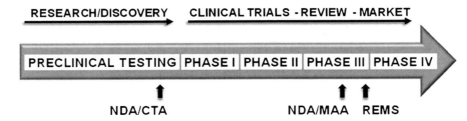

Fig. 5.1 The drug discovery pipeline. The preclinical phase covers the identification of suitable drug targets and the compounds/biologicals that interact with them. Once they have been checked for safety and efficacy, they are tested on human volunteers (phase I) and then on patients (Phases II–IV). The NDA/CTA applications are made to regulators to authorize clinical trials in humans. The NDA/MAA applications and REMS are required for marketing authorization. Further details are laid out in the main text and subsequent chapters

5.1.2 Preclinical Development

- DMPK (or ADME) and pharmacodynamics
  Drug Metabolism, Pharmacokinetics or Adsorption, Distribution, Metabolism and Excretion. Studies in animals to determine how rapidly the drug is absorbed, where it goes in the body, how it is broken down by metabolism and how rapidly it is cleared. Pharmacodynamics studies the effect of the drug on the body.

- Safety pharmacology and toxicology
  Determination of the maximum safe levels of drug in animals and any side effects that may prevent further development (e.g. causing birth defects or cancer)

- Process development
  Experiments to determine a cost-effective and environmentally sensitive way of manufacturing the drug

- Formulation development
  Determining the best way of formulating drugs for dosing in tablets, capsules, etc. This is designed to maximize the bioavailability and ease of manufacture.

- Application to conduct trials in humans
  If the drug candidate is judged to be potentially safe and effective in humans, an application is made to the regulators to authorize the testing in clinical trials. The main regulators are the American Food and Drug Administration (FDA), the European Medicines Agency (EMA) and the Japanese Ministry of Health, Labour and Welfare (MHLW). The application to the FDA is an Investigational New Drug (IND) and to the EMA, a Clinical Trial Authorisation (CTA).

5.1.2.1 Outcome

The decision (and permission) to progress a drug to clinical trials in humans, using a dose which is determined by the preclinical studies in animals

5.1.3   Clinical Development

- Phase I clinical trials
  The drug is administered to human volunteers to assess the maximum dose that can be tolerated without compromising safety. This information is used to select doses to test whether the drug works against the disease.
- Phase II clinical trials
  The stage at which the drug is tested for efficacy on patients with the disease that the drug is designed to treat. This information is used to plan a series of phase III trials of longer duration with more patients.
- Phase III clinical trials
  These trials can run for several years and are used to identify any safety issues that may arise over this period. At least two pivotal phase III trials are required to support an application to market the drug.

5.1.3.1   Outcome

A drug that has been shown to work according to the clinical trial design and that has the potential to make a return on investment for the manufacturer.

- Product approval and launch

  Marketing authorization
  A vast amount of documentation is put together during phase III trials to form a New Drug Application (NDA (FDA)) or Marketing Authorisation Application (MAA (EMA)). The NDA or MAA includes all of the relevant preclinical and clinical data that have been gathered over the years since the drug candidate was first identified.
- Phase IV and post-marketing surveillance

  Once the drug is in the market, companies may wish (or be obliged) to conduct further trials to compare its efficacy or safety profile with other medications or to test it in different patient groups (e.g. children or pregnant women). Even though the drug may have been approved for sale, the manufacturer is required to submit a strategy for monitoring and dealing with side effects; this is a Risk Evaluation and Mitigation Strategy (REMS (FDA)) or the EU Risk Management Plan (ERMP (EMA)).

5.1.3.2   Outcome

Ideally, a medicine that improves the lives of many patients with no safety problems arising in the long term. A commercially viable product that generates sufficient revenues before the patent on the medicine expires, when generic copies are then sold by other companies.

Chapter 6
Target Discovery

Abstract This chapter describes how drug targets are identified in the modern era of drug discovery. It starts with a general description of human disease processes and then leads through a series of investigations that progressively work towards the identification of a drug target protein. In doing so, it covers the key biological disciplines required to make this happen, such as cell biology, biochemistry, molecular biology and genomics. Finally, different classes of drug targets are described, including receptors, enzymes and ion channels.

6.1 Introduction

The impressive list of medicines developed in the twentieth century and beyond is testimony to the skill and dedication of the many thousands of drug discovery scientists who work in industry and academia. Despite these successes, the problem remains that many drugs are only effective in relieving the symptoms of disease and only few offer a complete cure. It is true that antibiotics and vaccination have proved highly effective in treating or preventing infectious diseases, but there are very few effective drugs for viral and fungal infections, let alone parasitic diseases such as malaria. Furthermore, there is still the likelihood of new infectious diseases appearing from nowhere to take the world by surprise, just as happened in the 1980s with AIDS. Those working in the biopharmaceuticals industry are fully aware of these issues and are trying to address them by increasing the efficiency of drug discovery at all levels. Sometimes the term "low hanging fruit" is used to describe the medicines that have already been discovered; the problem now is to reach the "fruit" higher up the tree that may actually cure serious diseases such as cancer and diabetes. This chapter presents an overview of how drug target discovery is currently undertaken in the biopharmaceutical industry and introduces some of the technical specialties, such as genomics, that are transforming the search for new medicines.

E.D. Zanders, *The Science and Business of Drug Discovery: Demystifying the Jargon,* 97
DOI 10.1007/978-1-4419-9902-3_6, © Springer Science+Business Media, LLC 2011

6.1.1 Modern Biomedical Research

In the mathematical sense, human biology is highly complex that a large number of variables, or interacting factors, operate together in ways that cannot be precisely modelled, even with the most powerful supercomputers. The field of complexity can be summarised by the phrase: "the whole is greater than the sum of its parts." In order to understand biology and, therefore, to design drugs that interfere with its processes in a predictable and precise way, it is necessary to have a detailed understanding of how the human body functions in health and disease. This is not a trivial undertaking, since each of us is genetically unique, with different likelihoods of succumbing to disease and having differing responses to the same medicine. Despite the challenges for drug discovery that arise from these complexities, a start along the road to fully understanding human biology has been made by scientists who are drawing up a "parts list" of the body (see the following section).

6.1.1.1 The Rise of "Omics"

The biopharmaceutical industry invests a vast amount of financial and intellectual capital in new technologies and procedures in the hope that drug discovery will become more efficient. Since the transition period between "traditional" pharmacology and biotechnology and the new molecular disciplines in the 1990s, the face of drug discovery has changed significantly, with the introduction of industrial-scale laboratory research underpinned by powerful computers. At the forefront of recent activity is the Human Genome Project, set up to determine the sequence of all 3 billion bases of human DNA, with the objective of understanding more about human biology in health and disease. A knowledge of the DNA sequence means that it is possible to build a catalogue of all human genes, and by implication, all proteins expressed in the body. The project's founders predicted that genome sequencing would benefit many branches of biology and medicine and this has indeed been the case. From a drug discovery perspective, knowing the full protein complement in human cells gives an upper limit on the number of possible drug targets (since most drug targets are proteins). It must not be forgotten, of course, that the genomes of other species are of considerable medical importance, particularly those belonging to pathogenic viruses and bacteria. The new molecular technologies have spawned a new lexicon based on the prototypic word genomics. The word was coined in 1987 as the title of a scientific journal dealing with DNA research; since then it has broadened out to define a scientific discipline that studies the genetic complement of an organism, in other words, the DNA sequences, their protein coding capacity, regulation and changes in disease. Genomics is distinct from genetics, the study of inheritance, whose basic principles were understood many years before DNA was shown to be the genetic material. The suffix "omics" has now been used to the point where there is an epidemic of "omics" technologies. Proteomics was one of the first, dealing, unsurprisingly, with the protein complement of an organism. The meaning of others, such as glycomics and metabolomics, can be deduced from the prefix in the name.

The extent to which new "omic" technologies have actually contributed to the development of new medicines has been the subject of much debate, not least among the investors who pay for the expensive technology. While it fair to say that the predicted flood of new products has not appeared at the time of writing this book, there is no doubt that a huge groundswell of knowledge continues to build up to a point where increased productivity is almost inevitable. It is worth noting that the life cycle of drug development can be as long as 15 years from discovery to market, so only a small number of product cycles have occurred in the 20 years since genomics technologies were first introduced into the biopharmaceutical industry.

6.1.1.2 Which Diseases to Treat?

The medical profession and the biopharmaceutical industry exist to provide treatments for the diseases that afflict human beings. Unfortunately, we are spoilt for choice when it comes to the number of different illnesses requiring new medicines (not counting surgical intervention or changes in the patient's lifestyle). According to the World Health Organization's International Classification of Diseases (ICD-10 2010), the number of classified conditions runs into the tens of thousands. Clearly, this is an impossibly large number for the biopharmaceutical industry to take on, however desirable this may be on humanitarian grounds; tough choices therefore have to be made based on both commercial and scientific grounds. This then generates controversy about the industry's lack of enthusiasm for discovering drugs that will not be profitable; this is the case with diseases that affect large numbers of people in the developing world, or small numbers of people in the advanced economies. Changes to this attitude are beginning to occur, as will be discussed later in Chap. 17. The biopharmaceutical industry is interested in the diseases listed in Table 6.1. These diseases are generally chronic degenerative conditions, such as arthritis, cancer and infectious diseases, such as influenza and hepatitis, all of which affect large numbers of people in the Western world. These disease areas are grouped into commercial franchises as listed in the table. Franchises are often associated with particular companies, for example respiratory medicines from GlaxoSmithKline and cancer (oncology) medicines from AstraZeneca. As the marketplace is very fluid, these associations are not fixed for ever, as some are lost and others gained (Glaxo, for example once held a huge gastrointestinal disease franchise because of its Zantac® drug, but once this patent protection was lost, the franchise all but disappeared within a few years).

6.1.1.3 Medical Terminology

The medical profession is intimately associated with the drug discovery industry both by using their products and by contributing to drug development through clinical

Table 6.1 Some of the diseases of interest to mainstream biopharmaceutical companies selling into Western markets

Disease	Franchise
AIDS	Infectious diseases
Hepatitis	–
Influenza	–
Septic shock	–
Tuberculosis	–
Hypertension	Cardiovascular
Atherosclerosis	–
Stroke	–
Solid tumours	Oncology
Leukaemia	–
Lymphoma	–
Rheumatoid arthritis	Arthritic diseases
Osteoarthritis	–
Osteoporosis	Metabolic diseases
Type II diabetes	–
Asthma	Respiratory diseases
Allergic rhinitis	–
COPD	–
Depression	Central nervous system (CNS)
Anxiety	–
Bipolar disorder	–
Epilepsy	–
Pain	–
Alzheimer's disease	CNS (neurodegeneration)
Parkinson's disease	–
Multiple sclerosis	–
Ulcerative colitis	Gastroenterology
Crohn's disease	–
Macular degeneration	Opthalmology

Although the list is not exhaustive, it does include the main illnesses suffered by an ageing population. The common endings in the name of the disease give a clue about the disease itself. Names ending in "itis", for example mean inflammatory diseases, "osis" a morbid process, "oma" a tumour and "emia" relating to blood. Interestingly, the medical profession considers pregnancy to be a condition, if not exactly a disease, but this is not a high priority for companies as existing preventative drug treatments are generally successful

research. Medical terminology is, therefore, employed a great deal in drug discovery and development, so some disease-related terms are highlighted as follows:

- Signs and symptoms
  Observations made by the doctor and the patient respectively.
- Aetiology
  The agent or mechanism that causes a disease. For infectious diseases, the aetiological agent is obvious; for example influenza is caused by infection with

influenza virus. The agents that cause diseases such as rheumatoid arthritis or diabetes are much more difficult to pin down. In fact, viruses and bacteria have been implicated in the aetiology of these diseases, but by the time the patient presents to the doctor, there is no trace left of the infectious agent.

- Pathogenesis
  The pathogenesis of a disease is the biological mechanism through which the disease occurs. The pathogenic mechanism for type 2 diabetes, for example is the development of resistance to insulin in the tissues.
- Morbidity and mortality
  A feeling of illness and death through illness.
- Comorbidity
  The occurrence of two or more diseases in the same patient.

6.1.1.4 Translational Medicine

A vast amount of public and private money has been invested in biomedical research over the past 50 years, and while the return on investment has been difficult to quantify in economic terms, most people would feel that it has produced a significant improvement in health care. The factors that limit the rate of progress in discovering new medicines are twofold, namely the rate at which new biological phenomena are discovered and the rate at which these findings can be translated into clinical practice. Those who undertake biomedical research are either scientists with degrees in subjects such as biochemistry or microbiology, or clinicians with medical degrees. Many clinicians have qualifications in both basic science and medicine and have made the transition between the clinic and the laboratory. There is a perceived cultural difference between the basic scientist and the clinician which is reflected in harmless stereotyping by both sides. Most bench scientists are expected to keep the laboratory tidy by doing their own clearing up. Clinicians, on the contrary, take some time to get used to this as they are used to having others do this for them. Of course, they have advantage of not being squeamish, so the sight of a medical colleague taking his own blood through a large syringe for his experiments was disturbing, but not surprising.

The interaction between basic and clinical scientists has been formalised in recent years by the term translational medicine. The Canadian physician Sir William Osler recognised that medicine is both a science and an art. His teachings to medical students in the early years of the twentieth century focused on the importance of listening to patients and carefully observing their signs and symptoms. This, in a sense, is the art of medicine, which recognises that each patient has a combination of different physical and psychological factors that is individual to them. The scientific aspect of medicine comes in the classification of disease and the technology used to diagnose and treat it. Eventually, it may be possible to call medicine a purely scientific enterprise, particularly when we fully understand the genetic and other factors that make each person unique, but this may not happen for many years. The point about this preamble is that drug discovery research can advance when clinicians, who see real patients, talk to scientists who work in the laboratory with more abstract models of biology and disease. If successful, this should accelerate the transfer of basic research findings into tangible products that can be tested in the clinic. This is why many biopharmaceutical companies have set up translational medicine departments, or have at least made sure that a clinician is closely associated with the drug discovery teams at an early stage.

6.1.2   Understanding Disease Mechanisms

The identification of suitable drug targets for a particular condition requires a detailed understanding of the molecular mechanisms of the disease. Where the disease is caused by infection, the drug target is most often part of the invading microorganism (although this is not always the case). For complex diseases such as cancer or diabetes, things get much more complicated because there are so many possible targets to explore. Where do you start?

Firstly, the features of the disease that are obvious to the patient and doctor are used as a starting point for a more detailed exploration. Rheumatoid arthritis (RA) will be used as an example throughout this chapter, as it is a representative example of a chronic disease that is high on the priority list of many biopharmaceutical companies. Patients with RA have swollen joints and suffer pain and immobility. This immediately focuses attention on the nature of the damage to the joints and how this compares with other joint diseases (arthritides) such as osteoarthritis. In other words, is there a specific pathogenesis for RA? From this point onwards, the clinician and scientist must examine a sample of tissue removed from the joint (synovial tissue) and analyse it using a range of sophisticated laboratory tools. Tissue removed from a living patient is called a biopsy, or biopsy material; if the person has died, it is called autopsy (or necropsy) material. It is always better to use biopsy material, if ethically possible, because cells (and the molecules within them) begin to degrade after death. If nucleic acids are being analysed, RNA must be extracted from tissue as soon as possible, as it is highly unstable (labile). In the past, I have gone to the extreme lengths of attending hip replacement operations so the surgeon could pass me some synovial tissue to freeze within seconds of it leaving the patient. This ensured that the RNA in the tissue was kept intact for later experiments, while, at the same time, introducing me to the more spectacular aspects of orthopaedic surgery.

Having obtained synovial biopsies from the patient, the next stage is to examine the material under a microscope to identify the different cells that make up the tissue. This introduces the discipline of cell biology, which will now be covered in some depth.

6.1.2.1   Cell Biology

Drug targets are proteins that are expressed inside and on the surface of cells, or are dissolved in biological fluids, such as blood or lymph. Cells are the fundamental units of living organisms and were first named by Robert Hooke in 1663 after examining a cork under the microscope, where he compared its structure to the small rooms occupied by monks (hence the derivation of the word from the Latin, *cellula* or small room). The cell theory was developed by Theodor Schwann and Matthias Schleiden in the nineteenth century and is stated as follows:

- The cell is the fundamental unit of structure and function in living things
- All organisms are made up of one or more cells
- All cells are derived from pre-existing cells through cellular division
- Cells carry genetic material passed on to daughter cells during cellular division

Cells are able to bind together in clumps or sheets to form tissues, or, if blood cells, to move freely within the circulation. The human body is comprised of approximately 200 different cell types, all of which arise from a single fertilised egg after conception. The way in which this happens is connected with stem cells, which are covered in Chap. 8. The reason for so many different cell types is that each has a specialised function in the body; for example red blood cells transport oxygen to the tissues and muscle cells create movement. Each cell type has the basic machinery of life in common, but can differ significantly in appearance and function. This is rather like a series of factories that make different products: they all have similar offices and eating areas etc, but are each set up to produce specific items such as cars or washing machines.

In order to study cells in more detail, they can be examined undisturbed in the tissue environment they occupy (examined *in situ*) or be purified from the tissue as a unique cell population. Tissue culture is then used to grow larger numbers of these cells in the laboratory for further study (see later). Some examples of different cell types are shown in Fig. 6.1.

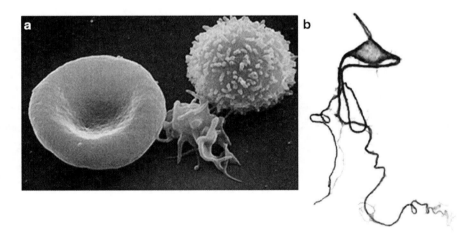

Fig. 6.1 Examples of different cell structures. (**a**) Scanning electron microscope image of blood cells; left to right: red blood cell (erythrocyte), platelet, lymphocyte. Image taken by Electron Microscopy Facility at The National Cancer Institute US. (**b**) Nerve cell showing long extensions that form a network that distributes signals throughout the nervous system

6.1.2.2 Imaging

Although science deals with abstractions and models, directly visualising the object under study is more satisfying than inferring its existence by other means. Cells are normally visualised under a microscope since they are well below naked eye visibility (a human cell is approximately 10 μm across, i.e. 10 μm or 10 millionths of a metre).

Modern imaging techniques allow the cell biologist to identify a cell by its shape (morphology) and by the types of molecules it expresses. Microscopes vary in sophistication, from the simple apparatus familiar to high school students which uses a white light to illuminate the specimen, to complex machines that use lasers or beams of electrons. The examination of cells and tissues under the microscope is known as histology, a procedure in which lumps of tissue are deep frozen or embedded in paraffin wax before being cut into thin sections using a very fine blade. The sections are stained with various dyes so that specific cell types are revealed according to the dye used. This histochemistry technique is routinely used in diagnostic laboratories to examine patient biopsies for abnormal cell types (as in cancer). It is also used extensively in the biopharmaceutical industry for target discovery and the analysis of animal and human tissues during the later stages of clinical development.

Returning to the RA example, histochemistry on synovial tissue taken from the joints of RA patients reveals the presence of large numbers of white blood cells (leucocytes) that are absent in un-inflamed tissues (Fig. 6.2). Leucocytes consist of a number of different cell types including T and B lymphocytes, monocytes and macrophages, and all of these are present in the inflamed synovium. Not shown in

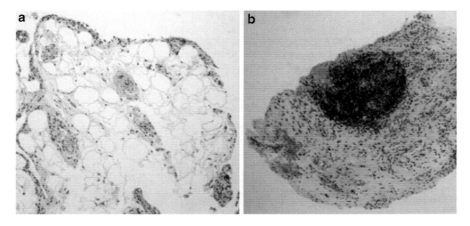

Fig. 6.2 Image of thin section of (synovial) joint tissue taken through a microscope. Tissue samples taken after joint biopsy or replacement surgery were sliced into sections less than 0.1-mm thick and treated with a dye (haematoxylin and eosin (H&E)) that stains cells a dark colour. (**a**) Uninflamed tissue showing a few cells as black dots. (**b**) Highly inflamed synovium showing massive infiltration of tissue with white blood cells, a hallmark of RA. Images kindly provided by Drs Andrew Filer and Dagmar Scheel-Toellner, University of Birmingham, UK, with permission

this figure is the visible damage to cartilage and bone in the RA joint, which again is absent in unaffected joints. This means that a hallmark of RA is the presence of these cells and the characteristic damage to joint tissue and bone. This points the search for drug targets in the direction of the leucocytes, although at this stage it would be too early to jump to conclusions. Their presence may not be the cause of the problem, but simply the consequence of (as yet unseen) damage, or insult, to the tissue. Despite this caveat, further examination of these cells would provide a useful starting point for more detailed cellular and molecular analysis of RA.

6.1.2.3   Cell (Tissue) Culture

As highlighted above, much useful information can be gained about the nature of disease by examining the cell types present in diseased tissues. Blood is also a tissue and its component cells can be readily separated into red and white cell populations (erythrocytes and leucocytes). Histochemistry is a valuable tool for investigating tissues, whatever their origin, but it does not provide information about the functions of each cell type and the molecules associated with them. This is best achieved by physically removing the cells from tissues and maintaining them in culture (tissue culture), using processes that are very similar to those used for growing bacteria and yeast (see Chap. 4). To illustrate the jargon, tissue culture produces cultured cells from cell cultures. In practice, cells are grown in sterilised plastic dishes or flasks containing a tissue culture medium consisting of sugars, salts, amino acids and other nutrients. All manipulations are kept sterile to avoid contamination by airborne yeast or bacteria, which grow much faster than the human (or other mammalian) cells in the cultures. For this reason, experiments are conducted in large stainless steel cabinets with special filters to keep contaminated air at bay. These laminar flow cabinets are often seen in TV clips about some new medical discovery with their white-coated operators. Despite the noise of the fan, the cabinets (or "hoods") provide a surprisingly meditative environment in which to escape from the distractions of the outside world.

Once the cultured cells are available in sufficient numbers, they can be used in a variety of ways, depending on the type of cell and the scientific questions to be addressed. Mammalian cell lines can be used for target discovery or screening, or else for producing genetically engineered protein drugs. The cell lines have the advantage of being essentially immortal so long as there is sufficient growth medium available to keep them alive; this means in practice that cell cultures are divided into more and more flasks or bottles until there are enough cells for the experiment. It is also possible to store cells in liquid nitrogen (at $-196°C$) and thaw them for re-culturing when needed. Many cell lines are derived from human or animal cells that have been transformed by viruses to grow indefinitely, so they are often described as transformed cells. A famous example is the HeLa cell derived from a tumour removed from an American woman, Henrietta Lack; for reasons that are not entirely clear, this line is so robust that it has been grown for decades in laboratories all over the world. Transformed cells are useful because they can be grown to very large numbers, or be used to study how cell transformation might lead to cancer. Primary cells, on the contrary, are cells that have been taken directly from tissues (such as blood) and should, in principle, retain the properties that they had in the intact body. Transformed cells do not retain these properties and are unlikely, therefore, to provide an accurate representation of a particular disease (possibly except cancer). Primary cells are, therefore, desirable for simulating diseases in as realistic a way as possible, but they are often difficult to obtain in quantity. Stem cells offer a way around this problem by providing a renewable source of different cell types that can be produced *in vitro* rather than from human donors. More recently, stem cells have been isolated from patients with genetic diseases, thus making it possible to create a range of primary cells that may be altered as a result of the disease. This is a very exciting development and is one reason, apart from their potential use in tissue repair, why biopharmaceutical companies are so interested in stem cells.

6.1.2.4 *In Vitro* Models of Disease

Many diseases are the result of complex interactions that occur between cells and molecules in the living person (*in vivo*). If these agents are removed from the body and examined in the test tube[1] (*in vitro*), some of this complexity will be lost. The *in vitro* model is, therefore, designed to be as near to the *in vivo* situation as possible, while recognising that any targets identified using this approach will ultimately have to be evaluated (*in vivo*) in living animals and eventually, in patients. Many *in vitro* models use cells that have been removed from tissues and then separated into their individual types before being placed in tissue culture. It is then possible to mix defined cell populations together in a precisely controlled manner and to observe their behaviour. One type of cell may cause another to grow, change shape or produce molecules with effects on other cells or tissues. The tissue culture medium in which the cells have been grown may contain molecules released by the cells. This medium, called the culture supernatant, contains many hundreds of different molecules, the majority of which are not relevant to drug discovery. However, a small minority (mostly proteins) have extremely significant biological activities. For example, they may stimulate cell division when added to non-dividing cells in culture, in which case they are called growth factors. These molecules are members of the cytokine family and are of fundamental importance to many aspects of disease, particularly cancer.

Some of these points are now illustrated using an *in vitro* model of rheumatoid arthritis as an example. Since the objective of the drug discovery scientist is to discover drug targets for RA, the model focuses on the cells and molecules that are most likely to produce the hallmark of this disease, namely destruction of the bone

---

[1] The glass test tubes of traditional chemistry are almost never used. The modern laboratory contains boxes of disposable plastic vessels in various configurations including flasks, plates, dishes and tubes.

and cartilage in the joint. Histological investigations have already revealed the presence of fibroblasts close to the cartilage, which suggests that these cells may be responsible for the damage to this tissue. Fibroblasts help to form connective tissues in the body and are important components of skin. When these cells are taken from the RA patient and placed in tissue culture, it can be shown that the culture supernatant contains molecules that directly break down cartilage (when added to the *in vitro* experiment). This implies that in some way, fibroblasts are activated by the local environment in the RA joint and then release factors that are responsible for the joint damage. Since leucocytes have already been shown to infiltrate the RA joints, it would be reasonable to assume that they may be responsible for activating the fibroblasts. As with the previous experiments with fibroblasts, the leucocytes from RA tissue are placed in tissue culture to observe the effect of the resulting culture medium on other components of the joint. The results of these *in vitro* experiments show that leucocytes in patients with RA produce factors that activate the fibroblasts in the joint, which in turn release other factors that cause the destruction of bone and cartilage. The experiment is summarised in Fig. 6.3.

Having identified molecules that may be responsible for the pathogenesis of a disease, the drug discovery scientists can then home in on the nature of these factors and demonstrate that inhibiting their production or action will also inhibit joint destruction. This logical cause and effect analysis is central to drug discovery. This real-life example with RA did result in the identification of a number of drug targets, one of the most promising being the receptor for a cytokine called tumor necrosis factor (TNF-α).

6.1.2.5   *In Vivo* Models of Disease

Once possible drug targets have been identified using clinical observation and *in vitro* models, they must be evaluated *in vivo* using a living organism. This is because the properties of the target in the living body may differ significantly from those observed in the test tube. A great deal of effort is put into target validation at the discovery phase of the pipeline, but true validation of a target really only occurs at the clinical trial stage when drugs are tested for their effectiveness in real patients.

Many different experimental designs are used to evaluate a drug target in whole organisms, but there are also some themes in common. Often, the first step is to create a disease model to test inhibitors of a drug target. Alternatively, the target itself can be removed by genetic manipulation. In both cases, the target is worth pursuing further if disease symptoms are ameliorated when the target is inactivated. The main concern for researchers is the relevance of the disease model to human beings, since the protein target may not be expressed in the model, or may be dissimilar to the human version (a common situation). In some cases, the disease occurs in a human being as the result of genetic mutation that alters a specific protein. Most genetic diseases of this type are monogenic, i.e. they are caused by a single gene defect. Examples include cystic fibrosis, muscular dystrophy and haemophilia. These result from "loss of function" mutations, where a particular protein is defective.

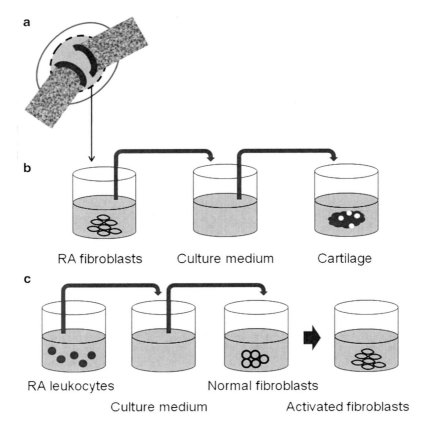

Fig. 6.3 An experiment to unravel the mechanism of rheumatoid arthritis *in vitro* and identify potential drug targets. (**a**) Schematic diagram of a knee joint with two bones joined inside a sealed membrane (*dotted line*) that contains a lubricating fluid (synovial fluid). The cartilage protecting the end of the bone is in black. The whole joint is enclosed in another membrane as further protection (*solid oval*). (**b**) A sample of the inflamed membrane from a patient with RA is placed in tissue culture and the RA fibroblasts allowed to grow. The cells are removed and the liquid is placed in a fresh tube where a piece of normal cartilage is added. The fibroblasts have produced agents that have eaten away at the cartilage just as in the patient's joints. (**c**) Leucocytes from the joints of a patient with RA are cultured to see if they produce a factor in the medium that will stimulate normal fibroblasts to become activated as in RA. In real-life experiments, these factors have been shown to be cytokines. The drug target is the receptor to which the cytokine binds and the drug itself is an inhibitor of this binding

Unfortunately, these conditions require the replacement of a defective gene (possibly with gene therapy) rather than the inhibition of an overactive one, which is something difficult to achieve with a medicine. In the latter case, proteins encoded by these "gain of function" mutations are much more useful as drug targets as they can be inhibited by drugs. These mutations occur in polygenic diseases such as cancer, autoimmune disease and many other serious chronic conditions, which is why these are of interest to the biopharmaceutical industry. While polygenic mutations have led investigators to new drug targets, most make a very small contribution to the overall disease and are, therefore, of limited utility, except possibly for biomarkers and diagnostics (see Chap. 14).

Model Organisms

Rodents

Model organisms are used to recreate aspects of human disease in species ranging from single-celled yeast all the way to mammals such as mice and rats. Larger animals are closer to humans in evolutionary terms and, therefore, are more likely to reflect human biology. Rodents, for example are the mainstay of the *in vivo* laboratory because they have a short life cycle and have organ systems and physiology similar to that of humans. They can also be bred into genetically pure lines with defined mutations induced with chemicals (chemical mutagenesis) or by using recombinant DNA technology. The latter process results in the creation of transgenic animals in which specific genes can be introduced (a human receptor, for example) or removed (a gene knockout). This is an enormously powerful technology because it can be used to observe the biological consequences of selectively removing every gene in a mouse (or rat). The disadvantages of using animals lie in their expense and the practical limitations of how many can be used when there may be a large number of conditions to test. Of course, there is also the ethical consideration of breeding animals for this type of research, something that will be raised again in Chap. 11. In order to overcome the limitations of working with larger animals, a number of small non-mammalian organisms are used in target discovery, the most popular of which are briefly described below. Given the rapid pace of research into this area, it would not be surprising if several new model organisms were introduced over the next few years.

Yeast

Yeast, being a single-celled fungus, is one of the simplest model organisms. It is popular with investigators because it grows rapidly and is highly amenable to genetic manipulation. Although it cannot mimic all the facets of a complex disease, it has been used to identify targets for a class of anti-cancer drugs known as the cell cycle inhibitors. The cell division cycle is the sequence of events that leads to the creation of two cells from one; this process is disregulated in cancer, so cell division becomes uncontrolled and leads to the growth of tumours. The mechanisms of yeast cell division are not dissimilar to those of humans, so it has been possible to identify key protein targets in this simpler organism by using genetic approaches and then use that information to produce drugs that interact with their human equivalents. Yeast is a single-celled eukaryote (see Microbiology, Chap. 4) but humans are eukaryotes made up of many different types of cells. This has prompted the search for model organisms that have the same versatility as yeast and yet also reflect the complexity of human biology. Some of the models used in basic and pharmaceutical research are based on flies, worms and fish, as outlined below.

Flies

The fruit fly *Drosophila melanogaster* has been used in pioneering genetic studies for over 100 years because of its ease of handling and short (2-week) life cycle. Many natural mutations that lead to changes in their body layout and behaviour have been catalogued and used for studies in basic and applied biology. The complete DNA sequence of fruit flies reveals a close similarity between the genes of this humble fly and those of far more complex human beings. It is estimated that more than 75% of human disease genes have a counterpart in *Drosophila*. Surprisingly, it is possible to observe a considerable range of behaviours in flies and relate them to defects in their nervous systems, something which is clearly relevant to target discovery for neurological diseases. Even drunken behaviour can be modelled in fruit flies, since they normally ingest large amounts of alcohol from fermenting fruits, which are their normal diet. They display features similar to those of human alcoholics (including alcohol tolerance), although it is not known if they can tell the difference between a bordeaux and a burgundy.

Worms

Another invertebrate model organism is the nematode worm *Caenorhabditis elegans* (*C. elegans*). This small (1 mm) worm grows with a three-day life cycle on agar plates covered with bacteria and can be frozen down for future use. This last feature is unique for a multicellular organism with a nervous system and other features of higher animals. Since *C. elegans* is transparent, each one of its 959 cells can be tracked *in vivo* throughout its development cycle. One high profile area of biomedical research is the mechanism of human ageing; *C.elegans* has provided some startling results that link metabolism to longevity and offers further evidence of a genetic component to ageing. Insulin and related proteins are important regulators of metabolism and energy balance, so the observation that worms with a defect in a member of the insulin receptor family live twice as long as normal worms is consistent with the fact that these animals live longer on a restricted diet. Unravelling the connections between these biological phenomena is highly complex, even with relatively a simple organism like *C. elegans*, but the power of modern cell and molecular biology makes it possible to make real progress in this area of research.

Fish

Although *C. elegans* worms are useful models, they are still a long distance from human beings in evolutionary terms: they do not have a heart, for example. This is why the tiny zebrafish (*Danio rerio*) has proved so popular in recent years. In addition to sharing many genes in common with humans, the fish is also a vertebrate animal and, therefore, has similar organs. Like *C. elegans*, zebrafish have small transparent embryos that are produced in large numbers; this combination of size and numbers means that zebrafish embryos can be used to screen compounds for activity against intact animals. The fish are easily manipulated using genetics, so panels of mutant fish with defects that include malformation of the heart and other organs have been used for a number of investigations into, for example heart regeneration and leukaemia. Zebrafish are also being evaluated as model organisms for toxicology screening in preclinical development (see Chap. 11).

Genetic engineering can be used for just about any application where DNA is transferred from one organism to another; if you can clone it, you can engineer it, hence the appearance of some seemingly bizarre modifications to experimental organisms. One prominent example is the introduction of a jellyfish gene encoding a fluorescent protein into specific zebrafish cells that can be followed as the fish develops to maturity. The protein emits a vivid colour when exposed to ultraviolet light, so the engineered cells literally light up. Green fluorescent protein (GFP) was the first of the jellyfish genes to be used in this way and has been so successful in advancing cell biology that it earned its discoverers a Nobel Prize for chemistry in 2008. Other proteins that glow red, green or orange have been expressed in transgenic zebrafish, and are sold to hobbyists and science educators by the US company GloFish.

Three of the model organisms described above are illustrated in Fig. 6.4.

Fig. 6.4   Three model organisms used in pharmaceutical research. Clockwise from top left: worm *Caenorhabditis elegans*, fruitfly *Drosophila melanogaster*, zebrafish *Danio rerio*. All are small multicellular organisms that reproduce rapidly in the laboratory and whose genetic and cellular composition is mapped out in great detail. Worm image is from the National Human Genome Research Institute in USA

6.1.2.6   Target Inhibition

Once a disease model has been established and a possible drug target identified, there is still some way to go before drugs are produced against that target. There has to be some confidence that changing the activity of the target (by activating or inhibiting it) will reduce the features of the disease displayed by the model. In the case of arthritis, this might be reduction of joint swelling. Three approaches are often used to achieve this change of activity, namely genetic engineering of transgenic animals, nucleic acid inhibition and antibody production.[2]

Transgenic Animals

These have already been introduced in the section on *in vivo* models of disease. Genetic engineering technology allows the investigator to add or remove genes from a model organism in a controlled way. If a drug gene is removed from the organism (a knockout), then the effect of this loss on the *in vivo* disease model can be observed directly. If the drug target is relevant to a disease, its removal should reduce the symptoms. Sometimes the genetic modification inhibits a vital biological function, in which case the embryo cannot develop into adulthood, making it impossible to perform the desired experiments. Even if the animals do mature in the usual way, the genetic defect may modify other genes and proteins as a compensatory mechanism, so the model may not be a true reflection of the normal biological state. This has lead to the development of conditional knockouts, in which the target gene remains unaltered throughout development into adulthood. Once the animal is mature, the gene is knocked out in the live animal using a genetic engineering process that is triggered by a small molecule (e.g. the antibiotic tetracycline) which can be added to the animal's drinking water. DNA technology can also be used to express or inhibit the expression of a particular gene within a defined cell type, rather than just randomly throughout the animal; this has proved to be particularly useful for studying the cells of the immune system.

Nucleic Acid Inhibitors

Transgenic model organisms are powerful tools for research into drug targets, but they are time consuming to generate and not always easy to produce. A simpler alternative is to administer some agent directly into the animal that could selectively remove or inhibit the drug target gene. These agents have already been introduced in Chap. 2 and are antisense RNA, small interfering RNA (siRNA), micro RNAs,

---

[2] Of course at this early stage of target selection a drug is not usually available to test in the model.

ribozymes, aptamers and zinc-finger nucleases (ZFNs). Out of all these, siRNAs are currently the most commonly used gene expression inhibitors for both cultured cells and model organisms.

Antibodies

The DNA sequences required for genetic modification of drug target genes are readily available from genome databases, and the experiments themselves are relatively straight-forward to perform. Unfortunately, altering a protein target by manipulating the expression of the gene that encodes it is not a reflection of what actually happens with most small molecule and biological drugs. The latter directly interacts with the drug target itself (a protein), rather than with the gene that encodes it. The ideal solution would be to generate molecules that interact specifically with any protein target of interest. Luckily, this can be achieved by harnessing the power of the immune system to generate antibodies that display exquisite specificity for almost any protein target of interest. Antibodies are large proteins (MW 150,000) that are produced naturally during infection, or artificially by immunising animals with proteins or cells. Antibodies can be added to tissue culture experiments *in vitro* or injected directly into animals to inhibit their target protein *in vivo*. This inhibition can occur through the direct blockade of a ligand binding to its receptor or through literally soaking up a protein ligand to remove it from the site of disease. Alternatively, if the target is on the surface of a cell, the antibody can recruit the immune system to destroy the cell in the same way as it would during a viral infection or during surveillance for tumours. It is important to note, however, that antibodies are unable to enter cells, so they are useful only when binding to targets that are present on the cell surface or dissolved in biological fluids such as blood.

The rheumatoid arthritis example mentioned earlier in the chapter is now used to illustrate some of these points as follows: the results of *in vitro* experiments (Fig. 6.3) indicated that leucocytes in the inflamed RA joint produce molecules that cause nearby fibroblasts to destroy bone and cartilage. The obvious next step is now to identify the actual molecules responsible for these effects and to see whether they could form the basis of a drug development programme. To cut a very long story short, the agents produced by fibroblasts which destroy cartilage were identified as enzymes (catalytic proteins) that break down connective tissue proteins such as collagen. Since these enzymes (technically, metallopeptidases) can be inhibited with small molecules, a number of drug candidates have been created over the years and tested in arthritis. Unfortunately, none have overcome side effect problems and other issues that make them unsuitable for clinical use. Another possibility is to identify the molecules produced by the leucocytes and inhibit those instead. Research on inflammation has been ongoing for years, so there is a long list of possible drug targets that might be involved in RA. One of these molecules is the cytokine TNF-α which was originally identified as a cytokine that killed tumour cells. Further research revealed that TNF-α has a role in inflammatory reactions, and the results of numerous investigations supported the idea that it might be activating the RA fibroblasts. Antibodies were, therefore, produced against this cytokine and added to the *in vitro* cultures of leucocytes and fibroblasts described earlier. This had the desired effect of reducing fibroblast activation, so the antibody was then injected into mouse or rat models of arthritis. These models produce swelling in the paw and bone erosion, both of which were reduced with the antibody to TNF-α but not a control antibody (which is made to an irrelevant protein).

The sequence of events that led to a promising drug target for RA started with the observation of patients, continued with the analysis of cells and molecules in joint tissues and finished with an animal model of the disease. The disease pathogenesis was shown to be caused by the overproduction of the cytokine TNF-α, so the drug target was the receptor to which it binds.[3] Antibodies to the cytokine reduced arthritis *in vivo* by soaking up the excess protein and preventing binding to the receptor. Another approach involved using receptor decoy proteins to act as receptor antagonists, just like the small molecules described in Chap. 4. In fact, both antibodies and decoys have been developed into biological drugs and have become major success stories in the treatment of arthritis. One of my former postdoctoral supervisors was responsible for some of this work and has been duly rewarded with a share in the Lasker Prize (the medical equivalent of a Nobel) and a knighthood from the British government.

6.1.3 Prospecting for Drug Targets

This chapter has so far described how drug targets are identified through an analysis of the disease to be treated. The investigator who uses this approach may have no idea what type of target will eventually emerge from laboratory investigations. The situation could be reversed, however, so that different classes of drug target proteins are defined at the outset and then assigned to different disease states. These two different approaches can be described as "lumping" or "splitting"; research departments in biopharmaceutical companies have been organised along either lumping or splitting principles, depending on the fashion of the day. The current trend is to lump different scientific disciplines together in order to study a particular disease area. GlaxoWellcome was one of the first to do this when it established self-contained "Centres of Excellence (Expertise) for Drug Discovery" (CEDDS); these focus on individual disease areas, such as respiratory or infectious diseases.

The remainder of this chapter covers the analysis of different types of drug target, or the "splitting." It is impossible to cover all of the technical background to this analysis, but an attempt will be made to explain the key features of the scientific disciplines that are relevant to this aspect of drug discovery. Since drug target proteins are mostly associated with cells, attention must now return to these fundamental units of life.

---

[3] This is actually far from being the whole story, as there is much more to learn about the causes and progression of RA; there are also many more target opportunities and drugs in development or in the clinic.

6.1.3.1 Looking Inside Cells: Sub-cellular Structures

Until the late 1940s, biologists were limited by the amount of detail that could be discerned in cells using conventional light microscopy. The invention of the transmission electron microscope meant that it was possible to use the high magnification and resolution of electron beams to image sub-cellular structures, otherwise known as organelles. These organelles have specific functions that contribute to the overall life of the cell, including its reproduction through division. The nucleus, for example contains the genetic material DNA, while the mitochondria are the powerhouses that produce energy. From the drug discovery perspective, the cell membrane is of vital importance, as it presents the outside face of the cell to its environment. This means that signalling molecules, such as hormones, neurotransmitters and cytokines, bind to the outside (extracellular) portions of their receptors embedded in the cell membrane. After binding has occurred, a signal is transmitted through the membrane to the inside of the cell to instruct it to perform a particular task, like making the cell divide.

Figure 6.5 shows a model of a human cell cut away to reveal the nucleus and other organelles.

6.1.3.2 Biochemistry

Biochemistry is the chemistry of life processes that examines all the large and small molecules that make up living organisms. Although biochemistry and organic chemistry are both based on the chemistry of carbon compounds, they differ in the conditions under which these compounds react together. Organic chemists synthesise compounds in the laboratory by using extremes of temperature and pressure, or highly reactive chemicals. This would obviously be impossible in living cells, since

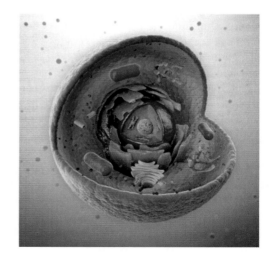

Fig. 6.5 Model of human cell with outer cell membrane cut away to reveal organelles. The nucleus containing chromosomes and DNA is also cut away and is the large artichoke looking structure in the middle. The small cylinders represent the mitochondria, and the membranous structure at the bottom is the Golgi apparatus involved in moving molecules through the cell

they would be completely destroyed. Instead, a large variety of chemical reactions occur at a benign 37°C without the need for harsh conditions. This is achieved through the action of enzymes, a large class of proteins that orchestrate nearly all of the chemical reactions in cells. Enzymes are biological catalysts which accelerate chemical reactions by lowering the amount of energy required for chemical substances to react together; the key point is that catalysts are not consumed in chemical reactions and can, therefore, be reused many times. Industrial catalysts for the manufacture of plastics or removal of car exhaust emissions are quite simple molecules, often based on the precious metals platinum or palladium; although enzymes may use similar catalytic mechanisms, they have an important extra feature. Being proteins, they can selectively bind to many different types of molecules, so they have evolved to catalyse highly specific chemical reactions. Enzymes of the protease class, for example catalyse reactions with proteins, while nucleases catalyse reactions with nucleic acids. It will be noticed that enzymes have a common suffix "ase" associated with the type of molecule with which it reacts. Some common names are still used, for example pepsin and trypsin, which are proteases found in the digestive system. Because of the large number of different chemical reactions catalysed by enzymes, the International Union of Biochemistry and Molecular Biology (IUBMB) (http://www.chem.qmul.ac.uk/iubmb/enzyme/. Accessed 12 Nov 2010) has devised the EC number system to create a logical classification; so pepsin becomes EC 3.4.23.1 and trypsin EC 3.4.21.4.

Enzymes are central to biochemistry, which was renamed from the earlier "physiological chemistry" by Carl Neuberg in 1903. Many of the chemical reactions occurring in cells, such as the conversion of sugars to energy and the creation of waste products such as urea, were described in the first half of the twentieth century. These reactions are collectively termed the metabolism of the cell, and occur in metabolic pathways, each step of which is driven and controlled by enzymes. As more and more reactions were discovered in different organisms, these pathways became highly complicated and even quite aesthetic when printed on a colour poster. At the time when I was a biochemistry student, these posters were sometimes displayed alongside the more conventional images of Led Zeppelin and other rock stars of the era. These charts have now been superseded by computer databases of metabolic pathways, such as the ones provided by the Kyoto Encyclopedia of Genes and Genomes (KEGG) (2010). A small part of a typical metabolic pathway is shown in Fig. 6.6. The lines in the figure represent a series of chemical transformations, each catalysed by an enzyme, which form a pathway from one molecule (represented by a dot) to another. The pathway can be linear, branched or even circular, as in the Krebs (or TCA) cycle illustrated in the figure.

Metabolic pathways were traced out by blocking the activity of individual enzymes in a pathway and then analysing the small molecules that accumulated in the cell as a result of the pathway being blocked. Alternatively, compounds labelled with radioactive atoms were added to cells and converted into new molecules by metabolism. In this procedure, a simple radioactive compound (e.g. glucose) was added to cells, which were then analysed at different points of time for the presence

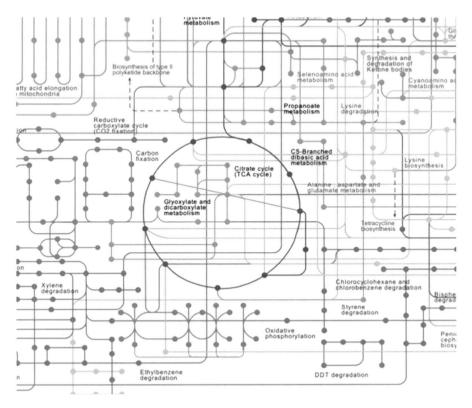

Fig. 6.6 Part of a metabolic pathway. Each enzyme that catalyses a biochemical reaction is represented as a dot linked in a specific path. The circular pathway is the Krebs cycle, a component of the system that converts glucose to energy. Original image courtesy of Kyoto Encyclopedia of Genes and Genomes (2010)

of new radioactive molecules. The radiolabel was "chased" into different compounds, so it was then possible to work out the flow of metabolism over time.

Compounds that are metabolised by enzymes in cells are called metabolites and account for about 10% of the mass of a cell. The rest of the cell, in comparison, is made up of approximately 60% protein, 16% lipid, 6% carbohydrates, 5% nucleic acids and 3% inorganic compounds such as metals. Metabolism and metabolites will be revisited in Chap. 11 when discussing drug metabolism in the liver.

The elucidation of metabolic pathways has been one of the great triumphs of biochemistry, leading, among other things, to improvements in nutrition through the discovery of vitamins and cofactors. Biochemistry has also revealed much about the structure of large molecules, such as proteins, nucleic acids, carbohydrates and lipids. Of these, the enzyme proteins, in particular, are central to many drug discovery programmes, as they are the targets of small molecule drugs. There are aspects of biochemistry other than just enzymes and proteins; these relate to the properties of nucleic acids, which are described in the sections below.

6.1.3.3   Molecular Biology

In the immediate years following World War II, many physicists turned their attention to biological problems, particularly the nature of the genetic material and the three-dimensional structures of large molecules. Although these activities were, strictly speaking, the pursuit of biochemists, they became subsumed within the term molecular biology, whose greatest triumph was the discovery of the double helical structure of DNA by Watson and Crick in 1953. This nucleic acid structure was determined through the use of X-ray crystallography, a powerful technique that was later applied to proteins. The structures gained through these experiments provided insight into how the shape of a large molecule determines its function. Macromolecular (i.e. large) structures of enzymes, structural proteins and nucleic acids are now determined routinely at the level of individual atoms using X-ray diffraction, NMR and other techniques. It is now even possible to determine the three-dimensional structures of sub-cellular structures comprised of dozens of individual proteins.

In addition to providing structural information, molecular biology also reveals how genetic information, encoded in the DNA molecule, is turned into protein. Francis Crick coined the term "central dogma of molecular biology"; this states that information flows from DNA through an RNA intermediate (messenger RNA) to specify the type and order of amino acids added to the final protein. Like most dogmas, this does not always hold true, since information can also flow backwards from RNA to DNA. Retroviruses, such as HIV, integrate their RNA genomes into the DNA of infected cells by a process of reverse transcription, i.e. they produce a DNA copy from an RNA template. This is catalysed by the enzyme reverse transcriptase, a prime target for small molecule drugs that inhibit the replication of HIV.

The actual mechanisms by which proteins are produced in the cell under the instructions of messenger RNA are well understood and described in many books and online resources. The following description of the way DNA sequences specify a genetic code is relevant to later sections on genomics and DNA sequencing. The basic principles are illustrated in Fig. 6.7 below.

The genetic code is made up of three letters (i.e. DNA nucleotides) that specify a single amino acid. In the example in Fig. 6.7, AAA on one strand (the coding strand) of DNA is copied into a messenger RNA intermediate. The AAA code then instructs the protein synthesis machinery to select the amino acid lysine (Lys) for inclusion into the growing protein chain. All twenty amino acids are specified by a particular triplet code (codon); in addition, there are start and stop codons that tell the cell when to start the protein chain and when to stop it. This genetic dictionary is extremely important for molecular biologists, as it allows them to predict the length of a protein and its amino acid sequence by just knowing the DNA sequence. This will be discussed later in connection with genomics and bioinformatics.

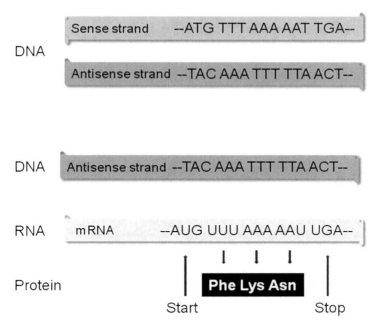

Fig. 6.7 Conversion of DNA code into protein via an RNA intermediate. Double-stranded DNA (*top*) with sense and antisense strands (see Chap. 2). Messenger RNA (mRNA) is transcribed (copied) from the antisense strand after the double helix has unwound. The nucleotides in the mRNA copy are read as groups of three letters (i.e. a triplet), each triplet specifying an amino acid or a stop/start signal

6.1.3.4 Genomics

In the pre-genomics era, it was possible for a biochemist or molecular biologist to devote almost an entire career to studying a handful of genes and proteins. Heroic efforts were made to purify microgram amounts of a protein of interest from tissues or cell cultures. This quantity was often far too small to be of much further use, so a strategy was employed to vastly increase the amount of protein that could be produced in the laboratory. Firstly, the amino acid sequence of the protein was determined, so that the DNA sequence of the gene that encoded it could be worked out using the dictionary of the genetic code. This DNA sequence could be turned into a physical sample of DNA, which was then introduced into bacteria to produce large amounts of recombinant protein. Although this brief description makes this to appear very straightforward, the library screening procedures were very time consuming and not easily scaled up to handle a large number of proteins. Despite these limitations, many cytokines and other proteins that were only present in minute amounts in tissues and cells could, for the first time, be produced in milligram to gram quantities. Some of these proteins became therapeutic proteins in their own right, in particular, the interleukin family of cytokines.

Now we are in the era of genomics, which is concerned with the DNA sequence and protein-coding capacity of an organism, as well as the way in which these sequences are regulated. Rather than studying a few genes at a time, as in the pre-genomic era, it is now possible to study the complement of an entire genome. Genomics makes it possible to calculate the number of proteins that an organism is capable of making, since DNA sequences can be used to infer protein sequences. In principle, this knowledge should provide an upper limit to the number of (protein) drug targets in an organism, and therefore the size of the "playing field" for drug discovery. Furthermore, the deduced amino acid sequences can be used to group proteins into families of known targets for drugs, such as receptors and enzymes. Surprisingly, the protein-coding regions only take up about 3% of the human DNA sequence of three billion base pairs. The rest, disparagingly referred to as junk DNA, encodes microRNA (and other) molecules (see Chap. 2) and is involved in gene regulation. This regulation can be illustrated by comparing a caterpillar and a butterfly. They both have identical DNA sequences and should, therefore, produce the same proteins, yet they clearly look quite different. This is because the proteins that specify the wings of the butterfly are turned on during development and those related to distinctive caterpillar structures are switched off. This regulation of gene expression occurs through the action of transcription factor proteins that bind to defined DNA sequences which are scattered around the genome; this binding results in the activation or repression of specific protein-coding genes.

Although transcription factor binding is a central mechanism for regulating gene expression, additional processes are involved, which come under the term epigenomics. More details will be given later, but it should be pointed out that there is literally more to life than raw DNA sequence: it is the regulation that turns a DNA code into a complex organism.

The development of genomics was possible because of the development of new technologies by scientists and engineers working in universities and instrumentation companies. Foremost among these technologies are automated chemistry, high-throughput DNA sequencing, bioinformatics and micro-fabrication, all of which are covered below.

Automated Chemistry

Sequencing the DNA of any genome would not be possible without the availability of oligonucleotides to both assist in the preparation of templates and for the sequencing process itself. Oligonucleotides are normally synthesised as strings of around 20 nucleotides (A, C, G, T) for use in a number of applications, including recombinant DNA production or for chemical reactions that synthesise DNA or RNA *in vitro*. One of these so-called priming reactions is part of the DNA sequencing process, first developed by Fred Sanger; this achievement won him a Nobel Prize to add to the one he had already received for obtaining the first protein sequence. The synthesis of oligonucleotides was not a trivial exercise in the early days of molecular biology. In 1972, an entire issue of the prestigious Journal of Molecular Biology was taken up with papers describing the creation of a synthetic gene built from synthetic oligonucleotides (e.g. ref. (Khorana 1972)). Although the size of this gene was modest by today's standards, it required a great deal of sophisticated chemistry, which was performed using standard laboratory procedures. This was acceptable for pioneering research, but not for routine use at high throughput. To overcome this limitation, engineers and chemists produced a small bench-top oligonucleotide synthesiser in which all the necessary chemical reactions were automated. Oligonucleotides can now be ordered on the Internet from supply companies and delivered by post in freeze-dried form, ready to be mixed with water and used in sequencing or other experiments.

DNA Sequencing

The first methods used to reveal the order of A, C, G and T nucleotides in a piece of DNA employed radioactive nucleotides, since these could be detected using medical X-ray film. The characteristic "DNA ladders" seen in sequencing images are the darkened areas of a photographic emulsion that correspond to a DNA fragment. The position of each fragment corresponded to a DNA letter, so by reading the film from the top and ending at the bottom, a scientist could obtain around one hundred nucleotides of sequence. This throughput was far too low to make sequencing of the genomes of even the simplest organisms remotely feasible. This only became possible with the invention of automated sequencing machines which used fluorescent dyes instead of radioactivity. Fluorescence can be readily detected with an electronic detector linked to a computer and a graphical output to display the sequence on a screen. Now that many sequencing reactions could be run in parallel, i.e. multiplexed, the number of bases that could be sequenced in a day rose to thousands; this paved the way to sequence entire genomes, consisting of megabases of DNA. An example of a sequence trace is given in Fig. 6.8 below.

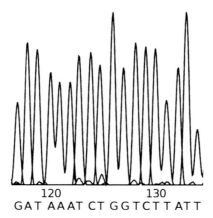

120   130
GAT AAAT CT GGTCTT ATT

Fig. 6.8 DNA sequencing trace showing part of a sequence starting 117 nucleotides into a piece of DNA and stopping at 134 nucleotides. Each peak corresponds to A, C, G or T depending on the colour of the trace (which cannot be shown in this greyscale picture). A sequencing machine will generate traces several hundred nucleotides long. The information is stored in a computer for later analysis

Bioinformatics

Strings of letters in DNA, RNA or proteins are strings of letters and nothing else, unless meaning can be extracted from them. One of the triumphs of molecular biology was the deciphering of the genetic code, so that DNA sequence could be used to predict the amino acid sequences of proteins. Sequence information was also used to understand gene regulation through identifying the stretches of DNA that are targets of transcription factors. Most importantly for medicine and drug discovery, sequencing could uncover genetic mutations. These are areas in DNA that differ between individuals, possibly at a single nucleotide or in larger stretches. Although mutations are important drivers of evolution, they can have serious consequences. Sickle cell anaemia, for example occurs in patients who have a single nucleotide mutation in the haemoglobin gene. A single nucleotide change will create a single amino acid change in the haemoglobin protein, which now aggregates (i.e. sticks together) and forces the red blood cells into a sickle shape. This is an example of a mutation in the coding region of a gene, but there are also mutations in non-coding regions that may affect gene regulation. These mutations can contribute to disease pathology by altering the expression of particular proteins.

A comprehensive analysis of DNA and protein sequences is only possible with the assistance of computers. The advent of powerful mainframe and personal computers in the 1990s helped to bring about the field of bioinformatics. Centralised computer databases of nucleic acid and protein sequences, such as GenBank and Ensembl, are freely available to the research community. Computer programs have been written to perform specific tasks like, for example the comparison of sequences between individuals or different species. One of the most widely used comparison tools is the Basic Local Alignment Search Tool (BLAST), developed in 1990 by the US National Institutes of Health (NIH). Commonly known as BLAST, it aligns sequences together to create the maximum overlap, so that if they are identical, they share 100% homology. BLAST also reveals mismatches that occur because the genes (or proteins) have altered through evolution (i.e. they come from different species) or they are altered between individuals as a result of mutation.

Bioinformatics opened up the field of comparative genomics, which is important for drug discovery; this is because it allows comparisons to be made between drug target sequences in humans and the same sequences in a model organism. For example if the target sequences differ significantly between species, it is unlikely that drugs directed against the human target will work in that model. Genome comparisons are also used to identify proteins that are only present in infectious microbes, as these could be new targets for antibiotics, antivirals or antifungals. Finally, sequence comparisons can be made within a species to classify proteins into families that share features in common, an important tool for the selection of drug targets.

A typical BLAST result is shown in Fig. 6.9. In this example, the sequence of the human CD4 protein is compared with the same molecule present in the mouse. The degree of homology (i.e. similarity) between the CD4 proteins from these two species is important when choosing animal models of HIV infection. The HIV virus uses the CD4 molecule as a receptor to bind to the human T lymphocyte prior to

Human Query 23   TQGKKVVLGKKGDTVELTCTASQKKSIQFHWKNSNQIKILGNQG-SFLTKG--PSKLNDR 79
                          TQGK +VLGK+G++ EL C +SQKK   F WK S+Q KILG G   L +G PS+ DR
Mouse Sbjct 24   TQGKTLVLGKEGESAELPCESSQKKITVFTWKFSDQRKILGQHGKGVLIRGGSPSQF-DR 82

          Query 80   ADSRRSLWDQGNFPLIIKNLKIEDSDTYICEVEDQKEEVQLLVFGLTANSDTHLLQGQSL 139
                          DS++ W++G+FPLII   LK+EDS TYICE+E++KEEV+L VF +T + T LLQGQSL
          Sbjct 83   FDSKKGAWEKGSFPLIINKLKMEDSQTYICELENRKEEVELWVFKVTFSPGTSLLQGQSL 142

          Query 140 TLTLESPPG-SSPSVQCRSPRGKNIQGGKTLSVSQLELQDSGTWTCTVLQNQKKVEFKID 198
                          TLTL+S   S+P +C+ +GK + G K LS+S L +QDS W CTV +QKK F +
          Sbjct 143 TLTLDSNSKVSNPLTECKHKKGKVVSGSKVLSMSNLRVQDSDFWNCTVTLDQKKNWFGMT 202

          Query 199 IVVLAFQKASSIVYKKEGEQVEFSFPLAFTVEKLTGSGELWWQAERASSSKSWITFDLKN 258
                          + VL FQ +   YK EGE EFSFPL F E   G GEL W+AE+ S   + WI+F +KN
          Sbjct 203 LSVLGFQSTAITAYKSEGESAEFSFPLNFAEE--NGWGELMWKAEKDSFFQPWISFSIKN 260

          Query 259 KEVSVKRVTQDPKLQMGKKLPLHLTLPQALPQYAGSGNLTLALEAKTGKLHQEVNLVVMR 318
                          KEVSV++ T+D KLQ+ + LPL L +PQ   Q+AGSGNLTL L+   G LHQEVNLVVM+
          Sbjct 261 KEVSVQKSTKDLKLQLKETLPLTLKIPQVSLQFAGSGNLTLTLDK--GTLHQEVNLVVMK 318

Fig. 6.9 A protein BLAST result taken from the NCBI online database (http://blast.ncbi.nlm.nih. gov/Blast.cgi?CMD=Web&PAGE_TYPE=BlastHome. Accessed 14 Nov 2010). Part of the protein sequence of the human CD4 protein (query) is aligned with the mouse equivalent (sbjct) using the single letter code for amino acids (Chap. 4). The numbers refer to the position of this stretch of sequence within the full length protein. Areas of identity and difference between the two species are shown in the middle line; a + indicates that while the amino acids may differ, they have similar chemical properties which may not significantly affect the protein structure. These are called conservative substitutions

entering the cell. However, since the protein sequence of the murine (mouse) CD4 is too dissimilar to the human homologue (equivalent), the virus cannot bind to mouse cells. The differences in the amino acid sequence are clearly shown in the figure (which could also have been constructed using nucleotide sequences). Genome databases are now so comprehensive that it is possible to compare sequences of a gene or protein of interest across the entire kingdom of life.

6.1.3.5 The Human Genome Project

The first genomes to be sequenced belonged to small viruses and then moved up in scale to those of microorganisms such as yeast. I vividly remember hearing the announcement, at a genomics meeting in Germany, that the full sequence of yeast had just been completed; the whole audience stood up and applauded. The yeast sequencing was a landmark in the progress of genomics, as it provided the first snapshot of a eukaryote genome with its 6,000 genes encoded in 12 Mb (million bases) of DNA. The sequences of other model organisms, such as *Drosophila* and *C. elegans*, soon followed, but the biggest prize was that of the human genome. This sequence consists of 3,000 Mb of DNA, which is 250 times the size of its counterpart in yeast. The task of sequencing the human genome was, therefore, considerable. In addition large amount of money was required, both to buy the sequencing machines (at a cost of over $100,000 each) and to support the production and analysis of large numbers of DNA fragments. There was also the need to re-sequence the entire genome more than once to iron out sequencing errors due to the limitations of the technology. The Human Genome Project began in 1990 and was funded by the Department of Energy and the National Institutes of Health in USA, along with the Wellcome Trust in the UK. Other countries such as Japan, China, Germany and France also contributed, thus making the project a truly international effort. At the same time that this publically funded effort was underway, the private sector realised that genomics could be exploited commercially by identifying and patenting genome sequences for use in developing novel drugs or targets. Companies such as Incyte Genomics and Celera sprang up to offer large pharmaceutical company clients full access to a database of genes (for a large fee) that were expressed in a whole range of disease states. They also filed patents for genes that they felt would be useful in drug discovery and, therefore, have commercial value. The stock market valuations of these companies were considerable, but there was an obvious tension between the public effort to allow free access to human genome sequence information and companies that wished to sell the information at a profit. This tension was not alleviated by Craig Venter's announcement that Celera would undertake the genome sequencing project itself and complete it sooner than the public effort. He proposed to use a technique of shotgun sequencing, in which the entire genome is broken into fragments, which are then sequenced and reassembled into the full genome sequence using computer algorithms. This announcement had the effect of invigorating both the public and private sequencing efforts which led to the project being completed in 2003, ironically the 50th anniversary of the work of Crick and Watson. The story of the Human genome Project has plenty of human interest and is worth exploring further.

Not long after the first human genome sequences were published, the commercial model of selling sequence data became untenable because the information was being made freely available. One of the legacies of the early genome projects was the greater industrialisation of biological research through the use of assembly line processes. I was made particularly aware of this during a visit to Celera in Rockville, Maryland, where the sequencing work was meticulously organised into compartments of activity that were coordinated by a huge suite of computers. I noticed that the control room for the computers was full of screens, but only one was being watched with any interest. This turned out to be the local news and weather channel, which had to be monitored for reports of electrical storms in the Maryland area; the consequences of damage to the computer systems due to a power surge could be extremely serious.

Once the human genome sequence was completed, many scientists were surprised to find that there are only about 23,000 protein-coding regions, since previous work suggested that there could be as many as 140,000. This comparatively small number of genes seems strange for such a complex organism as *Homo sapiens*; the answer lies, in part, with the complex regulation of cell function that occurs independently of genome sequence. This area of epigenomics or epigenetics, touched upon earlier, deals with the function of DNA that is independent of the gene sequences inherited from both parents. Epigenomics is attracting a great deal of interest from genomics researchers because of its relevance to diseases such as cancer (Kaiser 2010) and to the biology of stem cells. Epigenetic mechanisms are varied

Fig. 6.10 (**a**) Twenty-three pairs of human chromosomes imaged under a microscope (original image courtesy of NIH). Each pair has a number, and the sex chromosomes are labelled X. Females have two X chromosomes and males an XY pair. (**b**) Each chromosome contains genes in the form of double-stranded DNA that is supercoiled in combination with histone and other proteins to package a long strand into a small volume. Original image courtesy of National Human Genome Research Institute

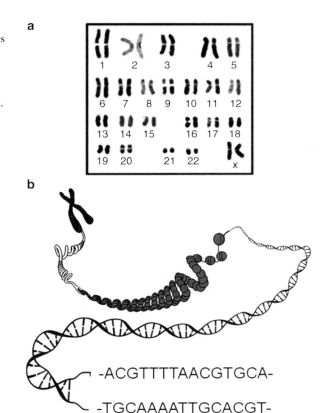

and complex, but involve proteins that are potential drug targets. The genetic material in a human cell is packaged into twenty-three pairs of chromosomes inherited from both parents. The chromosomes have the task of replicating the DNA each time a cell divides, which is quite an achievement since the length of the DNA in a cell would stretch out to about a metre if pulled apart. In order to compress this length of DNA into chromosomes, it is supercoiled, as shown in Fig. 6.10.

In addition to providing structure, the chromosomes also control the exposure of particular stretches of DNA to the enzymes that produce messenger RNA. These enzymes must physically interact with the DNA double helix, but they do so in conjunction with a class of chromosomal proteins called histones. The histone proteins are modified by the addition of specific small molecules to create a chemical code based on whether the small molecule is present or absent. The enzymes responsible for adding and removing these small molecules, histone acetyl transferase (HAT) and histone deacetylase (HDAC) respectively, are under intense scrutiny as targets for small molecule drugs that can alter the expression of specific genes through these epigenetic mechanisms.

Next Generation Sequencing

The Human Genome Project was a starting point on the road to understanding the natural world at a level of molecular detail that scientists could only dream of a few years ago. Since 2003, thousands of important genomes have been sequenced and the data deposited in online databases. The organisms studied include pathogens such as malaria parasites, and ones more likely to please the gourmet, such as the truffle genome. A new field of metagenomics has arisen, which uses sequencing technology to identify the genomes of individual microbes from within DNA that has been extracted from a mixture of organisms. Microbial DNA has been isolated from a variety of sources, both far away in the oceans and close to home in the human gut.[4] Identifying microbes, through their DNA sequence, is important from a general biology perspective because only a tiny proportion of this hidden world has ever been cultured; it is possible to identify many new species without even having to grow them on agar plates. Sequence information may also be used to identify novel metabolic pathways that could be activated by specialised growth media, thus in a sense bringing these microbes back to life. This is potentially useful for drug discovery, because microbes are sources of novel compounds. Furthermore, from the perspective of digestive diseases such as ulcerative colitis and Crohn's disease, these studies help to identify the microbes that reside in the human intestines, some of which may trigger the immune system in the gut to become overactive. Interestingly, sequencing has been used to identify bacteria associated with a particular type of seaweed used in sushi; these bacteria were found in the intestinal bacteria of Japanese but not North American subjects, so the effect of diet on human populations can be followed in great detail.

Despite the widespread interest in sequencing the whole of the living world, the human genome is still the main focus of attention from a medical, pharmaceutical and anthropological point of view. The original project to sequence this genome took 13 years and cost the US taxpayer approximately 2.7 billion dollars. This original feat provided a "reference genome" from which to identify possible protein-coding sequences and other features; it did, however, leave many questions unanswered about how genomes differ between individuals in health and disease. Clearly, the technology was available for generating more sequences, but at an unacceptably high cost and speed of progress. This desire for cheaper, faster sequencing has driven renewed competition in the field, with the stated goal of bringing the costs of sequencing a human genome down to $1,000. The first published human sequence was obtained from the pooled DNA of different individuals, but the first individual sequence was obtained in 2007 from Craig Venter's own DNA, followed by that of others including James Watson and Archbishop Desmond Tutu. Since then, thousands of full genome sequences have been obtained, including one from Ozzy Osbourne the rock singer, who was chosen because his "heroic" lifestyle makes his

---

[4] The adult human body is made up of about ten trillion cells, but ten times more bacteria live inside and on the skin, (the microbiota).

continued existence a medical impossibility. These later sequences were obtained using the so-called next-generation sequencing technology, which is a radical departure from the older procedures. The technology is advancing so rapidly that it is impossible to pick out any one system as an "industry standard". There is intense competition among instrument companies to produce machines that could one day be used for personalised medicine. Next-generation sequencing is already being used to compare the genomes of healthy individuals with that of those suffering from particular diseases, including cancer and multiple sclerosis. Cancer cells have about fifty different mutations but these vary between individuals, making it difficult, but not impossible, to identify specific drug targets. Next-generation sequencing is leading to a greater understanding of human biology and ancestry through the comparison of genomes from different ethnic groups and even from DNA extracted from Neanderthal bones. There can be no doubt that this era of high-throughput genome sequencing is one of the most exciting areas of biology and medicine, as the genetic origins and characteristics of people from all corners of the globe can now be determined in great detail.

Microarrays and Gene Chips

So far, this overview of genomics has focused on DNA sequencing as a tool for identifying drug targets, by using the genetic code to infer protein sequences. Once the gene sequence for a potential drug target has been identified, it is important to know where in the body it is expressed, so as to anticipate any side effects that might arise with a drug. For example if a drug is required to affect the lung, but the target is also expressed in the heart, there could be problems with cardiotoxicity during clinical development. Alternatively, it may be desirable to analyse the effect of existing drugs on gene (and protein) expression in the cell or animals; identifying drug-induced changes in specific genes or proteins can give clues about how the drugs are working in the body. Whichever question is asked, the answer depends on having technology that can reliably measure the expression of many thousands of different proteins or messenger RNAs. The total mRNA complement of a cell is called the transcriptome and the analysis is called transcriptomics. A number of well-established techniques for detecting mRNA and proteins are used routinely by biochemists in academia and industry. Genomics, however, is characterised by its high-throughput analysis of genes and genomes, so the low-throughput methods in routine use are unsatisfactory. This has lead to the development of microarrays, which allow the simultaneous measurement of the levels of thousands of different mRNA or protein molecules. It is easier to produce microarrays using DNA instead of proteins, because different DNA molecules are based upon a common chemistry and are therefore easier to synthesise. Microarrays for detecting mRNAs consist of DNA that has been arrayed in precise rows onto glass slides at very high density. For example one million DNA samples can be supported on a slide within an area about the size of a fingernail. This is achieved through either the inkjet technology used to spray ink onto printer paper, or through a process of photolithography that is used

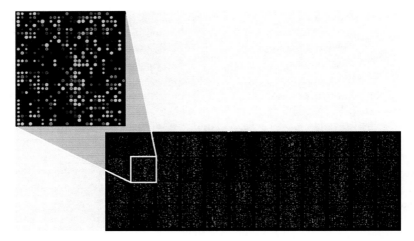

Fig. 6.11 DNA microarray showing the fluorescent signal created by the binding (hybridization) of cDNA copies of mRNA to DNA spotted onto a glass slide

to manufacture silicon chips. This latter procedure, developed by Affymetrix in the USA, gives rise to the gene chip, a term that is sometimes used to describe DNA microarrays. CCD-based imaging devices and computer software make it possible to detect and measure a fluorescent signal from each mRNA that binds to its correct target on the chip. In practice, the mRNA is converted *en masse* to a more stable DNA copy, called complementary DNA (cDNA), which is labelled with red or green fluorescent dyes. The use of different colours means that mRNAs from different sources can be compared on the same slide. For example mRNA could be extracted from a cancer cell and its cDNA labelled red; at the same time, a cDNA copy of the mRNA present in a normal cell could be labelled green. When mixed and applied to the same DNA microarray, genes that are present in the cancer cell will produce red dots and those expressed in the normal cell will produce green dots; genes expressed at the same level in both will produce a mixture of the two (yellow). Figure 6.11 is an example of a DNA microarray showing the fluorescent signals from thousands of different DNA-binding events on a glass slide.

In addition to detecting mRNA (via a cDNA copy), DNA microarrays are used to identify DNA mutations. The DNA can be extracted from a patient's blood, labelled with a fluorescent dye and then applied to a microarray that contains pieces of DNA with specific mutations. If the patient has a mutation in a corresponding piece of DNA, this will show up as a hybridization signal. This type of DNA microarray is an important tool for clinical development and personalised medicine, something that will be covered in Chap. 14.

Finally, despite the fact that DNA microarrays are easier to fabricate, many investigations will be concerned with proteins, rather than the genes that encode them. Proteins can be detected, in clinical and other samples, on microarrays containing immobilised antibodies. If a fluorescently labelled protein is recognised by an antibody, it will bind and, as with DNA arrays, give a coloured signal at a specific location on the slide. This large-scale detection of proteins is one of the characteristic features of proteomics.

6.1.3.6 Proteomics

Proteins are present in each of the 200 different cell types in humans, but can differ significantly in their level of expression. Some of them, the so-called housekeeping proteins, are expressed in all cell types, as they are involved in common processes such as replication and energy production. Other proteins are expressed in individual cell types, for example haemoglobin in red blood cells and myosin in muscle.

Since proteins are central to drug discovery, scientists realised that the approach that genomics took to DNA research could also be applied to proteins. The (inevitable) name proteomics was coined in the early 1990s and is still very much in use today. Proteomics is more challenging than genomics for a number of reasons, including the fact that the abundance of individual proteins in human tissues can vary from picogram to milligram levels, i.e. by a factor of a billion. Blood, for example contains hundreds of proteins that are swamped by comparatively enormous levels of albumen and immunoglobulins (antibodies). This can be a real problem when attempting to detect low levels of blood proteins for a diagnosis. Despite these challenges, a range of highly sophisticated proteomics techniques has been developed in order to separate proteins from cell extracts or biological fluids and identify them. These techniques will now be described in the following sections.

Gel Electrophoresis and Mass Spectrometry

Mixtures of proteins can be separated on the basis of their electrical charge, in a process called electrophoresis. The most common format is sodium dodecyl sulphate–polyacrylamide gel electrophoresis (SDS–PAGE), where polyacrylamide is a synthetic jelly-like matrix and SDS is a powerful detergent that is (rather alarmingly) used in shampoos. Proteins are dissolved by the SDS, which then confers on them a negative charge. This means that the proteins migrate through the polyacrylamide towards the positive electrode (anode) in the electrophoresis apparatus if an electric current is applied to both ends. The smaller the protein, the faster it migrates, so proteins are distributed through the gel at a distance that is proportional to their molecular weights. Once separated, the proteins can be stained with special dyes to reveal their positions. When standard proteins of defined molecular weight are run alongside the samples, the molecular weights of unknown proteins can be determined by simply comparing their migration relative to the standards. The identities of the separated proteins can be determined in a number of ways, one of which is through using specific antibodies and Western blotting (see Chap. 14). This, of course, can work only if such antibodies are available. Another technique for protein identification is protein mass spectrometry, which is one of the hallmarks of proteomics.

Mass spectrometry uses an electron beam to break molecules into charged fragments; these are accelerated through an electric field and separated according to their mass in a magnetic field. This provides highly accurate values for the molecular weights of the fragments that can be used to identify a protein through its amino acid sequence. The method of peptide mass fingerprinting (PMF) is now routinely used to identify proteins that have been literally cut out of the gel used for SDS–PAGE. The proteins are digested by the enzyme trypsin, which cuts the chain into peptides of defined size only where certain amino acids are present. The resulting peptides are passed through a mass spectrometer and their exact molecular weights determined. Protein sequences in the genome databases can be virtually "digested" by trypsin in the computer to create a set of peptides corresponding to all the proteins that the genome can encode. Each of these "virtual" peptides has a defined molecular weight which can be compared with that found in the real protein under investigation. If the peptides from the separated protein correspond with those obtained in the computer, the protein is identified. This powerful technique has been used to analyse highly complex mixtures of proteins from many different cell types and provides information about how these proteins interact together to perform their biological functions. These core technologies for proteomics are summarised in Fig. 6.12.

Proteins link together in specific complexes in the cell to form molecular machines, such as signalling pathways that transmit information from outside the cell to the inside. The association between proteins is a dynamic process that can occur very rapidly. This is important for drug discovery, since drugs that interact with a target that is part of a complex network may perturb other pathways in the cell. These off-target effects may, or may not, be desirable. In an ideal world, it would be possible to predict all off-target effects in advance of clinical trials, but our current understanding of complex biological interactions is inadequate. This is why a great deal of basic and applied research is being directed towards systems biology (see also Chap. 4). This approach to biological research is heavily reliant upon data generated from, among other things, genomics and proteomics experiments. The objective is to build models of how the cell operates, independently and within the intact body, so as to make drug discovery more predictive than is currently the case.

Structural Proteomics

A protein's function is related to the three-dimensional shape that is dictated by its primary amino acid sequence. The importance of protein shape for drug binding has been outlined already in Chap. 3 and highlights the importance of both structure and sequence. Structural proteomics is a term for the high-throughput generation and analysis of protein structures using tools such as X-ray crystallography and nuclear magnetic resonance (NMR). The former method requires, as the name implies, that the protein be crystallised before being bombarded with X-rays to determine the exact position of each atom within the molecule. Crystals can be very difficult to grow in the laboratory, particularly when the protein is normally found in cell membranes.

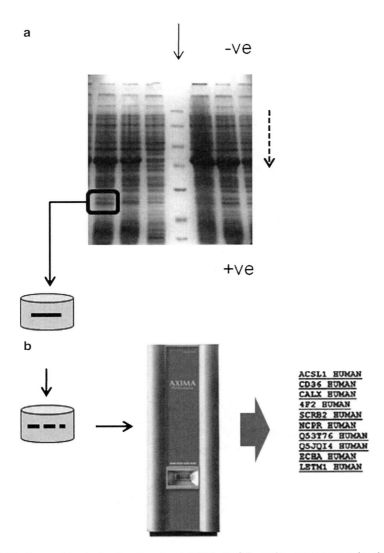

Fig. 6.12 Some of the tools of proteomics. (**a**) SDS–PAGE, used to separate proteins through a gel by applying an electric field from top to bottom; −ve indicates the negative connection and +ve the positive. The proteins are applied in separate lanes to the top and, being negatively charged, are attracted to the +ve end and migrate to the bottom. Each protein appears as a thin band that is revealed by staining the whole gel with a dye. The arrow at the top indicates where seven proteins have been separated within the gel. Their precise molecular weights are known already, so their relative migration can be used to determine the molecular weights of all the other proteins on the gel. (**b**) Determining the identity of proteins in each band. The box indicates where a protein band has been cut out of the gel. The piece of gel is then placed in a tube and the protein digested to smaller peptides using the enzyme trypsin. The peptides are introduced into a mass spectrometer instrument that precisely identifies the size of the peptides; a computer then searches the protein databases to identify the best matches. These are shown as a list of names to the right of the instrument. (**c**) A protein interaction map drawn using the STRING database (2010). Proteins that strongly associate together as a complex within a cell have been isolated and then analysed using SDS–PAGE and mass spectrometry. In this way, it is possible to draw a network of interactions between each component protein in the complex. In this example, the p53 protein that is involved in cancer is at the centre of the network

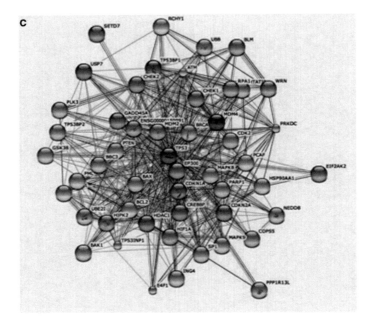

Fig. 6.12 (continued)

In addition, the crystal "freezes" the structure in a fixed position, so an X-ray structure is a snapshot of one moment in time. Proteins actually have flexible portions whose movement can be visualised using NMR; the preferred method of structure determination, however, is still X-ray crystallography because of its high degree of atomic resolution. Analyses of large numbers of structures (there are nearly 70,000 available in the main online database) have revealed particular protein folds or domains that are used like building blocks in different protein families. This "mixing and matching" of domains create a great variety of protein structures that can be grouped together in families by virtue of their similarity. As will be seen later, these protein families are important for drug target selection.

6.1.4   How Many Drug Targets Are There?

It is obviously impossible to give a precise figure, not least because many potential drug targets are associated with microorganisms, rather than human cells. It is possible, however, to give an approximate figure for the number of targets for current drugs. One of the most recent estimates was made in 2006 by Overington et al., who arrived at a figure of 248 unique targets for small molecules and 76 for biologicals (Overington et al. 2006).

These figures cover existing drugs, but if drug discovery is to be made more systematic, as its practitioners hope, then it would be useful to know the maximum number that could be discovered. The tools of genomics and proteomics now make it possible to make at least a rough estimate of this figure. Analysis of the human genome sequence using bioinformatics has identified around 23,000 protein-coding genes. On the face of it, there should be a maximum of 23,000 drug targets if every protein in the cell were involved in some disease. Unfortunately, biology is never this straightforward, there is always some complication. In this case, the number of possible proteins far exceeds the number of protein-coding genes. There are two reasons for this: firstly, the phenomenon of alternative splicing means that each gene can be processed into mRNA with different lengths, so some of the resulting proteins are derived from only a part of the original DNA sequence. It has been estimated that 95% of human mRNA molecules are spliced in some way. A second reason for the mismatch between the number of genes and proteins is the process of post-translational modification. This is where proteins are chemically modified by the addition of small molecules. One example of this is the addition of carbohydrate molecules (glycosylation) to proteins that are destined to protrude from the cell surface. Other important chemical modifications, such as phosphorylation, will be highlighted later. It is now clear then that the human proteome consists of hundreds of thousands of chemically unique proteins that are originally derived from only 23,000 genes. Estimates of how many of these might be drug targets range between one and ten thousand, which is quite enough to keep the drug discovery industry occupied for a few years yet.

6.1.4.1 Target Classes

Estimates of the number of possible human targets for drugs are based on a mixture of guesswork and prior knowledge of drug target families. This prior knowledge is summed up by the rather inelegant term druggable targets; these are proteins with structural features that allow strong binding by small molecules. Targets that are affected by marketed drugs are, by definition, druggable, so one way of identifying novel targets is to search for related protein family members and produce small molecules against them to test in the laboratory. Some of the main protein families that contain known drug targets are listed in Table 6.2.

The above list represents a small fraction of possible drug targets, but it does highlight the families that are still the subject of intense interest by the biopharmaceutical industry. This chapter will conclude with a brief description of each of these classes in turn.

- G protein-coupled receptors (GPCRs)
  Over twenty percent of marketed drugs bind to this class of receptor, which is expressed on the surface of many different cell types. The protein is anchored to the cell membrane by threading through it seven times, hence the alternative name seven transmembrane (or 7TM) receptor. G proteins are molecules that couple to

Table 6.2 Main protein families containing druggable targets

Target class	Representative example	Role in disease	Associated drug
Receptors			
GPCRs	Histamine H2	Stomach ulcers	Ranitidine
Nuclear	Oestrogen receptor	Breast cancer	Tamoxifen
Cytokine	TNF-α receptor	Rheumatoid arthritis	Enbrel (biological)
Enzymes			
Proteases	ACE	Hypertension	Lisonopril
Kinases	Abelson tyrosine kinase	Leukaemia	Gleevec
Phosphatases	Calcineurin	Transplant rejection	Cyclosporine A
Ion channels			
Ligand gated	GABA$_A$ receptor	Anxiety	Benzodiazepines
Voltage gated	Calcium channel	Angina/hypertension	Norvasc
Transporters	Monoamine transporters	Low serotonin depression	Fluoxetine

Cytokine receptors are the exception because they are not inhibited with small molecules, but they are an important target class for biologicals

this type of receptor in order to transmit the signals generated after ligand binding into the cell interior. The human genome contains over 1000 GPCRs, many of which are involved in sensing tastes and smells (i.e. gustatory and olfactory). However, around 400 GPCRs have potential as drug targets, although there is still much to learn about their normal roles in the body. All have the potential to bind ligands, but the proteins without a known ligand are called orphan receptors, until someone finds a home for them, which is happening with increasing frequency.

- Nuclear receptors (NRs)
  These small molecule receptors bind ligands inside the cell rather than on the surface. After ligand has bound, a complex formed between the ligand and the receptor moves into the cell nucleus to switch particular genes on or off. Nuclear receptors bind small lipophilic molecules such as steroids and retinoids (e.g. the sex hormones and vitamins A), which have profound effects on human physiology. The human genome codes for about 50 NRs of which as many as half are orphan receptors.

- Cytokine receptors
  A varied family consisting of more than one protein chain anchored into the cell membrane. The cytokine ligands are proteins such as interleukins, interferons and growth factors. As small molecules are not able to disrupt cytokine binding to its receptor, larger protein drugs have to be used. These are either antibodies or recombinant forms of the receptor that act as decoys to prevent ligand binding.

- Proteases
  These are enzymes that clip proteins at defined points by targeting specific amino acid sequences. Proteases have many roles in the human body, such as blood clotting, processing of peptide hormones and the life cycle of viruses such as HIV. Although inhibitors of proteases are challenging to produce as drugs, there are a number of highly successful medicines on the market that target this enzyme class.

- Protein kinases
  A large family of enzymes that attach a phosphate group (PO_3) to a protein molecule in order to change its activity in the cell. This process of protein phosphorylation is used by the cell to transmit signals from external receptors through the membrane and into the cell nucleus, where they switch on gene expression. Kinases are of particular importance in cancer; this is because cells grow independently of external growth factors as a result of specific kinase enzymes being permanently activated. Protein kinase inhibition is now a major area of small molecule drug discovery.

- Protein phosphatases
  Protein phosphatases are enzymes that perform the reverse role of protein kinases; that is, they remove phosphate groups from proteins instead of adding them. This is an important mechanism for cell signalling, as it acts as an "off switch" to keep control over cellular processes. Although phosphatase inhibitors would find use in a number of diseases, they have been difficult to turn into medicines. Despite this, there is still plenty of research activity aimed at producing drugs based on this target class, including, possibly, a small molecule substitute for insulin.

- Other enzymes
  The enzyme families listed above (with the exception of the phosphatases) make up the majority of current drug targets, but not all of them. Prominent examples are the HMGCoA reductase inhibitors (otherwise known as statins) that lower cholesterol and the phosphodiesterase (PDE) inhibitors, of which Viagra® is the most famous (infamous?) example.

- Ion channels
  Ions are atoms or molecules that bear a positive or negative charge. Metal ions, such as calcium (Ca^{2+}), sodium (Na^+) and potassium (K^+), play vital roles in many physiological processes. Ions pass through pores in cell membranes called ion channels. The two main types are known as ligand-gated and voltage-gated ion channels. Each channel is selective for a particular ion that moves from the outside of the cell to inwards, or vice versa. Ion movements are involved in the function of nerve cells and are implicated in conditions such as epilepsy, pain and heart arrhythmias. There is considerable interest in ion channels as drug targets, with a number of important drugs already on the market.

- Transporters
  Transporter proteins carry molecules within the body, specifically through the cell membranes which would normally block their passage into cells. For example nutrient molecules are carried across the stomach by transporters. Transporters are molecular targets in a number of diseases, the best known being depression, which is associated with low levels of serotonin in the brain. The monoamine transporter removes serotonin from nerve cells, but this neurotransmitter can be maintained at higher levels by inhibiting the transporter with drugs such as fluoxetine (Prozac®), thereby alleviating the symptoms of depression. Other transporter drug targets of interest include glucose transporters, whose inhibition could be useful for treating diabetes.

6.1.5   *Closing Remarks*

The search for drug targets that makes up the beginning of the drug discovery pipeline is complex and technically challenging, as has been made clear in this long chapter. This is only the beginning however, since enormous challenges lie ahead in finding drug molecules with all the properties required to turn them into safe and effective medicines. It is worth making this point, because however exciting a new target opportunity seems to its discoverer, the clinical reality can be disappointing. This could, of course, either be due to the target being unsuitable, or the drug itself being problematical. There is certainly no shortage of drug target ideas coming from academia and industry; a search for the term "potential drug target" using Google, for example, produces nearly 40,000 hits for the period 2009–2010. Obviously, this is an overestimate, because many links will be reports of the same published work, but nevertheless it gives some idea of the opportunities being presented to the biopharmaceutical industry. The description of how researchers approach the selection of drug targets is now concluded. The next stage in the drug development pipeline involves the discovery of small or large molecules that selectively interact with the targets.

Summary of Key Points

Observations of the signs and symptoms of disease give clues that allow the researcher to identify specific tissues in the patient, which can be further investigated at the level of cells and molecules. This process is formalised as translational medicine.

In vitro experiments are undertaken to test the hypothesis that a specific drug target protein is relevant to a disease mechanism.

In vivo experiments are undertaken in animals and other model organisms, such as zebrafish, to show that modifying the target with an antibody, or other agent, will ameliorate a disease symptom.

Modern biological disciplines, based on cell biology, biochemistry and molecular biology, provide the tools to understand diseases and drug targets at the level of genes, proteins and other molecules. More recent offshoots of these disciplines include genomics, epigenomics, transcriptomics, proteomics, systems biology and bioinformatics.

The Human Genome Project identified 23,000 genes that could encode human proteins, but the number of proteins actually produced by cells is much higher.

There are approximately 400 targets for current medicines, but there could be as many as 10,000 targets to be exploited in the future, based on estimates of protein numbers.

Drug targets are distributed in protein families, such as GPCRs and nuclear receptors.

References

ICD-10, http://www.who.int/classifications/icd/en/. Accessed 12 Nov 2010

Kaiser J (2010) Epigenetic drugs take on cancer. Science 330:576–578

Khorana HG (1972) Studies on polynucleotides. 103. Total synthesis of the structural gene for an alanine transfer ribonucleic acid from yeast. J Mol Biol 72:209–217

Kyoto Encyclopedia of Genes and Genomes (KEGG). http://www.genome.jp/kegg/. Accessed 19 Dec 2010

Overington JP et al (2006) How many drug targets are there? Nat Rev Drug Discov 5:993–996

STRING – Known and Predicted Protein-Protein Interactions, http://string-db.org. Accessed 16 Nov 2010

Chapter 7
Medicinal Chemistry

Abstract Medicinal chemistry is concerned with the synthesis of small molecules, which are then passed to biologists for testing against drug targets. The vastness of chemical space means that the number of different molecules that could theoretically be made is almost infinite; in reality, there are constraints based on the limitations of synthetic chemistry and the effects of certain functional groups on the human body. This chapter describes the goals of medicinal chemistry and introduces the range of technologies used to produce active drug molecules, including computer-aided drug design and natural product chemistry.

7.1 Introduction

The target discovery process at the beginning of the drug discovery pipeline was covered in some detail in the previous chapter. By this stage, it can be assumed that a suitable protein target has been identified, so the next challenge is to discover molecules that interact with the target; these molecules will then be turned into candidates for full clinical development. This chapter covers the discovery of the small molecule drugs that still make up the majority of medicines, despite the rapid rise of biotherapeutics (see Chap. 8). The primary aim of small molecule discovery is to provide compounds (leads) that can be further developed into the final medicinal product. It is quite possible, however, that the final medicine will differ significantly from the first identified compounds (hits) because of the modifications needed to improve their pharmacokinetic properties (such as adsorption and metabolism) that will be discussed in later chapters. Almost all small molecule drugs are produced using the tools of synthetic organic chemistry, which have been developed over approximately 200 years. Organic chemistry, like other sciences, has its own sub-divisions, which in the biopharmaceutical industry are medicinal, analytical and process chemistry. Medicinal chemists (sometimes referred to as pharmaceutical chemists) undertake the compound development work from the beginning, right up to the point where the compound is ready for clinical testing. Once a compound is

E.D. Zanders, *The Science and Business of Drug Discovery: Demystifying the Jargon*,
DOI 10.1007/978-1-4419-9902-3_7, © Springer Science+Business Media, LLC 2011

likely to be progressed further, process chemists start to plan a safe and cost-effective strategy for producing it in large amounts for clinical testing and ultimately manufacture. Analytical chemists are important at all stages of drug development, as they have to devise ways of testing the purity of compounds and measuring their concentrations in blood and other biological fluids.

7.1.1   The Vastness of Chemical Space

In Chap. 6, biological information was used to answer the question: "how many drug targets are there?" A related question could be asked of small molecules, this time based on chemical information, namely, how many organic molecules would it be theoretically possible to make? The term chemical space is used to describe all these possible combinations. Theoretical calculations of the number of possible structures of molecules with molecular weights of less than 700 have arrived at the staggeringly large number of 10^{60} combinations (Bohacek et al. 1996). In fact, just adding 150 common functional groups in combination to the simple n-hexane molecule (containing six carbon atoms in a chain) would alone produce 10^{29} combinations (Lipinski & Hopkins 2004). Chemists have produced roughly 80 million (8×10^7) compounds, a figure that is clearly a minute fraction of the total number that could theoretically be made.[1] In practice, organic synthesis is far from trivial exercise; this means that a realistic estimate of the number of possible small molecule drugs will be numbered in the millions, which is a minute proportion of the theoretical maximum.

7.1.2   The Goals of Medicinal Chemistry

The aim of medicinal chemistry is to produce compounds with the following properties:

• Potency *in vivo*
• Selectivity against the target
• Lack of toxicity
• Good pharmacokinetics (stability in body and other factors to be detailed later)

It is rarely possible to produce a molecule that immediately fulfils all of the above criteria. A useful analogy to compound optimization is the notorious Rubik's cube game devised by the Hungarian Ernő Rubik. The cube consists of six faces made up of nine stickers displaying one of a total of six colours. The colours can be mixed up through a series of independent turns and the objective is to produce a single colour on each face. An inevitable feeling of triumph ensues when one face has

---

[1] The mass of the visible universe is apparently about 10^{56} g so there wouldn't actually be enough material to make every compound even if the methods were available.

been manipulated into the same colour, followed by frustration when attempts to create further uniform faces result in the first face disappearing. This exactly parallels what can happen in medicinal chemistry when, for example a potent compound is identified that is not very selective. Subsequent efforts to improve selectivity by modifying the molecule may only serve to reduce potency, and so on.

7.1.2.1 Starting Points

Some medicinal chemistry case histories have already been described in Chap. 4. The histamine H2 antagonists, for example were discovered by modifying histamine and testing these modified compounds (i.e. analogues) in a biological assay to determine their activity. The starting point was therefore the natural molecule whose structure was already known. The type of starting molecule will vary depending on the drug target class. For receptors such as GPCRs and nuclear receptors, these will be ligands such as hormones, while for enzymes these will be the natural substrates. Taking proteases as an example, the enzyme binds to the substrate (i.e. a specific protein) and clips it at a particular amino acid, producing two or more smaller fragments. The starting point for medicinal chemistry is a peptide that contains a few of the amino acids on each side of the one that is cleaved by the protease. In many cases, however, it is not possible to use a natural molecule as a starting point. This may occur, where no such molecule exists, or where the natural molecule is too difficult to synthesize or modify. There may also be patent issues if other companies have covered the obvious features with their own drugs. The alternative method is to identify completely novel compounds that interact with the target by randomly screening large collections of diverse chemical compounds. This is one of the most common starting points in the industry and is often the first port of call for any small molecule discovery program. Screening will be covered in more detail in Chap. 9. Finally, it is possible to design molecules in the computer as starting points (*in silico* drug design). This is still at an early stage of development, but is used extensively in medicinal chemistry to optimize the interactions between drugs and their targets. The other starting point is, of course, the target protein itself. If a three-dimensional structure is available, this can provide details about the various binding pockets that could be accessed by small molecules. This is made more straightforward if the protein structure already has a small molecule bound to it, so much effort goes into producing crystals with both molecules bound together (co-crystallized).

7.1.2.2 The Search for Pharmacophores

The collection of molecular features contributing to the specific action of a drug on a target is known as a pharmacophore. The objective of a medicinal chemistry program is to identify a suitable pharmacophore and modify it to achieve the desired biological outcome (e.g. agonist or antagonist). The histamine H2 receptor case history given in Chap. 4 is a good illustration of this. The pharmacophore was identified as the imidazole ring in histamine which was then retained in cimetidine in a slightly modified form (addition of a methyl group) and replaced completely in ranitidine. This group (a furan) is known as an isostere since it has the same shape as the imidazole and can be substituted for it, producing a drug molecule with the activity as good as the original molecule, if not better. This process of isosteric replacement is widely undertaken by medicinal chemists who want to create greater compound diversity in order to improve biological properties and establish composition of matter patents.

Statin drugs provide another example where pharmacophores lead to useful drugs, in this case, amongst the best selling medicines of all time. Statins lower the level of cholesterol in the blood by inhibiting its synthesis, the result being a significant reduction in the incidence of coronary heart disease in high-risk groups of patients. Cholesterol is a lipid built up in a stepwise fashion from small chemical units by a series of enzymes, the key one being HMGCoA reductase, which controls the rate of cholesterol synthesis. Inhibition of the enzyme reduces cholesterol levels in the blood and the associated buildup of fatty deposits in the arteries (atherosclerosis). HMGCoA inhibitors have been developed by a number of companies and marketed as statin drugs. Figure 7.1 shows the molecular structures of the natural molecule HMGCoA, along with two of the best selling statin drugs marketed under the names Crestor® and Lipitor® by AstraZeneca and Pfizer, respectively. The pharmacophore in HMGCoA is indicated by the dotted box in the figure and is replicated (with some modification) in the two totally synthetic drugs. The resemblance between them and the natural molecule ends there, as will be obvious even to the untrained eye. In these examples, the addition of a fluorophenyl group (highlighted) has enhanced the binding of the synthetic statins to the enzyme target. The fluorine atom (F) is rarely found in natural molecules but is sometimes used in synthetic drugs to modify the charge of groups that interact with the protein target.

7.1.2.3   Visualizing Chemistry

The "think like a chemist" section in Chap. 3 highlighted the way in which a medicinal chemist can interpret two-dimensional chemical structure diagrams to identify different functional groups and get some idea of three-dimensional structure. This chemists' technique of visualization goes back to the nineteenth century, when pioneers like August Kekulé tried to determine the structures of organic molecules using the ideas about valency that were being put forward at the time. Kekulé is credited with working out the ring structure of benzene, apparently after visualizing it in a series of dreams (one of them on top of a London bus) (Rocke 2010; Robinson 2010). The routine use of computer graphics makes the visualization process much more straightforward, allowing different molecular features such as charge and shape to be added and subtracted at will. There is still, however, a place for the old fashioned plastic models of atoms and bonds that can be used to build compounds and examine their shape while holding them in the palm of the hand.

The chemical modifications that gave rise to histamine antagonists and the statin drugs are a reflection of the skill and knowledge acquired by medicinal chemists during the course of their work. This skill is almost like having a natural feel for

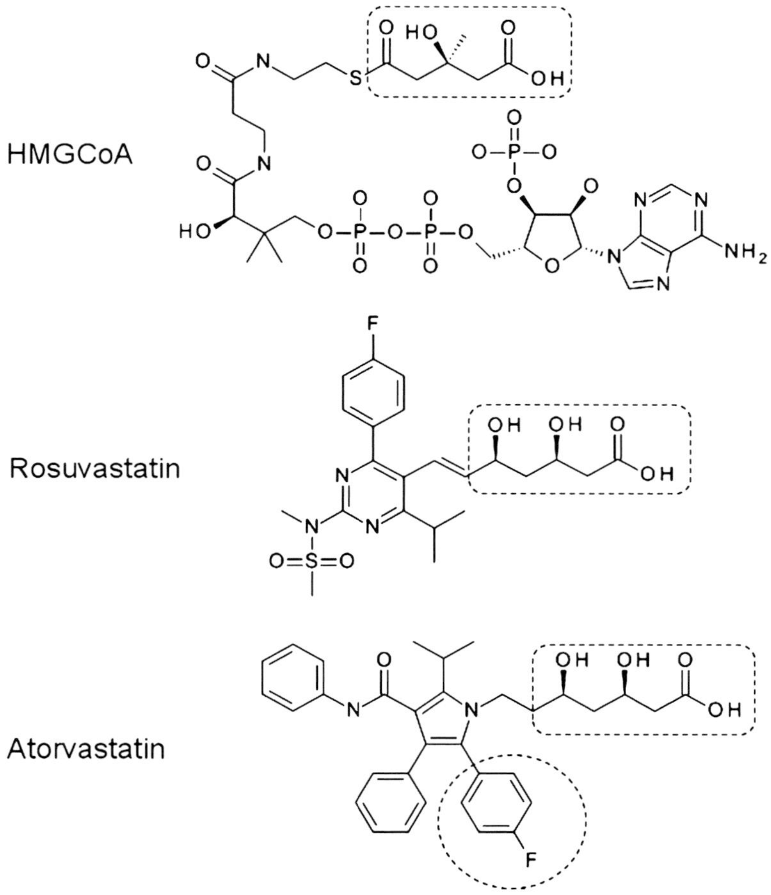

HMGCoA

Rosuvastatin

Atorvastatin

Fig. 7.1 Molecular structures of cholesterol lowering statin drugs and the pharmacophore present in the natural substrate for HMGCoA reductase. The fluorophenyl group is *highlighted* (see text). The reason why some bonds are drawn as *solid* or *dotted wedges* is explained later under stereochemistry

the system under investigation, rather like a gardener having "green fingers" for growing plants.[2] The structure–activity relationship (SAR) is central to medicinal chemistry; as the name implies, each structure chosen for biological testing will have a particular activity that varies in a defined way according to the type of chemical groups added to the starting molecule. This is illustrated by an example taken from a study of enzyme inhibitors by scientists at Wyeth Research. Full details are available in their publication (Douglas et al. 2007), a highly technical description of attempts to create potent inhibitors of the protein phosphatase

[2] Drug discovery scientists like James Black and Paul Janssen had this feel and, with their teams, were responsible for major pharmaceutical innovations.

enzyme PTP1B. There is considerable interest in this enzyme as a drug target, since its inhibition would enhance the response of cells to insulin signalling; this signalling defect is responsible for the insulin resistance that is central to type 2 diabetes. Compound 3 in Fig. 7.2 was used as a starting point for a series of modifications to the basic structure aimed at making the molecule large enough to bind to different parts of the enzyme and enhance its activity. Compounds 23 and 32 represent two such modifications, 32 being larger and more complex.

The activities of each compound against PTP1B and CD45, another protein phosphatase, are shown in Table 7.1. The smaller the figure, the more potent the inhibitor.

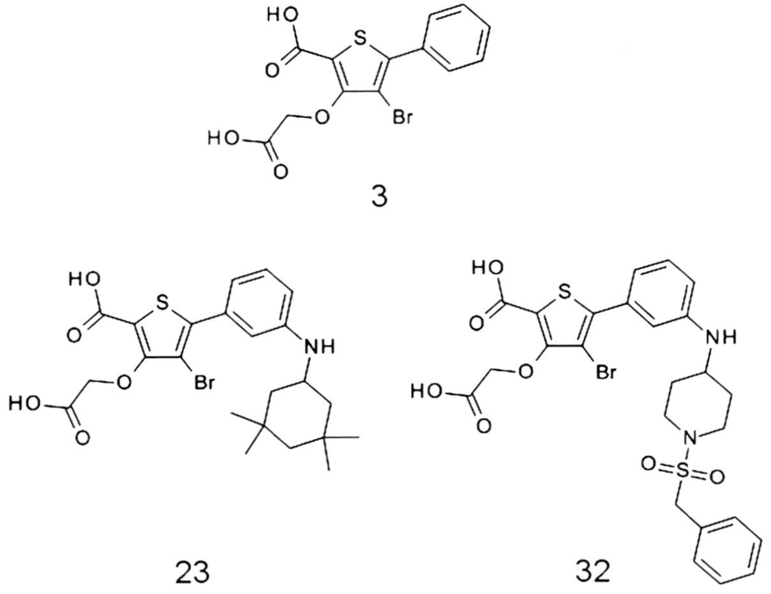

Fig. 7.2 Medicinal chemistry programme to produce PTP-1B inhibitors based on structure 3. Extra functional groups added to basic structure with compounds 23 and 32 are shown as examples. Adapted with permission from Douglas et al. (2007) Copyright 2007 American Chemical Society

Table 7.1 Activity of three inhibitors of PTP-1B from Fig. 7.2

Compound	PTP1B	CD45
3	3.2	280
23	0.036	151
32	0.004	77

Figures represent the potency of inhibition measured (in micromolar units) by a value called the K_i. The lower the value, the greater the potency (see any resource on enzyme kinetics). The potency of compound 32 is therefore much greater than compound 3, because of the difference between 3.2 and 0.004 μM, (or 4 nM). Adapted with permission from Douglas et al. (2007) Copyright 2007 American Chemical Society

It is clear that adding an extension to molecule 3 increases the activity about 100-fold with 23 and about 1,000-fold with 32. This brings the activity from 3.2 μM to 4 nM. This is the level of potency required for this type of inhibitor if it is to progress further in development. The table also shows the comparative lack of activity of all the compounds on the phosphatase CD45; this means that the compound is unlikely to cause side effects related to inhibition of this enzyme.

The quantitative structure–activity relationship (QSAR) is a key part of chemoinformatics, which is the analysis of virtual (imaginary) compounds using computer algorithms. QSAR involves some relatively complex statistical analysis, using values such as molecular weight and lipophilicity (solubility in fats) to predict the functional groups which are most likely to enhance biological activity. In addition to identifying groups with positive attributes, QSAR is used to eliminate potentially toxic groups, for example the thiourea group in the H2 antagonists (Chap. 4). Medicinal chemists have access to computer databases of known toxic groups, so they can pre-screen a collection of compounds before committing anything to synthesis and biological testing.

7.1.2.4 What Makes a Good Drug Candidate?

Not all compounds interacting with a selected target will be suitable for administration to human subjects. This has been understood, the hard way, by generations of drug discovery scientists and nothing has changed since. It is therefore important to define exactly what chemical properties a new compound must possess if it is to have any chance of reaching the marketplace. Medicinal chemists are rather like doctors, in the sense that it is always possible to get a second (or third or fourth) opinion on what they think is promising and what is not worth pursuing. I always used to feel dispirited in project meetings when the chemists would review just about every compound that we had selected with good biological activity only to reject it on the basis that it was "a Michael acceptor"; this is a chemical feature that usually raises problems during clinical development.

This rather ad hoc way of reviewing structures led Pfizer chemist Peter Lipinski to formulate the "Rule of Five" for selecting compounds for further development. This "Lipinski's Rule" states that for compounds to be orally active, they should have:

- A molecular weight of less than 500 Da
- No more than five hydrogen bond donor atoms
- No more than ten hydrogen bond acceptor atoms
- A $\log P$ of less than 5

This last point is a measure of the lipophilicity of a drug that is either determined theoretically, or by measuring how much dissolves in an organic solvent (octanol) compared with water. Being a logarithmic scale, it means that a compound with a $\log P$ of 6 is ten times more lipophilic than one with a $\log P$ of 5.

Other rules have been developed by the medicinal chemistry community and all serve a useful purpose if followed to the spirit, if not the letter, of the law.

At this point, it is important to stress that compounds selected initially for their potency and selectivity in biological assays may not be suitable as drugs because of pharmacokinetic or toxicity issues (see Chap. 11). If such issues do exist, it may be necessary to modify the chemical structure of the initial compound to a point where the structure of the final drug is significantly different.

7.1.2.5 Stereochemistry

The stereochemistry (i.e. shape) of small molecule drugs determines how they will bind to their target. Many molecules exist in forms that are a mirror image of each other, a phenomenon termed chirality, from the Greek for hand; this can be illustrated by looking at the left and right hand: the fingers are the same, but they are ordered as mirror images and cannot be superimposed. This has implications for drug binding, since only one mirror image form (enantiomer) will bind to a protein target, while the other is inactive, or will possibly interact with a totally different protein.

The chiral forms of the amino acid valine are shown in Fig. 7.3. The L and D enantiomers have identical atoms, but cannot be superimposed on each other. The drawing uses the Fischer projection, in which bonds projecting out towards the viewer are indicated with a solid wedge and those with a dotted wedge project backwards. The asterisk indicates the carbon atom positioned at the point of symmetry of the chiral molecule.

Many complex drug molecules have more than one chiral centre; mathematically if there are N chiral centres, there will be 2^N enantiomers, which becomes worryingly high for chemists planning the synthesis of a single chiral form. Examples of chiral drugs and their importance for toxicology and patent extension will be given later in the book.

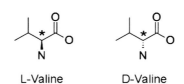

L-Valine   D-Valine

Fig. 7.3 Example of chiral forms of the amino acid valine with Hs omitted. The two molecules are mirror images of each other. Only the L-form of this and other amino acids are used in proteins, suggesting that this mirror image form was favoured during the early stages of life on earth

7.1.3 How Are Compounds Synthesized?

This is where the author has to concede defeat when trying to explain the ramifications of this vast and highly technical subject. However, some attempt has to be made to convey at least a feeling for how synthesis is performed in the modern chemistry laboratory.

The early literature on organic chemistry was written more than 100 years ago and is still referred to directly or indirectly by chemists wanting to convert one set of molecules into another. Many chemical procedures are used "off the shelf" to produce specific functional groups as required and are often named after the people who developed them. Examples include the Williamson ether synthesis and the Diels–Alder reaction. An illustration of how the Diels–Alder reaction can be used to form complex rings from simpler molecules is shown in Fig. 7.4.

Synthetic methods are still being developed to solve chemical problems which previously may have seemed intractable; one example is the selective breaking of C–H bonds to introduce new functional groups into molecules. Synthetic chemistry is one area in which innovation in academic and industrial laboratories can make a real impact upon the biopharmaceutical industry. New tools are appearing all the time, for example "click chemistry" used to produce complex compounds from simple modular units, often in the presence of metals as catalysts.

It is hard to overestimate the technical challenges of devising a reaction scheme for synthesizing drug compounds, particularly where chiral molecules are involved. The actual synthesis of organic compounds is not totally dissimilar to cooking, although the products of that pleasurable activity are unlikely to blow up in your face. The following example of a typical synthetic procedure is taken, more or less verbatim, from a paper published in the *Journal of Medicinal Chemistry* by a group investigating receptor agonists as potential treatments for multiple sclerosis (Bolli et al. 2010) (adapted with permission Copyright 2010 American Chemical Society).

To a solution of isopropylamine (1.31 g) in methanol (25 mL), phenyl isothiocyanate (3.00 g) is added portionwise. The mixture which became slightly warm (approximately 30°C) was stirred at room temperature for 3.5 h before bromoacetic acid methyl ester (3.39 g) followed by pyridine (2.63 g) was added. Stirring of the colorless reaction mixture was continued for 16 h. The resulting fine suspension was diluted with 1 N Hydrochloric

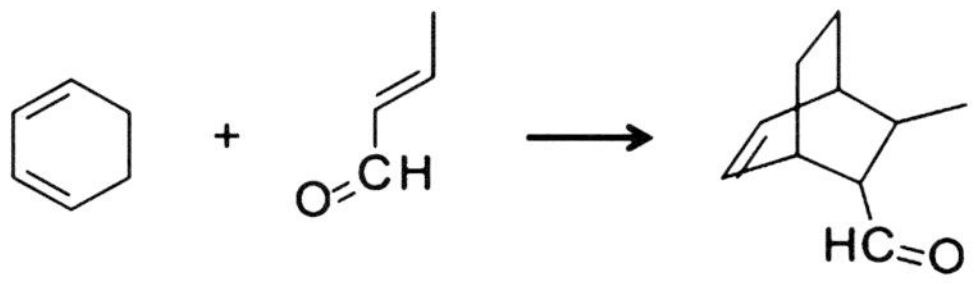

Fig. 7.4 Example of complex ring synthesis from simple alicyclic (non-aromatic ring) compound and a linear compound (an aldehyde). This uses the Diels–Alder reaction invented by two German chemists which earned them a Nobel Prize for chemistry

acid (100 mL) and extracted with diethyl ether (150 mL). The separated organic phase contains crude 4a. The pH of the aqueous phase was adjusted to pH 8 by adding saturated aqueous $NaHCO_3$ solution. The aqueous phase was extracted with diethyl ether (4 × 150 mL). The combined organic extracts containing crude 3a were dried over $MgSO_4$, filtered, and concentrated. The remaining crystalline solid was washed with heptane and dried under high vacuum to give 3a as an off-white crystalline solid.

This example illustrates the long cooking times which are sometimes needed to transform one compound into another. It also highlights the potential hazards and discomforts involved in working in a chemistry laboratory, as ether is explosively flammable and pyridine has a highly unpleasant smell. Industrial chemists and biologists have traditionally been kept well apart in separate buildings, partly because of sociological differences and more seriously, because of the nature of the science. This is beginning to change in some institutions, as scientists from different disciplines are becoming more integrated within single working areas to allow cross fertilization of ideas.

7.1.3.1 Analytical Chemistry

Once a compound has been synthesized, it is purified from all the other molecules present in the chemical reaction through a variety of well-established techniques such as filtration, crystallization or chromatography. Chromatography is widely used in chemistry and biochemistry and will be described in later chapters. Analytical chemistry is a key part of medicinal chemistry as it is used to ensure that a synthesized compound is actually what the chemist thinks it should be. It would obviously be impossible to obtain reliable data on compounds that have not been properly identified. Standard methods of analysis include the use of spectroscopy, which is based on the interaction of radiation with matter. Different forms of spectroscopy are listed below:

- UV spectroscopy
  Absorption of ultraviolet light by compounds to produce characteristic fingerprints relating to presence of specific chemical groups.
- IR spectroscopy
  The same principle as UV, but using absorption of longer wavelength infrared radiation.
- NMR spectroscopy
  Nuclear magnetic resonance (NMR) spectroscopy is one of the most commonly used techniques for identifying chemical structures. It is based on the interaction of certain elements with radio waves produced inside an NMR spectrometer.
- Mass spectrometry
  Its use for determining the identities of proteins by peptide mass fingerprinting has already been described in Chap. 6. It is also used for accurate structure determinations of small molecules.

- X-ray analysis
  This is used to determine the three-dimensional positions of atoms in a compound, thereby providing a definitive structural view called the absolute configuration.

7.1.3.2 Speeding Up Compound Synthesis

It should be clear from the foregoing section that small molecule drug synthesis can be highly complex and time consuming. The histamine H2 antagonist program, described in Chap. 4, took years to produce the breakthrough compounds that led to the final drugs. The slow rate of progress of traditional medicinal chemistry prompted the development of combinatorial chemistry (combichem) in the 1990s as a means of producing large collections of compounds (known as libraries) in a short period of time. The principle is very straightforward: one set of related chemicals is combined with another set that will react with the first to produce a product. Figure 7.5 illustrates this with an array of 3×3 reactions that will produce nine products. If the number of reagents is scaled up, the number of compounds produced for testing can run into millions.

Despite the attractions of having large numbers of compounds to test against drug targets, the early promise of combinatorial chemistry failed to materialize. Very few of the compounds which were active in initial biological tests could be converted into lead molecules for further development. In hindsight, this was because the structures of the individual compounds were not complex enough to serve as drug molecules; many did not fit in with Lipinski's rule, for example. This problem was later recognized by medicinal chemists, notably Stuart Schreiber in

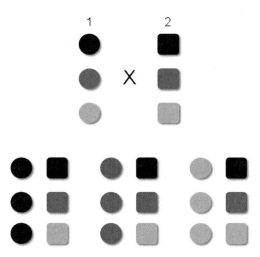

Fig. 7.5 Schematic diagram of combinatorial chemistry (combichem). Two groups of three similar compounds that react with one another will produce nine different combinations of product. This number can rise significantly as the numbers in each group are increased. The technical details of how compounds are reacted together and how the products are purified from the reactions can be found in external publications

Harvard, who began to design combinatorial libraries with much greater diversity, using a process called diversity orientated synthesis (Schreiber 2000). This is now a standard procedure for creating compound libraries that can be tested against a range of drug targets. Certain target classes, such as the protein kinases and ion channels (Chap. 6), contain binding sites that will accept a specific small molecule chemical scaffold, or pharmacophore; this may bind to every member of a particular protein family, but then can be made highly selective for individual family members by adding extra functional groups. These scaffolds form the basis of focused compound libraries which are commercially available from specialist medicinal chemistry companies.

Figure 7.6 shows a computer-generated model of about 200 individual compounds overlaid onto each other each sharing a scaffold ring structure that projects out to the bottom left of the picture. The various side chains that protrude round the edges can explore different binding pockets in the target protein, so that compound with the best fit should, in theory, have the best biological activity.

7.1.3.3 *In Silico* **Drug Design**

Medicinal chemistry requires a great deal of painstaking compound synthesis, biological testing and optimization to produce leads with the potential to become a drug. Despite genuine advances in the field, the medicinal chemistry process is still,

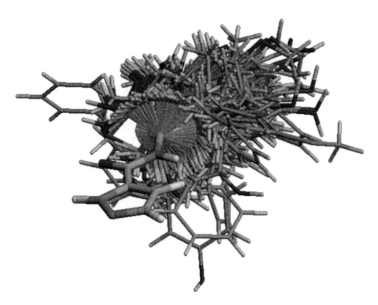

Fig. 7.6 Three-dimensional structures of compounds in focused library overlaid onto each other. The common ring structure faces towards the bottom left hand of the picture and the individual side chains protrude from the scaffold like a brush

to a large degree, hit and miss. In principle, it would be far better to "synthesize" compounds in the computer and then check them against target proteins for optimal binding prior to doing any laboratory work. This is a very important area of research that aims to minimize the number of compounds made and tested, but maximize the chance that a compound will be active. There are two main aspects to *in silico* drug design, namely virtual screening and *de novo* drug design. Both of these techniques require a prior knowledge of the three-dimensional structure of the target protein. Virtual screening involves docking small molecule structures into the binding pocket(s) on the protein and identifying those with the best fit. Unfortunately, there are number of different ways in which a single molecule can bind, so it is not always easy to select the one conformation that occurs in reality. In this case, it may be necessary to co-crystallize the compound with the protein and determine the structure of the small molecule bound into the protein; this is something that is not undertaken lightly. Despite this problem, virtual screening is routinely used to optimize the binding strength and selectivity of compounds during the early stages of drug discovery. Since the computing power required for large-scale virtual screening is quite considerable, some scientists have set up distributed computing using worldwide networks of personal computers linked to a central website. This harnesses the processing capability that would otherwise remain unused when PCs are not used to their full capacity.[3] These projects have been used for virtual screening against targets in cancer and HIV, as well as the search for extraterrestrial intelligence (no luck there so far).

De novo drug design can produce novel compounds in the computer that may bear no relation to any yet made in the laboratory. This makes it possible to explore chemical space in a significant way, since millions of compounds can be "made" every second. Another attraction is the ability to automatically reject those compounds with chemical groups that are known to cause problems with toxicity or other clinical development issues. Academic groups and small companies have been involved in *de novo* design for some years, but there are still significant technical challenges to overcome. First, protein structures often move during ligand binding and are therefore in a sense moving targets for *de novo* design. There are also unknown quantities, such as the number of water molecules that are bound and some features, like charge or hydrogen bonding, may not be adequately defined. Another key problem is whether it is possible to actually make the compounds once a design is available. Luckily, there have been successful attempts to train the computer with a set of synthetic rules that only select compounds which can be made in the laboratory. Although the full potential of *in silico* drug design has not yet been realized, this situation will almost certainly change over the coming years, with small molecule drugs of the future originating in a computer, rather than a bottle.

---

[3] See also Chap. 17.

7.1.3.4   Fragment-Based Design

Fragment-based screening is a combination of physical (i.e. laboratory) screening and *in silico* drug design that is used to create small molecule drug candidates. It works on the principle that very weak binding of small chemical groups to target proteins can be measured using techniques such as NMR or X-ray crystallography. This level of binding makes the compounds unsuitable as drugs, because they lack potency and selectivity. However, once a number of these groups have been identified for a single target, they can be joined together chemically to create drug-sized molecules with much higher binding affinity. This is illustrated in Fig. 7.7.

7.1.3.5   Inhibiting Protein–Protein Interactions

One of the greatest challenges for the medicinal chemist is finding small molecules to inhibit protein–protein interactions, in other words, the binding of proteins to other proteins. There are many examples of this, including the binding of cytokines to their receptors, or the interaction of cells via adhesion molecules. There are also many proteins that bind to each other to form a series of "on-off" switches inside cells; these are part of the signal transduction systems that regulate cell division and other cellular functions in health and disease. There is currently no universally applicable solution to the problem of protein–protein interaction inhibitors, despite

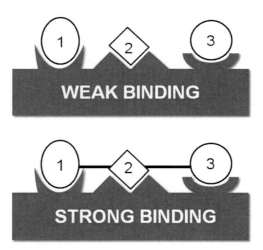

Fig. 7.7 Diagram of fragment-based drug design. Three small chemical fragments 1–3 bind to a protein target with very low, but detectable affinity. The fragments may be little bigger than the benzene ring (molecular weight 78, compared with 500 for an average drug). Once a group of fragments have been identified, they can be linked together in the laboratory to produce a compound with a higher molecular weight and much stronger binding affinity. This strategy can improve binding by nearly a million times and is being actively pursued by large pharmaceutical and specialist biotechnology companies

continuing efforts by medicinal chemists; this is a major reason for the development of protein drugs (see next chapter). All is not lost, however, as there are a few success stories of small molecules that inhibit these types of interactions. One example is the class of small molecule drugs based on a motif of three amino acids (RGD in single letter code). These drugs inhibit the protein–protein interactions that occur during thrombus (blood clot) formation. Other types of inhibitor are under development for oncology. Despite these limited successes, the search for inhibitors of protein–protein interactions is one of the greatest challenges faced by medicinal chemists however, the slow progress in this area is partly responsible for the current interest in proteins and other biologicals as alternatives to small molecule drugs.

7.1.4 Natural Products

The extraction of medicinal compounds from natural products formed the basis of early pharmacy and led to the development of many of the drugs in use today (see Chap. 4). The modern biopharmaceutical industry became strongly committed to natural products during the early days of antibiotic discovery, when thousands of cultured microorganisms were screened to find alternatives to penicillin. Antibiotics, and other natural products, are examples of secondary metabolites, as opposed to the primary metabolites of living cells, such as the amino acids, nucleotides, lipids and carbohydrates that are essential for basic cellular functions. The purpose of secondary metabolism in bacteria, fungi and plants has been debated, but with a consensus view that it is related to communication between living organisms. Microbes, in particular, use small molecules to communicate with each other; they live closely together in varying degrees of harmony, ranging from peaceful coexistence, to outright warfare. Some of their communication molecules have an effect on animals, including humans. As a result, there is some hope among scientists that an understanding of the basic ecology of plants and microbes will guide the search for natural products with medicinal properties.

7.1.4.1 Sources of Natural Products

The range of secondary metabolites that an organism can produce varies according to its environment, so in theory, the more exotic the habitat, the more chance of finding novel compounds. This is why there is such interest in prospecting for drugs from marine sources, or plants living in tropical rain forests. As an employee of a pharmaceutical company with a major interest in natural product drug discovery, I was encouraged, along with my colleagues, to bring back soil samples from holidays abroad; the purpose of this was to supply the microbiology department with new bacteria and fungi for their screening collections. This was presumably encouraged by the success of Sandoz (now part of Novartis) who, under a similar scheme, discovered the powerful immunosuppressant drug cyclosporine in extracts of a fungus.

The fact that cyclosporine was discovered in soil samples brought back from the USA and Norway shows that it is not necessary to go to really exotic places to discover useful natural products.

7.1.4.2 Natural Product Chemistry

Secondary metabolites are often highly complex chemical structures, which in terms of drug discovery, is part of their attraction. The more exotic the functional groups, the more chance of exploring novel chemical space. In the past, the determination of natural product structures was a major challenge, but modern analytical techniques (see "Analytical Chemistry" above) make this relatively straightforward. What is not so simple, however, is the total synthesis of complex molecules extracted from nature. These compounds have been created in living organisms through the action of specialized enzyme pathways that transform chemicals in ways that may never have been previously encountered in the laboratory. A number of heroic efforts have been made to synthesize useful compounds, but often the motivation of the chemists has been similar to that of mountaineers: "I did it because it was there," which, of course, is completely impractical for most commercial drug discovery efforts. This is not meant to be dismissive, since these individual challenges have resulted in new synthetic methods that are extremely useful for medicinal and process chemists. Furthermore, there are cases in which a biopharmaceutical company will manufacture a natural product by undertaking a complex multistep chemical synthesis. An example of this is the compound eribulin, derived from a sea sponge and marketed by Eisai Pharmaceuticals for the chemotherapy of breast cancer (Ledford 2010). The drug requires a massive 62 synthetic steps to manufacture, so this may prove to be an isolated case because of the seriousness of the disease.

The molecular structures of three natural products used directly or indirectly as drugs are shown in Fig. 7.8 to give an idea of their complexity.

Once an active natural product compound has been identified, it is necessary to find ways to scale up its production. Firstly, it may be possible to extract the intact compound directly from a plant, animal or fungal source; this assumes that there is enough of this source available to satisfy the demand for the drug by patients. Sometimes there may be large amounts of a naturally occurring precursor molecule, that is, a compound that requires some chemical modification in the laboratory for conversion into the final drug product. In this case, the conversion process is known as semi-synthesis. Secondly, the enzymes that synthesize the compound in the plant or microbe can be transferred to a simple bacterium or yeast using genetic engineering techniques; in this case, the natural product is produced in large amounts because the growth of the microorganisms can be scaled up considerably using large fermenters. It is, in effect, recombinant DNA technology applied to the production of small molecules, rather than proteins. Although this is technically challenging and far from routine, there have been some successes, for example in the production of the anti-malarial compound artemisinin extracted from the sweet wormwood plant. A Californian group has engineered yeast to produce artemisinic

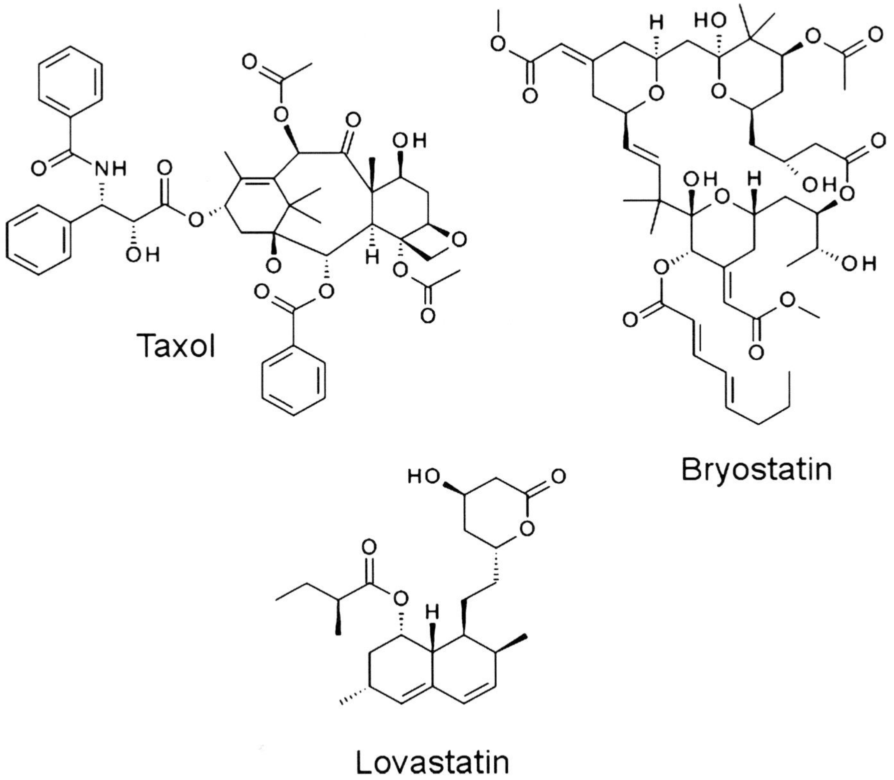

Taxol

Bryostatin

Lovastatin

Fig. 7.8 Some compounds extracted from natural sources showing the complexity of their structures. Taxol is derived from yew bark and has powerful anti-tumour properties. Bryostatin is derived from a marine invertebrate and inhibits a cell signalling enzyme. Lovastatin was isolated from fungi and was the first HMGCoA reductase inhibitor developed to lower blood cholesterol

acid from simple sugars, using a series of enzymes cloned from the *Artemisia annua* plant (Ryo et al. 2006). In an example of a semi-synthesis, the artemisinic acid is subsequently converted to artemisinin in the laboratory to produce the drug in quantity. This is illustrated in Fig. 7.9.

Since the demand for this anti-malarial drug is understandably high, and the cost to patients in the developing world has to be kept low, alternative sources are being actively explored, including genetically engineered organisms and cultured plant cells.

Finally, the structures of natural products have been used to identify pharmacophores that can then be synthesized in the laboratory and used in a conventional medicinal chemistry program. The synthetic statin drugs were based on a pharmacophore discovered in lovastatin (see Fig. 7.8) produced by the fungus *Aspergillus terreus* and oyster mushrooms (see Fig. 7.1).

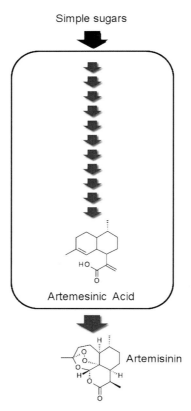

Fig. 7.9 Production of antimalarial drug artemisinin using genetically engineered yeast cells. Each *grey arrow* in the metabolic pathway represents a conversion of one compound into another that is catalyzed by a specific enzyme. The first steps in the pathway use pre-existing yeast enzymes to convert simple sugars (i.e. glucose or similar) to FPP, a precursor of cholesterol and other lipids. The remaining enzymes have been introduced from the *A. annua* plant to convert FPP to arteminisic acid which can be purified from the yeast cells after they have been harvested. Some chemical manipulations in the laboratory convert arteminisic acid to arteminisin (Ryo et al. 2006)

7.1.4.3   Natural Product Discovery in the Biopharmaceutical Industry

It should be clear from the foregoing sections that natural product chemistry has played a major part in small molecule discovery by biopharmaceutical companies. This was certainly the case from the 1940s to the 1990s, but the advent of combinatorial chemistry and other sources of synthetic compounds, led to the closure of many natural product discovery departments in the major companies. There was frustration with the fact that it was almost impossible to consistently produce measurable amounts of active compounds in crude extracts of plants and microbial cultures. These extracts were also difficult to test in sophisticated biological assays because of the presence of interfering substances, like tannins in plants, which generated false hits. Sometimes researchers could be led in the wrong direction; I recall the excitement of having a good clear "hit" in a screen of fungal media on an immunology target only to find, after exhaustive purification and analysis, that the active compound was a non-specific inhibitor of cellular respiration, something that was totally unexpected.

The situation is beginning to change however, despite the fact that the basic problems outlined above still remain. Firstly, there is recognition that most of the synthetic compounds produced for screening do not have sufficient structural complexity to make useful leads, so there is no escaping the fact that natural products are a rich source of chemical diversity. Secondly, the capabilities of the analytical instruments at the disposal of the natural product chemist have increased out of all recognition. High throughput chromatography, coupled with mass spectrometry, has made it possible to analyze thousands of components in complex mixtures and to identify novel structures to explore in the laboratory. Finally, the full extent of microbial and plant diversity is nowhere near being fully explored, for natural products, or for anything else. Only a tiny fraction of the World's species of microbes have ever been grown and tested, so there is still a lot to play for.

Summary of Key Points

The diversity of chemical structures of small molecules based on carbon is known as chemical space.

Chemical space is vastly greater for compounds that could theoretically be made compared with approximately 80 million compounds made in the laboratory.

Medicinal chemistry aims to produce small molecules to interact with a drug target with high potency and selectivity.

Chemical modifications are made to pharmacophores from natural ligands (e.g. histamine), random screening hits, natural products or molecules designed *in silico*.

Efforts are being made to increase the number of compounds available for testing by creating chemical libraries using combinatorial chemistry.

Drug design in the computer is in its early stages, but is helping to create novel compounds to test against drug targets or to optimize existing molecules.

Natural products derived from plants, animals and microbes are a rich source of drugs, either as starting points for medicinal chemistry, or as drugs in their own right.

References

Bohacek RS, McMartin C, Guida WC (1996) The art and practice of structure-based drug design: a molecular modeling perspective. Med Res Rev 16:3–50

Bolli MH et al (2010) 2-Imino-thiazolidin-4-one derivatives as potent, orally active S1P1 receptor agonists. J Med Chem 53:4198–4211

Douglas P et al (2007) Structure-based optimization of protein tyrosine phosphatase 1B Inhibitors: from the active site to the second phosphotyrosine binding site. J Med Chem 50:4681–4698

Ledford H (2010) Complex synthesis yields breast cancer therapy. Nature 468:608–609

Lipinski C, Hopkins A (2004) Navigating chemical space for biology and medicine. Nature 432:855–861

Robinson A (2010) Chemistry's visual origins. Nature 456:36

Rocke AJ (2010) Image and Reality: Kekule Kopp and the Scientific Imagination. University of Chicago Press, Chicago, IL

Ryo D-J et al (2006) Production of the antimalarial drug precursor artemisinic acid in engineered yeast. Nature 440:940–943

Schreiber SL (2000) Target-oriented and diversity-oriented organic synthesis in drug discovery. Science 287:1964–9

Chapter 8
Biotherapeutics

Abstract Biotherapeutics are large molecule drugs which are developed against targets that are not readily affected by small chemical compounds. This chapter covers mainly protein drugs, as well as the recombinant DNA technology used to produce these molecules in large quantities. Several sections are dedicated to the antibody drugs that are beginning to take a significant share of the pharmaceuticals market.

8.1 Introduction

The creation of small chemical molecules for testing against biological targets was covered in the last chapter. While orally active small molecules are still the preferred offering of the biopharmaceutical industry, the larger molecules of nature are being used to literally access the parts of drug targets that small molecules cannot reach. Figure 8.1 illustrates this point; the so-called "druggable targets" for small molecules have well-defined pockets into which a compound can insert itself and bind via the electrical forces outlined in Chap. 4. These small molecule targets have served the industry well for many years and will continue to do so. There are, however, many important targets which have points of interaction so widely spaced apart, that a small molecule cannot bind to them with sufficient affinity. These are mostly targets for protein ligands and include the cytokine receptors associated with cancer and autoimmune diseases.

From the 1960s onwards, drug discovery chemists invested a great deal of time and effort trying to find agonists or antagonists of small peptide hormones; as a result, there was a certain amount of medicinal chemistry expertise in this area of (small) protein ligands. Unfortunately, the technical difficulties experienced by these earlier researchers were forgotten by a newer generation of scientists. There was, in the words of the British writer Samuel Johnson, a "triumph of hope over experience" in trying to find small molecules that could inhibit the binding of larger proteins (e.g. the cytokines) to their receptors. Large pharmaceutical companies and some of the new biotechnology start-ups, screened thousands of compounds in

E.D. Zanders, *The Science and Business of Drug Discovery: Demystifying the Jargon*,
DOI 10.1007/978-1-4419-9902-3_8, © Springer Science+Business Media, LLC 2011

Fig. 8.1 (**a**) Small molecule with tight binding to a drug target protein (*grey image*). Both points of binding on the small molecule (*black spheres*) have engaged with complementary areas on the receptor. (**b**) The binding site on the protein is now spaced further apart so that only one part of the small molecule can bind. The resulting loss of binding affinity means that the small molecule will not be effective as a drug

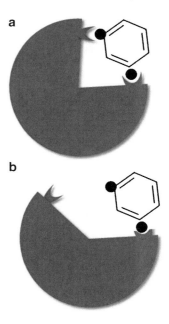

an attempt to find small molecules that could block the binding of protein ligands to their receptors, but to no avail. This was immensely frustrating, because discoveries of new targets for protein ligands were being made on a regular basis. Furthermore, the cell biology and clinical work in industry and academia made it quite clear that drugs affecting these targets could provide enormous medical benefit to patients; the example of tumour necrosis factor (TNF-α) inhibitors for rheumatoid arthritis has already been given in Chap. 6. Something had to be done to get around this problem, and eventually a solution, or at least a partial one, was found that is beginning to change many aspects of the traditional chemistry-based pharmaceutical business.

8.1.1   Terminology

There are several ways of describing biotechnology-based medicines; some common terms are listed as follows:

- Biologicals
- Biologics
- Biotherapeutics
- Protein therapeutics
- Antibody therapeutics (antibodies are also proteins, so can be included in all of the above categories)
- Cell therapeutics

8.1.2 The Emergence of Protein Therapeutics

Protein drugs, such as insulin, have been introduced already in Chaps. 2 and 4. In the early years of the new biotechnology industry (1980s), large pharmaceutical companies were wary of becoming involved with protein drugs, since their whole business had been founded upon small molecule chemistry. There were good reasons for their concerns about protein drugs, since these products cannot be administered by mouth and are difficult to consistently manufacture to the purity standards that are demanded of small molecule drugs. Nevertheless, large pharmaceutical companies began to notice the commercial success of the first recombinant protein drugs and so began the now established practice of buying small biotech companies to acquire the drugs and molecular technology behind them.

The early biologicals were mostly genetically engineered replacements of natural growth factors and enzymes which could be produced in large quantities in fermentation tanks; this avoided the need to purify them from human or animal tissues. Several hematopoietic growth factors were developed as medicines designed to stimulate the growth of red or white blood cells in cancer patients undergoing radiotherapy or chemotherapy. One of the most successful of these is erythropoietin, a hormone that stimulates the growth of red blood cells; a recombinant form is used to treat anaemia in patients with kidney disease as well as cancer. It also has the dubious honour of being yet another illegal performance-enhancing drug that sports authorities have to watch out for. Erythropoietin, brand name Epogen®, was a great commercial success for its developer Amgen Inc; it allowed the company to grow from a small "pure" biotechnology company to a significant pharmaceutical business, with products in the top ten of prescription drug sales. This level of sales means that the consequences of generic competition are now the same with protein drugs as they are already with small molecules. There is one difference, however; when patents on small molecule medicines have expired, competitors can manufacture a generic product that is chemically identical to the original, but this is not so easy with protein drugs. This is why the industry is now grappling with biosimilars, a term used to describe generic copies of biotherapeutics. Some examples of recombinant protein drugs are given in Table 8.1.

Table 8.1 Some of the first generation recombinant therapeutic proteins

Name	Disease
Somatotropin	Growth retardation
Insulin	Diabetes
tPA	Cardiovascular
Streptokinase	Cardiovascular
Erythropoietin	Cancer
Interferon beta	Multiple sclerosis

All are relatively small cytokine/growth factor-like proteins, except for tPA and streptokinase which are enzymes

8.1.3   Technical Aspects of Recombinant Protein Production

Some of the basic elements of molecular biology and protein biochemistry which are relevant to genetic engineering have been touched upon earlier in this book. What follows is a fuller description of the process that begins with the identification of a protein of interest and continues with the genetic engineering needed to produce it in industrial quantities for use as a medicine. In this example, the cells used for protein expression are the *E. coli* bacteria, which were used for the first recombinant protein drugs.

Recombinant protein expression involves the following experimental steps:

1. Isolate human DNA that codes for the protein of interest (e.g. human insulin)
2. Stitch the human DNA into a vector that will "carry" the DNA into bacteria
3. Grow the bacteria to produce the human protein
4. Purify the human protein

8.1.3.1   Step 1. Finding the Needle in the Haystack

The length of DNA encoding an average sized protein is about 1,000 bases, which corresponds to about 350 amino acids (because of the three letter genetic code). Total human DNA contains about 3,000,000,000 bases, so locating a sequence of interest is rather like finding a needle in a haystack. Luckily, techniques have been developed which make it a relatively simple task to locate and amplify a DNA sequence of choice, however low its abundance. The most important method is the polymerase chain reaction, commonly known as PCR; this is based on the hybridization of specific oligonucleotide primers to DNA, followed by the synthesis of new strands using an enzyme called DNA polymerase. At this point, the reader is referred to the many Internet resources which use animations to illustrate the PCR process. The sequences of the oligonucleotide primers correspond to the beginning and end of the desired protein sequence, so the end result is a fragment of double-stranded DNA containing only the protein coding information. If 10 mg of total human DNA is isolated from a tissue such as blood, it will contain roughly 40 pg (million millionth grams) of DNA coding for the specific protein sequence. The amount of amplified fragment required for inserting into a vector is in the order of micrograms, so the original gene has to be amplified at least a million times. One of the powerful features of PCR is its ability to add any desired sequence to the oligonucleotide primers so that they are incorporated into the final DNA product. This can be very useful for attaching linkers, which allow the fragment of copied human DNA to insert into vector DNA at exactly the right place. PCR can also be used to introduce mutations into the DNA, making it a central part of the genetic engineering toolbox now used to manipulate the genomes of everything from viruses to humans.

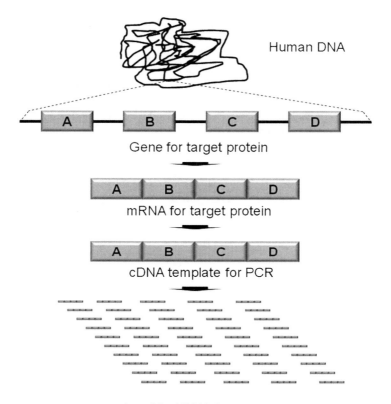

Human DNA

Gene for target protein

mRNA for target protein

cDNA template for PCR

Amplified DNA fragments

Fig. 8.2 Amplification of DNA fragments containing the gene to be introduced into bacteria to produce human protein. The gene to be amplified is broken up into four exons (A–D) separated by introns (*solid line*). During the process of mRNA formation in the human cell, the introns are removed (spliced out) and the exons joined into one piece of RNA with all the genetic code in place to specify a protein. An exact cDNA copy of the mRNA is made *in vitro* and is amplified many times in a PCR reaction to physically create enough DNA for the next step

While the principle of amplifying protein-coding fragments of DNA is straight-forward enough, there is a slight complication; it is not possible to do this directly on the DNA isolated from human cells. The reason is that protein coding genes are split into sections called exons which are separated by regions of DNA called introns. The introns are later removed in the messenger RNA (mRNA) intermediate that is used to prime the synthesis of proteins, while the exons are joined together to give the correct sequence for amplification. Unfortunately, PCR cannot be performed directly on the RNA, so a DNA copy called complementary DNA (cDNA) is created as a template for amplification. The steps described above are summarized in Fig. 8.2.

8.1.3.2   Step 2. Introduce the Human DNA into an Expression Vector

The human DNA fragment from step 1 contains all of the sequence information required to express the human protein of interest, but further manipulation in the form of genetic engineering is required before it can program the synthesis of protein in other cells. Genetic engineering was built upon the practical application of microbiology, i.e. the study of bacteria, viruses and fungi, to the problem of moving DNA from one cell to another. Viruses use their coat proteins to inject their own DNA into cells during the process of infection. The viral DNA is then turned into mRNA and translated into viral proteins that are used to build new viruses. Viruses infect many cells from plants and animals, but they also target bacteria, in which case they are called bacteriophages or phages. These have been used for much of the pioneering work on molecular biology and were later employed as vectors that could transfer foreign DNA into bacteria. Although viruses that infect bacteria and other cell types are used extensively in genetic engineering, they are not the only vectors available to the molecular biologist. Bacteria contain a small piece of circular DNA, called a plasmid, which is separate from the main chromosomal DNA that contains most of the bacterial genes; actually, bacterial DNA is not packaged into separate chromosomes like in eukaryotes, but the term is used all the same. The circular plasmid DNA can be purified from bacteria, cut into fragments and then reformed with foreign genes to produce a recombinant plasmid vector.

8.1.3.3   Step 3. Transformation

The plasmid DNA can be introduced into bacterial cells by one of two processes, both of which may seem rather bizarre at first sight. Bacteria are enclosed in a cell wall, a protective barrier which is impermeable to many different molecules, DNA included. The first method of introducing DNA into bacteria involves treating them with a chemical to allow the cell wall to open up at elevated temperatures. The treated *E. coli* cells are simply mixed with the DNA in a tube and then briefly incubated at 42°C to allow the plasmid DNA to enter. Although this is a highly inefficient process, the number of added DNA molecules is so great, that enough get inside the bacteria to produce a reasonable number of recombinant colonies on agar plates. The other method of bacterial transformation uses an electric current in a process called electroporation. This rather Frankenstein-like process stretches the DNA out into a thread and creates pores in the bacterial cell wall; the DNA is then literally threaded through the cell wall under the influence of the electric current. Whichever transformation method is used, the bacteria that have successfully taken up the plasmid (bacteriophage enter the cells naturally) will have also taken up a gene that confers resistance to an antibiotic (e.g. ampicillin). This gene is built into the plasmid or phage vector to allow antibiotic selection of recombinant bacteria. If ampicillin is added to the growing culture, the untransformed cells will die because they are sensitive to the antibiotic and only the transformed ones will survive and grow.

8.1.3.4 Step 4. Production of Recombinant Protein

Transformed bacteria are grown in laboratory-scale cultures of a few hundred millilitres of culture medium before being analyzed for the expression of human protein. The resulting protein will either be associated with the bacterial cells, or will have been secreted into the culture medium. In either case, it should be easily detectable using the gel electrophoresis technique described in Chap. 6. The next stage involves the purification of the human recombinant protein from the proteins and other molecules present in the cells and growth medium. This is accomplished by chromatography (discussed in later chapters) and must be conducted to rigorous standards if the protein is to be administered to human subjects. This is because bacteria contain various molecules, such as lipopolysaccharide (LPS), which are powerful stimulators of the immune system and are potentially dangerous, even in trace amounts.

Once a purification scheme for the protein has been established, the production is scaled up inside the production plants using large fermenters. The volumes of culture media used to produce protein on the kilogram scale can be as high as 27,000 litres per fermenter. The different stages of recombinant protein production in the laboratory are summarized in Fig. 8.3.

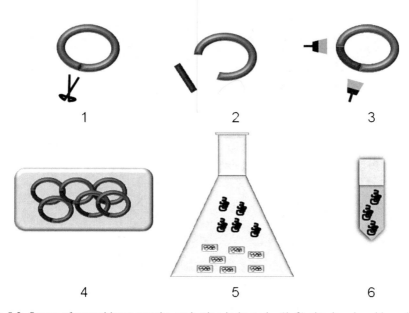

Fig. 8.3 Stages of recombinant protein production in bacteria. (1–3) circular plasmid or phage DNA is cut and a piece of human DNA (produced according to Fig. 8.2) pasted into reseal the circle. The "cutting and pasting" is performed *in vitro* using special DNA modifying enzymes. (4) The circular DNA with the human gene is introduced into bacteria and the cells grown in flasks (5). The bacteria multiply in the growth medium and produce human protein as well as proteins encoded by the bacterium's own DNA. (6) The recombinant human protein is purified away from the other proteins in the bacteria and growth medium

8.1.3.5   The Problem with Sugars

Bacterial expression of recombinant proteins in *E. coli* is routinely performed in the research laboratory and is generally a quite efficient process. Unfortunately, there are many proteins of pharmaceutical interest that have complex sugar molecules (glycans) attached at various points along the chain of amino acids. Such proteins, called glycoproteins, are only present in eukaryotes, because the (glycosylation) machinery required to produce them is absent in bacteria. Figure 8.4 shows the

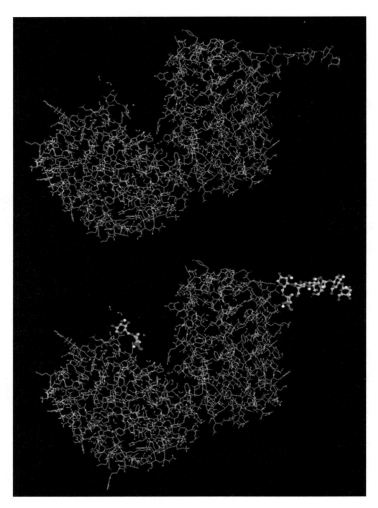

Fig. 8.4 Three-dimensional structure of interferon-1a showing two protein subunits with carbohydrate side chains highlighted as *ball and stick displays*. Structure 1AU1 from Karpusas, M et al. (1997) The crystal structure of human interferon beta at 2.2-A resolution. Proc. Natl. Acad. Sci. USA 94:11813–11818 deposited in the Protein Data Bank

three-dimensional structures of glycosylated and non-glycosylated interferon beta-1a, highlighting a chain of sugars that extends from the basic protein core.

The therapeutic efficacy of proteins can be significantly improved by the presence of sugars; this is because of improved stability in the blood, resistance to heat and, in the case of antibodies, higher biological activity. The requirement for fully glycosylated proteins has driven the search for expression systems that add sugars onto recombinant proteins. This can only be achieved in eukaryotic cells, so one of the first systems to be used was based on *S. cerevisiae*, or baker's yeast. This single-celled fungus can be grown in large amounts, so it seemed to be ideal for the large-scale production of recombinant proteins. Unfortunately, *S. cerevisiae* introduces sugars that are significantly larger than the natural forms, so alternative species of host cells have been evaluated, including another type of yeast, *Pichia pastoris*. Although yeast has the desirable property of rapid growth in simple media, the problem with unnatural glycosylation is a real handicap when considering proteins for therapeutic use. This problem does not occur in higher organisms, so cell lines have been produced from both insects and mammals which can produce recombinant glycoproteins in quantity after transformation by genetically engineered plasmids or viruses. The most commonly used cell line was originally derived from the ovary of a Chinese hamster (a typically exotic source of biological material) and is called CHO. For industrial-scale production of proteins, CHO cells are suspended in large bioreactors; these are regularly replenished with fresh growth medium to produce recombinant proteins in yields of up to 5 g of protein per litre of culture.

Finally, protein expression in insect cells, while a well-established laboratory tool, is now being evaluated as a system for producing biopharmaceutical proteins. The insect cell expression system is based on a virus, called a baculovirus, which infects the Sf21cell line that is derived from the ovaries (again) of the moth *Spodoptera frugiperda*. Genetic engineering is used to modify baculovirus DNA, allowing the expression of human proteins in large-scale insect cell cultures. There is interest in the baculovirus system as a source of vaccines, since it can produce very pure antigen preparations in a relatively short period of time when compared with conventional production methods, like for example influenza vaccines in chicken eggs. This means that, in theory at least, vaccines against new strains of infectious agents could be rapidly made to order, something that would speed up the responses of governments to global pandemics.

8.1.4   Antibodies

On the face of it, antibodies do not look very promising as drugs because of their size (150,000 Da) and complexity. The fact that antibody drugs are now one of the best selling medicines in the world is testament to the fact that they can offer features that are not found in other types of biologicals. The main characteristic of antibodies is their ability to bind with exquisite specificity to a protein which can differ from other proteins by only a few atoms. They are also unique in being designed by nature, figuratively speaking, to attack and destroy cells that have been infected by viruses. Once an antibody binds to the surface of an infected cell, it recruits white blood cells to literally break open the cell and clear up the debris afterwards. Therapeutic antibodies, such as Herceptin®, bind to cells (in this case, from breast tumours) and cause their destruction through the above mechanisms.

Other antibodies, such as infliximab, are designed to "mop up" cytokines, such as TNF-α, to prevent them binding to their receptors. Infliximab marketed as Remicade®, was among the first wave of therapeutic antibodies to be introduced into the clinic. The antibody was developed by the US biotech company Centocor, now a subsidiary of Johnson and Johnson, and commercialized in partnership with large pharmaceutical companies. This was a new territory for the traditional biopharmaceutical industry which, at best, was lukewarm about protein drugs, particularly antibodies. The financial success of Remicade®, and other emerging antibody therapeutics, finally encouraged the large companies to take these products more seriously. The acceptance of proteins as products on an equal footing with small molecules, and the later acquisition of antibody companies to develop the technology, all stemmed from this period in the mid-1990s.

8.1.4.1 Terminology

The word antibody is used to describe the class of proteins called immunoglobulins. These proteins are divided into different subclasses, or isotypes, called immuno-globulins A, D, E, G and M (shortened to IgA, IgD, IgE, IgG and IgM). Nearly all therapeutic antibodies are of the IgG isotype, while those responsible for allergic reactions, such as hayfever, are IgE antibodies. The isotypes are themselves subdivided into subtypes, e.g. IgG1, IgG2, IgG3 and IgG4 in humans.

8.1.4.2 Generating Antibodies

Immunology is a large and complex subject which is medically important because of the immune system's central role in fighting infection, rejecting organ trans-plants and causing a wide range of allergic and autoimmune diseases. Antibodies are produced by a class of white blood cells called B lymphocytes and are a cen-tral part of the adaptive immune system. There are many sources of information about antibodies and the white blood cells that produce them, most of which are outside the scope of this book. However, in order to understand how therapeutic antibodies are produced by the biopharmaceutical industry, it is necessary to pro-vide some background information. Antibodies are produced in mammals and birds, either by natural infection, or by deliberate immunization. It is generally unethical to deliberately immunize human beings with a protein for research pur-poses, so animals such as mice and rats are normally used instead. There is another reason: if a human protein is injected into a human, the immune system recognizes that protein as "self," or a harmless part of the body. This phenomenon is called immunological tolerance and is the reason why we generally do not mount an immune response to ourselves, unless we suffer from an autoimmune disease such a multiple sclerosis.

In practice, antibodies are generated over a period of a few months by injecting animals with antigens, that is purified proteins, or cells that bear protein targets on their surface.[1] It is certainly possible to create antibodies to proteins which reside on the inside of cells, but these will not be useful therapeutically as they cannot penetrate the cell membrane. Once the immune system has been stimulated with repeated doses of antigen for a sufficiently long time, the amount of antibody that has been generated is measured in blood samples using immunoassays (see Chap. 14). Immunoassays are very important for analyzing therapeutic antibodies during the preclinical development phase (Chap. 11) and for diagnostics (Chap. 14). Once animals have been identified that produce large amounts of antibody to the antigen of interest (i.e. they have high titres), they are sacrificed (standard terminology) for their spleen cells. The spleen contains large numbers of antibody-producing B lymphocytes, each one of which produces a single unique antibody; because there are many different B cells in a living spleen, the overall repertoire of antibodies produced against a single antigen is quite varied. This is called a polyclonal response and is the sum of all the antibody-producing activity of single (monoclonal) antibody-producing cells. Since only one specific antibody is required for development as a protein drug, individual B cells have to be isolated and grown in culture. This was first achieved by Koehler and Milstein, who developed the technique of producing monoclonal antibodies from spleen cells, which involves immortalizing the clones of antibody-producing B cells isolated from spleen; this is achieved by fusing them with a tumour cell line to create a hybrid cell, i.e. a hybridoma, which can be grown indefinitely in large numbers. The monoclonal antibody is secreted into the tissue culture medium used to grow the cells; this medium is the starting material from which therapeutic antibodies are purified during the manufacturing process (see Chap. 10).

8.1.4.3 The Importance of Being Human

Since antibodies are usually produced in mice or rats, the immunoglobulin proteins will have amino acids specified by mouse or rat DNA; the proteins will therefore be seen as foreign by the human immune system. This is a highly undesirable property for a therapeutic antibody that will be repeatedly injected into patients; their own immune system will generate antibodies to the antibody, thereby neutralizing its beneficial effect. This problem has forced companies to devise ways of making antibodies that are indistinguishable from the version that would be produced if human beings were injected with the protein antigen. This process of humanization

---

[1] It is possible to produce antibodies to carbohydrates and other molecules, but protein antigens make up by far the greatest number of targets for antibody drugs.

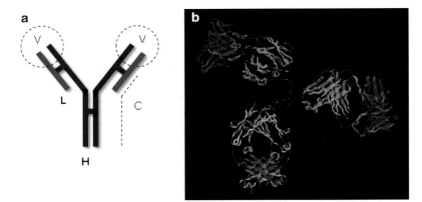

Fig. 8.5 Structure of an antibody molecule. (**a**) Schematic diagram of immunoglobulin G (IgG) molecule showing two heavy (H) and two light (L) chains linked together. The top parts of the H and L chains have amino acid sequences that vary to create a unique binding site for target antigens (V regions). The rest of the molecule is the same for all immunoglobulins from the same species and with the same isotype. (**b**) Ribbon diagram of IgG molecule with the structure determined by X-ray crystallography (PDB structure (1IGT) of an intact IgG2a monoclonal antibody. Harris LJ et al. (1997) Biochemistry 36:1581–1597). The strands represent the amino acid backbone of each of the four protein chains. Each chain is folded into protein domains with characteristic structures. The whole antibody molecule has a molecular weight of 150,000, which is significantly greater than most cytokines and hormones

involves the application of genetic engineering technology to monoclonal antibody production and is otherwise known as antibody engineering (Kim et al. 2005).

Figure 8.5 is a schematic diagram of the immunoglobulin molecule; it shows the structure of an IgG antibody as four protein chains tightly linked together by covalent bonds (Chap. 3). The large and small components are called heavy and light chains (H and L chains), respectively. The arms of the Y-shaped molecule contain stretches of amino acids that make up variable regions (V regions) which, as the name suggests, vary between individual antibodies. It is these regions that make up the antigen binding site, each having a unique shape and charge in the same way as drug target proteins.

When a therapeutic antibody is produced in mice or rats (hereafter referred to as rodents), these V regions contain amino acids relating to these species; as already discussed, these rodent sequences will eventually cause problems when the antibody is administered to patients. The remainder of the antibody contains constant regions (C regions) that are the same for every antibody of a given subclass. If the rodent constant regions can be changed to human sequences without compromising the ability of the antibody to bind to its target, this will make it more useful as a biological drug. Such molecules are known as chimeric antibodies, one example being Remicade®. They are quite acceptable as therapeutics, particularly if they are not repeatedly injected over a long period, but there is still the risk that the human immune system will make antibodies to the rodent variable regions. The solution is to progressively change the rodent variable regions into human sequences, until the antibody is fully humanized, as illustrated in Fig. 8.6.

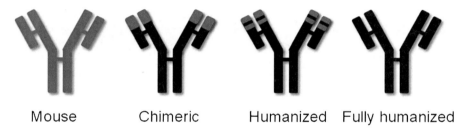

| Mouse | Chimeric | Humanized | Fully humanized |

Fig. 8.6 Modifications of mouse antibodies to create human therapeutic antibodies. Mouse (or rat) antibodies will provoke an immune response if injected into humans; chimeric antibodies use all of the rodent variable (V) regions joined to a human constant region. Humanized antibodies have rodent sequences removed from the V regions to make them even less likely to stimulate the human immune system. This is completely eliminated by fully humanizing the antibody

Chimeric and humanized antibodies are produced using genetic engineering to manipulate the DNA sequences that code for constant and variable regions. The techniques require PCR and cloning in bacteria, both of which have been introduced earlier in the chapter. The outcome, after a complex set of procedures, is the creation of two heavy and two light chains expressed in mammalian cells; the chains are correctly glycosylated and ready to be assembled into antibodies which are almost identical to their natural counterparts.

8.1.4.4 An Immune System in a Test Tube

Immunizing rodents to produce antibodies has served basic and applied biological research well, and will continue to do so for a long time. Millions of lives have been saved, or improved, by therapeutic antibodies that were originally created in these animals (sometimes irreverently called "furry test tubes"). The downside is the time taken to produce antibodies and the fact that not all human molecules will stimulate the rodent immune systems (i.e. they are not immunogenic). An ideal solution would be to avoid the use of animals altogether and to create the antibody *in vitro*. This is not so farfetched, given the versatility of genetic engineering and the ingenuity of scientists. A system called phage display was invented by McCafferty in 1990 to exploit the properties of a particular bacteriophage known as M13 (McCafferty 1990). Phages are used as vectors to carry human DNA into *E. coli* bacteria which then express a human protein. For antibody engineering, the M13 phage are constructed, not with a gene-like human insulin, but with genes coding for the huge number of V regions present in human heavy and light chains. These phage DNA libraries may contain 10^{11}, or more, individual sequences which are expressed as proteins on the surface of the phage virus itself. The technical details of how these V regions are identified in the first place are quite complex, but the end result is a collection of phage that can bind to target antigens in the test tube, just like natural antibodies. In practice, a protein of interest is attached to a solid support and then covered with a solution of phage particles to allow binding. The phage with the appropriate V region sequences will stick to the target, while the rest are washed away. Since the bacteriophages that stick are fully capable of infecting bacteria and growing up to large numbers, they can be amplified in this way and used for further experiments. The binding process is usually repeated several times to select the strongest and most specific phage binding. Throughout this process, the investigator has no idea of the sequence of the V region DNA, since its selection has been an entirely random process. Once a candidate phage has been identified, however, its DNA sequence is determined and used to construct synthetic V regions. These can then be inserted into genuine human immunoglobulin protein scaffolds that have been engineered to lack V regions; in this way, a fully humanized antibody can be constructed without having to immunize an animal.

A summary of the phage display process is shown in Fig. 8.7.

The first antibody produced in this way was developed by Cambridge Antibody Technology (now MedImmune/AstraZeneca) and marketed by Abbott as HUMIRA®. It is one of several antibodies to TNF-α developed for treating arthritis and other inflammatory diseases. This illustrates the fact that the commercial attractions of a particular target are now stimulating competition in the biologicals marketplace, as has already been the case with small molecule drugs for many years.

8.1.4.5 Next Generation Antibodies

Although antibodies have proven their worth as drugs, they do suffer from a number of technical problems, including their slow clearance rate after injection into the body. Furthermore, an IgG molecule is over five times larger than the average therapeutic protein and if used against solid tumours, will not fully penetrate the cancerous tissue to destroy it. This has prompted the search for much smaller proteins that retain both the antigen-binding capability of large antibodies and their ability to remove invading organisms (i.e. their effector functions). A new generation of antibody-like proteins is under development that retains V region sequences within a much smaller protein framework. One of these is the single domain nanobody, developed by Ablynx, which has antigen-binding capability in a molecule of around 12,000 Da (Ablynx Website 2010). Nanobodies, or similar antibody fragments, can be modified by genetic engineering to create bi-specific antibodies that consist of two chains linked together, each recognizing different antigens. This is a promising approach to cancer therapy, as it targets both the surface of the white blood cells primed to destroy tumours and the surface of the tumour cell itself; the result is that the two cell types are drawn into close proximity to allow the cell killing to take place.

Other antibody engineering programs are underway to improve the biological function of antibodies, their antigen-binding affinity and their handling by the body once injected. There is even the possibility of using small antibody fragments as oral drugs if they can be formulated in such a way that prevents them being digested in the stomach.

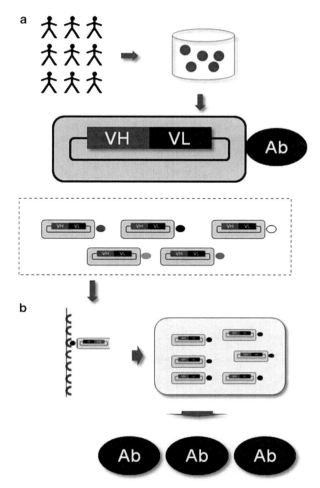

Fig. 8.7 Production of antibodies using phage display. (**a**) Lymphocytes isolated from the blood of human donors. These contain random V regions on both H and L chains (VH and VL). The DNA coding for these regions is amplified using PCR and inserted into the M13 bacteriophage where the antibody protein (Ab) is expressed on the surface. The M13 phage library contains many different combinations of VH and VL sequences, so it is like an immune system in a test tube. (**b**) The phage library is mixed with target antigen on a solid support (which could also be whole cells) and the single phage that recognizes the antigen is bound to it while all the others are washed away. The single phage is removed from the support and grown to larger numbers (amplified) in bacteria. This is like the normal process of recombinant protein production, so the antibody protein is purified in the conventional way. The VH and VL genes in the M13 can also be used to build a full-sized humanized IgG molecule using genetic engineering techniques

Therapeutic antibodies have now come of age and are one of the most significant classes of biological drugs in the current marketplace. The technology is being rapidly developed by specialist biotechnology companies, who are either partnering with the traditional chemistry-driven corporations, or have been acquired by them.

Table 8.2 Examples of therapeutic antibody nomenclature

Generic name	Brand name	Derivation
Infliximab	Remicade®	Chimeric antibody for immune system
Bevacizumab	Avastin®	Humanized for cancer
Adalimumab	HUMIRA®	Fully humanized for immune system
Efungumab	Mycograb®	Humanized for fungal infection

The first part of the generic name is specific for the drug, the second for the condition (e.g. "im" or "lim" for immune system) the third for type of antibody, "xi" chimeric and "umab" for humanized

Nomenclature of Antibody Drugs

Therapeutic antibodies have a non-proprietary or generic name assigned to them by the same organizations that control the nomenclature of small molecule drugs (Chap. 3). They also have a brand name, like Humira® or Remicade®, described earlier. The generic name is built up from a group of word elements that describe the type of antibody (e.g. chimeric, humanized) and the indication that it is used for (e.g. cancer, respiratory). The resulting names are frankly a bit of a mouthful and quite ugly, as shown in the examples given in Table 8.2.

8.1.5   Other Large Molecule Drugs

Although most biological drugs are proteins (this includes vaccines), other large molecule drugs, such as nucleic acids and gene therapy vectors are also being developed. Chapter 2 contained some basic background to these agents, so these will not be discussed much further, except to say that both of these are designed to alter drug targets at the level of the genome. Both use technology described earlier in this chapter, including bioinformatics to choose the correct DNA sequences, oligonucleotide synthesis to create the siRNA or antisense drugs and vector engineering for gene therapy.

Apart from proteins and nucleic acids, some carbohydrates and lipids are molecules with large molecular weights. Lipids are used more for drug delivery than as drugs in their own right, something which will be covered briefly in a later chapter. Carbohydrates are molecules consisting of individual saccharide units that link together to form complex polymers with a variety of functions. The anticoagulant drug heparin, which has been in use for many years, is an example of a large molecule carbohydrate drug. It is related to the glycosaminoglycan (GAG) family of molecules built up from the small molecules N-acetylglucosamine or N-acetylgalactosamine.

One of the functions of carbohydrates is to create adhesion between viruses or bacteria and the surfaces of cells. This makes them interesting from the point of view of infectious diseases, where carbohydrates may be present either on the cell being infected, or else on the virus or bacterium. The anti-influenza drugs Relenza® and Tamiflu® are both small molecule inhibitors of the sialidase enzyme that breaks down a carbohydrate molecule on the surface of infected cells. Inhibiting this enzyme then prevents viral entry into the cell and reduces the duration of flu symptoms. Carbohydrates are also involved in the adhesion of white blood cells to blood vessels during acute inflammation and have been seen as potential drug targets for many years. Unfortunately, for technical reasons, carbohydrates are not easy to turn into inhibitor drugs with high affinity for their protein target; this, however, has not discouraged researchers from trying to make breakthroughs in this area.

8.1.6 Cell Therapy

The drugs covered in this and the previous chapter are all generated in the early preclinical discovery phase of the drug development pipeline. Once these have been produced in the laboratory, the next stage involves screening them for biological activity and assessing their potential as medicines (covered in later chapters). The development of cell therapies follows a somewhat different path and has the more complex objective of regenerating cells and tissues, rather than exploiting individual drug targets. In an ideal world, tissue regeneration would be achieved by swallowing an orally active drug to stimulate the growth of new tissues in specific places, like the brain. Unfortunately, tissue growth during development depends on many complex interactions between growth and differentiating factors (like cytokines), signalling pathways, cell adhesion molecules and the programmed death of unwanted cells. This last process, known as apoptosis, (Greek for falling of leaves) is critical for maintaining constant levels of cells in the body. For example, if rapidly dividing blood cells were not killed off on a regular basis, the human body would soon fill up with them and eventually explode. Apoptosis is also important in tissue modelling, for example in removing cells from the primitive hand of the embryo during development to form the individual fingers out of a web-like structure. The point of this brief diversion is that there is no single protein target in cells that is responsible for creating new tissues, instead there is a complex interplay between many different genes, proteins and other molecules.

Since it is hard to envisage any way of repairing tissues other than through using stem cells, there is an enormous worldwide effort to understand what makes these cells special and how can they be coaxed into forming new tissues to order. The starting point is the population of pluripotent stem cells that arise in the early cell division stages of the fertilized egg (described in Chap. 2). The origin of these cells during early embryogenesis is illustrated in Fig. 8.8.

8.1.6.1 Sources of Stem Cells

The problem with natural stem cells is that they have to be isolated from human embryos that have been discarded during *in vitro* fertilization (IVF) procedures. This is both ethically controversial and impractical if these cells are going to be developed and marketed by the biopharmaceutical industry. There is also the major problem of the donor cells being rejected by the immune system of the recipient

Fig. 8.8 Pluripotent stem
cells. After fertilization, the
egg (ovum) keeps dividing
until the blastocyst stage is
reached. In normal development, this ball of cells will
implant into the uterus and
develop into an embryo. All
of the different tissues in the
embryo (and adult) derive
from the pluripotent stem cells
present in the blastocyst. If
these are removed in the laboratory and cultured under
special conditions, they can be
turned into tissue-specific stem
cells and ultimately new tissues
such as blood, bone, muscle,
etc. in a way that mimics
embryonic development

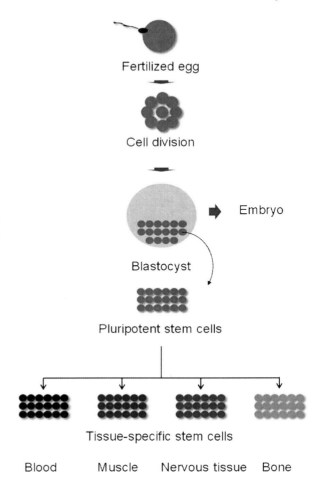

patient. The only practicable way of getting round this situation is to somehow
create stem cells from a patient's own adult cells. There is no easy answer to this,
as embryonic stem cells (ES cells) have all the correct molecular systems in place
to perform the task of creating different tissues; alternative sources will almost
certainly differ in subtle ways that could lead to clinical problems emerging in the
longer term. Despite this caveat, there is an enormous amount of research directed
at finding stem cells that do not require the use of embryos. A breakthrough
occurred in 2006, when Shinya Yamanaka and colleagues in Japan succeeded in
creating stem cells from adult mouse cells (Takahashi and Yamanaka 2006). These
were named induced pluripotent stem cells (iPS) and created a great deal of excitement
in the field of regenerative medicine. The process of creating them required the
introduction of a series of genes that control other genes critical for the formation
of ES cells in the embryo. Unfortunately, at least one of the introduced genes is
implicated in cancer, so it is far too risky to make iPS cells for human therapy using

this method. This has not, however, deterred researchers from devising new ways of making iPS cells in a way that reduces the possibility of them causing cancer (i.e. their oncogenic potential). The result of these researches is a range of human iPS cells which can be used for research and maybe ultimately, for therapy.

Another active area of research is the manipulation of stem cells with small molecules in order to affect various cell signalling pathways. Although the idea of swallowing a pill to repair damaged tissue is fanciful, it certainly does appear that small molecules can be used to drive stem cells down a particular route towards mature tissues. This could be very useful for creating specific cell types in "factories" prior to injecting them into patients.

There is understandable caution from the regulatory authorities about proceeding with clinical trials of stem cell products. At the time of writing, early safety trials for ES cells to treat stroke and spinal cord injury are about to go ahead using products developed by specialist biotechnology companies. As with the history of therapeutic antibodies, if these trials lead to clinical and commercial benefit, the biopharmaceutical industry will undergo yet another shakeup away from its traditional comfort zone of small molecule development.

Summary of Key Points

Many drug targets are too large to be effectively modified by small molecules.

Large molecule drugs like proteins are proving to be effective and commercially successful medicines.

Therapeutic antibodies (immunoglobulins) are large proteins that are providing new treatments for cancer, arthritis and other major conditions.

Antibody engineering is used to create humanized versions of immunoglobulins as well as produce antibody fragments using phage display technology.

Stem cell therapy shows great promise for regenerative medicine, but there are many technical obstacles to overcome before it can become routine in clinical practice.

References

Ablynx Website (2010). http://www.ablynx.com/research/. Accessed 20 Nov 2010

Kim SJ et al (2005) Antibody engineering for the development of therapeutic antibodies. Mol Cells 20:17–29

McCafferty J (1990) Phage antibodies: filamentous phage displaying antibody variable domains. Nature 348:552–554

Takahashi K, Yamanaka S (2006) Induction of pluripotent stem cells from mouse embryonic and adult fibroblast cultures by defined factors. Cell 126:663–76

Chapter 9
Screening for Hits

Abstract This chapter describes the process of screening that is undertaken once the target for a drug has been identified and the compounds or biologicals have been produced to test against it. Different laboratory assays are used to measure interactions with the target, and depending on the throughput of the screen, may require robotics to automate the process. These technologies along with the relevant terminology used in this particular aspect of drug discovery are described in this chapter.

9.1 Introduction

The identification of drug targets, small-molecule synthesis and the production of large molecules have already been covered. This chapter introduces the screening assay (or just screen) that is used to identify either compounds or biologicals that interact with a chosen target. Screening is the primary strategy for small-molecule drug discovery by the biopharmaceutical industry, despite the element of chance associated with it. Random collections of small molecules (synthetic or natural products) are screened against the targets to identify pharmacophores which can then be modified by medicinal chemists to create drug candidates for full clinical development. Biological products, such as antibodies, are screened in a similar way to small molecules, but the lead candidates are progressed to development along a different path (antibody humanization, for example).

9.1.1 Terminology

Screening has its own particular terminology, which may vary somewhat from company to company:

- Active
  The first stage of screening produces an "active" that has an effect on the target in question. This active could be a false positive; in other words, it has affected

the target in a non-specific way. This is a common problem, as many compounds stick non-specifically to proteins or act like detergents; there may, therefore, be a high rate of attrition of such compounds in a screen.

- Hit
  If the active effect is repeated in a second screen (i.e. is reproducible), the compound becomes a "hit". Before a hit can become a lead, it must be selective against the target and must have a clearly defined structure activity relationship (SAR) with related compounds (see Chap. 7). Quite often, a screening collection that produces an active contains several related compounds which can be tested at the same time to provide some initial SAR information.

- Lead
  The desired outcome of a screening campaign is the identification of a lead compound (or lead) that can be further evaluated *in vitro* and in animal models of the disease. Leads are hits that have been chemically modified in the laboratory to optimize their biological properties.

- Primary, secondary and tertiary screens
  The primary screen is the initial survey of compounds using the drug target alone. Active compounds are then tested in secondary screens to measure the selectivity of the compound by using different protein targets or cell types. This is crucial for ensuring that the active compound is working on the target and not through some non-specific disruptive effect. It is particularly important for whole cell screens, since many compounds may simply be toxic. Further (tertiary) screens may be performed to ensure that the active is a real hit.

The size of a screen is determined by its throughput, i.e. the number of compounds that are tested in a given campaign. The throughput is determined by the type of screen being undertaken and is summarized as follows:

- Low throughput
  A maximum of around 200 compounds are tested. Often, these are not small molecules picked at random, but highly biased towards a particular chemical structure, such as those used for focused compound libraries (Chap. 7). It is also possible that the screening target is difficult to set up for more than a few tests, a situation that arises when screening whole tissues or organs. Because the number of tests is low, there is normally no requirement for automation.

- Medium throughput
  Compounds (and microbial extracts) are screened in low thousands. This screen is used when the target is not easily set-up in large numbers, for example with live model organisms, like zebrafish embryos (Chap. 6). Even with several thousand compounds, it is possible to perform the screen without automation, but as I know from bitter experience, the process becomes extremely tedious if performed manually.

- High throughput
  This has been the mainstay of biopharmaceutical screening and is now increasingly being taken up by academic institutions. Large collections of compounds

Fig. 9.1 Screening flow chart. Compounds or extracts of natural products (cultured bacteria or fungi, or plant/ animal extracts) added to the drug target protein and effect measured (see details in text). If the desired effect is observed, the compound is retested against the same target. If the effect is reproducible, the compound is tested against an irrelevant target. If no effect is observed, the hit compound is modified by medicinal chemistry to generate a series of compounds for retesting on the target. If a clear structure activity relationship (SAR) is observed between the different compounds, the most promising examples are selected as lead compounds for further development into drugs

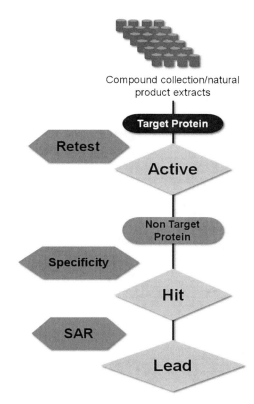

Compound collection/natural product extracts

(up to 1 million) are screened with the assistance of robotic workstations to manipulate compounds and target samples (see later).

- Ultra-high throughput screening

  The problem with screening random compounds is that the chance of finding a useful hit is much lower than if the inputs were carefully pre-selected to eliminate poor candidates. Obviously, the more compounds screened, the more chances of finding something useful; however, the adage "rubbish in, rubbish out" definitely applies to screening (actually, this is usually described in more "robust" language by drug discovery scientists). Ultra-high throughput screening (UHTS) of several million compounds certainly increases the input, but only large companies, such as GlaxoSmithKline and Pfizer, have the resources to pay for the materials and robotics required for such a huge enterprise.

The basic outline of a screening strategy is shown in Fig. 9.1.

9.1.2 Screening in Practice

The different classes of drug targets detailed in Chap. 5 have their own particular characteristics which determine how a screen (at any throughput) is configured.

For example, screens for inhibitors of enzymes are different to those designed for receptor agonists or antagonists. The target itself may be a purified protein or might remain in the environment of the cell in which it is normally expressed. In both cases, there is a need to use as little biological and chemical materials as possible in order to keep the cost of each screen at a minimum. This is achieved by using disposable plastic vessels, known as microplates, which hold very small volumes of liquid. Screening plates are moulded with 96, 384 and 1,536 wells which are suited to different degrees of throughput. The amount of plastic used for a large screen is daunting; screening 1 million compounds without any duplication or extra samples would require about 650 1,536-well plates.

Compounds to be screened are dissolved in small volumes of liquid and added to the primary assay at a fixed concentration (normally 10 μM). This figure is a compromise between having too many false positives because the concentration is too high and not picking up useful starting points if the concentration is set too low. The storage and manipulation of compounds can be extremely challenging, particularly when as many as 100,000 are being screened each day, so robotic workstations are needed to automate the process. An example of a 96-well microtiter plate and a screening robot is shown in Fig. 9.2.

Large collections of compounds have been built-up by large pharmaceutical companies over periods of many years and include those bought from academic institutions and specialist collections. The majority, however, emerge from internal company research programmes; this has tended to bias the screening results towards the type of target in which the company has had a historical interest. I discovered this with my screens for immunosuppressant compounds, where most of the actives turned out to be steroid-like molecules produced for other programmes in the past. Unfortunately, they were of no interest and had to be weeded out. Modern compound collections have been pre-screened to remove the compounds likely to produce non-specific or undesirable effects. A more recent development is the use of highly focused screening collections consisting of small-molecule libraries built-up from pharmacophores discovered in the nature or designed in the computer (see Chap. 7). This chemoinformatics approach ensures that the chance of finding a useful hit is much greater than through searching at random.

9.1.2.1   What Is Actually Measured?

The main requirement for a screen is a simple and robust system that generates a signal in a reproducible way. Depending on the target being screened, this signal may be anything from a colour change to the growth of cells. Antibiotics were discovered by measuring the inhibition of growth of whole bacteria when screening natural product extracts. Other cell-based screens use mammalian cell cultures to measure growth or some specific aspects of their function. The immunosuppressant drug cyclosporine A, for example, was discovered by inhibiting the function of whole lymphocytes which had been artificially activated in the screening assay to mimic an immune reaction. There are different techniques to measure these cell

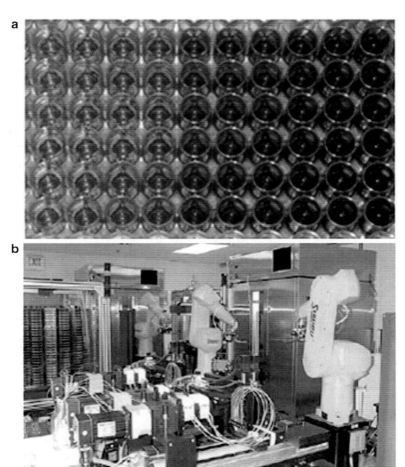

Fig. 9.2 (**a**) 96-well plastic microtiter plate with coloured liquid. This is used as a vessel to hold the screening reactions in small volumes (in this case, up to about 250 µl). (**b**) A screening robot for automating the addition of liquids to screening plates and measuring responses to different compounds. Three robot arms that manipulate the plates (in racks, *left side* of image) and position them are shown

effects, some of which involve the uptake of small amounts of radioactivity using labelled nucleotides or amino acids that are incorporated into DNA and proteins, respectively. Radioactive compounds, however, have to be handled with great care under strict regulations for monitoring and disposal; this has prompted the search for non-radioactive alternatives, such as a range of small organic compounds that change colour when modified by the cells undergoing division. The intensity of a colour change can be quantified in a spectrophotometer, which measures the absorbance of light by a sample and expresses this absorbance as a number.

Spectrophotometers are the mainstay of the screening (and biochemistry) laboratory and can be designed to measure the colour absorbance of many samples in parallel, such as those dispensed into multi-well screening plates.

The use of live cells to screen drugs should, in principle, provide a more realistic picture of how an active compound is likely to behave in a patient. Unfortunately, the cell-associated target is also in the presence of many other molecules which can interfere with a screening reaction through creating false positive results or producing results that are difficult to interpret. Furthermore, the compounds being screened may not penetrate the cell membrane and get to their target (if it resides inside the cell), so potentially interesting hits may be missed. The alternative to whole cell screens is to use the isolated target protein in varying degrees of purity. Screens for the GPCR class of receptors, for example, are often set up using cell membranes to express the protein that is then mixed with radioactive ligands as described in Chap. 4. It is now quite routine to express human receptor proteins in animal cells (such as CHO or COS cells, Chap. 8) through the use of recombinant DNA technology. This means that almost any GPCR, or other receptor type, can be screened as long as its DNA sequence is available.

Screens for both inhibitors and activators of enzymes are often set up with the purified protein dissolved in a solution of water and various salts, known as a buffer. Both enzymes and other biological molecules are highly sensitive to changes in pH (acidity and alkalinity, see Chap. 4) temperature and concentrations of salts, such as sodium chloride. Buffers are designed to maintain the solution at a constant pH, hence their use for any biochemical reaction that has been set up *in vitro*, such as an enzyme screen. The activity of an enzyme is determined by the conversion of a substrate into a product. The substrate for a protease enzyme (pepsin in the stomach, for example) is protein, and the product is a collection of smaller peptides formed by breaking the protein chains. In a screen for protease inhibitors, an artificial substrate is produced in the form of a small peptide synthesized in the laboratory with a coloured dye molecule attached. When the peptide is cut by the enzyme, the dye molecule is released and registers as a colour that can be accurately measured in a spectrophotometer. Any screened compound that inhibits the enzyme stops the colour increase and, therefore, registers as an active. Figure 9.3 shows a basic screening format for compounds that bind to a target which has been immobilized in a microtiter plate.

9.1.2.2   Advanced Screening Technologies

Modern screening operations are constrained by cost and safety issues, particularly when applied at very high throughputs. The unit cost of a screen can be reduced by using smaller amounts of precious reagents in each well. Safety is a particularly important issue with radioactivity because experiments have to be performed in dedicated facilities and everything must be monitored for accidental spillage. This has encouraged the search for labels that have equal or greater sensitivity to radio-isotopes without the need for special precautions in their use. These labels and

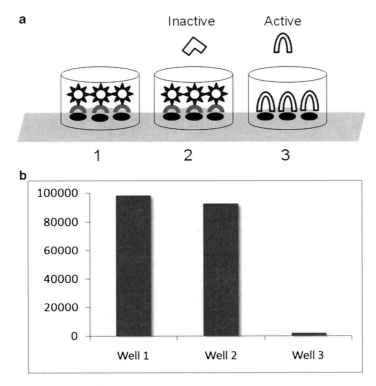

Fig. 9.3 Basic screening layout for compounds that bind to a drug target. (**a**) Three wells of a microtiter plate are shown with the target protein immobilized on the bottom (*black ovals*). Whole cells or cell membranes could also be used. A compound that is known to bind to the target (e.g. a hormone) is tagged with a radioactive or a colorimetric label and added to the well; excess material is washed away and the bound ligand is detected by a radioactivity counter (or spectrophotometer if a coloured label is used). If a compound with a stronger binding affinity is then added to the target, the label is displaced and the amount of radioactivity in the sample falls. Well 2 has a compound added that fails to bind, and therefore the radioactivity remains the same as if nothing had been added. Well 3 has an active compound which displaces the labelled ligand and reduces the radioactivity. (**b**) A graphical representation of each well. The radioactivity in wells 1 and 2 is around 100,000 units, and the active compound reduces this to about 2,000 units. If many more samples are looked at, it would be easy to pick out the active compounds by looking at a graph of this type or even just at the rows of figures printed out by the radioactivity counter

detection systems exploit known physical phenomena related to the interaction between radiation (of all types) and matter. Some of these detection systems are listed as follows:

- Fluorescence
  This occurs when light with one wavelength (colour) stimulates a fluorescent molecule to emit light of another wavelength. Fluorescent labelling is very sensitive, and is widely used in screening and diagnostics (Chap. 14). A related technology, fluorescence resonance energy transfer (FRET), is widely used to

measure the interactions between large molecules; positive contact between molecules labelled with particular elements (e.g. Europium or Terbium) results in a reduction of the fluorescent signal.

- Phosphorescence
  This is similar to fluorescence in that light of a specific wavelength is emitted from phosphorescent materials, but the duration and nature of the emission are different. Phosphorescence is used in specialized assays and for imaging radioactivity.

- Chemiluminescence
  The wonderful glow of fireflies at night results from the conversion of chemical energy to light, aided by the enzyme luciferase. The biochemical mechanism behind this has been exploited in many screening formats which use recombinant firefly luciferase in conjunction with light-emitting compounds. The sensitivity of these labels is extremely high and can exceed that of some radiolabels.

- Surface Plasmon Resonance
  This, rather complex, phenomenon is extremely useful for measuring the interaction between different molecules, since there is no need to tag them with any sort of label. The instrumentation required for surface plasmon resonance (SPR) is expensive and unsuited for very high-throughput applications, but is being increasingly used in the screening laboratory.

High-content screening is a screening technology that involves the use of sophisticated microscopes and imaging systems to simultaneously visualize multiple events occurring inside cells that have been treated with different compounds. A screening compound can be evaluated for its effect on many different processes occurring inside cells, in addition to those caused by the primary drug target. This has an advantage over simpler screens in that mechanisms of action or possible toxicity can be evaluated at a very early stage. *In vivo* screening offers the ultimate test of a compound's activity, but is normally impractical to perform on more than a few animals. This has begun to change, with the introduction of the small model organisms discussed in Chap. 6. Prominent among these is the zebrafish whose embryos are small enough to be screened in 384-well microplates. The embryos can also be manipulated using recombinant DNA technology to express fluorescent marker proteins in specific body structures in order to observe the effects of compounds on their appearance and function. This approach has been used to highlight blood vessels in zebrafish by using genetic engineering to express a gene called green reef coral fluorescent protein (GRCFP), which is derived from a marine organism. The vessels shine green under fluorescent light and can be imaged with a microscope and CCD device to show the blood vessel growth (angiogenesis) over several days. A medium-throughput screen of a compound library produced known inhibitors of angiogenesis, plus a novel compound that also inhibited human angiogenesis in secondary assays (Tran et al. 2007). Inhibitors of this type have the potential to treat cancer by preventing the growth of new blood vessels, thereby starving tumours of their blood supply.

9.1.3 Chemical Genomics and Proteomics

The interaction between small molecules and proteins encoded by the genes of organisms is not only important in drug discovery, but also in the understanding of fundamental biological processes. There is nothing new in this, but over the last 10 years or so, the use of small molecules to probe biological function has been termed chemical genetics or chemical genomics. Chemical genetics is simply the process of altering biological function with small-molecule probes instead of through genetic mutations. Just as genomics is genetics on a genome-wide scale, chemical genomics (sometimes called chemical proteomics) is the search for small molecules that interact with all the proteins encoded by the genome. This makes chemical genomics a central part of small-molecule drug discovery as it overlaps considerably with target discovery, compound synthesis and screening. Although most proteins are not likely to be drug targets, chemical probes made for each of them can provide valuable information about basic human cell biology. This could be exploited in pharmaceutical research for target identification as well as to identify proteins that are the targets for toxic drugs, as exemplified later in this chapter. The success of the Human Genome Project in identifying human genes has prompted similar (but smaller scale) initiatives in chemical genomics. In the USA, the National Institutes of Health (NIH) and the National Cancer Institute (NCI) have established centres for chemical genomics to identify small molecules that interact with many thousands of proteins and make the information available to researchers online. Some of the characteristic tools of genomics, such as microarrays, have been exploited in the chemical genomics research. For example, it is possible to immobilize small molecules at high densities on specially treated glass slides in a microarray format. A protein under investigation can then be labelled with a fluorescent tag and passed over the chemical microarray to generate a signal where binding occurs. Since the identity of the compound is known at each position on the slide, it is possible to determine which one(s) is responsible for binding. The miniaturization of this binding assay makes it possible to screen many thousands of compounds simultaneously.

9.1.3.1 Immobilized Compounds

When a purified protein is used in a screen for small molecules, the results are relatively straightforward to interpret; if the protein is a drug target, then molecules that bind to it will be of interest as potential drugs. The situation is quite different with screens that use the function of live cells as readout. Sometimes, the precise molecular target may not be known, and there is no guarantee that compounds are active just because they interact with it. In this case, the screen has to be deconvoluted; in other words, the complex web of proteins in the cell has to be unravelled to reveal the true drug target. Although modern understanding of the chemistry and biology of the cell has accelerated the process of deconvolution, it is still a major undertaking for any research group. There is, however, a technique called affinity selection that can be used to literally pull the drug target protein out of an extract of broken cells. This approach has been used for target discovery by academic groups and commercialized by companies, such as

Cellzome. It has also been successfully used by Serenex (now part of Pfizer Inc.) as a low-throughput screening system. A compound that has been shown to have an effect on a particular cell function is linked to a solid support in a similar way to the chemical microarrays; the difference is that the support is a bead of cellulose or a similar inert material that can be packed into a glass column. When human cells are broken up into mild detergents, their proteins are dissolved into a solution that can be poured onto the top of the column and allowed to pass slowly into a collection vessel. Most of the proteins do not bind to the compound in the column, but those that do can be recovered and identified using the mass spectrometry approach outlined in Chap. 6. One way of recovering the protein from the column is to add a large excess of the same compound that is also immobilized on the beads. This has the effect of competing for the protein-binding sites and makes it possible to screen other compounds by assessing their ability to displace the protein. This is the procedure that Serenex used to identify novel compounds against a cancer target protein of interest. The affinity selection process is illustrated in Fig. 9.4.

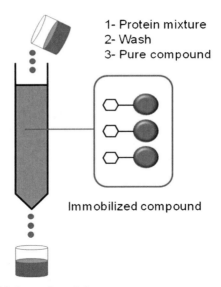

1- Protein mixture
2- Wash
3- Pure compound

Immobilized compound

1- Unbound proteins
2- Unbound proteins
3- Specifically bound protein

Fig. 9.4 Affinity selection of proteins on small molecule columns. A small molecule is immobilized on a solid support using a chemical linker. The support could be a synthetic or natural polymer (e.g. cellulose) that can be suspended in buffer and packed in a column (plastic or glass tube). Liquid is poured into the top of the column; it then passes over the compound and emerges at the bottom, where it is collected for further analysis. The experiment starts with a protein mixture from cells or other sources being poured over the column, where most pass straight through without binding. Any non-specific binding is reduced by washing the column with more buffer. Finally, the protein that binds specifically to the small molecule on the column is eluted by adding a large excess of the compound in solution. Alternatively, different compounds can be added to see if they compete for the binding site on the target protein, thus providing valuable information for further drug development

Finally, affinity selection has been used with the so-called off-target effects, where compounds act on proteins that are not their primary targets. This has recently been illustrated with the drug thalidomide which gained notoriety in the 1960s because of its teratogenicity (i.e. it caused birth defects that included characteristic limb malformations). Thalidomide was prescribed as a sedative to pregnant women and for preventing morning sickness; it is currently used under strict controls to treat leprosy and multiple myeloma. It would be desirable to create thalidomide analogues that are safe to use in pregnancy, hence an interest in finding the protein target responsible for birth defects. This could be used to select compounds that had the beneficial effects of thalidomide, but showed no binding to this protein. The protein, cereblon (CRBN), has been identified in the extracts of human cells using thalidomide attached to beads in a column and has been shown to be part of a signalling pathway involved in limb formation (Ito et al. 2010).

Summary of Key Points

Screening is used to randomly select small and large molecules as leads for further development.

The number of samples tested can range from a few hundred to millions.

Different physical phenomena are used to detect the binding or modifications of molecules in screening assays; these include radioactivity and fluorescence.

Chemical genomics focuses on the interactions between small molecules and proteins on a genomic scale.

Affinity selection is a method of purifying a target protein from a complex mixture using immobilized small molecules.

References

Ito T et al (2010) Identification of a primary target of thalidomide teratogenicity. Science 327:1345–1349

Tran TC et al (2007) Automated quantitative screening assay for antiangiogenic compounds using transgenic zebrafish. Cancer Res 67:11386–11392

Chapter 10
Process Chemistry and Formulation

Abstract This chapter covers the scale up and manufacturing of drug molecules, using process chemistry for small molecules and large-scale expression systems for antibodies and other proteins. The second part deals with the formulation of active pharmaceutical ingredients into a dosage form that is suitable for administration to patients. The chapter concludes with a brief review of nanotechnology and its role in drug delivery. This is particularly important for the delivery of new biotechnology products, such as nucleic acids.

10.1 Introduction

Once a compound or a biotherapeutic molecule has been selected as a lead for further development, it is ready to leave the discovery phase and move into preclinical development. The end of the discovery phase signifies a major transition between unregulated, sometimes "blue sky" research and the heavily regulated process of producing and marketing a medicine that may be sold to millions of people worldwide. Decisions and actions taken at these latter stages now have major legal, moral and financial implications for a biopharmaceutical company.

There has always been a gulf between discovery scientists and those involved in the development because the working ethos of each group is driven by different requirements. The discovery scientists, almost by definition, are more freewheeling and experimental in keeping with the "discovery" in their job title. There is nothing more frustrating to such scientists than having to perform a prescribed set of experimental procedures that have to be rigorously followed to the letter. Development scientists, on the other hand, must possess the same experimental skills, but use them in very clearly defined processes that have to be performed in a uniform and consistent manner. In the past, this cultural gap was enormous, with each side understanding their part of the drug development process, but having little inclination to learn from each other's experiences. Discovery scientists would metaphorically throw the compounds over a wall to development teams and then forget about them; equally, there was no real appetite in the development for exploiting the latest findings in basic research to improve their processes and procedures. All these began to change in the 1990s, the result being a much closer integration between early discovery and the later stages of drug development. Included in these later stages are the manufacture and formulation of compounds and biologicals. These are critical parts of the development process, since a whole programme can fail simply because the drug is impossible to formulate or too expensive or hazardous to manufacture.

This chapter describes some of the basic processes used in the scale up and manufacture of small molecules and therapeutic proteins and then covers their formulation into the products that are sold in the pharmacy. These particular development functions are encompassed by the term "pharmaceutical development".

10.1.1   Scale Up and Manufacture

Compounds and biologicals (like antibodies) are normally produced in milligram-to-gram quantities for primary testing and evaluation in disease models. Once a lead compound has been identified, its production must be scaled up from grams to kilograms to provide enough materials for preclinical evaluation in animals as well as for formulation.[1] Clinical trials and commercial production require multi-kilogram quantities produced under strict guidelines, collectively known as Good Manufacturing Practice or GMP (also current GMP or cGMP). The main regulatory authorities responsible for their administration are the American Food and Drug Administration (FDA), the European Medicines Agency (EMA) and the Ministry of Health, Labour and Welfare in Japan. These agencies are covered in more detail in later chapters, along with a description of the regulatory submission process. Manufacturers are now encouraged by the FDA and others to follow the principles of Quality by Design (QbD) using Process Analytical Technology (PAT) to ensure that the quality of the drug is optimized during the process of development and not subsequently at the production stage.

10.1.1.1   Small Molecule Process Chemistry

Medicinal chemists have a reasonable amount of freedom in the choice of synthetic routes and materials used to produce the small quantities of compounds required for initial screening. This freedom is lost when the compounds have to be scaled up in a pilot plant, since the number of synthetic steps has to be kept within reasonable

---

[1] To put these amounts in perspective, a daily 10 mg dose of an average-sized, small-molecule drug administered to 1 million patients chronically over 1 year requires about 4 tons of materials (Marti and Siegel 2006).

bounds (normally five to ten steps). The choice of raw materials for the synthesis is also important, since these must be readily available, inexpensive and compatible with environmental regulations. The term "green chemistry" is becoming more widely spread as the biopharmaceutical industry responds to the changing expectations of the outside world.

In practice, the initial scale up of compounds is undertaken by the process chemist who later partners with chemical engineers to design manufacturing schemes for the marketed drug. Since the manufactured compounds must be as pure as possible, analytical chemists are employed to liaise closely with the chemists and engineers in the process teams. A great deal of creative effort goes into developing new synthetic routes for compounds using novel catalysts or other techniques. One of the main concerns of the process chemist is the behaviour of chemical reactions on a large scale. For example, a small reaction may give off some heat as it proceeds; on a larger scale, however, this heat output could be highly dangerous, so this has to be anticipated in advance.

Process chemistry also has to be as efficient as possible in order to keep costs down to a level that the pharmaceuticals market will bear. The sum of all the manufacturing and licensing costs of a compound is known as the cost of goods, which would normally be less than $5 per gram. This is made even cheaper once a drug comes off patent and is taken up by generic manufacturers, since the cost per dose must come down to make it commercially viable. This has put pressure on the generic companies to design synthetic routes that are cheaper than those used initially for the branded medicine. The painkiller ibuprofen is a case in point. This was produced by Boots in the late 1960s using a chemical synthesis involving six individual reactions. Although the process created enough materials for the marketplace at the time, it required large amounts of chemical reagents and produced an excess of aluminium salts. Later on, the BHC process was developed by the Boots-Hoechst-Celanese company and used in 1992 in a Texas plant to produce around 4,000 tons of the drug per annum. The synthesis employed only three steps and used a solvent that was itself a part of the reaction process and which could be recycled with minimal waste (Fig. 10.1).

10.1.1.2 Manufacture of Biologicals Versus Small Molecules

Drug compounds and biologicals are created in different ways because the synthesis of small molecules and large molecules requires separate processes. As described in earlier chapters, small molecules can be synthesized in a laboratory, or a factory, using quite harsh conditions and can then be purified to a very high degree. In addition, the level of purity can easily be monitored using sensitive analytical methods. On the other hand, most biological products are produced in living organisms and are far less forgiving of mistreatments, such as variations in temperature during manufacture or storage. There are also two major issues with biological sources: the consistency of production and the purity of the final product. Even cloned (genetically uniform) cell lines are liable to variations in their yield of recombinant protein

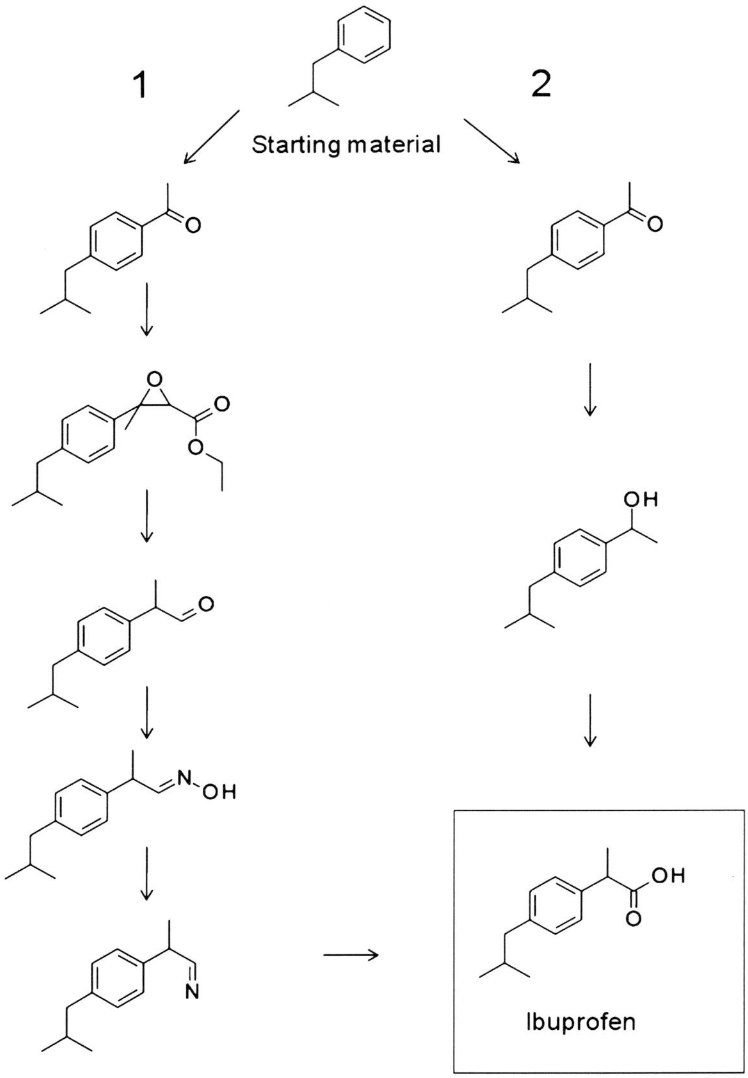

Fig. 10.1 Process chemistry for Ibuprofen. Two schemes for manufacturing the painkiller from a common starting material are shown. The first involves six reactions which were reduced to three using scheme (2). Reaction conditions are not shown, but can be found in Sheldon (2010). Figure adapted from Sheldon (2010) with kind permission of Wiley-VCH Verlag GmbH & Co. KGaA

and cannot be kept growing continuously. They have to be grown from batches of cells that have been stored frozen in liquid nitrogen. Batch-to-batch variation is a major concern, since a sudden change in protein expression during any phase of the development process could have a significant impact on the approval process by the regulatory authorities. The problem with purity stems from the fact that cells contain materials that are difficult to fully remove from the finished product.

Bacteria contain molecules called pyrogens which cause fever in humans and are responsible for the fatal sepsis that can occur after infection with gram-negative bacteria like *Escherichia coli*. The mammalian cells used to produce recombinant proteins, including antibodies, contain viruses that might conceivably integrate with the patient's DNA with unknown consequences. The downstream processing of biological molecules produced in large batch cultures is, therefore, of considerable importance.

Antibodies

Since antibodies are the fastest-growing class of protein therapeutics, a great deal of experience has been gained in their scale up and manufacture by the biopharmaceutical industry. Despite this, producing antibodies for clinical trials and beyond is a highly complex process involving many different steps that impose great demands on a company's manufacturing capacity. This means that the cost of goods is significantly higher than that of small molecules, being as much as $1,000 per gram, although process optimization can bring this down to around $300.

A typical production scheme for a humanized therapeutic antibody is shown in Fig. 10.2. The starting point is a master cell bank (MCB) of CHO cells expressing the H and L chains of the antibody. These cells are carefully selected for their ability to produce high levels of antibody protein in simple growth media that is free of animal-derived materials. The working cell bank (WCB) is taken from this master stock and grown in successively higher volumes of growth medium; these volumes start from a few tens of millilitres and move up to thousands of litres held in bioreactors. Once the cells have produced sufficient antibody in the culture medium, they are removed using a centrifuge, and the culture supernatant is filtered through a very fine membrane filter (0.2 μm or one twenty thousandth of a millimetre). This is the first of the downstream processing steps that leads to the final purified antibody.

The antibody is purified from the rest of the materials in the culture fluid using an immobilized protein called protein A, which has the property of binding tightly to human IgG antibodies. This selective binding is exploited by immobilizing the protein in a column (a similar principle to the immobilized compound in Chap. 9) and then passing the culture fluid through it to pull out the antibody. Once most of the host cell proteins (HCPs) have been washed off the column, the antibody is recovered by lowering the pH (thereby increasing the acidity). A low pH step is also used to inactivate any virus that may have been carried through from the CHO cells. A set of polishing procedures are then used to reduce virus, HCPs and DNA to levels that are acceptable to the FDA and others. This is achieved by using a range of chromatography techniques followed by filtration. The antibody is then concentrated and formulated, prior to sterilization by further filtration.

Nucleic Acids

Finally, it is worth briefly describing the production of nucleic acid drugs at scale, since these could become the "breakthrough drugs" in the same way that antibody therapeutics were in the late 1990s. Nucleic acid drugs (oligonucleotides of the type

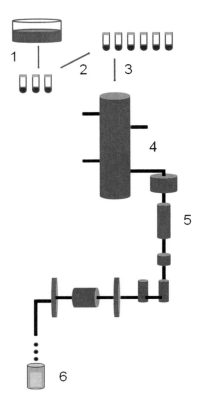

Fig. 10.2 A highly schematic illustration showing the principle of antibody manufacturing: (**1**) CHO cells producing the antibody grown in laboratory to produce enough cells to store as a master cell bank in liquid nitrogen; (**2**) a working cell bank used to start the manufacturing process; (**3**) cells grown in successively larger volumes until there are enough to add to a large bioreactor; (**4**) a recombinant antibody is produced in the bioreactor growth medium which is separated from cells and pumped off into the purification chain; (**5**) a series of filters and chromatography columns are used to purify the IgG from the growth medium and remove viruses and other hazardous materials and (**6**) the end result is sterile antibody in the correct formulation and ready for clinical use

described in Chap. 2) are synthesized from small molecules (nucleotides) using the techniques of organic chemistry. However, the starting material for these large-molecule drugs is extracted from biological materials like salmon sperm and calf thymus, both of which have been known to generations of molecular biologists as rich sources of DNA.

10.1.1.3 Production of Proteins in Animals and Plants

Although cultures of genetically modified cells are currently the method of choice for producing therapeutic proteins, issues with cost and complexity have driven the search for alternative sources. One possibility is to use transgenic animals or even plants, since they can be engineered to produce large amounts of correctly glycosylated human protein. This area is known as pharming and is still in its infancy because of regulatory, safety and political issues, particularly in the case of genetically modified plants. Nevertheless, the human clotting factor, antithrombin III, has been purified from the milk of genetically engineered goats and marketed by GTC Biotherapeutics as ATryn® for use in patients with an inherited clotting disorder (http://www.gtc-bio.com/products/atryn.html). Plants, such as tobacco, and also animals are being considered as hosts for the production of many other proteins and vaccines, so it is possible that products derived from these sources could be approved and manufactured over the next few years.

10.1.2 Formulation

A small molecule or a biological drug is never administered to patients on its own, but is mixed with other ingredients in a dosage form that reflects the intended route of administration. Dosage forms for compounds taken by mouth are tablets[2] or capsules and make up the majority of currently prescribed medicines. Dosage form design uses the formulation process to ensure that the medicine can enter the circulation in a controlled way with maximal bioavailability and in a form that is acceptable to the patient. This latter point is particularly important in the case of injectable or inhaled products, where patient compliance may become an issue because of the fear of needles, etc.

10.1.2.1 Terminology

The drug part of a formulation is called the active pharmaceutical ingredient (API), while the remainder is formed with inactive compounds called excipients. The latter are classed by the regulators as generally regarded as safe (GRAS) and are required to ensure that the API is bioavailable. Excipients are also important for the actual manufacturing process, since the tablet must be formed in a machine in a consistent way. Information and industry standards on excipients are available from organizations, such as the International Pharmaceutical Excipient Councils Federation (IPEC Federation 2010) and listed in reference manuals, such as the United States Pharmacopeia–National Formulary (USP–NF) (United States Pharmacopeia–National Formulary 2010).

The various types of formulation ingredients and some representative examples are listed in Table 10.1.

---

[2] The term "pill" is used colloquially, but this actually refers to a type of sugar-coated preparation that is no longer produced.

Table 10.1 Different classes of formulation ingredients

Class	Function	Examples
Fillers	"Bulk up" tablet or capsule	Cellulose, lactose and vegetable oils (diluents for capsules)
Solubilizing agents	Help solubilize lipophilic drugs	Cremophor EL
Binders	Hold tablet together	Sorbitol, gelatin and PVP
Disintegrants	Encourage break-up and dissolution of drug in stomach	Carboxymethyl cellulose
Lubricants	Stop powder sticking to tablet die	Talc and silica
Glidants	Promote powder flow during manufacture	Magnesium carbonate
Antiadherents	Prevent tablet sticking to punch	Magnesium stearate
Sweeteners	Mask unpleasant taste of API	
Colouring	Visual appeal and drug identification	FD&C Red No. 40
Sweeteners	Mask unpleasant taste in liquid formulations	Aspartame
Preservatives	Resist microbial contamination	Benzoic acid and vitamin E
Coating agents	Resist moisture in the air and hide unpleasant flavours	Hydroxypropyl methyl cellulose and gelatin (capsules)

10.1.2.2   Formulation Development

Formulation development is undertaken at several different phases of the development process. The first significant involvement of formulation scientists/pharmaceutical chemists really begins after a lead compound or a biological has been chosen for further development. At this exploratory stage, there are a number of key criteria that have to be established to produce a workable formulation. These are:

- Solubility and lipophilicity
  Most drug candidates are lipophilic (fat soluble, Chap. 3), since highly charged molecules do not generally penetrate the cell membrane. This can cause problems with the formulation since the drug may not readily dissolve in the stomach.

- Solubility at different pHs
  This is an important property, as the degree of acidity and alkalinity can vary significantly in different body compartments. For example, the stomach has a very low pH between 1.0 and 3.0 while the duodenum is at pH 6.0 to 6.5. This means that an orally available drug could experience a major change in solubility as it migrates (transits) through the stomach and into the small intestine.

- Physical form of drug
  Chemical substances exist in different forms (polymorphisms) that can have profound effects on their physical properties. Carbon, for example, is found as a crystal (diamond), powder (soot) and layered sheet (graphite), along with exotic forms, such as fullerenes, graphenes and nanotubes. Pharmaceutical compounds are also polymorphic, being either amorphous, like a powder, or crystalline. Two important factors in the formulation of a small molecule drug are particle size and

crystal habit (i.e. the shape of the crystal). Formulations used in dry powder inhalers (DPIs), for example, require very careful control of particle size. When crystals are used in drug formulations, they are micronized (ground into a fine powder using a mill). Whether a drug is developed as a powder or in crystalline form has profound consequences on drug development, since the different forms determine the solubility in the body and the ease of manufacture. Since polymorphic forms can appear and disappear in different preparations of the same compound, there is a danger that this could happen in the middle of a clinical trial; it would then be impossible to know the exact dose of drug administered to patients, and the trial data could be completely invalidated. The experience of Abbott Laboratories with its drug Ritonavir (marketed as Norvir® for HIV infection) is an example of how polymorphisms can adversely affect the manufacturing stage as well. Ritonavir was produced as a semi-solid form in capsules because the drug was not bioavailable in a tablet. Since it was in liquid form (dissolved in alcohol/ water), there was no regulatory requirement for checking the crystalline form. Two years after the launch in 1996, a new crystal form appeared in manufacturing batches that greatly reduced the solubility of the compound; this form rendered the drug unmanufacturable and held up supplies until a new formulation was devised to overcome the problem (Bauer et al. 2001).

• Physical and chemical stability
  The physical form of a medicine must confer stability as well as resistance to breakdown during storage. Some compounds, particularly in amorphous form, are liable to absorb water from the atmosphere (they are hygroscopic) which can affect the shelf life of the compounds as well as the ease of manufacture. A drug product requires a shelf life at room temperature of at least 18 months, so stability testing is an important factor in the overall development process.

• Salt selection
  Different salt forms (and hydrates) of small molecules have already been described in Chap. 3. If a salt form is required at all, each type will cause the above properties (stability, physical form, etc.) to vary, so evaluation of different salt forms is important at an early stage.

Once the above evaluations have been made and suitable formulations identified, the experimental drug can be submitted to the preclinical development process that involves toxicology and other animal studies (Chap. 11). The final formulation into a tablet or a capsule is not completed until well into the clinical development phase; prior to that, the compound is administered to phase I clinical trial volunteers in a capsule that is filled by hand. One challenge for formulation scientists is the preparation of tablets and capsules containing placebos for clinical trials. These formulations must have an identical appearance and taste to those containing the drug. Another, unrelated, concern is the possible chemical interaction between plastic in the bottle used to store the medicine and the medicine itself. This even extends to concerns about the adhesive in the label; this highlights the level of detail required for the regulation of drug development and the emotional stability required by the pharmaceutical scientists concerned.

10.1.2.3 Formulation of Biologicals

Mention has already been made in Chap. 2, and elsewhere, about the lack of oral bioavailability of nearly all protein and nucleic acid-based drugs and vaccines. This means that the formulation must be compatible with parenteral administration, i.e. administration through the skin or into the airways. Nucleic acids, such as the siRNAs, present additional challenges, as they must penetrate the cell membrane in order to reach their target. Since antibody proteins are administered at high concentrations, these large molecules can stick together (aggregate), thereby reducing the stability and creating unwanted stimulation of the immune system (immunogenicity). In fact, all protein therapeutics must be checked carefully for aggregation and immunogenicity during both the clinical and manufacturing phases of development.

10.1.2.4 Protein Formulation

Unlike tablets that are swallowed, proteins are directly introduced into the normal blood circulation by injection, so the pH encountered is around 7.0 and the concentration of salts in the plasma is at the normal physiological level. Administration of the drug at a different pH causes the patient to experience pain at the site of injection, so proteins are formulated to maintain physiological levels of pH and salts. Further ingredients, including amino acids, mannitol, glycerol and trehalose, are used to stabilize the protein during the process of freeze–drying (for storage) and reconstituting in buffer prior to injection. This is because proteins are susceptible to denaturation, the process by which chains of amino acids are unfolded by heat or mechanical agitation into an inactive form. Boiled eggs and melted cheese represent extreme examples of this, but therapeutic (and other) proteins dissolved in liquids can readily denature at the interface between the liquid and air. Special detergents, such as the polysorbates, are added in order to reduce this specific problem.

Proteins have a tendency to stick to containers and seemingly disappear completely if formulated in low concentrations. This has proved to be the downfall of many a biochemist who may have spent weeks isolating small amounts of a protein of interest only to wonder where it went once it was stored in a glass bottle. The loss of material can be a problem with proteins like erythropoietin or interferon beta that are injected in small amounts; in these cases, gelatin or human serum albumen (the main protein in blood) is used as a bulking agent. Although these proteins are effective, the emergence of spongiform encephalopathies (e.g. "mad cow disease") has been a cause for concern, since the prions that cause this disease have been found in both bovine and human tissues. One way round this problem is to produce recombinant gelatin or albumen that can be manufactured in bioreactors instead of an animal. A small (8.5 kDa) fragment of recombinant human gelatin produced by FibroGen Inc. in California has been tested in safety studies using human volunteers and found to be safe and well tolerated.

Another way of enhancing the stability of protein drugs in the circulation is to attach small molecules of polyethylene glycol (PEG). This process of PEGylation has been used in marketed drugs, such as PEGASYS interferon alpha produced by Hoffman-la-Roche for treating hepatitis C infection.

10.1.3 *"There's Plenty of Room at the Bottom"*

This was the title of a talk given by the Nobel Laureate, Richard Feynman, to the American Physical Society in 1959, where he introduced the basic ideas behind nanotechnology (Feynman 1959). The name is derived from the Greek for dwarf, and is concerned with producing materials and devices at nanometre (one billionth of a metre) scales; Feynman speculated that it would be quite feasible to print the entire edition of the Encyclopedia Britannica on the head of a pin. Since then, remarkable strides have been made in micro-fabricating machines and devices at the near-atomic scale. This has a relevance to pharmaceuticals, since there is a great deal of interest in using nanotechnology in formulations that enhance the delivery of drugs to target tissues. A common formulation is based on liposomes; these consist of minute phospholipid spheres that have encapsulated small-molecule drugs and then fuse with cell membranes to allow the compound to enter the cell. Liposomes are also used for the delivery of nucleic acids; this is of increasing importance, given the current interest in RNA drugs. Alternative delivery agents are being developed from different polymeric materials, one example being the plastic microspheres used in depot formulations designed to control the release of drugs after being implanted in the body.

One particular drug delivery problem is the introduction of small molecules into the brain to treat CNS diseases. The blood brain barrier (BBB) is a physical structure of vessels that keep the general circulation of blood separate from the fluid in the brain and spinal cord (cerebrospinal fluid). It acts as an important barrier to bacteria and molecules that would be harmful if introduced into the brain. These molecules have a relatively high charge which places restrictions on the structures of drugs that can target the brain because they have to be lipophilic, unless a way is found to bypass the BBB using liposomes or other nanoparticles.

Nanotechnology is definitely one of the major growth areas of research in drug discovery and might well make the dream of orally available proteins and nucleic acids a reality. The possibilities of manipulating materials at the molecular level are almost endless, as illustrated in the following report of a "plastic antibody" by Japanese and American scientists (Hoshino et al. 2010). They designed a nanoscale organic polymer which could bind to mellitin, a protein found in bee venom. The objective was to remove this protein from the circulation of mice as a proof of concept for treating humans suffering from serious reactions after receiving bee stings. Using whole animal imaging, they showed that the mellitin was bound by the polymer and transported to the liver for removal by excretion. Although the pharmaceutical industry is a long way off marketing "plastic antibodies", this example just illustrates some of the creativity and ingenuity that will lead to new products in the decades to come.

Summary of Key Points

Scale up and manufacture of small molecule drugs require the input of process chemists to devise safe, efficient and environmentally friendly reaction schemes.

The cost of goods is an important factor in deciding whether a drug discovery project is commercially viable.

Recombinant protein manufacture employs large bioreactors and downstream processing to remove contaminants from cells and culture medium.

Transgenic animals and plants are being investigated for production of drugs by "pharming".

Drug formulation of the API requires inert excipients.

Nanotechnology is being investigated as a means of improving drug solubility and delivery into different parts of the body.

References

Bauer J et al (2001) Ritonavir: an extraordinary example of conformational polymorphism. Pharm Res 18:859–866

Feynman RP (1959) Plenty of room at the bottom. http://www.zyvex.com/nanotech/feynman. html. Accessed 24 Nov 2010

GTC Biotherapeutics ATryn – Recombinant human antithrombin. http://www.gtc-bio.com/products/ atryn.html. Accessed 23 Nov 2010

Hoshino Y et al (2010) Recognition, neutralization, and clearance of target peptides in the bloodstream of living mice by molecularly imprinted polymer nanoparticles: a plastic antibody. J Am Chem Soc 132:6644–6645

IPEC Federation (2010). http://www.ipecfed.org/. Accessed 24 Nov 2010

Marti HR, Siegel JS (2006) Process chemistry in API development. Chimia 60:516

Sheldon R (2010) Introduction to green chemistry, organic synthesis and pharmaceuticals. In: Dunn PJ, Wells AS, Williams MT (eds) Green chemistry in the pharmaceutical industry. Wiley-VCH Verlag gmbH KgaA, Weinheim

United States Pharmacopeia National Formulary (2010). http://www.usp.org/USPNF/. Accessed 24 Nov 2010

Chapter 11
Preclinical Development

Abstract This chapter describes the preclinical studies that must be performed on drug candidates before they can be administered to human volunteers. Investigations are made into how the drug affects the body (pharmacodynamics) and how the body affects the drug (pharmacokinetics), as well as safety pharmacology and toxicology. All of these investigations are laid out in the chapter, which concludes with a description of how the preclinical information is used to estimate the dose of a drug that is administered in the first human trials.

11.1   Introduction

This chapter marks the point in the drug discovery pipeline where animal studies are used to gather all the information required to plan clinical trials in human subjects. Moving towards this stage is sometimes referred to as "entering the valley of death". This is not meant to convey sinister undertones about the outcomes of clinical trials, but to highlight the fact that many drugs fail to make it into full clinical development for reasons that will become clear later on.

Before discussing these reasons, it is assumed that a drug candidate is potent (ideally at the nanomolar level) and specific for its target. It should also have been subjected to *in vitro* and *in vivo* tests that show that the target is affected, ideally in a model of the disease. Manufacturing and formulation issues may also have been resolved at this early stage, but none of the preceding work guarantees that the drug candidate will become a medicine. For this to happen, the candidate must do the following:

- Get to the target
- Stay there for the required time
- Be eliminated sufficiently quickly to allow the next dose to be taken
- Be sufficiently stable, i.e. resistant to metabolism
- Be safe

E.D. Zanders, *The Science and Business of Drug Discovery: Demystifying the Jargon*, 203
DOI 10.1007/978-1-4419-9902-3_10, © Springer Science+Business Media, LLC 2011

The procedures used to check whether the drug fulfils these criteria come under the umbrella term preclinical development (which includes the scale-up and formulation reviewed in the previous chapter). Preclinical development is used to gather all the information needed to support a regulatory application for administering a drug to humans for the first time. This goal is known as first time in humans or FTIH.[1] The applications themselves are termed Investigational New Drug (IND) and Clinical Trial Authorisation (CTA) for the FDA and EMA, respectively.

Different animal species are used in preclinical development to examine the following:

- Pharmacodynamics
  The effect of the drug on the body
- Pharmacokinetics
  The effect of the body on the drug
- Safety pharmacology
  Any undesirable effect of drugs on body functions
- Toxicology
  Any undesirable effect of drugs on body structures

11.1.1 Basic Requirements

11.1.1.1 Good Laboratory Practice

Once a decision has been made to move a compound or a biological into full development, the precise demands of the regulatory agencies have to be met. Good manufacturing practice (GMP) has been mentioned already in this context, but laboratory procedures are also regulated. These come under the term, good laboratory practice or GLP. This is employed at the preclinical phase to ensure that clear, validated operating procedures are followed in the laboratory and that management structures have legal accountability. GLP procedures help to anticipate and respond to the accidental mislabelling of samples and other routine errors that can occur in any laboratory. Site inspections are carried out by the regulators to enforce GLP regulations, and the condition of all the apparatus and materials used in the lab is monitored and recorded to a much higher degree than that would be considered normal in a research laboratory. This high level of regulation exists because of the high stakes involved, both legal and ethical.

---

[1] This used to be "first time in man", but presumably changed to reflect modern social attitudes.

11.1.1.2 Harmonization of Procedures

The need to coordinate drug development activities in a globally consistent way has prompted governments and regulators to collaborate on a series of industry guidelines. The result of this collaboration is the International Conference on Harmonisation of Technical Requirements for Registration of Pharmaceuticals for Human Use (ICH) based in Geneva (ICH 2010). Some of the extensive documentation available on the ICH Web site is referred to in this and subsequent chapters; these guidelines provide detailed information on required procedures and a useful indication of the current thinking in the regulatory field. Despite these harmonization initiatives, there are still procedural variations between the different regulators. It is not possible to cover these differences in any detail, but the Web sites of the FDA and EMA contain a great deal of information about the entire regulatory process, from preclinical development to marketing authorization.

11.1.2 Preclinical Testing in Animals

All experimental drugs must, by law, be tested on animals prior to the administration to humans. This is an area of great controversy outside the drug discovery industry, since animal experimentation has tarnished the image of scientists for over 100 years. Many drug discovery scientists have become used to checking for bombs under their cars and working in highly secure environments. However, if we want to continue to produce drugs with any kind of safety profile, there is currently no alternative to using animals. Despite all the sophisticated knowledge and technologies at our disposal, it is still scientifically impossible to make exact predictions about how drugs will interact with the human body. While most, if not all, pharmaceutical industry scientists would be more than happy to dispense with animals altogether, the much discussed alternatives of *in vitro* tests and computer simulations are simply not acceptable substitutes for live animals at the present time. I have had personal experience with compounds that appeared to be safe and effective *in vitro*, being lethal when given to rodents. Obviously, this animal test had to be in place to ensure that the compound did not reach the clinic. In summary, few people in their right mind would risk taking a drug that had not been through at least some basic screening in animals.

Despite this somewhat forthright statement of current realities, there is undoubtedly a genuine need to minimize or eliminate the use of animals in preclinical development. This is not only to predict a drug's effect on humans as accurately as possible, but also to avoid ethical dilemmas and save costs.

One problem with testing drugs in animals is that the results do not always correlate with those obtained later in human subjects. This issue of concordance has been reviewed by drug discovery scientists, academics and regulators, who have surveyed human toxicities relating to 150 compounds (Olson et al. 2000). The toxicities were picked up in 71% of tests using rodents and non-rodents (63% non-rodents alone, 43% rodents alone). Of all toxicities detected in animals, 94% occurred within 1 month of testing.

These figures offer support for the continued use of animals in toxicology, but nobody can doubt that there is enormous room for improvement. Research in predictive toxicology is recognized as a high priority by both academia and industry. There are also umbrella groups, such as the National Centre for the Replacement, Refinement and Reduction of Animals in Research (NC3Rs), that were formed after a UK Government initiative. While *in vitro* and computer models have real potential to reduce the uncertainty in preclinical evaluation, there will be a need for a whole organism model for some years to come. Model organisms, like the zebrafish (described in Chap. 6), offer the possibility of a genuine compromise between the desire to avoid experiments on higher mammals and the need to use living organisms to screen for organ toxicity. Some of these new technologies are discussed later in this chapter.

11.1.2.1 Which Species Are Used?

The following table lists the animal species normally used for drug development. In the case of antibodies and other biologicals, which do not bind to non-primate tissues, there is no advantage to be gained by using animals, like mice and rats, so these species are not used (see Table 11.1).

11.1.3 The Preclinical Development Process

The commitment to take a lead compound or a biological through preclinical evaluation towards the first exposure to humans is not taken lightly. Even with a standard set of test packages, it can take up to 1 year to complete and show little change from 2 million dollars; this is assuming that no problems occur on the way. The tests are designed to establish that the dose of the drug affects the right target while at the

Table 11.1 List of animal species used in preclinical development

Animal	Comment
Rat	Commonly used small animal species
Mouse	Alternative to rats and used when compound is limiting
Dog	Commonly used large animal species
Rabbit	Used for reproduction toxicology
Hamster	Large rodent model used for oral dosing and carcinogenicity
Guinea pig	Used to test for allergic reactions
Pig (minipig)	Similar organ layout and skin to humans
Non-human primates	
Cynomolgus monkey	Most commonly used macaque for compounds/biologicals
Rhesus monkey	Used for biologicals and HIV drugs
Marmoset	Small primate, but more distant relative of humans

same time being safe enough to administer to human volunteers. The preclinical development process is now considered in some detail.

11.1.3.1 Pharmacodynamics

Initial investigations of the effect of the drug on the body will have already been undertaken in animal models of the disease; this should, in principle, give investigators some idea of the dose of drug that works against the target in patients. The amount of drug required for optimal activity in an animal model depends on different factors, including the number of drug targets in the animal and the strength of binding. To estimate how much drug would be required for human use, the dose must be scaled up from the dose in animals in proportion to the weight of the patient. A rat weighs about 150 g while an average human is 60 kg (and rising). This allometric scaling is not necessarily straightforward, however, as the pharmacodynamic response of the drug depends upon its fate in the body (pharmacokinetics, see below) and a number of other factors that influence the responses of human patients. These factors include the age of the patient and the pre-existing conditions which may be unrelated to the disease to be treated. Pharmacodynamics becomes an important issue in clinical trials and subsequent marketing, since different groups of patients can exhibit different responses to the drug.

11.1.3.2 Pharmacokinetics

The effect of the body on the drug is one of the most import go/no go areas in drug development. Pharmacokinetic analysis looks at the way in which compounds or biologicals are processed after they have been administered to animals. This gives some idea of the bioavailability of the compounds, and is also used to study potential interactions between different drugs or foodstuffs.

Terminology

- Drug metabolism pharmacokinetics (commonly referred to as DMPK)
  This refers to the chemical reactions in the body that modify an administered drug.
- Absorption, distribution, metabolism and excretion (commonly referred to as ADME)
  This covers the uptake of a drug into the circulation and its distribution within the body tissues, followed by its metabolism and then removal from the body.
- ADMET or ADMETox
  ADME packaged together with toxicology

11.1.3.3   How ADME Studies Are Carried Out?

Drug candidates are given to experimental animals intravenously and by mouth (if the compound is designed to be orally active). Biologicals are normally injected. Samples of blood are taken from the animal before drug administration and then at several time points thereafter so that the speed at which the drug enters and leaves the circulation can be measured. The laboratory procedures involve adding an anti-coagulant to blood, spinning out the cells in a centrifuge and analyzing the straw-coloured plasma by liquid chromatography coupled with mass spectrometry (LC-MS). The result is a precise measurement of the concentration of drug in the sample (more details are given later in Drug Metabolism). A simple pharmacokinetic experiment is shown in Fig. 11.1, where a compound is administered, either orally or intravenously, and plasma samples are taken over at different time points to measure the amount of drug in the circulation. Not surprisingly, intravenous administration gives the highest level of drug at an early time point; but with oral administration, there is a lag time before the drug enters the circulation.

The size and shape of these concentration curves provide a set of numbers that describe the ADME properties of the administered drug. Some of the important values are as follows:

- Cmax
  Maximum plasma concentration of the drug
- Tmax
  Time taken to achieve Cmax

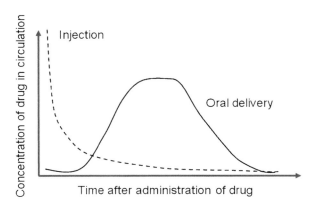

Fig. 11.1 Pharmacokinetics: Changes of drug concentration in the circulation over time. Blood samples are taken at regular time intervals after the drug is administered to the animal by oral and parenteral routes. The concentration of drug is measured in the plasma, and is plotted against time. The curves are characteristic of the different routes of administration and reflect both the uptake and elimination of the drug *in vivo*

- $T_{1/2}$
  Half life of the drug or the time taken for the drug to be reduced to 50% of its starting concentration

- AUC area under the curve
  AUC is used in non-compartmental analyses to estimate the total amount of drug administered. The area is calculated by using integration (mathematical formulae based on integral calculus). Compartmental analysis is potentially more accurate over different time points and uses terms, such as rate constants and other kinetic parameters. More detailed descriptions of the pharmacokinetic equations described in this section can be found in external sources of information about drug development. The information gained after measuring the above values in an animal model determine whether a drug candidate can progress through the remainder of the preclinical evaluation process. A candidate should ideally be well absorbed (by mouth if relevant), distributed evenly throughout the body and then eliminated in a timely way. The factors that influence each of these actions are now covered in turn:

Absorption

If a drug is to be taken by mouth, it must be absorbed through the stomach or small intestine. Drugs that are designed to treat CNS diseases must also cross the blood brain barrier; alternatively, some medicines (like the non-sedating antihistamines) are designed to not enter the brain.

Absorption through the gut is assessed in laboratory models that mimic the cells which control the movement of compounds across the human intestine. The industry standard model uses a human cell line (Caco-2), originally derived from a cancer of the colon. This line is grown as single sheets (monolayers) in a special apparatus that measures the amount of drug moving from one side of the layer to the other. A compound that is likely to be well absorbed in the living animal moves freely across the cell layers. These layers (and the human gut) are not just passive barriers, however; some compounds are driven across using energy provided by the cells, a process called active transport. Other compounds are literally pumped back out of the cells by a protein called P-glycoprotein (P-gp) which can be a major barrier to intestinal absorption. Some drugs, however, are inhibitors of P-gp and, therefore, have increased permeability through the gut wall. P-gp is part of a defence mechanism that has evolved to protect the body from noxious chemicals produced by outside sources (xenobiotics). It is a major contributor to the multidrug resistance that arises in cancer chemotherapy and, as a result, has been investigated as a drug target in its own right for many years.

Protein Binding

Drugs normally exert their effects on the tissues of the body after leaving the circulation, which is rich in plasma proteins, such as albumen (sometimes called human serum albumen or HSA). Many compounds bind to these plasma proteins, thereby reducing the amount of materials that is available for interaction with the drug target. Protein binding studies are, therefore, carried out to guide the selection of drug doses for later studies, since it may be necessary to use larger amounts of the drug in animals and the clinic if protein binding is high. Protein binding is measured in a laboratory process called ultrafiltration, which employs a plastic filter to separate small molecules bound to plasma proteins from those that are free in solution. High levels of protein binding do not necessarily preclude further development of a compound, however, since marketed medicines, such as diazepam and warfarin, show greater than 98% binding (Brunton et al. 2005).

Drug Metabolism

Cellular metabolism is controlled by enzymes which conduct a wide range of chemical reactions that build up or break down molecules of all sizes. This allows the cell to function as a living entity. Drug metabolism also uses cellular metabolism, but in a series of specialized chemical reactions that are designed to clear xenobiotic compounds from the body. As already outlined in Chap. 2, small molecule drugs pass from the stomach into the liver prior to reaching the general circulation. The liver is the primary site for drug metabolism, in which chemical transformations occur to produce a number of metabolites, which are closely related in structure to the administered drug. Sometimes, a metabolite has more biological activity than the parent compound, which can cause difficulties with dose estimation later on. The administered drug can actually be inactive until subjected to metabolism, in which case it is known as a prodrug; one example is acyclovir, which is used to treat *Herpes simplex* infections. Drug metabolism can be exploited in various ways, for example, by creating prodrugs that enter cells only after being modified by enzymes present in the target cell itself. Of course, there may be a downside to drug metabolism, particularly if the compound is rapidly broken down to an inactive form, or else produces a toxic metabolite.

The general scheme of drug metabolism is illustrated in Fig. 11.2. Compounds entering the liver are subjected to Phase I and Phase II metabolism by separate groups of enzymes.

Phase I reactions break down the compounds through oxidation or other chemical reactions. The enzymes that perform this task are from the cytochrome P450 family (shortened to CYP450). Drug conjugates are produced in Phase II reactions, where chemical groups are added to drugs as a type of sorting code that allows the compound to be directed towards elimination in either the faeces or urine. The enzymes have complex names and exist in multiple forms (isoforms) within a large family. The main examples are UDP-dependent glucuronosyl transferase (UGT), glutathione-S-transferase (GST) and phenol sulphotransferase (PST).

Fig. 11.2 Two phases of drug metabolism in the liver. Compounds entering the liver are subjected to a series of chemical reactions catalyzed by specialized enzymes, including the CYP450 system. Drugs and metabolites from phase I may be further modified by phase II enzymes that add chemical groups to produce conjugates. Polar (water soluble) metabolites and conjugates are excreted in the urine while non-polar compounds (soluble in the detergent-like bile produced by the gall bladder) are excreted in the faeces

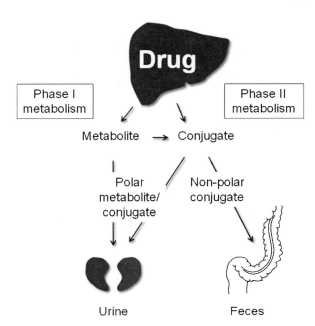

CYP450 Enzymes

The importance of these enzymes in drug development cannot be overemphasized, as they can have a profound impact upon the way different people respond to the same medicine (covered in Chap. 14). CYP450 enzymes are also responsible for the interactions that may occur when drugs are taken with particular foods or when more than one medicine is taken at the same time. Figure 11.3 shows the possible outcomes of a single drug interacting with CYP450 enzymes in the presence of another medicine or foodstuff.

In the first case, drug 1 inhibits a particular CYP450 enzyme that metabolizes drug 2, leading to a rise in the level of drug 2. This may either be beneficial or potentially dangerous due to toxicity. Alternatively, drug 1 might increase the level of the CYP450 in the liver (induces it) and, therefore, reduce the level of drug 2, again with potential benefits or downsides.

Some examples of drug or food interactions are given in Table 11.2.

Laboratory Evaluation of Drug Metabolism

Bioanalysis

The process of ADME evaluation depends on the ability to measure the concentrations of drugs and their metabolites in plasma and other body fluids, such as urine. The range of techniques available for this, which include chromatography and mass spectrometry, come under the heading of bioanalysis.

Fig. 11.3 The importance of CYP450 enzymes in drug interactions: (**a**) drug 1 inhibits a CYP450 making it less active on drug 2, so the latter is poorly metabolized and (**b**) drug 1 induces more CYP450 activity which then breaks down drug 2. The induction of CYP450 enzymes in the liver occurs over several days in contrast to inhibition which occurs more rapidly

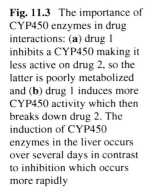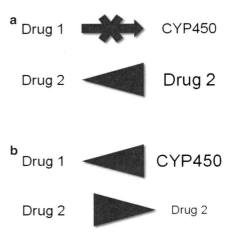

Table 11.2 Major CYP450 isoforms and some agents that affect them. More examples are given in Ogu and Maxa (2000)

CYP450	Comments
1A2	Inhibited by tobacco smoke
2C9	Inhibited by fluvastatin (Lescol®)
2C19	Induced by norethindrone (oral contraceptive)
2D6	Inhibited by fluoxetine (Prozac®)
3A4	Inhibited by grapefruit juice

Chromatography is used to separate molecules from complex mixtures. The name derived from the Greek means colour writing, so called because the first chromatography experiments, performed early in the twentieth century, separated mixtures of coloured substances, such as plant dyes. In order to separate compounds that are mixed together in a solution, the mixture is poured into a column (i.e. a tube made of glass, plastic or metal), which contains an insoluble material called a chromatography matrix. The matrix is chemically modified in such a way that different classes of molecules (both large and small) bind to it. This binding is reversible and dependent on the chemistry of the individual compounds, so each one can be successively eluted from the column and collected in separate tubes. The elution process can be monitored by continuously measuring a property, such as light absorbance, using a spectrophotometer (Chap. 9). The result is the display of a series of peaks on a graph, each peak representing a purified molecule. If the separated compounds have to be identified, they are subjected to standard analytical chemistry techniques, such as mass spectrometry. Normal liquid chromatography relies upon gravity to force the samples through simple columns for the separation. While this is acceptable for many applications, this method really lacks the sensitivity needed for the detection of minute quantities of drugs and metabolites in plasma. Instead, high pressure liquid chromatography (HPLC) is used for drug analysis. The principle is the same as normal chromatography, but high pressures are used to force small volumes of

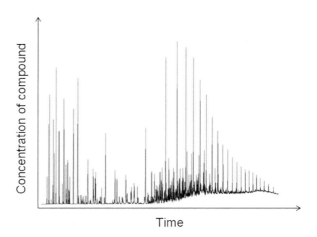

Fig. 11.4 An HPLC trace showing individual compounds, separated from a mixture, as sharp peaks on a graph. Each peak elutes at a very specific and reproducible time after the mixture has been applied to the HPLC column so that each peak can be identified by comparing the migration of standards, i.e. compounds whose identity is known

plasma through strong steel columns. Different types of matrices are packed into each column, according to the types of compounds to be analyzed. These matrices come under the general headings of ion exchange, reverse phase, size exclusion or hydrophobic supports. An example of an HPLC analysis is shown in Fig. 11.4.

In Vitro Metabolism

While the first metabolism studies on compounds are conducted on live animals *in vivo*, it is normal practice to assess the metabolic stability of drugs *in vitro* using human liver cells (hepatocytes). Although it is preferable to use isolated hepatocytes of humans, rather than those of animals, these are not always readily available, in which case, liver microsomes are used. These are isolated from the whole liver and contain the relevant enzymes for drug metabolism; unlike hepatocytes, they can be stored frozen in batches for use at any time. Microsomes from rat liver are often used for a preliminary metabolic screen, as human liver is less readily available.

Human microsomes are also used as a source of different CYP450 isoforms which vary in expression according to the genetic background of the donor. These isoforms contribute to the individual responses that patients have to particular medicines (see pharmacogenetics, Chap. 14). Some CYP450 enzymes are available as purified proteins, produced using the genetic engineering technology, thus obviating the need to use enzymes derived from human liver donors.

Drug Clearance

The final part of the ADME analysis is elimination, in which drugs are removed from the body via the liver and kidneys. The time taken for this to occur and the amount of compound that is cleared are both measured in at least two animal species. Drug clearance (Cl) is a measure of the efficiency by which a drug is removed from the plasma. Hepatic and renal clearance rates are defined as the volume of plasma that is cleared of drug after flowing for 1 min through the liver and kidneys, respectively. These rates depend upon a number of factors, including plasma flow and protein binding. The clearance rates of experimental compounds are classified as high, medium or low; those with high clearance rates are unlikely to be useful medicines, as they do not remain in the body for long enough to provide a useful therapeutic effect. On the other hand, drugs with low clearance rates could be difficult to control during regular dosing, as levels could exceed the required margins of safety.

11.1.4   Drug Safety

At the same time as ADME studies are being performed, the safety assessments are initiated and carried on through the rest of preclinical development. The main objective is to ensure that the amount of drug required to have a therapeutic effect is significantly lower than the amount that provokes a toxic reaction in the body. This difference, known as the therapeutic window, is illustrated in Fig. 11.5. The amount of drug that produces a toxic response must be determined in order to establish an important value, the No Adverse Effect Level or NOAEL. This value is used to calculate the dose of drug that is given to human volunteers (see later).

The results of drug safety studies provide information on effects on the following:

• The organ systems of the body
• The relationship between toxicity and exposure to the drug
• The dose dependence of the toxic effect
• The potential reversibility of the toxic effect

Fig. 11.5 Therapeutic window between drug efficacy and toxicity. Increasing amounts of drugs are administered to an animal or a human to measure the maximum therapeutic responses (i.e. desired change in disease symptoms, etc.) and then the point at which serious toxicity occurs. The difference in dose between the two gives a measure of the therapeutic window. It is obviously desirable to develop drugs with as wide a window as possible, although all drugs are toxic at some level

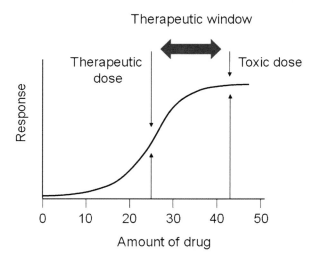

The remainder of this chapter covers the procedures used to assess drug toxicity and concludes by showing how all of the ADME Tox information is used to estimate the dose of a drug that is administered to human volunteers. Further information about each of the safety pharmacology and toxicology procedures is available from the ICH, through the detailed guidance documents on its Web site (ICH 2010).

11.1.4.1 Safety Pharmacology

Drug candidates are normally tested for their effects on all organ systems in experimental animals under the umbrella term, safety pharmacology (also known as secondary or general pharmacology). This is conducted under GLP guidelines where possible, and is run separately or as part of a general toxicology programme. Formal safety pharmacology is not required with drugs that are administered through the skin (dermally), into the eye (ocular) and with cytotoxic cancer drugs and biologicals that do not interact with non-primate tissues. Safety pharmacology studies are normally conducted in rats (or sometimes mice) and a large animal species, like dogs. In some cases, it may be necessary to use a non-human primate, such as the marmoset. Compounds are administered by the route expected to be used in the clinic, i.e. oral or intravenously, depending on the drug's bioavailability. The amount of drug delivered is normally a multiple of the anticipated clinical dose (ACD), or human equivalent dose (HED), which has been estimated from the ADME data and earlier disease models. In practice, the investigations may use 10, 30 and 100 times the ACD to create a wide margin of safety for the final dose estimation.

The safety pharmacology package is divided into a core battery, plus follow-up or secondary tests as summarized in Table 11.3.

Core Battery

This provides a first look at the effect of a compound on vital body functions, such as heart rate, respiration, blood pressure and nervous system function. This last category requires the use of a functional observation battery (FOB) or Irwin profile that is designed to monitor basic coordination, behaviour and nervous reflexes. The core battery studies require electronic instruments to measure the different parameters under investigation.

Table 11.3 Safety pharmacology tests according to ICH S7A guidelines (2011)

Core battery	Follow-up and supplemental studies
Central nervous system	Renal/urinary system
Cardiovascular system	Autonomic nervous system
Respiratory system	Gastrointestinal system

Follow-Up and Supplementary Tests

Sometimes, a class of compound or biological has safety issues associated with it; in this case, the core battery may be extended with follow-up studies. These provide more details about particular functions, such as blood pH, cardiac output and learning ability. Supplemental studies are also designed to observe the effects of drugs on organ systems that are not already covered by the core battery. These include a detailed analysis of urine, responses to nerve stimulation and secretion/transit times in the stomach and intestine.

Cardiac Rhythm and Q-T Interval

One of the most important safety issues relates to the effect of drugs on the rhythm of the heart. This is a complex area, but one that has to be carefully examined, as particular classes of drugs can induce *torsade de pointes*, a potentially fatal heart arrhythmia. This also occurs in a genetic condition, long Q-T syndrome, so called because the trace on an electrocardiogram (ECG) shows an increase in the distance between the Q and T peaks resulting from a delayed repolarization in the heart ventricle. The heart muscle is controlled by electrical signals that are conducted through ion channels (Chap. 6), one of which, a potassium (K^+) channel (called hERG), is implicated in the Q-T effect.[2] Safety pharmacology should, therefore, include *in vivo* evaluation of the heart function using ECG, as well as *in vitro* testing for the effect of drugs on the hERG channel in cell lines. Detailed guidance is given in ICH document S7B (2011).

11.1.4.2 Toxicology Package

While safety pharmacology covers the effect of drugs on major organ functions, there are a number of defined procedures that must be carried out as part of a toxicology package (see ICH M3(R2) (2011)). These include detailed analyses of animal tissues taken *post mortem*, as well as studies on the potential of drugs to cause birth defects or cancer. Firstly, however, there is a need to determine the toxicokinetics of a drug by dosing up to the maximum level tolerated by the animal.

---

[2] The naming of hERG is a good example of the sense of humour exhibited by scientists working with model organisms. The name means human ether-à-go-go-related gene originally found in the fruit fly, Drosophila (Kaplan and Trout 1969). When mutant flies were given ether (as part of a normal laboratory analysis), their legs began to shake in the same way as dancers at the Whisky à Go Go nightclub in Los Angeles.

Acute- and Repeat-Dose Toxicity Studies

Acute dosing of different amounts of compound will have already been performed in rats as part of the safety pharmacology process. This helps to determine the maximum tolerated dose (MTD) of the drug, which could be administered at up to 1,000 mg/kg per animal. While acute toxicology is not seen to be particularly valuable if chronic studies are going to be undertaken anyway, it can be used on its own for testing drugs that are administered to volunteers at very low doses in exploratory clinical trials (Chap. 12).

A chronic repeat-dose study is undertaken in two species (rat, dog or rat, primate), run under GLP conditions, to provide enough regulatory information for human trials. In addition to taking measurements of body weight and food consumption, investigators have to analyze the body tissues and fluids of each dosed animal in great detail. Over forty tissues are examined using histology (Chap 6), adding to the enormous amount of experimental data that will already have been accumulated during preclinical development.

The exact duration of the repeat-dose study depends on the envisaged duration of the clinical trial. These ICH guidelines are shown in Table 11.4.

Genetic Toxicology (Genotox)

If a drug causes physical damage to DNA, it may result in harmful mutations and, possibly, cancer. Since this is a real concern in drug development, a key part of the toxicology package involves screening drug candidates to identify those compounds which may be genotoxic or mutagenic. A "Standard Battery" of tests is employed, involving the use of bacteria, animal cells and whole animals, as described in ICH S2(R1) (2011).

Bacterial Ames Test

This assay was devised by the American scientist, Bruce Ames, to monitor the damage to DNA in *Salmonella typhimurium*. A particular strain of this bacterium is selected

Table 11.4 ICH recommendations for the duration of repeat dose toxicity trials in animals according to the clinical trial design

Maximum duration of clinical trial	Minimum duration of repeated-dose toxicity studies to support clinical trials	
	Rodents	Non-rodents
Up to 2 weeks	2 weeks	2 weeks
2 weeks to 6 months	Same as clinical trial	Same as clinical trial
>6 months	6 months	9 months

to grow on agar plates (Chap. 4) only when the amino acid histidine is present in the growth medium. This is the result of a genetic mutation in the bacterial DNA that prevents it from producing its own histidine. To test for genotoxicity, the bacteria are spread onto plates that lack histidine and then incubated with test compounds. If a compound is mutagenic, it will alter the bacterial DNA and reverse the histidine mutation, so the bacteria can then grow independently of this amino acid. The number of bacterial colonies that appear on the plate is related to the degree of genotoxicity. This assay is a useful primary screen for compounds, and is also used to check for drug metabolites that may themselves be mutagenic. In this case, liver microsomes (see earlier) are added to the bacteria, along with the test compound, to metabolize the drug *in situ*.

Mouse Lymphoma Assay

While the Ames test is an important first screen for genotoxic compounds, it is important to confirm any positive results using animal cells, the most widely used being the mouse lymphoma L5178Y$^{tk+/-}$ cell line. This line has a mutation in the thymidine kinase (tk) gene that causes the cells to die if they are grown in the presence of the synthetic compound, trifluorothymidine. Using the same principle as the Ames test, any drugs that damage DNA reverse the tk mutation and allow the cells to grow in the presence of the toxic compound. Instead of counting bacterial colonies on a plate, the mouse cells are counted in a liquid culture medium.

11.1.4.3 *In Vivo* Micronucleus Assay

In addition to causing DNA damage, genotoxic compounds also damage chromosomes (i.e. they are clastogenic). This can be seen not only directly by examining chromosomes under a microscope, but also indirectly by using the micronucleus assay. A test drug is administered to rats or mice, and their bone marrow cells are removed for examination under a microscope. Under normal conditions, blood cells are produced in the bone marrow by cell division and then become mature red blood cells after expelling a nucleus (these cells are the only ones in the body that do not have this structure). If any damage to chromosomes occurs during this division process, the cells release small fragments, called micronuclei, which can then be counted under a microscope.

Carcinogenicity

While the tests outlined in the previous sections are useful for the screening of potentially genotoxic compounds, they are conducted over a short time frame and cannot fully mimic the chronic administration of a drug to humans. Long-term carcinogenicity studies (18–24 months) are, therefore, undertaken in mice and rats of both sexes, using compounds at the maximum tolerated dose. Since this time frame is longer than the preclinical development phase, these "lifetime studies" provide further safety information while the drug candidate is proceeding through clinical trials. There is some debate about the usefulness of using both mice and rats over this time period; as a result, a number of more sophisticated models of carcinogenesis are being evaluated by the regulators (see ICH S1A, S1B, S1C(R2) accessed through links for ICH S1 A-C guidelines (2011)).

Reproductive Toxicology (Reprotox)

The thalidomide tragedy focused minds on the teratogenic potential of drugs, i.e. their potential to cause birth defects. This area of reproductive toxicology is clearly important not only for women of childbearing age, but also for men, whose fertility may be affected by experimental drugs. As with carcinogenicity studies, Reprotox is conducted in parallel with clinical development and requires only some basic information on embryonic development in animal studies prior to first human trials (for guidelines, see ICH S5(R2) (2011)).

Studies on the effects of drugs on embryo development (embryotoxicology) are often undertaken in rats and rabbits, where all aspects of embryonic development are studied from conception to birth. For male fertility, sperm samples are obtained from rodents during chronic toxicology studies.

Safety Tests for Biologicals

Most of the drug candidates passing through safety pharmacology and toxicology are small molecules, rather than biotherapeutics, such as antibodies, nucleic acids and vaccines. Safety assessment is of paramount importance for these latter drug types as well, but many, like antibodies, are agents which interact specifically with human targets. This means that many biotherapeutics do not bind to body components in animals other than those derived from the primate family (which consists of monkeys, apes and humans). The degree of crossreactivity between species is assessed at an early stage in order to select the appropriate animal species for toxicology. The scale of these tests is often limited, however, by the need to restrict the use of non-human primates. The ICH guidelines, S6 (2011) and S6 (R1) (2011), cover the safety evaluation of biologicals and include the requirement to test forimmunogenicity and local tolerance. Immunogenicity is the degree to which the drug provokes an antibody response in the animal (which has already been mentioned in Chap. 8), and is covered in ICH S8 (2011). Local tolerance is the response to the administration of the biotherapeutic at the site of injection. Some inflammation may occur, depending on the formulation used or through the possibility that drugs designed to modify the immune system may provoke inflammation through some unanticipated mechanism. Reproductive toxicology may have to be undertaken in a non-human primate, but, for practical reasons, these are more limited than the equivalent rodent or rabbit studies. Finally, genotoxicity and carcinogenicity are evaluated according to practical circumstances. Some biologicals may be inherently unable to damage DNA or cause cancer, but others, like nucleic acids, may do so. These have to be assessed on a case-by-case basis.

11.1.4.4 New Technology

Preclinical safety evaluation is time consuming, expensive and not always predictive of later problems. A number of drugs have been withdrawn from sale over recent years because of fatal adverse reactions in a number of patients; examples include the antidiabetic drug Rezulin® and the statin Baycol®. These considerations, including the need to reduce and replace animals where possible, have driven research into finding better ways of predicting toxicity. There is no shortage of ideas in this field, but the demands of formal regulations make it difficult to introduce new technologies into the standard battery of procedures. Any variation in the existing methodology has to be rigorously tested before being acceptable to the regulatory authorities. A review of recent ICH guidelines, however, does show that new technologies, such as transgenic animals, are being recognized as potentially useful, and a forward-looking approach by the FDA and others will help. A brief mention is now made of some promising new approaches to toxicology.

Toxicogenomics

Genomics and microarrays have already been introduced in Chap. 6. These technologies allow researchers to measure the (mRNA) expression of many thousands of genes in parallel and provide information about cellular function in health and disease. Toxicogenomics employs microarrays to measure gene expression in the liver, kidneys and other target organs, after administering a drug to experimental animals, such as rats. Animals dosed with different drugs and toxins display the characteristic patterns of gene expression (gene expression signatures) that relate to the type of compound administered. This means that signatures from known toxins can be identified and used to flag up a warning if an experimental drug shows a similar pattern. This is illustrated in Fig. 11.6 using the data from a study by Ovando and colleagues at the University of Buffalo (Ovando et al. 2010). They examined gene expression signatures from the livers of rats treated with dioxin-like compounds (DLCs), the aim being to unravel the mode of action of these environmental toxins. These signatures are often displayed as "heat maps", in which the level of expression of individual genes is represented by rectangles that are coloured according to whether the gene is up or downregulated in response to chemicals. In this example, the two DLCs, TCDD and PCB126, give signatures that are completely distinct from the non-DLC compound PCB153 that does not cause liver toxicity.

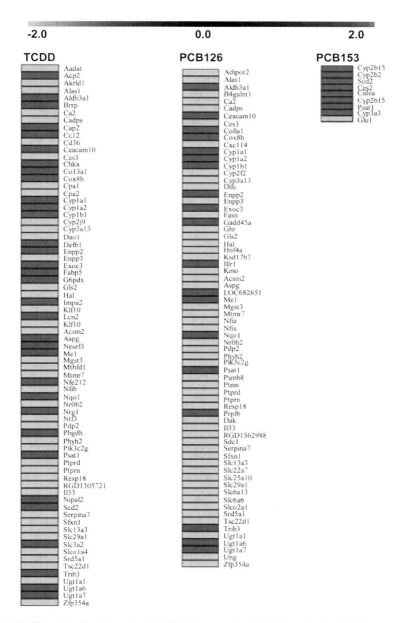

Fig. 11.6   Heat map showing upregulated (*dark rectangles*) and downregulated (*light rectangles*) rat liver genes measured after the exposure of animals to three compounds, the first two of which cause liver damage. From Ovando et al. (2010) under open access

This toxicogenomics approach encompasses protein and metabolite expression, as well as mRNA, but it is vital that the laboratory model accurately reflects the situation in human beings. For example, rats are used for many of these experiments, including the example above, but they still belong to a different species. Even if human cells are used for *in vitro* tests, they are still cultured under highly artificial conditions. In real life, a given cell type is associated with other cell types within a three-dimensional matrix; many attempts are being made to recreate this complexity in the laboratory as a step towards producing a fully predictive and reproducible test system.[3] Much of this research is being undertaken by consortia of regulators, biopharmaceutical companies and academics and should provide valuable data to support the modernization of preclinical toxicology.

Zebrafish

While the small model organism, *Danio rerio*, has already been described as a model organism for drug target discovery, it is attracting a great deal of attention as a possible alternative to large animal toxicology. The fish has a small transparent embryo that rapidly develops the organs found in conventional test species. The zebrafish heart, for example, has a very similar structure to that found in mammals and can even be monitored by ECG. Compounds that damage the mammalian heart also damage this organ in zebrafish embryos; this damage can be directly visualized under the microscope, even while the fish is alive. Despite many unanswered questions about the suitability of zebrafish for toxicology screening in a regulated drug development environment, this organism appears to be one of the most promising alternatives to traditional rodent toxicology. Companies have been set up to provide compound screening services in zebrafish to large biopharmaceutical companies (Phylonix 2010); at some point in the future, there should be a clear answer to the question of how effective these model organisms are in predicting human toxicity.

11.1.5 Estimating the Dose for First Time in Humans

The data gained from the studies described in this chapter are used to estimate the maximum recommended starting dose (MRSD) for human volunteers. This is not a straightforward area, since drugs differ from each other in their potential toxicity and other properties, so a single method of calculating this dose is not ideal. There is a danger that the starting dose could be underestimated, so there is little chance of a therapeutic effect once the drug enters patients; equally, of course, there is a danger

---

[3] A recent article describes an "organ on a chip" that mimics the function of the human lung and provides a proof-of-principle for creating other artificial tissues that could be used in toxicology (Huh et al. 2010).

that unforeseen toxicities emerge in humans if the dose is set too high. This is why biopharmaceutical companies are investigating different ways of making the MRSD prediction as accurate as possible for the full range of compounds and biologicals that are being submitted for clinical trials. One approach is to use mathematical techniques to provide more refined estimates of pharmacokinetic and pharmacodynamic data (this is known as pharmacometric analysis). The FDA document, "Estimating the Maximum Safe Starting Dose in Initial Clinical Trials for Therapeutics in Adult Healthy Volunteers" 2005, provides guidance on how to select the dosage for humans (FDA Guidance for Industry 2005). The process is summarized as a flow chart in Fig. 11.7.

The first step is the calculation of an HED based on the dose used in animal models for safety pharmacology and toxicology. The animal dose is determined as the NOAEL or the maximum amount of drug (in mg/kg) that produces no adverse effect (a NOEL is a no-effect level, which is different).[4] It has been suggested that a comparison between human and animal doses is best made by comparing body surface area rather than weight, so NOAEL can also be converted to mg/m^2. Each animal species requires a different conversion factor as shown in Table 11.5.

Fig. 11.7 Calculation of the maximum recommended starting dose (MRSD) for human clinical trials based on preclinical animal data. The No Adverse Effect Level (NOAEL) is used as the starting point to generate a human equivalent dose (HED) that is then divided by a safety factor to derive the MRSD

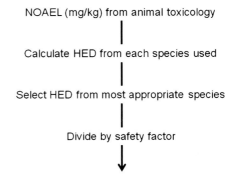

NOAEL (mg/kg) from animal toxicology

Calculate HED from each species used

Select HED from most appropriate species

Divide by safety factor

Maximum recommended starting dose (MRSD)

Table 11.5 Figure used to divide NOAEL value to obtain an equivalent dose in humans

Species	Conversion factor
Mouse	12.3
Hamster	7.4
Rat	6.2
Rabbit	3.1
Dog	1.8
Cynomolgous monkey	3.1

---

[4]The acronyms can be quite amusing, for example, SNARL – "suggested no adverse response level".

Once an HED value has been calculated for each animal species used (e.g. rat and dog), the lowest value is used in combination with a safety factor to calculate the final dose. The safety factor is normally 1/10 of the HED, although this can vary according to the particular class of drug under investigation. Once the MRSD has been estimated, the time comes for preclinical development to end and make way for the lengthy clinical development process.

Summary of Key Points

Preclinical development is used to assess the potential suitability of a compound or a biological as a medicine prior to testing in humans.

Pharmacodynamics and pharmacokinetics relate to the effect of the drug on the body and the body on the drug, respectively.

Pharmacokinetics is reflected in the ADME properties of the drug.

Toxicology is undertaken with a standard series of tests, including safety pharmacology, acute- and repeat-dose studies.

The toxicology data help to determine the maximum dose of drug that can be given to human volunteers.

References

Brunton L, Lazo J, Parker K (2005) Goodman & Gilman's The Pharmacological Basis of Therapeutics. McGraw-Hill, Columbus, OH, USA

FDA Guidance for Industry (2005) Estimating the Maximum Safe Starting Dose in Initial Clinical Trials for Therapeutics in Adult Healthy Volunteers. http://www.fda.gov/downloads/Drugs/GuidanceComplianceRegulatoryInformation/Guidances/ucm078932.pdf. Accessed 25 Nov 2010

Huh D et al (2010) Reconstituting organ-level lung functions on a chip. Science 328:1662–1668

ICH (2010) www.ich.org. Accessed 24 Nov 2010

ICH M3(R2) (2011). http://www.ich.org/fileadmin/Public_Web_Site/ICH_Products/Guidelines/Safety/M3_R2/Step4/M3_R2__Guideline.pdf. Accessed 16 Jan 2011

ICH S2(R1) guideline (2011). http://www.ich.org/fileadmin/Public_Web_Site/ICH_Products/Guidelines/Safety/S2_R1/Step2/S2_R1__Guideline.pdf. Accessed 16 Jan 2011

ICH S5(R2) guidelines (2011). http://www.ich.org/fileadmin/Public_Web_Site/ICH_Products/Guidelines/Safety/S5_R2/Step4/S5_R2__Guideline.pdf. Accessed 16 Jan 2011

ICH S6 (R1) guideline (2011). http://www.ich.org/fileadmin/Public_Web_Site/ICH_Products/Guidelines/Safety/S6_R1/Step2/S6_R1_Step2_Guideline.pdf. Accessed 16 Jan 2011

ICH S6 guideline (2011). http://www.ich.org/fileadmin/Public_Web_Site/ICH_Products/Guidelines/Safety/S6_R1/Step4/S6_Guideline.pdf. Accessed 16 Jan 2011

ICH S7A guideline (2011). http://www.ich.org/fileadmin/Public_Web_Site/ICH_Products/Guidelines/Safety/S7A/Step4/S7A_Guideline.pdf. Accessed 16 Jan 2011

ICH S7B guideline (2011). http://www.ich.org/fileadmin/Public_Web_Site/ICH_Products/Guidelines/Safety/S7B/Step4/S7B_Guideline.pdf. Accessed 16 Jan 2011

ICH S8 guideline (2011). http://www.ich.org/fileadmin/Public_Web_Site/ICH_Products/Guidelines/Safety/S8/Step4/S8_Guideline.pdf. Accessed 16 Jan 2011

Kaplan WD, Trout WE (1969) The behavior of four neurological mutants of Drosophila. Genetics 61:399–409

Links for ICH S1 A-C guidelines (2011). http://www.ich.org/products/guidelines/safety/article/safety-guidelines.html. Accessed 16 Jan 2011

Ogu GC, Maxa JL (2000) Drug interactions due to cytochrome P450. Proc Bayl Univ Med Cent 13:421–423

Olson H et al (2000) Concordance of the toxicity of pharmaceuticals in humans and in animals. Regul Toxicol Pharmacol 32:56–67

Ovando BJ et al (2010) Toxicogenomic analysis of exposure to TCDD, PCB126 and PCB153: identification of genomic biomarkers of exposure to AhR ligands. BMC Genomics 11:583–598

Phylonix (2010). http://www.phylonix.com/. Accessed 25 Nov 2010

Part III
The Drug Development Pipeline:
Clinical Trials to Marketing Authorization

Chapter 12
Clinical Trials

Abstract This chapter outlines the different phases of clinical trials, starting with phase I human volunteer studies through to phase III studies using large numbers of patients. The overview includes case histories of a phase I and a phase III trial to illustrate their design and implementation. Also covered are the regulatory applications for the first time in human studies.

12.1 Introduction

The drug discovery process moves towards its culmination in the clinic. This is the ultimate proof of concept for a new drug; does it work in patients? This chapter describes the different clinical trial phases that lead from initial studies of a drug in volunteers to its evaluation in patients with a specific disease. Also covered are the key regulatory applications that have to be approved before a drug is administered to humans for the first time (later applications to market the drug are covered in the next chapter). Like many other aspects of drug development, there are variations in procedures that apply to individual types of medicines, diseases or patient population. This means that some trials do not neatly fit into a particular phase; late-stage cancer patients, for example, may be treated in a phase I study that looks for efficacy, as well as for drug safety and tolerability.

A great deal of information about the conduct and regulation of clinical trials is available on the Web sites of the FDA and ICH (FDA clinical trials links 2010; ICH Guidelines Efficacy topics 2011); further information is available from trials managed by the NIH's ClinicalTrials.gov (2010) and the World Health Organization's International Clinical Trials Registry Platform (ICTRP) (2010).

Clinical trials are conducted in different phases as listed in Table 12.1.

Table 12.1 Phases of clinical testing human subjects

Clinical Phase	Comment	Timescale
Phase 0	Preclinical pharmacokinetics using humans instead of animals	Weeks
Phase I	Dose-ranging study in human volunteers	Weeks
Phase II	Testing drug in up to approximately 100 patients for proof of concept	Months
Phase III	Testing drug in 100s to 1,000s of patients over a longer period	Years
Phase IV	Postmarketing studies	Years
Phase V	Postmarketing surveillance	Years
Application		
IND	Investigational New Drug – FDA	Pre phase I
CTA	Clinical Trial Application – EMA	Pre-phase I
NDA	New Drug Application – FDA	During phase III
MAA	Marketing Authorization Application – MAA	During phase III
REMS	Risk Evaluation and Mitigation Strategy – FDA	During phase III

Applications are documents required by the regulatory authorities at different stages of clinical development

12.2   Preparation for Clinical Testing

Information about the pharmacokinetics, pharmacodynamics and safety of experimental drugs will have already been gained from animal models; this information is used to guide the selection of a dose that will be used in the first time in human (FTIH) studies. ADME studies are now repeated by clinical pharmacologists, using human volunteers instead of animals, to provide information that supports further clinical development of the drug. The clinical department is responsible for establishing the clinical endpoint of a trial. Some diseases, like migraine, have a clear manifestation that can be measured – in this case, headache and visual disturbances. Other conditions, however, may have to be measured indirectly, using surrogate endpoints, such as lowering of blood glucose for diabetes or reduction of pathogen levels in infectious diseases. This area of surrogates and biomarkers is discussed later in the book.

12.2.1   Good Clinical Practice

Unsurprisingly, clinical trials are highly regulated, so they are subject to harmonization and quality control rules in the same way as manufacturing and laboratory analysis (see ICH E6 (R1) (2011)). Good clinical practice (GCP) is required for the design, implementation and reporting of drug trials on human subjects, who must be treated with the ethical considerations required by the Declaration of Helsinki.

This declaration was drawn up by the World Medical Association (WMA) in 1964 to act as a set of guidelines for physicians wishing to conduct research on human subjects. Some of the main requirements for GCP as applied to clinical trials are listed below:

- Adherence to ethical standards
- Careful analysis of risk/benefit
- Informed consent of patients
- Fully qualified personnel
- Review by the Institutional Review Board (IRB) or Independent Ethics Committee
- Clear reporting of data
- Materials produced under GMP conditions

12.2.2   Terminology

Some basic terms are now listed, before moving on to the design and implementation of clinical trials:

- SAD – single ascending dose
- MAD – multiple ascending dose
- Randomization

The random assignment of patients into different treatment groups

- Stratification

  The separation of patient types into categories (e.g. male and female)

- Placebo

  Literally, "I shall please". A dummy pill, capsule or injectable formulation, designed to look and taste identical to the drug compound. Placebos are used in all clinical trial phases to counteract the powerful placebo effect that can profoundly influence the outcome of some trials.

- Active comparator

  Instead of using a placebo, which gives no benefit to the patient, a medicine that is commonly used for the condition under investigation may be used. This active comparator, or active control, is being increasingly used in clinical trials which would previously have been designed with placebo arms.

- Blinded trial

  – Single: A trial in which the subject does not know whether they are taking drug or placebo, but the clinical investigator does.
  – Double: A trial in which both the subject and the investigator do not know which is placebo and which is drug (obviously, a third party has to know!).

- Open label study
  An unblinded trial in which patients know which medicine they are taking. This can be used for comparing different doses, very similar drugs or for situations where placebos would be inappropriate (e.g. in advanced disease or where a suitable active comparator is available).

- Crossover trial
  A trial in which one group receives placebo and the other the drug for a certain time period, after which the treatment is reversed. In this way, placebo-controlled groups should improve after transfer to drug, and the clinical improvement should cease when drug group is given the placebo. These trials can be double-blinded to add further objectivity to the clinical assessment.

- Adaptive clinical trial
  Adaptive trials are a comparatively recent initiative, in which a study may be modified in mid-stream as a result of early clinical results. This could mean changing the dose of the drug or the number of patients in the trial.

- Bridging study
  A study performed in a new marketing region or population (e.g. paediatric or geriatric) to provide data on safety and efficacy that can be related to the pre-existing clinical trial information. This may be necessary if there are significant differences in pharmacokinetics between these different groups.

- Washout period
  Before new drugs are administered to clinical trial subjects, any pre-existing medicines should be cleared from the body (unless part of the trial). The time period that is set by the clinical trial organizers is called the washout period.

- Adverse event (AE)
  An untoward symptom or a laboratory finding that occurs after drug administration and which may not be necessarily caused by the treatment. A Serious Adverse Event (SAE) may result in death or major disability. The Medical Dictionary for Regulatory Activities (MeDRA) is used as a standard reference for describing adverse events.

- Adverse Drug Reaction (ADR)
  All unintended and noxious responses to a drug administered at any dose. A serious ADR may result in death or major disability.

- Sponsor
  Any company or organization, such as clinician networks, that finances and organizes a clinical trial. If a trial is sponsored by a Contract Research Organization (CRO) working under contract (e.g. to a biopharmaceutical company), then ultimate legal responsibility lies with the latter organization. The sponsor is also required to take out insurance as an indemnity against claims due to the trial itself, but this does not cover medical malpractice.

- Investigator
  The individuals who actually perform the trial; their leader is called the Principal Investigator.

12.2.3 Regulatory Requirements Before First Human Exposure

Before a drug can be administered to humans for the first time, a set of documents must be drawn up for submission to the regulatory authorities. In the USA, these are specified in Section 21, part 312 of the Code of Federal Regulations (CFR) and form the Investigational New Drug (IND) application. In the European Union (EU), the regulations come under Directive 2001/20/EC of the European Commission and form the Clinical Trial Application (CTA). In case there is any doubt about the seriousness with which these regulations are viewed, a few dishonest clinicians have found themselves in prison for misleading the authorities.

Although there are some differences between the IND and CTA applications, essentially the same type of information is required for both, so the IND is used here as a representative example of a formal application for FTIH trials.

12.2.3.1 The Investigational New Drug Application

This application (submitted to the FDA) is a key set of documents which support the case for trialling an experimental drug in human subjects. It may also support the use of an existing drug for another indication (i.e. disease). Since the application consists of over 2,000 pages, it will take several months to compile prior to submission. The main categories (apart from administrative details) are listed as follows:

Introductory Statement and General Investigational Plan

This includes the name, formula and nature of the drug, as well as its formulation, routes of administration and dosage. Also submitted is a general plan for how the trial is going to be conducted and whether there are any known risks associated with the drug.

Investigator's Brochure

This contains a summary of the drug and its formulation as well as the pharmacokinetic, pharmacodynamic and toxicology data gathered to date. It also describes possible side effects and any special monitoring required during the trial.

Protocols

Descriptions of how the studies are going to be carried out, with more details required as the trials progress through different phases. All aspects of patient recruitment, monitoring procedures and flexibility in study design are covered, including the formal qualifications of the proposed investigators.

Chemistry, Manufacturing and Control (CMC) Information

This contains detailed information about the chemical nature of the drug and its purity as well as the associated excipients and the placebos used in the trial. The drug must also be tested for stability over at least the duration of the trials. At present, the FDA does not require GMP quality for phase I, unlike the EMA, but this may change with harmonization.

Pharmacology and Toxicology Information

This not only requires the relevant ADMET and other laboratory data, but also the names, qualifications and locations of the individuals who evaluated it.

Previous Human Experience with the Investigational Drug

The drug may have been already marketed, in the USA or elsewhere, and have background information on safety which should be submitted.

Additional Information

Information on abuse potential, use in children or use of radioactive drugs, all fall into this category.

The application is normally reviewed within 1 or 2 months and, if approved, the first clinical trial can then commence.

12.3   Clinical Trial Phases

12.3.1   Phase 0 (Microdosing)

As mentioned in Chap. 11, the animal models used for ADMET in the preclinical development are not always predictive of human reactions to the drug. One possibility, therefore, is to administer very small doses of compound or biological to human volunteers in order to obtain valuable pharmacokinetic data before committing large resources to a phase I trial. This is called microdosing or phase 0. A microdose is a maximum of 100 µg of drug, or less than one hundredth of the dose required to generate a pharmacological effect. Preclinical toxicology requirements are, therefore, limited to single-dose administration to animals without the need for genetic toxicology; this means that preclinical development times can be cut from 1 year to about 4 months and involve considerably less effort. Since the drug is present at a very low concentration in the human plasma, it is tagged with trace amounts of carbon 14 (^{14}C) that can be detected and measured using accelerator mass spectrometry (AMS). This highly sensitive technique is used for carbon dating of archaeological samples and, because the amount of radioactivity in the drug is too low to detect, does not require special regulatory approval. The potential value of microdosing in early clinical development has been recognized by the FDA and EMA, as well as through initiatives, such as European Microdosing AMS Partnership Programme (EUMAPP) (2011). Although microdosing is not yet a routine part of drug development, there is no doubt that it may become more commonplace as biopharmaceutical companies gain confidence in the ability of the technique to provide an accurate picture of drug disposition in the human body.

12.3.2   Phase I: Human Pharmacology

A typical phase I trial is conducted with up to 100 human volunteers assembled at a hospital or specialized contract research unit. The objective of such trials is to assess the maximum dose of experimental drug that can be safely tolerated and to ensure that there is a sufficiently high concentration in the plasma to generate a pharmacological effect in patients. These volunteer trials are not usually designed to look for clinical effects (they generally use healthy people after all), but there may be a pharmacodynamic effect that can provide the encouragement to commit resources to phase II trials. Some trials of vaccines, anticancer agents and other situations where efficacy must be rapidly determined are often reported as Phase Ib trials or Phase I/II.

12.3.2.1   Phase I: Case History

To give an idea of how phase I trials operate in practice, this example is taken from the trial of a compound designed to increase the number of platelets in the blood of patients with disease or undergoing chemotherapy (Jenkins et al. 2007). Platelets are the small cell-like bodies in blood that aggregate together to form clots, so reduced platelet counts can increase bleeding times. The GlaxoSmithKline drug, eltrombopag or SB-497115,[1] is a small molecule agonist for the thrombopoietin receptor on platelets. Preclinical work established that the compound worked with human cells *in vitro* and also increased the number of platelets when given orally to chimpanzees.

---

[1]The code can indicate where the compound was originally developed. In this case, SB means SmithKlineBeecham.

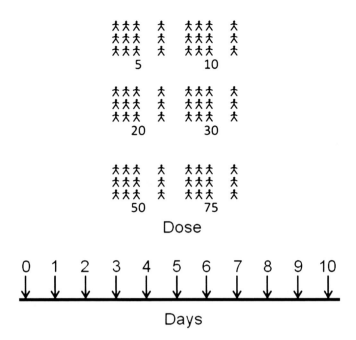

Fig. 12.1 Study design of phase I clinical trial of eltrombopag. Each group of nine volunteers was given the drug at the indicated doses (in mg/kg). Three individuals receiving placebos were added to each group. Drugs or placebos were given daily over ten days with blood and urine sampled at regular intervals

Phase I studies were performed with male volunteers in a London hospital after full ethical approval had been obtained in advance. Volunteers were pre-screened for the existing conditions that might affect blood clotting or related phenomena; the mean age, height and weight of the volunteers were 27.5 years, 1.8 m and 79.8 kg, respectively. The placebo-controlled trial design is illustrated in Fig. 12.1.

Six groups of twelve subjects were assigned daily oral doses of eltrombopag, from 5 to 75 mg in capsules; nine received the drug and three a placebo. The study was blinded so that only the subjects did not know whether they were receiving drug or placebo. Safety assessments (ECGs, blood and urine chemistry and reporting of adverse events) were made throughout the trial. Blood and urine samples were taken at regular intervals during the treatment and analyzed for drug levels while platelet numbers were monitored in the blood. In this way, the phase I study was used to study pharmacokinetics (by looking at drug levels) as well as pharmacodynamics (increases in platelet numbers). The results of the trial indicted that the pharmacokinetics were consistent with the animal data, since the drug was orally bioavailable and increased in concentration in proportion to the dose given. Furthermore, the dose-dependent rise in the number of platelets showed that the drug was working in the expected way. No safety issues were reported that could be related to the medication and the small numbers of AEs, such as headache or tiredness were independent of drug dose or placebo.

12.3.2.2 Dealing with the Unexpected

Most phase I trials proceed without any serious adverse reactions, but one trial, conducted in 2006 with a therapeutic antibody, nearly cost the lives of six volunteers. This was an almost unique occurrence, but it revealed gaps in a regulatory process that is more geared towards conventional small molecules than the newer biological drugs. The antibody in question, TGN1412, was unusual in that it was an agonist, rather than antagonist, for receptors on the surface of lymphocytes (almost all therapeutic antibodies inhibit or destroy cells rather than stimulate them). TGN1412 was designed to direct the immune system to destroy cancer cells or to rebalance it to stop the progression of autoimmune diseases like rheumatoid arthritis. The preclinical development of the antibody, conducted in cynomolgous and rhesus monkeys, showed that the antibody reacted positively with the blood cells in these species without causing any toxicity. The NOAEL level (Chap. 11) was determined to be 50 mg/kg, so 1/500th of this dose was selected for a trial with six volunteers (plus two on placebo). The trial was run in a clinical trials unit, within a London hospital, and planned in such a way that the remote possibility of a cytokine storm could be dealt with by having drugs and other interventions on standby. Unfortunately, within hours, the volunteers suffered fever, low blood pressure and other symptoms of septic shock, which had to be controlled in an intensive care unit. This outcome was entirely unexpected, given the conventional safety assessment of the drug, but it caused enormous suffering as well as the demise of the small company that developed the medicine. Another consequence was the re-evaluation by the regulators of how biologicals are tested in phase I trials; this policy change was based on an expert report sponsored by the British Government (Duff 2006). For example, the dose of TGN1412 was clearly too high, despite the preclinical results in monkeys, so the dose selection criteria would have to be modified if potentially dangerous agonist antibodies are to be tested again; furthermore, all six volunteers received the drug at the same time, so it would be sensible to dose each one sequentially to minimize the number that could suffer serious adverse reactions.

12.3.3 Phase II: Exploratory

Once a compound, or a biological, has been shown to be safe and well tolerated at doses likely to have a clinical effect, planning for phase II trials can begin. Unless the earlier phase I trial had been specifically designed to look for efficacy, this is the first point at which the proof of concept is tested on patients to see if there is any hope of moving on to phase III and beyond. Clinical trials on patients require huge resources of time, money and effort and take up a large proportion of the total drug development budget. Phase II testing is normally undertaken on a closely defined set of 50–100 patients who suffer from the disease that the drug is designed to treat. This relatively small number reduces the risk of unexpected ADRs or lack of efficacy, both of which could be very expensive to the sponsoring organization.

Phase IIb trials can extend earlier studies by including placebos and establishing a dose–response relationship prior to selecting the appropriate dose for the much larger Phase III studies. Each study is designed to assess the safety and effectiveness of a treatment regime, which could be of the following type:

- A single medicine for a specified disease
- An altered dose of medicine
- A marketed medicine for a new indication
- A new drug compared with a gold standard medicine
- Two or more different medicines

The gold standard medicine, referred to above, is a drug that is generally considered to be the most effective treatment for a particular disease at the time of the trial; this means that an experimental drug has a significant hurdle to overcome before it can show a convincing improvement over an existing medicine. Antibiotics are good examples of gold standard drugs, since the existing compounds like penicillin are highly effective in killing bacteria; a new product have to show a significant clinical advantage, perhaps through overcoming the problem of antibiotic resistance. The option of testing two or more different medicines as combination therapies is highly relevant to diseases, such as AIDS, where three different drugs are formulated together to reduce the problem of drug resistance to the HIV virus. Current thinking about the cancer treatment strategies is also moving towards multiple drug therapies (see section about James Watson in the introduction). While the thought of using drugs in combination may have scientific logic, the regulatory situation is not straightforward. The problem with drug combinations (in the form of one tablet or several) is that they have to be evaluated in separate phase III studies for both the combination and separate drug components. This obviously increases the time and expense of drug development and could discourage companies from producing combination therapies that work well in cancer and other diseases (hepatitis infection for example). These concerns have been recognized by the FDA who, after discussion with the drug industry and other relevant parties, will draw up suitable guidelines (http://edocket.access.gpo.gov/2010/pdf/2010-13769.pdf, Accessed 26 Nov 2010).

12.3.3.1   How Is Drug Effectiveness Measured?

This question could be rephrased: "How do you know when a drug has worked in patients?" The answer may seem obvious, "the patient gets better", but of course that leads to the question: "How do you define better?" The other problem is the separation between the proposed mechanisms of the drug and the actual clinical effect. In many cases, a drug that has a measurable effect on a particular protein target in patients may make no difference to the symptoms of the disease in which the target has been implicated. Alternatively, the disease symptoms may be reduced, but the target is unchanged, a consequence of the limits to our understanding of the molecular mechanisms of disease.

The formal design of clinical trials requires the specification of variables that define the desired clinical endpoint of a study as objectively as possible. The variables have to be presented in a form that can be analyzed using statistics (see later). More details about the different types of variables described below are available in ICH E9 (2011).

- Primary variable
Normally, this is a single measurement that defines the effectiveness of the drug. This can be very wide ranging according to the type of disease or question asked by the investigator. Examples include: survival after a certain period of time, quality of life improvements, number of heart attacks over a defined period and the slowing down of tissue destruction.

- Composite variable
In many cases (arthritis or psychiatric diseases, for example), a number of separate measurements are used to assess the clinical state of the patient, and it may not be possible to identify a single primary variable. In this case, a composite variable consisting of all the different factors in combination is used for the trial analysis.

- Global assessment variable
This is similar to the composite assessment, but includes a more subjective analysis of the disease by both physician and patient as to the effectiveness of the treatment.

- Categorized variable
This is a requirement that a disease measurement falls into a particular category. This is illustrated by a trial that requires diastolic blood pressure to fall below the fixed value of 90 mmHg.

- Surrogate variable
There are cases in which it is not possible to directly observe clinical effects during the course of the clinical trial. In this case, a surrogate marker of the disease has to be employed (see also Chap. 14). One of the best known of these is the surrogate marker of AIDS used to speed up the development of drugs against the causative HIV virus. The symptoms of AIDS are expressed slowly in different ways, so rather than just showing that drugs reduce levels of HIV virus, investigators use a surrogate of the immune deficiency that is the hallmark of the disease. Immune deficiency is caused initially by depletion of the CD4 T lymphocyte population in white blood cells, since these are the direct target of the HIV virus. The surrogate variable for clinical trials is, therefore, the level of CD4 lymphocytes in AIDS patients compared to uninfected individuals. Despite cases like this, the choice of surrogate markers has to be made extremely carefully as these are not always predictive of clinical outcome. Nevertheless, some diseases such as neurodegeneration are so complex and difficult to assess in an objective way that the search for predictive surrogate markers may offer the best way forward in drug development.

- Secondary variable
  As the name implies, secondary variables are considered after the primary variable but may provide new information about a drug that can be exploited in further trials. One example is the reduction in the incidence of strokes (secondary) as a result of bringing blood pressure below a certain value (primary variable).

12.3.3.2   Basic Clinical Trial Actions

If clinical trials are to be performed on patients, the following actions have to be taken:

- Identify hospitals and clinical investigation teams
- Recruit a suitable cohort of patients
- Conduct the trial
- Use biostatistics to determine the effectiveness of the trial
- Monitor and report ADRs
- Present a full report of the trials to the regulatory authorities

The above items are covered in the remainder of this chapter and in the next.

12.3.3.3   Hospitals

The nature and size of the study determine whether single-centre or multi-centre trials are performed. In the latter case, there may be contributions from hospitals in several different countries. The geographical location of the hospital is very important, since the ethnic background of the local population of patients may vary widely, along with the potential responsiveness to a drug treatment (see Chap. 14). Countries such as India have become very attractive to clinical trial sponsors because of their low cost base and ready access to patients, but there is concern that drugs tested on one population may not be as effective on another. Given that the main markets for prescription medicines are still the USA, Europe and Japan, this is an important issue that can be resolved only by conducting more research into population genetics and genomics.

12.3.3.4   Patient Recruitment and Selection

Once a clinical team and plan are in place, patients have to be identified and recruited for trials that may require many months of repeated visits to hospital. Although many patients are willing to submit to repeated interventions in the hope that their contribution will be of use to themselves and others, there are several reasons why they may not be selected for trial or be compliant once enrolled. The inclusion or exclusion criteria used to select patients are defined by the nature of the study. Patients should obviously be included if their condition fits with the trial objective, but they may be excluded for a variety of reasons, including having other diseases that may confound the study. Since patients are also human, they have free will to conduct their lives as best they can. This means that they may choose not to "play ball" with the trial investigators and be non-compliant with their medication or hospital visits. This can be understandable, particularly if unpleasant side effects arise as part of the treatment. There may, however, be logistical problems; for example, some patients with rheumatoid arthritis have such severe disability in their joints that they require most of the morning just to get to a position where they can leave their homes to be taken to the clinic. This limits the number of hours available to the investigator and increases the time taken to complete the trial. Sometimes, the reverse occurs, when patients actively look forward to attending the clinic, as one patient said in a trial which I was familiar with: "to get away from the wife for a few days!" Although non-compliant trial participants inevitably reduce the quality of the data, an Intention-To-Treat Principle is applied to subjects assigned to a treatment group. This means that they are assessed as part of that group, regardless of whether they actually completed the treatment.

The issue of patient recruitment is of great concern to sponsors and investigators; a study of recruitment to multi-centre clinical trials funded by the UK healthcare agencies between 1994 and 2002 showed that fewer than 31% managed to recruit their original target number of patients (McDonald et al. 2006). When difficulties with recruitment do occur, the trial may be delayed or abandoned or else decrease in value because the statistical power of the study is reduced by having fewer patients. Patient recruitment may be increased through an efficient management of processes and the use of different media, including interactive Web-based media or Web 2.0 (covered in Chap. 17). One example of what can be achieved is demonstrated by a UK-based trial designed to assess whether screening the whole female population for ovarian cancer actually reduces the mortality from the disease (Menon et al. 2008). The consortium of the UK hospitals contacted one out of every 6.5 women aged between 50 and 74 in the UK (excluding Scotland) and managed to recruit around 200,000 women within 5 years. Subjects were assigned into control groups (~100,000) and two screening groups, of 50,000 each, for the prospective 10-year study which is still ongoing at the time of writing.

12.3.3.5   Biostatistics

People differ from one another in many ways, including their responses to drug treatment. This means that the variability that occurs in clinical trials has to be measured and analyzed using statistics. This branch of mathematics has sometimes suffered from an image problem; witness, for example, British statesman Winston Churchill's remark about "lies, damn lies and statistics". Even biologists have come up with the (rather weak) joke that "if the experiment needs statistics, it means it hasn't worked". This, of course, is an exaggeration and perhaps reflects the frustrations that living organisms cause biologists through refusing to behave with the same precision and predictability as the inanimate objects studied by physicists.[2]

---

[2] This is only to make a point. Statistics is actually fundamental to physics.

The biostatistics department in a company is responsible for the statistical analysis needed prior to the recruitment of patients (or volunteers) and for analyzing the data as the trial proceeds. Statistics deals with likelihoods or probabilities that a certain event or events will occur, with a certainty being 1 and a "no chance" being 0, with all points in between. Probabilities in clinical trials are expressed as decimals, like my chance of winning the UK National Lottery being about 0.0000000714 (or 14 million to one). The main objective of biostatistics in clinical trials is to obtain a measure of the statistical significance of an effect that is measured after drug administration. This measure may compare the responses of the drug treatment to that of the placebo and produce a probability that the observed response to treatment is greater than what would have been observed by chance; this is known as the null hypothesis. Of course, there may be no significant difference or indeed a worsening of the patients' condition, but whatever the result, the statistical analysis enables the investigators, sponsors and regulators to assess whether the treatment has actually worked. The accuracy of the significance measurement is related to the sample size, in other words the more people tested in the trial, the greater the accuracy. This is referred to as the power of a planned study: too low and the conclusions are ambiguous, too high and the resources are expended unnecessarily. There is a real danger with underpowered studies that the results are scientifically meaningless, but sometimes the problem of patient recruitment is so great that investigators are tempted to proceed with the trial anyhow. As always, a compromise between the desired outcome and the real world situation has to be made.

12.3.3.6   Statistics Terminology

A number of tests of significance are referred to by name in biostatistics reports; while it is not the intention to offer more than a very brief description, some are listed below and can be studied in detail by accessing the many statistics resources available elsewhere, including ICH E9 "Statistical Principles for Clinical Trials" (ICH E9 guidelines 2011).

- Chi squared or χ^2-test
  This is commonly used to compare variable data between groups by assigning a probability that the observed variability is likely to be true (see P-value below). The variables in a clinical trial designed to assess the ability of a drug to lower blood pressure are the blood pressure measurements in a group of treated subjects compared with those in a placebo (or active)-controlled group.

- ANOVA – Analysis of Variance
  This is a statistical method related to the χ^2 test that allows comparisons of multiple sets of data. This is useful for trials with more than just a treatment and a placebo arm.

- *P*-values

  A *p*-value is the probability that there will be a difference between different groups (e.g. drug-treated and placebo) in a situation when no difference exists. In other words, a high *p*-value (high probability) implies that the trial has not worked, and a low *p*-value gives the investigator confidence that any difference between groups is likely to be real. *P*-values are quoted in clinical trial reports and publications to give the readers a number which allows them to judge whether the drug treatment actually worked. Typical *p*-values quoted might be something like $p<0.05$ or $p<0.001$. In the last case, this indicates that the chance of the difference between groups not being real is less than 1 in 1,000, and therefore the result is considered meaningful.

- Type I and type II errors

  Tied up with the comparisons of different sets of variable data is the false positive or type I error, written as the Greek letter α. A false positive might present itself as a lessening of symptoms in a trial for reasons unrelated to the drug. This happens to a surprisingly large degree of patients treated with placebos, possibly related to the extra care and attention they receive in hospital. Type II errors are false negatives written as β. These, of course, mislead investigators in thinking that the treatment has not worked when in fact it has. All of the above statistical tools (and more) are used to determine the optimal power of the study (number of patients and groups) as well as interpreting whether the drug has really worked in patients and therefore worth pursuing further.

12.3.3.7 The Structure of a Clinical Trial Report

In case there has been some doubt about the amount of paperwork required for drug development, the following ICH recommendations for the structure of a clinical trial report should correct any misconceptions (from ICH E3 "Content of Clinical Study Reports" (2011)).

Title Page, Synopsis, Table of Contents and List of Abbreviations Ethics

IRB, Declaration of Helsinki followed, patient information and consent are given.
Investigators and study administrative structure.
Investigators and observers, such as nurse, physician's assistant, clinical psychologist, clinical pharmacist, or house staff physician and biostatistician(s).

Introduction, Study Objectives, Investigational Plan, Study Design and Plan Description

Drugs: doses and procedures, patients, blinding: single/double blind, open label, controls: placebo, active drug, etc., method of patient assignment: randomization, stratification, sequence and duration of all study periods.
Discussion of study design, including the choice of control groups.
Selection of Study Population.
Inclusion criteria, exclusion criteria, removal of patients from therapy or assessment.

Treatments

Treatments administered, identity of investigational product(s), method of assigning patients to treatment groups, selection of doses in the study, selection and timing of dose for each patient, blinding, prior and concomitant therapy and treatment compliance.

Efficacy and Safety Variables

Efficacy and safety measurements assessed and flow chart, appropriateness of measurements, primary efficacy variable(s) and drug concentration measurements.

Data Quality Assurance

Statistical methods planned in the protocol and determination of sample size.
Statistical and analytical plans and determination of sample size.
Changes in the conduct of the study or planned analyses.
Study patients, disposition of patients and protocol deviations.
Efficacy evaluation and data sets analyzed.
Demographic and other baseline characteristics.

Measurements of Treatment Compliance

Efficacy results and tabulations of individual patient data.
Analysis of efficacy, statistical/analytical issues, adjustments for covariates, handling of dropouts or missing data, interim analyses and data monitoring, multi-centre studies, multiple comparison/multiplicity, use of an "efficacy subset" of patients, active-control studies intended to show equivalence, examination of subgroups, tabulation of individual response data, drug dose, drug concentration and relationships to response, drug–drug and drug–disease interactions, by-patient displays and efficacy conclusions.

Safety Evaluation, Extent of Exposure and Adverse Events

Brief summary of adverse events, display of adverse events, analysis of adverse events and listing of adverse events by patients.
Deaths, other SAEs and other significant adverse events.
Listing and discussion of deaths, other SAEs and other significant adverse events.

Clinical Laboratory Evaluation

Listing of individual laboratory measurements by patient and each abnormal laboratory value, evaluation of each laboratory parameter, laboratory values over time, individual patient changes and individual clinically significant abnormalities.

Vital Signs, Physical Findings and Other Observations Related to Safety

Safety conclusions.

Discussion and Overall Conclusions

Data figures, tables, graphs, forms, references and appendices.

12.3.4   Phase III: Confirmatory

The following section covers the design and conduct of phase III clinical trials; these are designed to replicate the phase II efficacy data for the drug candidate in a larger number of patients over a longer period of time.[3] This design (generally) ensures that any safety issues that may have been absent in smaller trials can be identified before the drug reaches the market. Unfortunately, many phase III trials fail to confirm efficacy or they reveal safety problems to such a degree that the drug development programme has to be terminated. When phase III trials are designed to support a marketing application to the regulators (regulatory submission, covered in next chapter), they are described as pivotal studies. These trials are large, randomized-controlled trials in multiple centres that are either coordinated into one study or treated as multiple independent single-centre trials with similar objectives. Sometimes, a phase III trial is designed to support a particular marketing approach or to extend the use of the drug to different types of patients (label expansion), in which case the term phase IIIb is sometimes used.

12.3.4.1   Case History: Phase III Trial of an Antibody to Treat Osteoporosis

Background

The following case history describes the phase III trial of denosumab, a fully humanized monoclonal antibody developed by Amgen Inc in California. This product was approved for the treatment of osteoporosis, by both the EMA and FDA, in 2010 and is marketed under the brand name Prolia®.

Osteoporosis is a condition in which the density of bone (bone mineral density) is reduced from normal levels, leading to an increased risk of fractures. It is common in the elderly, particularly postmenopausal women, as well as in patients with sex hormone deficiency, such as men undergoing treatment for prostate cancer. The level of mineral in the bone is controlled by a balance between its production by osteoblasts and breakdown by osteoclasts. These cells work in tandem to maintain a constant level of bone density, so osteoporosis ensues if the activity of osteoclasts predominates. From a drug discovery and development perspective, the therapeutic objective for osteoporosis is a reduction in osteoclast activity brought about by affecting a target associated with this particular cell type. The current "gold standard" for osteoporosis treatment is the bisphosphonate class of small molecules that inhibit the enzymes used by osteoclasts to break down bone. The Merck product alendonate (now off patent) is a typical example of the orally available molecules that are effective in preventing the loss of bone mineral.

---

[3] The phase II and III trials are designed and conducted in a very similar way, so there is a significant overlap between them.

Although these drugs are generally well tolerated, they do have side effects, and some patients are unable to take them over long periods. In a highly competitive field like this, biopharmaceutical companies are trying to develop drugs that have improved efficacy and fewer side effects. Basic research on cytokines and their receptors provided a suitable opportunity for this, since a cytokine named RANKL was found to activate osteoclasts in preclinical models. It was reasoned that an inhibitor would prevent osteoclast activation and therefore reduce bone thinning. Since the target molecule is a cytokine receptor, it cannot be readily inhibited with small molecules, so Amgen developed a fully humanized monoclonal antibody to RANKL (code name AMG162). The antibody worked in laboratory studies and passed through preclinical development ready for clinical evaluation. A phase I trial was conducted on 49 postmenopausal women randomized into 12 placebo and 6 treatment groups that received escalating doses of antibody (Bekker et al. 2004). The study was conducted over 9 months and used biomarkers in the urine to assess how effective the treatment was in preventing bone turnover. The results showed a dose-dependent effect of the antibody, as well as a satisfactory pharmacokinetic and safety profile.

Having established that the antibody was safe, well tolerated and had an effect on markers of bone turnover related to dose, a phase II efficacy trial was initiated using 412 women with low bone mineral density (Lewiecki et al. 2007). These subjects were recruited from 29 clinical centres in the USA, and the study was conducted over 2 years using placebo groups and groups receiving increasing doses of antibody over a period of either 3 or 6 months. This phase II trial also included an active comparison between patients given the antibody and those given the drug alendronate; this was to compare efficacy and the number of adverse events. In addition to measuring markers of bone turnover, the clinicians also measured the actual density of bone using a technique called DXA, which is based on X-ray imaging. The results of this trial showed that AMG 162 was at least as effective as alendronate in increasing bone mineral density over a period of 2 years, so the scene was set for the pivotal phase III trials that would satisfy the regulators.

The FREEDOM Trial

Doctors love using acronyms to describe large-scale clinical trials, and the phase III evaluation of AMG 162 (now given its INN name denosumab) was no exception. It was named the FREEDOM trial: "Fracture Reduction Evaluation of Denosumab in Osteoporosis Every 6 Months" (Cummings et al. 2009). A total of 7,868 women were enrolled in this trial which was designed to measure the number of new bone fractures that arose over a 3-year period in subjects taking denosumab, or placebo, every 6 months. A single 60 mg subcutaneous dose of antibody was chosen because the phase II trial had established that this was likely to be effective and well tolerated.

The trial patients, recruited from the Americas, Europe and Australasia, were stratified into different age bands as illustrated in Fig. 12.2.

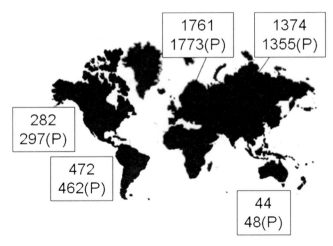

| 1761 | 1374 |
| 1773(P) | 1355(P) |

| 282 |
| 297(P) |

| 472 |
| 462(P) |

| 44 |
| 48(P) |

Age	Placebo	Denosumab
<70	1028	1030
70-74	1642	1637
≥75	1236	1235

Fig. 12.2 Patient recruitment for the FREEDOM clinical trial of denosumab for osteoporosis. Patient stratification into different age groups is shown along with the global distribution of drug-treated and placebo (P) groups (Cummings et al. 2009)

To give an idea of the scale of the task for sponsors and investigators, just organizing ethical approval required the consent from 139 separate IRBs and ethics committees. A diagram of the study design with primary and secondary endpoints is shown in Fig. 12.3.

Not shown in the diagram is the separate assessment of changes in bone mineral density, using DXA and markers of bone turnover measured in the blood. Taken together, all these measurements were designed to provide a comprehensive assessment of the efficacy of denosumab when compared with placebo. Physicians were required to report adverse events (including deaths) during the course of the study. Specific expert committees were set up to determine whether the SAEs and deaths were caused by the pre-existing conditions or as a result of the drug treatment. The results of the trial were presented as a series of graphs and tables in the Amgen publication. For simplicity, only the 3-year primary endpoint is shown in Fig. 12.4. Here, denosumab has significantly lowered the number of new vertebral fractures over the 3-year trial period compared with placebo. Notice the p-value which indicates the significance of the difference between the percentage of the antibody and placebo groups who suffered new vertebral fractures over 3 years.

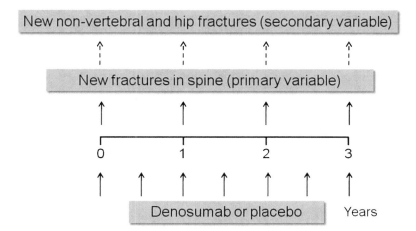

Fig. 12.3 Study design for phase III trial of denosumab for osteoporosis. Drug or placebo were given every 6 months over 3 years while assessing the number of new fractures occurring over that period

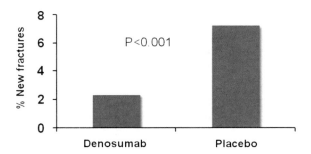

Fig. 12.4 Number of new fractures in subjects given denosumab or placebo over 3 years. The *p*-value gives a measure of the significance of difference between the two groups. Data from (Bekker et al. 2004)

Table 12.2 Adverse events recorded during FREEDOM trial (Bekker et al. 2004)

Event	Denosumab	Placebo
All	3,605	3,607
Serious	1,004	972
Fatal	70	90

These are not adverse drug reactions as values for placebo and drug are similar. Serious events include cancer, infection, stroke and heart disease

Antibody treatment did not give rise to more adverse events than placebo during the course of the study, except for a slightly higher incidence of eczema and cellulitis. There were deaths and serious events in both groups (see Table 12.2).

This phase III pivotal trial was considered a success because of the statistically significant reduction of fractures in the antibody-treated group and absence of significant drug-associated adverse events (i.e. ADRs). It is sobering to note the number of years that passed between the submission of the phase I publication to a journal in 2003 and the marketing approval that was given in 2010. It should be clear that part of the reason for this is the time taken to recruit patients and organize trials, let alone to conduct the study, which, in the case of osteoporosis, is required by the regulators to be of 3-years duration.

12.3.4.2   Specialized Patient Groups

The general clinical trials process described up to now is applicable to the majority of patients, but there are specific groups where variations in disease manifestation and responses to drugs can be highly significant. These groups are the elderly, children and the male and female genders.

Paediatrics

Children have not reached full biological maturity and are still in the development stages that were initiated during embryo formation (embryogenesis). This means that they may respond to medicines in a different way to adults and not just because they are smaller. One much-quoted example is the different pharmacodynamics of the antibiotic tetracycline between adults and children, where the drug causes permanent staining in children's teeth as they develop. Although there are about 75 million children (aged 0–18) in the EU (http://www.mhra.gov.uk/Howweregulate/Medicines/Medicinesforchildren/index.htm, Accessed 26 Nov 2010), the biopharmaceutical industry has been reluctant to invest as much effort in providing medicines for them as compared with adults. There is, however, specific guidance on paediatric drug development provided by the regulators and the ICH (ICH E11 (2011)). In general, studies of many drugs on adults form the basis of later evaluation on children. If, however, the intention is to treat life-threatening diseases where there is no cure, then children can be used at the outset. There may also be some treatments (such as gene therapy) that are more specific for children, so testing in adults would be inappropriate. Other considerations include formulation, where some excipients may be harmful to developing children or where it might be necessary to make the product more palatable.

Geriatric Population

At the other end of the age spectrum, anyone over the age of 65 is classed as elderly or geriatric, according to the ICH E7 clinical trial guidelines (2011). This figure does seem rather on the low side, considering the upward trend in life expectancy (see introduction), and think of Mick Jagger. Nevertheless, as a group, the elderly is differentiated from younger adults by virtue of the fact that they may have chronic age-related conditions, such as reduced kidney function (renal insufficiency), and be prescribed several different medicines at the same time. The ageing population is important to the biopharmaceutical industry, as its scientific and commercial focus is on the chronic diseases such as Alzheimer's and cancer that normally occur later in life. This is well illustrated by the case history of osteoporosis treatment, where the majority of the trial subjects were over 70. The ICH E7 guidelines provide information on specific aspects of clinical trials with geriatric patients that need to be considered by sponsors and investigators. Particular emphasis is placed on metabolism and drug–drug interactions (see Chap. 11).

Vive la Différence

The biological differences between men and women are generally something to be celebrated, but from the perspective of drug development, these can be complications. The large changes in hormone levels during monthly cycles and pregnancy, for example, make it important to use female animals or human subjects, yet most preclinical models and human trials use males (unless the intention is to treat females predominantly, as with the denosumab example). There appears to be an increasing realization on the part of clinicians and regulators that gender differences must be taken more seriously when conducting drug development programmes. These differences are manifested as changes in pharmacokinetics and pharmacodynamics, as well as conditions, such as cardiovascular disease, which may present quite differently between men and women. There has also been a political drive towards increasing the representation of women in clinical trials and paying more attention to specific diseases, such as breast cancer. This shift in emphasis has meant that investigators have to think carefully about how to conduct trials with pregnant women, or those who may get pregnant, while taking the drug under evaluation. One answer may be to conduct small phase I trials after phase III studies are underway with male patients; in any event, extreme rigour in safety monitoring is required to ensure that no harm is done to mother or foetus (Baylis 2010). Basic research in the detailed differences between male and female biology and pathology will help to guide future preclinical and clinical trial designs, perhaps through identifying new biomarkers using proteomics or other technologies (Chap. 14).

12.4   The Need to Improve Efficiency

Every time a new drug-related scientific breakthrough is featured in the media, it is nearly always qualified by the phrase "but it will be many years before a treatment is available for patients". This is obviously true because of the preclinical and clinical hurdles involved, but it is also dispiriting; there is a general feeling, among those involved, that processes could be improved and regulations made more efficient. One study of phase III cancer trials organized by the Eastern Cooperative Oncology Group (ECOG) in the USA gives an idea of the scale of the problem (Dilts et al. 2008). By studying 16 trials in detail, the group concluded that it took as much, or more time, to activate a trial (ranging from 435 to 1,604 days) as it did to conduct the study itself. Since more than 481 distinct processes were required, including 61 major decision points, this is not too surprising. To make the point even more forcefully, a process diagram capturing all the interactions, if printed out in 8 point type, would measure a staggering 5 by 50 feet (http://www.cmrhc.org/processmaps.htm, Accessed 29 Nov 2010). This may, for all I know, be quite normal when designing an airplane, but frankly most people would rather wait a bit longer for a new jumbo jet than for a new cancer treatment. Anyone who contributes to a multidisciplinary project in any field will feel a shudder of recognition after discovering why the timelines were so extended. This was because of the need for review boards and agencies from multiple locations who were all expected to operate with identical procedures and approaches, an almost impossible objective. The biopharmaceutical industry, regulators and clinicians are all aware of the problem and are making attempts to streamline processes and even question the value of some types of trial. There is also a strong financial incentive to speed up clinical trials, since every month of delay causes revenue loss to the sponsoring company as the patent life of the drug ticks away. It is not unreasonable to suggest that the topic of clinical trial efficiency is very near the top of a list of concerns felt by the biopharmaceutical industry.

Summary of Key Points

Clinical trials are conducted in several distinct phases, starting with phase I studies on human volunteers to determine the maximum tolerated dose and other clinical pharmacology parameters.

Phase II trials use patients to check efficacy and safety and phase III to confirm both of these in large number of patients over a longer time period.

Clinical trial documentation is complex and extensive.

Biostatistics is used to analyze trial data to measure differences in responses between placebo-controlled (or active-controlled) and drug-treated groups.

Patient enrolment is a major factor in the efficient running of clinical trials.

References

Baylis F (2010) Pregnant women deserve better. Nature 465:689–690
Bekker PJ et al (2004) A single-dose placebo-controlled study of AMG 162, a fully human monoclonal antibody to RANKL, in postmenopausal women. J Bone Mineral Res 19:1059–1066
Cummings SR et al (2009) Denosumab for prevention of fractures in postmenopausal women with osteoporosis. N Engl J Med 361:756–765

Dilts DM et al (2008) Development of clinical trials in a cooperative group setting: The Eastern Cooperative Oncology Group. Clin Cancer Res 14:3427–3433

Duff G (2006) Expert scientific group on phase one clinical trials. The Stationery Office, London

EUMAPP (2011). http://www.eumapp.com/. Accessed 17 Jan 2011

FDA clinical trials links (2010). http://www.fda.gov/ScienceResearch/SpecialTopics/RunningClinicalTrials/default.htm. Accessed 25 Nov 2010

ICH E11 guidelines (2011). http://www.ich.org/fileadmin/Public_Web_Site/ICH_Products/Guidelines/Efficacy/E11/Step4/E11_Guideline.pdf. Accessed 17 Jan 2011

ICH E3 guidelines (2011). http://www.ich.org/fileadmin/Public_Web_Site/ICH_Products/Guidelines/Efficacy/E3/Step4/E3_Guideline.pdf. Accessed 17 Jan 2011

ICH E6 (R1) guidelines (2011). http://www.ich.org/fileadmin/Public_Web_Site/ICH_Products/Guidelines/Efficacy/E6_R1/Step4/E6_R1__Guideline.pdf. Accessed 17 Jan 2011

ICH E7 guidelines (2011). http://www.ich.org/fileadmin/Public_Web_Site/ICH_Products/Guidelines/Efficacy/E7/Step4/E7_Guideline.pdf. Accessed 17 Jan 2011

ICH E9 guidelines (2011). http://www.ich.org/fileadmin/Public_Web_Site/ICH_Products/Guidelines/Efficacy/E9/Step4/E9_Guideline.pdf. Accessed 17 Jan 2011

ICH Guidelines Efficacy topics (2011). http://www.ich.org/products/guidelines/efficacy/article/efficacy-guidelines.html. Accessed 17 Jan 2011

WHO International Clinical Trials Registry Platform (2010). http://www.who.int/ictrp/en/. Accessed 25 Nov 2010

Jenkins JM et al (2007) Phase 1 clinical study of eltrombopag, an oral nonpeptide thrombopoietin receptor agonist. Blood 109:4739–4741

Lewiecki EM et al (2007) Two-year treatment with denosumab (AMG 162) in a randomized phase 2 study of postmenopausal women with low BMD. J Bone Miner Res 22:1832–1841

McDonald AM et al (2006) What influences recruitment to randomised controlled trials? A review of trials funded by two UK funding agencies. Trials 7:9, doi:10.1186/1745-6215-7-9

Menon U et al (2008) Recruitment to multicentre trials-lessons from UKCTOCS: descriptive study. BMJ. doi:doi: 10.1136/bmj.a2079

NIH's Clinicaltrials.gov (2010). Accessed 25 Nov 2010

Chapter 13
Regulatory Affairs and Marketing Approval

Abstract This chapter gives some background to the main regulatory agencies and then provides details of the applications required to gain permission to market a drug. The post-marketing surveillance phases are also covered, and the chapter concludes with a brief overview of marketing to physicians.

13.1 Introduction

The clinical trials process now continues through the late stages of phase III trials and on to the marketing and post-marketing surveillance phases. This chapter provides some background to the key regulatory agencies and describes the formal application process needed to gain marketing authorization for a drug. Once a medicine has been approved for sale, the regulatory process does not end there; a number of high-profile product withdrawals on safety grounds have prompted the demand for increased monitoring of the drug's effects on the population at large. This surveillance by physicians and the producer companies is undertaken in phase IV and V trials, which are conducted once the drug is in the market. Pre- and post-marketing regulations come under the term "regulatory affairs", which, given their central importance in getting a drug into the market, is a significant business function within a biopharmaceutical company. This chapter marks the final stage of the drug discovery pipeline and concludes with a brief description of the marketing process.

13.1.1 Regulatory Agencies

It should now be clear to the reader that the regulations covering drug discovery and development create huge demands on biopharmaceutical companies, in terms of both time and money. The agencies that issue these regulations for the USA, Europe and Japan have the most influence on global drug development and are covered in

E.D. Zanders, *The Science and Business of Drug Discovery: Demystifying the Jargon*,
DOI 10.1007/978-1-4419-9902-3_13, © Springer Science+Business Media, LLC 2011

the next section. The responsibility for authorizing drug sales in individual countries lies with national agencies, including those representing each European country. Some of these agencies are responsible for significant markets in their own right, for example, Canada and the BRIC countries of Brazil, Russia, India and China.

13.1.1.1   The Food and Drug Administration

Since the USA is the world's largest market for prescription medicines, the views of the country's regulator, the Food and Drug Administration (FDA), are followed closely by the global biopharmaceutical industry. The modern form of this US government agency was born out of tragedy in 1937, when 107 people died of poisoning by Elixir of sulphanilamide. The following year, President Roosevelt signed the Food Drug and Cosmetic Act to create the FDA. The organization is headed by the Commissioner of Food and Drugs, who is responsible for a number of offices and centres covering both aspects of consumer regulation. The two most important centres for pharmaceuticals are the Center for Drug Evaluation and Research (CDER) and the Center for Biologics Evaluation and Research (CBER), both of which deal with the IND and New Drug Applications (NDAs). The agency has had to keep up with advances in science and medicine, as well as respond to the political and economic pressures through the introduction of new laws and directives. A full historical list of the US regulatory agencies and laws, going back to the founding of the US Pharmacopeia in 1820, is available on the FDA Web site (http://www.fda.gov/AboutFDA/WhatWeDo/History/Milestones/ucm128305.htm. Accessed 27 Nov 2010).

The FDA has to deal with the competing demands of companies wishing to develop and sell products as quickly as possible and patients who expect high levels of drug safety. This requires greater public transparency on the part of the biopharmaceutical companies and acceptance of new technologies on the part of the regulators. In response to the latter, the FDA launched the Critical Path Initiative in 2004 with the aim of using modern technologies to improve various aspects of the drug development process. These include the conduct of clinical trials, drug manufacturing procedures and electronic data management. Open access to clinical trial information is provided by a joint FDA-National Institutes of Health (NIH) Initiative, ClinicalTrials.gov. This online resource contains data on over 90,000 clinical trials conducted in more than 170 countries worldwide (ClinicalTrials.gov 2010).

13.1.1.2   The European Medicines Agency

The creation of the European Union (EU) and its recent expansion have created a pharmaceuticals market to challenge that of the USA. Each member country has its own regulatory body, such as the Medicines and Healthcare Products Regulatory Agency (MHRA) in the UK, and, of course, each has its own language. The European

Medicines Agency (EMA), based in London, acts as a hub to coordinate a network of national agencies from all the EU countries and their political bodies. The EMA is headed by an Executive Director who oversees a group of six committees, made up of experts and representatives from all the EU members. CTA and Marketing Authorisation Applications (MAAs) are made to the Committee for Medicinal Products for Human Use (CHMP). Despite this centralization, the EMA does not authorize the marketing of every medicine in the EU, but leaves this to individual member states. A full list of National Competent Authorities for each country is available on the EMA Web site (National Competent Authorities in Europe 2011). Like the other agencies, the EMA is concerned with improving the efficiency of the drug development process, so it has published the "Roadmap to 2015" that mirrors the FDA's critical path initiative.

13.1.1.3   Japan's Ministry of Health, Labour and Welfare

Japan is a significant market for pharmaceuticals, partly because of its ageing population and a strong biomedical science base. The Ministry of Health, Labour and Welfare (MHLW) is run by a minister in the Japanese Government and consists of a number of different bureaux, including the Pharmaceutical and Food Safety Bureau responsible for drug development authorization (http://www.mhlw.go.jp/english/index.html, Accessed 27 Nov 2010). The MHLW is also a contributor to the ICH Harmonisation Initiative, along with the FDA and EMA.

13.1.2   The New Drug Application

This major regulatory submission process begins during the pivotal phase III clinical trials, where it is hoped that the experimental drug will prove to be safe and effective in a large number of patients. The FDA requires an NDA and the EMA, an MAA. The purpose of an NDA, as summarized here by the FDA, is to determine:

- Whether the drug is safe and effective in its proposed use(s), and whether the benefits of the drug outweigh the risks
- Whether the drug's proposed labelling (package insert) is appropriate, and what it should contain
- Whether the methods used in manufacturing the drug and the controls used to maintain the drug's quality are adequate to preserve the drug's identity, strength, quality and purity

The tangible end product of this process is a package insert (in the USA) that accompanies the medicine in order to provide prescribing information. This is sometimes referred to as "the label", as in the phrase "off-label" use of medicines. The EMA equivalent is the Patient Information Leaflet (PIL), which is an abbreviated form of the Summary of Product Characteristics (SPC) document written for prescribers.

The main headings required for an FDA-approved package insert are as follows:

- Product Names, Other Required Information
- Boxed Warning[1]
- Recent Major Changes
- Indications and Usage
- Dosage and Administration
- Dosage Forms and Strengths
- Contraindications
- Warnings and Precautions
- Adverse Reactions
- Drug Interactions
- Use in Specific Population

13.1.2.1   The Common Technical Document

The NDA and its European equivalent are based on the Common Technical Document (CTD). This consists of separate modules containing the information about drug manufacture, efficacy and safety that is required for marketing authorization. Each module is so extensive that the whole application may run to over 100,000 pages. In order to increase efficiency, as well as to save a few forests and acres of storage space, the regulators are introducing a submission process based on electronic CTDs (eCTDs). Although the exact contents of the CTD differ according to the requirements of a given regulator, the ICH M4 documents (ICH M4 CTD guidelines 2011) specify a common set of guidelines, which are summarized as follows:

Module 1: Administrative Information and Prescribing Information

Table of contents of the whole submission
Specific information for each country, where the drug is to be registered (which means that module 1 is not strictly part of the CTD)

Module 2: CTD Summaries

Table of contents
Introduction
Quality overall summary
Nonclinical overview

(continued)

---

[1] These are warnings about serious risks, the most serious being the black box warning, so-called because of the border around the printed text.

Module 2: CTD Summaries   (continued)

Clinical overview
Nonclinical written and tabulated summaries
Pharmacology, pharmacokinetics and toxicology
Clinical summary
Biopharmaceutic studies and associated analytical methods, clinical pharmacology studies, clinical efficacy and clinical safety
Literature references
Synopses of individual studies

Module 3: Quality

Table of contents
Body of data
Literature references

Module 4: Nonclinical Study Reports

Table of contents
Study reports
Literature references

Module 5: Clinical Study Reports

Table of contents
Tabular listing of all clinical studies
Clinical study reports
Literature references

Pharmacovigilance

An important part of the marketing application process is the submission of a pharmacovigilance plan for monitoring the safety of a drug after its introduction to the general population. The ICH E2E guidelines cover the types of materials that must be submitted to the regulators, either as part of the CTD or as separate documents (ICH E2E 2011). These contain a Safety Specification and a Pharmacovigilance Plan for monitoring the drug after launch.

The Safety Specification

This contains some or all of the following, depending on the drug in question:

Nonclinical (Animal Models)

Safety pharmacology, toxicology and drug interactions

Clinical

Limitations of the human safety database
Numbers treated so far versus population likely to receive drug and any new
  or different safety issues identified
Population not studied in the pre-approval phase, e.g. children, elderly and
  different ethnic groups
Adverse events (AEs)/adverse drug reactions (ADRs)
Identified and potential risks that require further evaluation
Identified and potential food–drug and drug–drug interactions

Epidemiology

Incidence and prevalence of the disease to be treated in different regions

Pharmacological Class Effects

Particular drug classes may have similar risks (e.g. causing heart arrhythmias)

Summary

Pharmacovigilance Plan

This is structured as follows:

Summary of Ongoing Safety Issues

Routine pharmacovigilance practices
Expedited ADR and periodic safety update reports (PSURs)
Action plan for safety issues
Action(s) proposed and rationale, monitoring by the sponsor and proposed
  action and milestones for evaluation and reporting

Summary of Actions and Milestones

Pharmacovigilance methods
Design and conduct of observational studies

Pharmacovigilance is undertaken by passive or active surveillance of the patient
population taking the drug. Spontaneous reporting of an adverse event to the regulators by patients and doctors is a common example of passive reporting; although

clearly useful, it is random and unstructured. Active reporting overcomes this problem by collecting the adverse event data from patients enrolled in risk management programmes or who contribute to surveys about the drug. This brief description belies the considerable amount of detailed epidemiology that is undertaken by pharmacovigilance experts in support of the marketing of a new medicine.

The regulatory authorities have specific mechanisms for reporting adverse events, for example, the Adverse Event Reporting System (AERS) for the FDA (FDA Adverse Event Reporting System), the EudraVigilance network for the EMA (EudraVigilance 2010) and the Yellow Card scheme in the UK.

The Drug Master File

It is quite normal for the biopharmaceutical company submitting a marketing application to be concerned about revealing proprietary information to the external committees appointed by the regulators. This is prevented by submission of a Drug Master File (DMF) to the regulators; this document is based on the CTD and contains restricted and non-restricted information in separate sections. The EMA equivalent is the Active Substance Master File (ASMF) or European Drug Master File (EDMF).

Variations in the NDA

The marketing application for patented medicines is covered by the NDA or MAA, but there are variations which cover generic medicines and biologicals, such as vaccines. The Abbreviated New Drug Application (ANDA) is used for generic copies of medicines that are already in the market and, therefore, have been through a full review process (generic medicines are covered in Chap. 16). The only requirement on the manufacturer is to be able to demonstrate the bioequivalence of the generic product. In practice, this means showing that the generic product has the same absorption properties as the patented medicine when administered to 24–36 volunteers (FDA generics approvals 2010). Bioequivalence is relatively straightforward to demonstrate small molecules, but not at all for biologicals, as mentioned in Chap. 8. The approval of blood products, vaccines, cell therapy and gene therapy is made by the FDA's CBER, with the marketing application being called a Biologics License Application (BLA). This requires essentially the same types of information and clinical trial structure as the NDA. The design and interpretation of vaccine trials are, of course, quite specialized, so the expert review panel includes immunologists and microbiologists.

The Approval Process

The documentation for an NDA is sent to the CDER division of the FDA. The MAA is submitted to CHMP of the EMA. After the classification into standard or priority review (for FDA, see below), the submission is reviewed by internal and external

Fig. 13.1 Timelines for NDA review by the FDA

experts who require meetings with the sponsors to discuss and clarify any technical points that may arise. When the FDA requires clarification from the sponsor, it sends out an "approvable letter" requesting further information. Once all issues have been clarified to the satisfaction of the regulator, an "approval letter" is sent out to the sponsor to signal that the NDA has been accepted. In the case of EMA approval, the CHMP issues an "assessment report", possibly along with a "request for supplementary information", which will lead to approval or otherwise.

The huge amount of information that has to be reviewed inevitably means that the approval process is time consuming and may take over 1 year. The regulators do provide an option to prioritize the application if the drug is likely to make a significant difference to serious diseases or has a better safety profile than existing marketed drugs. The biopharmaceutical company must request a priority review and wait for 45 days to receive a decision. The timings for standard and priority review are illustrated in Fig. 13.1.

Fast Track Review

If a drug candidate is likely to fulfil an unmet medical need and treat a serious illness like cancer, the FDA is able to fast track the review by committing more resources and increasing the number of meetings with the sponsors. It may also be possible to use a rolling review, in which time is saved by reviewing the applications section by section as they are submitted, rather than waiting for the whole document. Fast track review is requested by the sponsor at any time during the drug development process, and a decision as to whether the drug does fulfil an unmet medical need is made by the FDA after 60 days.

Accelerated Approval

Even though phase III clinical trials can take several years, this may still not be sufficient time to determine whether a drug confers real benefits to patients through
increasing life expectancy or quality of life. However, in the case of drugs for some
cancers, where the main clinical outcome may be patients' survival times, the FDA can
follow a process of accelerated approval; this system accepts the use of drug-induced
changes in biomarkers or surrogates of the disease to provide a more rapid measure of
the clinical outcome. The markers for cancer, for example, could be tumour shrinkage
or biochemical measures of drug activity, such as target enzyme inhibition. Having
passed through accelerated approval, a drug can be marketed, but on the condition that
it is reviewed in phase IV studies (below). These studies are performed in the general
patient population, and they determine whether the drug makes a long-term difference
to the disease; if not, it could lead to the product being withdrawn from the market.

The following examples of FDA-approved cancer drugs illustrate both the advantages and pitfalls of fast track review. Imantinib (Gleevec®, see Chap. 3) was developed by Novartis as a small-molecule drug for a particular type of leukaemia and fast
track-reviewed in just 4 months. This meant that the life-saving medicine was rapidly
introduced to patients and provided real clinical benefits, despite the problems with
drug resistance that emerged later on. The other example is gefitinib, marketed as
Iressa® by AstraZeneca, which was granted accelerated approval for treating a type
of lung cancer after it completed phase II trials. The small-molecule drug was successful in shrinking tumours and given marketing approval in 2003 on condition of
running a confirmatory trial. Unfortunately, this trial failed to show survival benefit,
so Iressa® was withdrawn from the general patient population, thus casting a shadow
over the accelerated approval process. The situation with this drug has now improved,
however, after the discovery that it only works on patients with a particular genetic
mutation in the Iressa® protein target. Iressa® was approved in 2010 as a first-line
treatment for lung cancer patients with the target mutation, so all was not lost with
this drug. This example demonstrates the importance of pharmacogenetics and how
it can be used to improve the efficiency of clinical trials by selecting only those
patients who are likely to respond to the drug (covered further in the next chapter).

13.1.3 Phase IV: Post-Marketing Studies

Once a medicine is in the market, the biopharmaceutical company may be obliged
to invest in clinical studies that extend the number of patients in order to confirm
safety and efficacy; in the case of safety, this is called a Post Authorization Safety
Study or PASS.[2] It may also test the drug in specific population, such as pregnant

---

[2] The FDA may require "post-approval commitments" and the EMA the CHMP's "follow-up
measures" (FUMS).

women or ethnic groups. Phase IV studies are conducted under GCP conditions in hospitals, or other healthcare centres, and are designed to go beyond phase III trials. This may be through increasing the number of active comparators, comparing the drug against more marketed products, or extending the treatment times.

An example of a phase IV trial to test a marketed drug in a particular population comes from Forest Laboratories in the USA with its anti-hypertensive drug, Bystolic® (http:// www.frx.com/news/PressRelease.aspx?ID=1421500, Accessed 29 Nov 2010). This was trialled over 8 weeks in a placebo-controlled randomized study, using 277 Hispanic patients with high blood pressure. This beta blocker drug adrenaline receptor antagonist was shown to reduce blood pressure and display the same proportion of adverse events as placebo. This kind of positive result in a different patient population is clearly helpful to Forest in supporting the marketing of this drug, but there is also a regulatory imperative to monitor safety, which begins before the medicine is marketed (see REMS later).

13.1.3.1   Post-Marketing Surveillance (Phase V)

Once a medicine has received the marketing authorization and has been approved for reimbursement by healthcare providers, it will start to generate revenues with or without phase IV trials. Although a great deal of money and time will have been spent over the period from the first clinical trials up to the marketing authorization, the responsibility of the manufacturer for monitoring safety does not end there. This is because of the risk that serious adverse reactions, which may be very rare and not detectable in small numbers of patients, could show up when significant numbers of people are treated with the drug. This has occurred in a number of high-profile cases, such as with the Merck drug Vioxx® that was developed as a "safer aspirin" for arthritis; the drug was withdrawn from the market after reports that patients had an increased risk of heart attacks while taking the medicine.

Meta Analysis

Sometimes, ADRs come to light only after the data from a number of trials are pooled together and carefully examined using statistics. Studies of this type use a technique called "meta analysis", which can be useful for increasing the power of the analysis by studying data from more patients. It can also, however, be subject to bias and inaccuracy, particularly if the studies are selectively excluded from the analysis. A meta analysis of clinical trials by clinicians who have concerns about a marketed drug can have a major impact on the fate of that drug, as witnessed by Merck with Vioxx® and, more recently, GSK with Avandia®.

Risk Evaluation and Mitigation Strategy

In light of increased concerns about drug safety, the regulators are encouraging drug companies to devise a strategy for monitoring and reporting adverse events that may arise once the medicine is in the market. This Risk Evaluation and Mitigation Strategy (REMS), or the EU Risk Management Plan (EMA), is put in place during phase III trials. An example is provided by post-marketing plans for the therapeutic antibody denosumab (marketed as Prolia®) that was developed to treat osteoporosis (see previous chapter). Its manufacturer Amgen Inc. was granted the marketing authorization for the antibody by the EMA and FDA in 2010; the company has put in place the following strategies to assist the medical profession in its choice of treatment and to provide commercial support for its product (Amgen Press 2010) (quotation courtesy of Amgen Inc., Thousand Oaks, California):

> A Risk Evaluation and Mitigation Strategy (REMS) to communicate the risks of Prolia®, which consists of a communication plan for health care providers and a medication guide for patients.
>
> Comprehensive post-marketing surveillance.
>
> Amgen continues to gather data from extension studies in more than 4,500 women with postmenopausal osteoporosis who will have exposure to Prolia® for up to 10 years. In addition, Amgen will implement an international Prolia® long-term safety observational study to assess pre-specified adverse events of special interest based on seven existing data systems from five countries, which will include healthcare administrative databases, electronic medical records, and national health registries. These women with postmenopausal osteoporosis who received Prolia® will be followed long term. Finally, Amgen is launching the Prolia® Post marketing Active Safety Surveillance Program to monitor the long-term safety of Prolia® and improve the quality of data collected in the post-marketing setting. This program is intended to enhance the adverse event reporting system by soliciting reports of pre-specified adverse events of special interest.

13.1.4   Marketing the Drug

Although the commercial aspects of drug development will be covered in more detail later on, this chapter concludes with some comments about marketing a drug to clinicians.

Patients are obviously the end-users of prescription medicines, but these products are available only from the medical profession that helped to develop them in the first place. Clinicians make decisions about which drugs are appropriate for certain groups of patients using their personal experience in the clinic and the opinions of their peers. The biopharmaceutical industry, therefore, devotes considerable resources to informing doctors about its products; this may involve direct visits from sales personnel, published materials in journals and magazines or sponsorship of conferences. Panels of experts, consisting of specialists with senior appointments in hospitals or universities, advise companies about the need for a new medicine and give their professional judgment as to how it should be used in clinical practice. The relationship between the biopharmaceutical industry and clinicians has not been without controversy, particularly in terms of financial inducements used to promote a product. Whatever the details of particular cases that emerge in the media from time to time, it must be sensible to form close ties between the medical profession and those who supply the tools to treat their patients. As an industry scientist, who has interacted with many research clinicians over the years, I (nearly) always felt that the relationship was based on a shared interest in the science behind our activities, with the understanding of who held the purse strings kept well in the background.

Scientists and doctors communicate their results by means of publications and oral presentations at conferences and seminars. The publications include peer-reviewed papers in journals, magazine articles, online blogs, wikis and Webinars. The articles used for the clinical trial examples in the last chapter were all submitted to journals, where the editor used external experts to "peer review" the article before agreeing to publication. This is accepted as being the most rigorous method of quality control even though authors, including me, complain if the referees reject the paper or make unreasonable demands for more data. The biopharmaceutical industry often employs medical writers to produce scientific communications of all types, including the thousands of pages of regulatory materials required during drug development. These medical writers may be directly employed by the company, or be part of a specialist agency, where the writing is outsourced. Apart from regulatory documentation, this writing covers everything from marketing advertisements to peer-reviewed articles. There is a danger, however; some journal articles have been authored by "ghost writers", and this lack of transparency can lead to a loss of confidence by the scientific and medical profession. Journals are tackling these issues head-on by requiring full author transparency and financial disclosures of conflict of interest.

Summary of Key Points

The key global regulators are the FDA, EMA and Japan's MHLW.

The NDA or European MAA are drawn up and submitted to the regulators during phase III trials.

Depending on the severity of the disease, the application may receive fast track review and accelerated approval.

Pharmacovigilance is an important part of pharmaceutical development both during and after the clinical trials.

An REMS is required by the FDA before marketing approval is granted.

Phase IV studies may be conducted, once the medicine is in the market, to go beyond the phase III trial by using different patient groups or other changes, such as increased duration.

Post-marketing surveillance (phase V) involves feedback from doctors and patients to identify adverse reactions.

Medical writers are employed to publicize the new medicine using scientific and educational media.

References

Amgen Press Release (2010). http://wwwext.amgen.com/media/media_pr_detail.jsp?year=2010& releaseID=1433162. Accessed 29 Nov 2010

ClinicalTrials.gov. (2010). http://www.clinicaltrials.gov. Accessed 26 Nov 2010

EudraVigilance (2010). http://eudravigilance.ema.europa.eu/highres.htm. Accessed 7 June 2011

FDA: Adverse Event Reporting System (2009). http://www.fda.gov/Drugs/GuidanceCompliance RegulatoryInformation/Surveillance/AdverseDrugEffects/default.htm. Accessed 2 Jun 2011

FDA generics approvals (2010). http://www.fda.gov/Drugs/DevelopmentApprovalProcess/How DrugsareDevelopedandApproved/ApprovalApplications/AbbreviatedNewDrugApplication ANDAGenerics/default.htm. Accessed 7 June 2011

ICH E2E (2011). http://www.ich.org/fileadmin/Public_Web_Site/ICH_Products/Guidelines/ Efficacy/E2E/Step4/E2E_Guideline.pdf. Accessed 17 Jan 2011

ICH M4 CTD guidelines (2011). http://www.ich.org/products/ctd.html. Accessed 17 Jan 2011

National Competent Authorities in Europe (2011). http://www.ema.europa.eu/ema/index. jsp?curl=pages/medicines/general/general_content_000155.jsp&murl=menus/partners_and_ networks/partners_and_networks.jsp&mid=WC0b01ac0580036d63. Accessed 17 Jan 2011

Chapter 14
Diagnostics and Personalized Medicine

Abstract The drug discovery landscape is changing with the advent of personalized medicine and companion diagnostics that are used to identify patients who will respond to a marketed drug. This chapter provides an overview of the techniques used in the diagnostics laboratory and moves on to discuss personalized medicine in the form of pharmacogenetics and single nucleotide polymorphism analysis. Mention is also made of the surrogate markers and biomarkers used in clinical trials.

14.1 Introduction

The previous chapters in this section have covered the drug discovery pipeline from target to marketed medicines, with occasional reference to diagnostics and the differing reactions of patients to the same drug. Diagnostics and personalized medicine are becoming more important to the biopharmaceutical industry for several reasons. Firstly, serious adverse drug reactions, the so-called iatrogenic diseases, account for over 100,000 deaths annually and 1.5 million serious injuries at a cost of approximately 3.5 billion dollars (Committee on Identifying and Preventing Medication Errors 2007). Secondly, many drugs work against only a proportion of patients, so it is, therefore, wasteful and unethical to prescribe such drugs to those who do not respond to them. Thirdly, selecting patients for clinical trials would be made more ethical, scientifically rigorous and cost-effective if patients are pre-screened to provide a genetically uniform pool of subjects, rather than a random selection who suffer from the same disease. Finally, it is often difficult to make an objective measurement of whether a treatment has actually worked in clinical trials; this is particularly true with neurodegenerative conditions, such as Alzheimer's disease, where the restoration of brain function is difficult to measure objectively (see next chapter). These various topics, which come under the broad headings of diagnostics and personalized medicine, are described in some detail in this chapter.

E.D. Zanders, *The Science and Business of Drug Discovery: Demystifying the Jargon*, 269
DOI 10.1007/978-1-4419-9902-3_14, © Springer Science+Business Media, LLC 2011

14.1.1   Background to Diagnostics (D$_x$)

Diagnosis of disease is as old as medicine itself; it may be performed during a consultation with a physician or in specialized hospital laboratories. Strictly speaking, diagnostics development and drug development are quite separate activities, the former being concerned with the identification, rather than the treatment of disease. The diagnostics industry is very much the poorer cousin of the biopharmaceutical industry, since the unit cost of a diagnostic kit is considerably less (100-fold) than that of a patented medicine. The diagnostics market is mostly driven by the demand for reagents and instrumentation by hospital laboratories and retailers of home diagnostic kits. Because of this, the products have to be robust, cheap and straightforward to use, which is in contrast to the expensive products of the biopharmaceutical industry. This is not, however, to underestimate the importance of diagnostics in supporting public health or the sophistication of the technology that is used to create the required tests and instruments. These products are also used for the analysis of preclinical and clinical samples during drug development, where tests are conducted in centralized service laboratories.

Routine diagnostic tests, such as measurements of blood pressure, or levels of cholesterol, glucose and other substances, all help the clinician to make a diagnosis or to offer the patient advice on changes of lifestyle. Another important area of diagnostics concerns infectious diseases, where the specific infectious agent must be identified before the appropriate drug is prescribed. Finally, some diagnostic procedures do not require clinical input, for example, the pregnancy testing kits used at home.

14.1.1.1   Point-of-Care Diagnostics

It is in the obvious interest of the patient that a diagnosis is made rapidly, particularly if it is related to a life-threatening condition. However, even the most efficient hospital laboratory cannot provide the speed or convenience of a diagnosis in the primary care practice or even at home. This is why point-of-care (POC) diagnostics, which can be performed away from the hospital, is such a fast-growing area and one in which there is great scope for innovation.[1] From the drug discovery perspective, POC diagnostics are going to be important for personalized medicine; in this scenario, the primary care physician may have diagnosed a particular disease in a patient and then will perform a further test to see which medicine would be the most appropriate for that patient. This is sometimes referred to as "prescribing the right drug to the right patient"; this topic is discussed later under "Personalized Medicine".

---

[1] POC diagnostics are also used in hospital emergency rooms, where rapid diagnosis of conditions is clearly important.

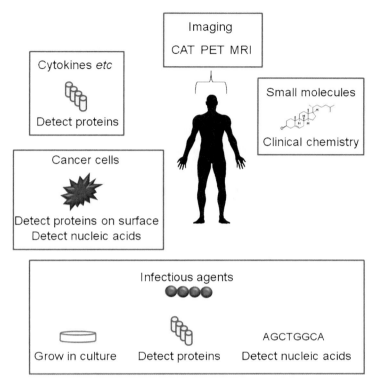

Fig. 14.1 Main categories of diagnostic tests. Various forms of imaging are used, particularly to examine the brains of living subjects. The other techniques are used on blood, urine, cerebrospinal fluid or tissue samples

14.1.2   Technology

Although it is impossible to describe even a fraction of the diagnostic tests that are available, or under development, it is possible to make some generalizations, since many share common design principles. In broad terms, the diagnostic test (assay) may be based on a physical measurement, such as blood pressure, volume of air breathed out, an image in a computerized axial tomography (CAT) scan or the amount of glucose in the blood. Figure 14.1 shows a schematic overview of some of the most important areas.

14.1.2.1   Imaging

Where diseases are manifested by changes in the living body, such as the appearance of tumours, the obvious way of detecting this is through direct observation using X-rays or other techniques. Although not always easy to quantify, imaging has the potential to rapidly determine the effect of a drug on, for example, tumour size in cancer or tissue destruction in arthritis. The use of radiography to measure bone fractures has already been mentioned in Chap. 12 in connection with the development of denosumab. While X-rays are used routinely for many diagnoses, other imaging techniques exist that can visualize soft tissues and even the exact area where a drug binds to its target. These techniques are briefly summarized as follows:

- CAT or CT scans
  Multiple X-ray images are taken of the affected part of the body and the images reconstructed to form a highly detailed view of the bones, blood vessels and organs. Image contrast agents are often used to provide a clearer distinction between different structures, with much research being undertaken to develop novel agents which can highlight specific tissues and even cells.

- Optical imaging
  Fluorescent molecules attached to proteins are visualized by shining light (normally infrared) on the surface of the body. The technique is limited by the poor penetration of light below the body surface, but it is versatile and can be used with genetically engineered animals that express fluorescent proteins (see animal models Chap. 6).

- Ultrasound and photoacoustic imaging
  Ultrasound imaging (sonography) exploits the echo created when sound is reflected off different structures. Specific contrast agents containing microscopic gas bubbles are injected into the circulation to create a high contrast between the blood vessels and surrounding soft tissue. Microbubbles can also be attached to probes which target specific areas of the body.

  Photoacoustic imaging is based on the photoacoustic effect, in which light from a laser shines on a specimen; this heats up and emits sound waves which are detected with special sensors.

- Magnetic resonance imaging (MRI) scans
  This is based on the interaction between radio waves and certain elements, such as hydrogen. MRI produces very high-resolution images of body tissues by detecting the hydrogen in water molecules. Images can be further enhanced using contrast agents containing elements such as gadolinium. Functional MRI (fMRI) is used to detect changes in blood flow in the brain to reveal areas of neuronal activity; it may, as a result, identify the anatomical sites of certain human actions and behaviours. Not surprisingly, this is an area of intense research interest, but is not without some controversy, as some findings relating to behaviour may have been over-interpreted.

- Positron emission tomography (PET) scans
  Certain radioisotopes emit positively charged electrons (positrons) which interact with electrons to produce gamma radiation. This radiation can be detected using specially designed cameras and processed to create 3-dimensional body images. PET scans use tracker molecules which are firstly tagged with radioisotopes and then injected into the circulation. The choice of molecules is almost limitless, but

the one most commonly used for medical imaging is ^{18}Fluorodeoxy glucose, which is taken up by actively metabolizing tissues. PET scans are also used to image the binding of labelled drugs and probes to precise areas in the body. Although PET scanning has the advantages of high sensitivity and resolution, it comes at the price of producing the radioisotopes used to incorporate into different molecules. The half life of the commonly used ^{18}F isotope is 2 h while that of the ^{11}C, ^{15}O and ^{13}N isotopes is less than 30 min; these very short half lives mean that the isotopes must be generated in a cyclotron situated very near to the hospital or research facility used for the study.

14.1.2.2 Diagnostic Tests for Small Molecules

The blood levels of small molecules, like glucose, cholesterol or creatinine, give an indication of the health of the patient in routine clinical practice or during clinical trials. These molecules are usually detected in a system that generates a coloured product, whose intensity is measured by light adsorption (see spectrophotometry, Chap. 9). The system that generates the product is usually an enzyme, which converts the test molecule (analyte) into a product that reacts chemically with another compound to form a dye. The various components of the assay may be bound onto a paper and a plastic test strip; this is then dipped into blood or urine to produce a colour change if the analyte is present. The strips can then be "read" in small hand-held devices that provide a numerical display of the analyte concentration.

14.1.2.3 Antibody-Based Assays (Immunoassays)

Antibodies are exquisitely specific for their targets (antigens) and are ideally suited for diagnostic applications. An antibody created against a hormone in blood, for example, can be used to discriminate between that molecule and the hundreds of other proteins that may be present in the blood sample. Tests that employ antibody-based detection of analytes (which are usually proteins) are called immunoassays. The most important requirements for the assay are sensitivity to low levels of analyte and the specificity for it; the assay must also operate over a wide range of analyte concentrations, in other words, it must have a large dynamic range. One example of how this is applied in practice comes from the clinical trial of the therapeutic antibody, TGN1412, in phase I volunteers; this trial resulted in a near-fatal cytokine storm (described in Chap. 12). The levels of different cytokines were measured in blood samples, before and during the treatment (Suntharalingam et al. 2006), and illustrated the low levels that can be detected in healthy subjects (2.8 pg/ml); this rose to 1,760 pg/ml after 1 h and 4,675.9 pg/ml after 4 h.[2]

---

[2] This 4 h level of around 4.6 ng TNF-α per millilitre of blood illustrates just how potent and destructive these cytokines can be.

Immunoassays are produced in different formats, depending on the specific requirements of the analysis; the main assays are described below:

Enzyme-Linked Immunosorbent Assay

This immunoassay format is actually more straightforward than the name would imply and is used to detect and measure different hormones, cytokines and other proteins in solution. It has become the method of choice for the screening for diagnostic proteins in blood, urine or other fluids, replacing the older radioimmunoassay that employed antibodies labelled with radioactive iodine (^{125}I). A typical sandwich Enzyme-linked Immunosorbent Assay (ELISA) system is illustrated in Fig. 14.2 (the sandwich refers to the two antibodies that form a sandwich with the antigen (analyte) as the filling).

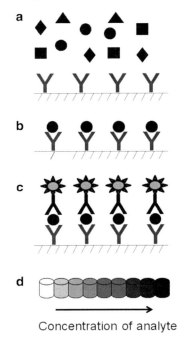

Concentration of analyte

Fig. 14.2 A sandwich ELISA format. (**a**) An antibody (*Y shape*) is attached to the bottom of a plastic well to capture (pull out) the analyte protein that it specifically binds to. The protein (*solid circle*) is mixed with other molecules, as would be the case in blood or other tissues. (**b**) The analyte protein binds to the immobilized antibody, and all other proteins are washed away. (**c**) A second antibody is bound to the analyte; this one is conjugated (tagged) with a label that generates a signal which can be measured in a spectrophotometer. In an ELISA, the label is an enzyme (hence, enzyme-linked) that converts a colourless substrate to one with a colour, whose intensity is proportional to the amount of enzyme present. (**d**) A series of plastic wells in a 96-well plate, where increasing amounts of analyte have been added from *left* to *right*. The colour intensity is proportional to the amount of analyte and can be converted into a number (absorbance value) by using a spectrophotometer

This basic system is often configured to produce greater sensitivity or improved discrimination between the analyte and interfering substances in blood. Highly sensitive detection systems can be produced that use antibodies against antibodies, or else exploit the very strong interaction that exists between the small molecule biotin and the protein streptavidin. These will not be elaborated upon any further, but details can be found in the many external resources that cover immunoassays, e.g. Genway Immunoassay Wikipedia 3.0 (2011).

Cytometry

The ELISA system described above is configured to detect hormones and other signalling proteins that are present in solution (e.g. in the blood). However, many important proteins are expressed on the surface of living cells and can act as markers for diseases, like cancer. The CD4 molecule is an example of such a marker protein, in this case, for the immunodeficiency that results from infection with the HIV virus. CD4 is expressed on the surface of about 40% of the T lymphocytes circulating in the blood. If an individual is infected with the HIV virus, the levels of CD4 cells are severely reduced, thus compromising the ability of the immune system to fight infection, which eventually results in AIDS. The diagnosis of patients with AIDS, as well as monitoring the effects of anti-HIV drugs, requires a suitable immunoassay that can rapidly count the number of CD4 cells in a sample of blood. This is achieved using a technique called flow cytometry, in which cells are labelled with an antibody specific for the molecule of interest (CD4 in this example). The cells are then passed through a machine called a flow cytometer. The process of flow cytometry conducted in this machine is illustrated in Fig. 14.3. In this example, white blood cells (leukocytes) are isolated from blood and stained with an antibody to CD4, which is tagged with a fluorescent molecule that glows green when illuminated by laser 1. A second antibody, labelled with a fluorescent molecule that glows red under laser 2, is used to stain another population of blood cells, called CD8; the process of staining cells using fluorescently labelled antibodies is called immunofluorescence. The cells are forced through a tube into a single file and then passed through the laser beams. When a cell with the right colour is detected, light is emitted and a signal passed to a computer for analysis and display.

Each cell is displayed on the computer monitor as a dot, whose position reflects the colour of the label attached via the antibody. It is then straightforward to identify the area in the display where CD4 positive cells have been identified (circled) and also the areas for CD8 and those blood cells that bear neither of the molecules; not shown here is a small proportion of cells that are positive for both CD4 and CD8. Finally, the machine counts the number of cells in each area, so the proportion of blood cells that bear CD4 can be readily determined. Two different fluorescent dyes were used for the example above (two-colour immunofluorescence), but it is possible to label at least ten different cell types simultaneously as long as the flow cytometer has multiple lasers and filters.

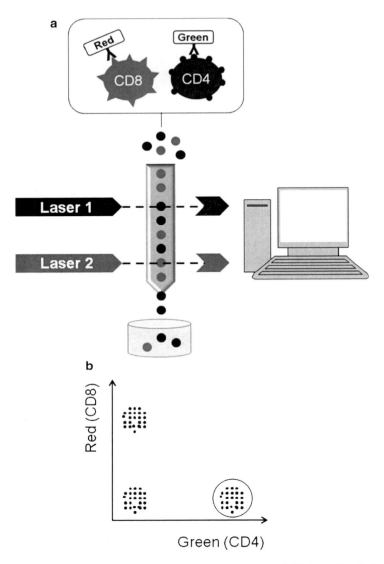

Fig. 14.3 Diagram of flow cytometry used to count the number of CD4 +ve T cells in blood. (**a**) White blood cells are isolated from blood and mixed with antibodies to CD4 and CD8 proteins on the cell surface. Each antibody has a molecule attached that emits a signal (red for CD8 and green for CD4) when the labelled cells are passed through a flow cytometer. The cells flow down a tube, where they are illuminated by lasers. Every time a red label passes the red laser, a fluorescent signal is registered by the detector and sent to the computer; the same occurs with green cells and the green laser. (**b**) The computer plots each cell as a dot on a 2-dimensional display, where each axis is the intensity of fluorescence. In this way, cells labelled with green are separated from those labelled with red and those labelled with both red and green together

Immunohistochemistry

Immunohistochemistry (IHC) (or immunohistology) is a key part of the drug development process; it is used to examine tissues from animals and human subjects for adverse effects during drug development, as well as for diagnostics. The technique is based on histochemistry (introduced earlier in Chap. 6), where thin sections of tissues are attached to glass microscope slides and stained with dyes to reveal different cell types. IHC is based on similar principles, except that antibodies, tagged with a fluorescent or enzyme label, are used instead of a coloured dye. Because antibodies bind to different cells with great selectivity, individual cell types can be readily identified in tissue sections. As with flow cytometry, antibodies used for IHC can be tagged with fluorescent molecules (fluorochromes), but they can also be tagged with enzymes that create an insoluble coloured product at the site of antibody binding. This is illustrated in Fig. 14.4, where an enzyme-labelled antibody has been applied to a section of breast tissue. The sites of antibody binding are revealed as dark areas in a lighter background.

Modern developments, like the introduction of laser scanning confocal microscopy, have enormously improved the quality and resolution of cell and tissue images; as well as being scientifically useful, they can be real works of art. Diagnostic specimens are normally checked by pathologists who assign a score that depends on the intensity of staining of particular cell types. This is a subjective

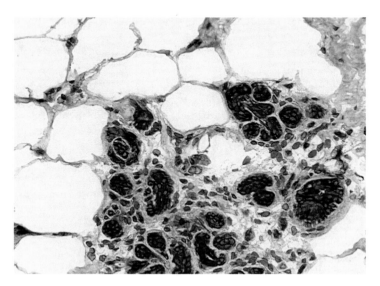

Fig. 14.4 Immunohistochemistry used to visualize cells in breast tissue. A thin section of tissue on a microscope slide is mixed with the antibody that can discriminate between fat cells (clear structures and cells surrounding ducts). The dark brown colour is produced at the site of antibody binding by a coloured product produced by the enzyme attached to the antibody

process, so attempts have (and are) being made to automate the process by using image processing computer algorithms; while there has been undoubted progress in this area, the fully automated IHC laboratory is not yet in routine use.

Western Blotting

There are some situations where the natural antibodies produced by human subjects can be used for diagnosis. This is particularly relevant for infectious diseases, where the patient will have produced antibodies as a response to the viruses, bacteria or parasites that may have infected them. The protein targets of these antibodies can be identified using Western blotting, which is based on the deposition of proteins onto a plastic membrane, followed by detection using specific antibodies. Samples of bacterial or viral proteins are separated on a gel matrix using an electric charge [SDS polyacrylamide gel electrophoresis (SDS-PAGE) described in Chap. 6]. The Western blotting procedure[3] is designed to produce an exact copy of the separated proteins on a plastic membrane; this is achieved by layering the membrane over the gel and applying an electric current across its entire surface. The proteins then migrate out of the gel and onto the plastic, where they bind tightly, but still maintain exactly the same pattern as in the original gel. The reason for making this copy is that the plastic membranes are stronger and thinner than the polyacrylamide gel; this means that vigorous washing steps can be performed without the risk of breaking the gel and that antibody reactions will occur quite rapidly. Western blotting has an advantage over ELISA assays in that it provides information about the size of each protein, as well as the number that may react with the same antibody; however, it requires a specialized apparatus and is less straightforward to perform. The basic principle is illustrated schematically in Fig. 14.5.

Western blotting forms a part of the standard test for HIV infection, where the patient has produced antibodies to the virus in the blood; these are used to probe HIV proteins separated on the membranes, and if virus protein bands appear, it means that the donor is HIV positive. The method is also used to detect misfolded proteins, for example, the prion proteins that are responsible for degenerative brain diseases, such as Creuzfeldt–Jakob. Protein-folding diseases are of great interest to the biopharmaceutical industry, as they may be responsible for some of the features seen in the brains of patients with Parkinson's and Alzheimer's diseases (see next chapter).

---

[3] Western blots are named after the compass point – the concept of blotting molecules onto membranes was exploited by Dr Ed Southern in the form of the Southern blot used for analyzing DNA fragments. Someone, with a particular brand of humour, subsequently named the transfer of RNA a Northern blot, so Western blots are followed for proteins (the naming is actually getting out of hand with the introduction of Eastern and Southwestern blots).

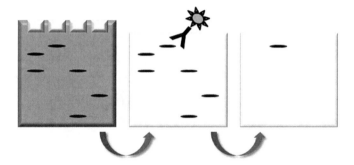

Fig. 14.5 Schematic diagram of the Western blotting procedure. Four separate protein samples are separated through an electric field in an SDS PAGE gel and transferred to a plastic membrane to produce an exact replica of the original gel. The membrane (nitrocellulose, nylon or PVDF) is easier to manipulate than the gel, and it can be incubated with antibodies to a protein of interest. In this case, a labelled antibody binds to the protein band in the second sample and is revealed as a coloured deposit on the membrane. This gives a value for the molecular weight of the antibody target if standard marker proteins are run in parallel

Nanoparticles: Beads and Dots

A great deal of ingenuity has been applied to improve the sensitivity of immunoassays through the use of nanotechnology. Magnetic and semiconductor materials created for the electronics industry have been formed into particles with sizes ranging from nanometres to micrometres; these are used for capturing antibodies that are bound to their target or act as supports for fluorescent probes. Antibody capture can be accomplished with magnetic particles (beads) coated with an antibody or any molecule that binds specifically to the target protein. The beads can then be isolated to remove everything, except the target molecules of interest, by simply applying a magnet. Magnetic particles can also be used to create ultrasensitive assays that reproduce the interactions between a magnetic recording head and a computer hard disc drive. These magnetonanosensors can detect protein levels in the attogram range (10^{-18} g or one million trillionth of a gram) (Gaster et al. 2009).

Quantum dots are another type of nanoparticle which can be attached to antibodies to produce a signal, in this case, emission of fluorescent light. The dots are made of semiconductor materials that emit light of different wavelengths (colours) depending on the size of the particle. This makes quantum dots particularly useful as multicolour probes for different immunoassay formats, since a range of sizes can be linked to specific antibodies and used in combination (Invitrogen (Life Technologies Inc.) 2010).

Lab-on-a-Chip

The lab-on-a-chip (LOC) is an example of microfluidics technology that enables biological and chemical reactions to be performed in extremely small volumes.

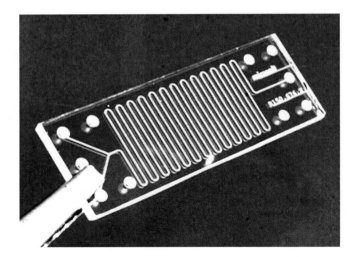

Fig. 14.6 A microfluidics chip used to perform small-scale reactions produced by Micronit Microfluidics (Micronit 2010). Note the size of the unit compared with the tweezers. Two channels for pumping in separate reagents are visible on the *left hand side* of the chip. Image courtesy of Micronit Microfluidics

This is ideally suited to immunoassays, where different reagents (antibodies, proteins, enzymes, etc.) are reacted together and the waste products removed by washing. Conventional immunoassays can take several hours, both because of the time needed for the antibody to bind sufficiently to its target and because of the need to perform multiple washing steps. LOC devices are under development for POC diagnostics and for research applications in the biopharmaceutical industry and academia (Fig. 14.6).

Molecular Diagnostics

This term is generally applied to the detection of nucleic acid molecules derived from microbes or human tissues. It is particularly useful for detecting genetic sequences from viruses and bacteria in a much shorter time than that taken to culture these organisms in the laboratory. Molecular diagnostics of human nucleic acids is used for detecting the characteristic DNA rearrangements and mutations that occur in cancer cells. Nucleic acid-based diagnostic techniques for specific cells or organisms employ an amplification stage from the DNA or RNA present in clinical samples. This is achieved using the polymerase chain reaction (PCR) to amplify DNA, followed by oligonucleotide hybridization to specific sequences in the target DNA (Chap. 6). The power of the technology means that infectious organisms, such as new strains of influenza virus, can be characterized in great detail while a viral epidemic is unfolding. Many molecular diagnostic applications are based on quantitative PCR, in which the absolute amount of DNA present in a sample of tissue or microbe can be determined by measuring the level of binding of fluorescently labelled probes.

14.1.3 *Regulation of Diagnostics*

Just as the regulation of drug development is designed to ensure that marketed products are safe and effective, so it is with diagnostics. A false diagnosis based on an erroneous positive (or negative) result can have catastrophic consequences for the patient. A number of possible scenarios can be envisaged, such as inaccurate HIV tests or prognostic screening tests for cancer that lead to the unnecessary removal of tissues. This potential hazard with unregulated products is the reason why the FDA has a dedicated section to cover diagnostics, the Office of *In Vitro* Diagnostic Device Evaluation and Safety (OIVID). In Europe, the *In Vitro* Diagnostics Directive (IVDD), which was passed into the EC law in 2000, is applied by competent authorities in individual member states, rather than through the EMA. The directive requires that diagnostic devices to be sold in the European Union (EU) must be self-certified as compliant with the IVDD. The self-certification is indicated by Conformité Européene (CE)-marking. Certain tests that fall into higher risk categories, such as those for infectious agents, must register for a CE mark via a notified body rather than through self-certification.

14.1.3.1 Office of *In Vitro* Diagnostic Device Evaluation and Safety

OIVID is part of the Centers for Devices and Radiological Health (CDRH) and has three divisions; these cover diagnostic devices for different conditions as follows:

- Division of Chemistry and Toxicology Devices (DCTD)
  Tests for therapeutic and illegal drugs, hormones and specialist chemistry tests
- Division of Immunology and Hematology Devices (DIHD)
  Tests for cancer, blood and immunological diseases and genetic disorders
- Division of Microbiology Devices (DMD)
  Tests for known and emerging infectious diseases

Diagnostic devices are assigned to one of three classes for review according to the potential risk: class I devices include reagents for routine testing, class II for moderate risks (e.g. mutations in blood-clotting proteins) and class III for high-risk procedures, such as automated analysis of cervical smears for cancer diagnosis (Mansfield et al. 2005).

Class III devices require premarket approval (PMA) by the FDA and often require data from clinical trials to show their effectiveness. Under certain circumstances, however, an Investigational Device Exemption (IDE) may be granted if the test is to be used, for example, to select a specific group of patients with serious diseases for a clinical trial. This scenario is likely to be more common as pharmacogenomics (PGx) and biomarker tests become a routine part of clinical trial design.

14.1.4 Personalized Medicine

14.1.4.1 Theranostics

All of the diagnostic techniques described in the preceding sections are applied at some point or the other in the drug development process whether it is in the basic target discovery, preclinical toxicology or clinical trials. While this has been the case for a long time, interest in new diagnostic technologies and applications has intensified quite recently. This is largely because the biopharmaceutical industry recognizes that medicines do not work for all patients with the same disease; this is driving the search for diagnostic tests which predict responses to specific drugs, an area, rather inelegantly, called theranostics. The products of this personalized approach to medicine, known as companion diagnostics, are the subject of intense interest by both the drug discovery and diagnostics industries. The few companion diagnostics currently in the market are designed to support anti-cancer drugs, but many others are under development. Assuming that technical obstacles can be overcome, the main issues with companion diagnostics will be the willingness of healthcare providers to pay for them and the provision of financial incentives for manufacturers. These, and related issues connected with the commercial aspects of personalized medicine, are outside the scope of this chapter, but have been thoroughly reviewed in a recent article (Blair 2010).

Companion Diagnostic Example: HER2 Test

This test is designed to support the use of the therapeutic antibody, trastuzumab, marketed by Roche as Herceptin® for the treatment of metastatic breast cancer. Approximately 25% of breast cancer cases involve cells that over-express a protein called Human Epidermal Growth Factor Receptor 2 (HER2). The function of HER2 in normal cells is to act as a receptor for epidermal growth factor (EGF), a cytokine that stimulates cell division. In breast cancer, the HER2 gene has been altered by a mutation that results in the production of an excess of active receptor protein; this amplification results in an unregulated cell division and the formation of tumours. The therapeutic antibody, Herceptin®, is designed to bind to HER2 and bring about the destruction of the breast cancer in the same way as antibodies do with cells infected with viruses. It is clearly pointless to prescribe this expensive drug to patients who do not express high levels of HER2 protein, so companion diagnostic tests have been FDA-approved and marketed to determine which patients should receive the medicine. The HercepTest®, produced by Dako, uses IHC to visualize the binding of antibodies against HER2 to the sections of breast cancer tissue. The surface membranes of cells that are positive for HER2 are labelled with a brown colour and observed under a microscope. The interpretation of these results requires an expert pathologist, who is aware of potential artefacts that could lead to false (positive or negative) results. Since the image under the microscope has to be interpreted subjectively, it is given a score of 0, 1+, 2+ or 3+ according to the intensity of staining. Quite often, an alternative test is used to support the diagnostic prediction obtained using IHC. This second test measures the amplification of DNA for HER2; this amplification can be observed directly under the microscope using a technique called Fluorescence *in Situ* Hybridization (FISH). *In situ* hybridization just means that a nucleic acid probe binds to DNA or RNA, which is still located in the cell (*in situ*), rather than in purified form. The fluorescent probes used for the FISH technique bind to the target genes, in this case, HER2, which are still associated with the chromosomes; the signal appears as a coloured dot of light under the microscope. Probes labelled with different coloured fluorescent dyes can be mixed together to detect multiple targets simultaneously by analogy with the multicolour flow cytometry or IHC used for proteins. The basic outline of the PathVysion®, the test marketed by Abbott for the detection of HER2 gene amplification (Abbott Path 2011), is shown in Fig. 14.7.

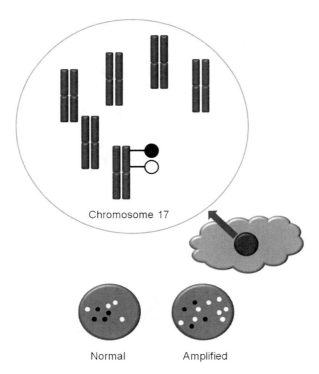

Fig. 14.7 The FISH method for detecting amplification of the HER2 gene in breast cancer cells. The cell nucleus is magnified to show pairs of chromosomes, including chromosome 17, the site of the HER2 gene. DNA probes containing the HER2 sequence (*white circle*) and a probe specific for chromosome 17 (*black circle*) are labelled with different coloured fluorescent markers and applied to sections of tissue. The nuclei are examined under a fluorescent microscope, and the small dots corresponding to the binding of each probe counted. In normal tissue, the number of HER2 and chromosome 17 dots should be the same; in HER2 +ve breast cancer, the former should outnumber the latter because of amplification

14.1.4.2 Biomarkers

The term biomarker is being heard more frequently in the biopharmaceutical industry, as new molecular and imaging tools are being used to identify changes in the human body associated with specific diseases. These changes may take the form of increased (or reduced) levels in the blood, or other body compartments, of cells, proteins, nucleic acids, lipids or small molecules. The ideal biomarker is easily measurable, with minimal inconvenience to the patient, and can be highly accurate in defining disease status. Biomarkers, such as glucose or cholesterol levels, are routinely measured during the drug development programmes for cardiovascular diseases and diabetes. The search for biomarkers of complex diseases, such as cancer, arthritis and Alzheimer's disease, is almost as challenging as the search for treatments. Cancer biomarkers are particularly difficult, as there are large differences in the genetic make-up of tumours taken from different tissues and patients. Because cancer cells rearrange and delete many genes as part of the process of oncogenesis (tumour formation), it is difficult to identify a set of expressed genes or proteins that reliably associate with a particular type of tumour. This has not deterred investigators from trying, however; as a result, molecular technologies, such as gene and protein expression microarrays and protein mass spectrometry, have been used to identify interesting biomarkers that may turn out to be clinically useful. These techniques can also identify prognostic markers which are particularly relevant to life-threatening diseases, such as cancer; this is because patterns of gene or protein expression may be associated with high or low chances of survival. At the time of writing, translation of research on cancer biomarkers into clinical practice has been limited. This is because each marker, or group of markers, has to be extensively validated in patients over several years. Assuming that a biomarker has been validated for clinical application, a suitable biomarker test kit has to be developed and clinicians trained in its use; this extends the timescale from lab to patient even further. Despite this, in June 2010, the FDA approved the Pathwork® Tissue of Origin Test, produced by Pathwork diagnostics in California. The test is designed to determine the tissue origin of tumours by using DNA microarrays (gene chips) to compare the profile of mRNA expression in the test sample with patterns of gene expression from well-defined tissues. The heads of both the FDA and the US National Institutes of Health (NIH) recognize the need for rapid and efficient approval of biomarkers while, at the same time, ensuring patient safety; it is, therefore, reasonable to expect that more high-technology tests of this type will enter the clinic over the next few years (Hamburg and Collins 2010). Indeed, Genomic Health (the USA) and Agendia (the Netherlands) produce prognostic tests for metastatic breast cancer that have been approved by the regulators and sell for more than $3,000 a test.

The "Stratified Medicines Innovation Platform" is an early example of how a personalized medicine is being developed for national healthcare systems (Technology Strategy Board 2010). This initiative is funded by the British Government with the aim of developing diagnostics and biomarkers for cancer treatment through accessing thousands of patients treated in hospitals run by the National Health Service.

The above comments apply equally to surrogate markers, which are used to monitor the progress of a disease during some clinical trials and are not necessarily based on current molecular technology; the marker may simply be survival time. The search for novel surrogates follows the same path as biomarkers in general, with genomics and proteomics being used to identify suitable molecules in human tissues.

14.1.4.3   Pharmacogenetics and Pharmacogenomics

Gene sequencing provides insight into how individuals vary at the level of DNA and how this variability can be linked to responses to drugs, as well as to disease. This has spawned the field of pharmacogenetics (PGt), which can be roughly defined as the inheritance of drug responses, while PGx is the relation between drug responses and the genome. In an attempt to produce a consistent definition for regulatory purposes, the ICH E15 (ICH E15 guidelines 2011) document uses the following definitions:

- PGx
  The study of variations of DNA and RNA characteristics as related to drug response.
- PGt
  A subset of PGx defined as the study of variations in DNA sequence as related to drug response.

There is essentially a complete overlap between molecular diagnostics and PGx, at least as far as the technologies are concerned, so attention will now be focussed on PGt, a discipline that promises to turn the vision of personalized medicine into reality. PGt actually predates DNA sequencing by many years, since the first recorded case of different individual responses to an ingested chemical reported by Arthur Fox (1932). The first paragraph of Fox's paper sums up the situation:

> Some time ago the author had occasion to prepare a quantity of phenylthio carbamide, and while placing it in a bottle, the dust flew around in the air. Another occupant of the laboratory, Dr C.R. Noller, complained of the bitter taste of the dust, but the author, who was much closer, observed no taste and so stated. He even tasted some of the crystals and assured Dr Noller that they were tasteless but Dr. Noller was equally certain it was the dust he tasted. He tried some of the crystals and found them extremely bitter. With these two diverse observations as a starting point, a large number of people were investigated and it was established that this peculiarity was not connected with age, race or sex. Men, women, elderly persons, children, Negroes, Chinese, Germans and Italians were all shown to have in their ranks both tasters and non tasters.

This paper was followed by the one written by A.F. Blakeslee, who showed that this variation had a genetic explanation. Many years later, the gene that differs between tasters and non-tasters was shown to encode a taste receptor protein (a GPCR).

In the intervening years between this first description of a pharmacogenetic response and the advent of whole genome sequencing, clinicians began to notice

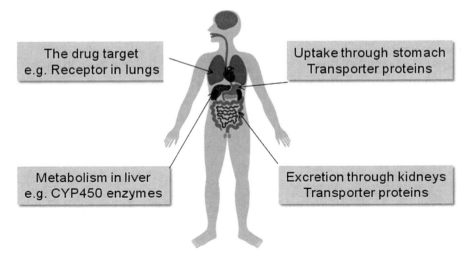

The drug target
e.g. Receptor in lungs

Uptake through stomach
Transporter proteins

Metabolism in liver
e.g. CYP450 enzymes

Excretion through kidneys
Transporter proteins

Fig. 14.8 Anatomical sites with specific functions that may contribute to individual responses to medicines

examples of inherited responses to medicines that related to their effectiveness and safety. Now that it is possible to compare genes at the level of DNA sequence, the stage is set for a new era of personalized medicine, based on the use of genetic information to guide drug prescription.

The Targets of Pharmacogenetic Mutations

Since mutations in DNA lead to altered levels or functions of proteins, the targets of these mutations relating to drug responses are to be found in the proteins that affect both the pharmacodynamics and pharmacokinetics of the drug. Figure 14.8 shows the different points where DNA changes could influence drug efficacy or toxicity:

It's a Snip

Pharmacogenetic differences between individuals are determined by isolating DNA from blood samples. The DNA is then analyzed for changes in nucleotide sequence between different individuals that may relate to the different drug responses. Despite the advances in Next-Generation Sequencing (Chap. 6), it is currently uneconomical and impractical to sequence the entire genome of every patient who is prescribed a drug by their doctor. In fact, it is not necessary to look at the entire genome sequence, but instead to look only at that part of the genome that is relevant to the disease, or drug, under consideration. Differences between individual

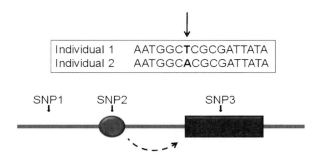

Fig. 14.9 Different types of single nucleotide polymorphisms (SNPs). The *oval* represents a protein (transcription factor) that binds to DNA and affects the activity of genes further away. In this example, the affected gene (represented by the *black rectangle*) produces a protein. SNP1 is located in a piece of DNA, where mutations have no effect (they are silent). SNP2 modifies the binding of the transcription factor and, therefore, modifies the level of expression of the protein. SNP3 directly modifies the amino acid sequence of the protein

genomes come in the form of deletions or duplications or through substitutions of one nucleotide base by another. Substitutions of one nucleotide are called single nucleotide polymorphisms or SNPs (pronounced "snips"), and their detection is one of the main ways in which genetic variability is measured. The possible effect of SNPs on genetic function is illustrated in Fig. 14.9, where a sequence of DNA from two individuals is identical, except for a change in a single base (nucleotide).

In this example, the T in individual one has been substituted with an A in individual two. If the SNP was present in the vast amount of human genome sequence that does not encode proteins, then it may have no effect on either individual (SNP1). Alternatively, the SNP may affect the DNA involved in regulating the amount of a protein that is made by a cell, and therefore the levels will differ between individuals (SNP2). Finally, the SNP may directly alter the genetic code that specifies the amino acids introduced into the protein (SNP3). This last change may have profound consequences if the function or stability of the protein is altered significantly, so investigations into the PGt of drug responses focus on SNPs that may be present in drug target genes or genes that encode metabolic enzymes, like CYP450. Whole genome sequencing of 179 individuals has revealed approximately 15 million SNPs in the human genome (The 1000 Genomes Project Consortium 2010). Some of these are found together in blocks on chromosomes called haplotypes, which are useful for mapping genes associated with disease and drug responses (The International HapMap Consortium 2011).

Examples of SNPs Associated with Drug Responses

- Drug targets
  Changes in genes for drug target proteins could affect the actual binding site for the drug or the amount of protein produced by the relevant cell. Despite the

extensive SNP analysis of a variety of drug target genes, there is little firm evidence that consistently associates these types of mutations with the clear variation in drug responses that are observed clinically. However, there is evidence for genetic variation in the response to asthma medication; SNPs in the genes encoding adrenaline receptors in the lung and the enzyme 5-lipoxygenase lead to variations in patient responses to the drugs that affect these targets.

• Drug transporters
Transporter proteins act as gatekeepers to control the entry of drug compounds into different tissues as well as their exit during excretion. Genetic variation, in the form of SNPs and other mutations, could limit the efficiency of uptake or clearance of a drug and, therefore, affect its efficacy or safety. The uptake of the immunosuppressant drug tacrolimus, used in organ transplantation, appears to be affected by ABCB1 transporters in the intestine; this knowledge could, therefore, be applied to limit the dose of drug given to patients who might otherwise suffer from kidney toxicity. One transporter that has been fully validated has nothing to do with drug responses, but controls whether earwax is wet or dry. The ABCC11 transporter has an SNP that affects the rate of transport of fluids in the ear, and hence the state of the wax, which is dry in East Asians and wet in other populations who have a G instead of an A in the transporter DNA.

• Drug metabolism enzymes
So far, the most useful and informative pharmacogenetic targets have been the enzymes which are involved in both phase I and phase II drug metabolism (Chap. 11). The FDA is now sufficiently confident of the genetic association between certain drug responses and the rate of metabolism that it is allowing genetic data to be included in the package insert provided with the drug. The following example concerns the metabolism of the drug warfarin, marketed as Coumadin® by Bristol-Myers Squibb. Although originally used as a rat poison, warfarin is an effective anticoagulant (blood thinning) drug, but one in which the effective dose may vary as much as tenfold between patients. If too much drug is given, the patient may haemorrhage uncontrollably with fatal consequences. The large dose variation is due to differences in warfarin metabolism, which are associated with SNPs in two enzymes, CYP2C9 and VKORC1. These variants have been used to guide warfarin dosing in clinical trial settings to see whether PGt offers any advantage over conventional dose estimation. The results of a recent trial in the USA indicate that prior knowledge of the CYP2C9 and VKORC1 genetic variants (or genotypes) reduces the admissions of patients to hospital for adverse bleeding events by over 30%. This type of clinical analysis provides the evidence needed to support the introduction of this pharmacogenetic test into routine clinical practice (Epstein 2010). Studies of this type and others linking CYP2C19 to adverse reactions to clopidogrel (another anticoagulant) suggest that cardiovascular medicine may join oncology at the forefront of real-world pharmacogenetic testing.

Summary of Key Points

Diagnostics are fundamental to clinical practice and are increasingly being used to support drug development.

The technology is wide ranging and includes imaging, biochemical assays for small molecules, immunoassays for proteins and nucleic acid detection.

DNA sequence information is being used for personalized medicine through the identification of SNPs and other mutations which associate with responsiveness to drugs, as well as certain diseases.

The integration of biomarkers and companion diagnostics into personalized medicine is dependent on clinicians establishing the clinical validity and utility of the tests.

References

Abbott Path Vysion (2011). http://www.abbottmolecular.com/PathVysionHER2DNAProbeKit_5138.aspx. Accessed 18 Jan 2011

Blair ED (2010) Molecular diagnostics and personalized medicine: value-assessed opportunities for multiple stakeholders. Per Med 7:143–161

Committee on Identifying and Preventing Medication Errors (2007). In: Aspden P, Wolcott J, Bootman JL, Cronenwett LR (eds) Preventing medical errors: quality chasm series. The National Academies Press, Washington DC

Epstein RS (2010) Warfarin genotyping reduces hospitalization rates results from the MM-WES (Medco-Mayo Warfarin Effectiveness study). J Am Coll Cardiol 55:2804–2812

Fox AL (1932) The relationship between chemical constitution and taste. Proc Natl Acad Sci USA 18:115–120

Gaster GS et al (2009) Matrix-insensitive protein assays push the limits of biosensors in medicine. Nat Med 15:1327–1332

Genway Immunoassay Wikipedia 3.0 (2011). http://www.genwaybio.com/gw_file.php?fid=6056. Accessed 18 Jan 2011

Hamburg MA, Collins FS (2010) The path to personalized medicine. N Engl J Med 363:301–304

ICH E15 guidelines (2011). http://www.ich.org/fileadmin/Public_Web_Site/ICH_Products/Guidelines/Efficacy/E15/Step4/E15_Guideline.pdf. Accessed 18 Jan 2011

Invitrogen (Life Technologies Inc.) (2010). http://www.invitrogen.com/site/us/en/home/brands/Molecular-Probes/Key-Molecular-Probes-Products/Qdot/Technology-Overview.html#structure. Accessed 30 Nov 2010

Mansfield E et al (2005) Food and drug administration regulation of in vitro diagnostic devices. J Mol Diagn 7:2–7

Micronit Microfluidics (2010). http://www.micronit.com. Accessed 29 Nov 2010

Suntharalingam G et al (2006) Cytokine storm in a phase 1 trial of the anti-CD28 monoclonal antibody TGN1412. N Engl J Med 355:1018–1028

Press release Technology Strategy Board (2010). http://www.innovateuk.org/content/news/healthcare-initiative-could-enhance-uk-position-as.ashx. Accessed 13 Dec 2010

The 1000 Genomes Project Consortium (2010) A map of human genome variation from population-scale sequencing. Nature 467:1061–1071

The International HapMap Consortium (2011). http://hapmap.ncbi.nlm.nih.gov/. Accessed 18 Jan 2011

Chapter 15
Pulling It All Together: A Drug Development Case History

Abstract This chapter presents a drug development case history that aims to consolidate the information that has been previously given on drug target discovery, selection of compounds or biologicals, clinical development and personalized medicine. It takes the form of a hypothetical programme to discover and develop a medicine to treat Alzheimer's disease. It aims to be as realistic as possible, mixing current research findings with comments about the strategic thinking that would occur in a biopharmaceutical company while undertaking a project of this type.

15.1 Introduction

The purpose of this chapter is to consolidate into a single case history the various aspects of drug discovery and development that have been described previously. This illustrates the scientific and commercial processes that would be used to develop a medicine to treat Alzheimer's disease, a major cause of suffering for patients and their families and also a financial burden on health and welfare systems. While the drug described in this example sadly does not yet exist, the background to its development is intended to be as realistic as possible, based on the current literature and the author's own experiences in the biopharmaceutical industry. Of course, the logical progression of the activity laid out in this example is an idealized situation that rarely occurs in real life. The former British Prime Minister, Harold MacMillan, when asked to name factors that make a government go off course, replied, "Events, dear boy, events". This is as true for drug discovery as it is for politics, and of course human behaviour always plays its part. Nevertheless, the objective here is to show how the key scientific areas covered in the preceding chapters are integrated with the commercial decision making that is central to the drug discovery industry.

E.D. Zanders, *The Science and Business of Drug Discovery: Demystifying the Jargon,*
DOI 10.1007/978-1-4419-9902-3_15, © Springer Science+Business Media, LLC 2011

15.1.1   Discovery and Development Strategy

Once the idea of developing a novel drug to treat Alzheimer's disease has been accepted in principle, a number of actions will have to be taken to turn this into practice. The main headings for these actions will are summarized in Fig. 15.1.

Before the project is approved by the company management, it has to be evaluated on its scientific and commercial merits; if either one of these is lacking, it is unlikely that the necessary human and financial resources will be forthcoming. These deliberations are covered in the following section.

15.1.2   Scientific and Commercial Analysis: The Product Profile

Since the development of prescription medicines is market-driven, it is important to take this into account at the outset of a drug discovery programme. A decision on whether to invest years of time and millions of dollars in a drug for a particular disease area depends upon a number of factors, including the likelihood of success and the commercial return. The decision-making process starts with the drawing up of a product profile that should answer the following questions:

- Is there an unmet medical need?
- Will a new drug show significant advantages over the existing medicines?
- How does it fit into the company's research and commercial portfolio?
- Will a new drug make a return on investment?
- How will the drug be administered?

Fig. 15.1 Main components of a drug discovery and development programme

15.1.2.1 Unmet Medical Need

Most people in the developed world are aware of the impact that dementia has on an ageing population. This topic has become the subject of a great deal of media attention, mostly focused on the disease described by Alois Alzheimer at the beginning of the twentieth century. The fact that the prevalence of all dementias is increasing suggests that medical intervention is not working well enough. The current medicines for Alzheimer's disease treat the symptoms of memory loss, but do not arrest the breakdown of nerve cells in the brain (neurodegeneration), so progression of the disease is inevitable. There is, therefore, a considerable unmet medical need for effective treatments.

15.1.2.2 Comparison with Existing Medicines

Given the nature of Alzheimer's disease and the commercial opportunities for effective drugs (see later), it is no surprise that there is a great incentive for the biopharmaceutical industry to introduce new treatments as quickly as possible. The mainstay of the current treatment is a range of drugs, such as Aricept® and Namenda®, that improve symptoms (i.e. loss of memory and cognition) by increasing neurotransmitter levels in the brain. This could be compared with trying to keep a car with a faulty engine from stopping completely by pumping the accelerator to increase the level of fuel; unfortunately, this only serves to postpone the inevitable failure of the engine. The two available classes of memory-enhancing drugs are enzyme inhibitors (of acetylcholine esterase) and receptor antagonists (NMDA). Acetylcholine esterase inhibitors work by increasing the levels of neurotransmitter acetylcholine in the brain, and the NMDA antagonist may regulate the levels of neurotransmitter glutamate. While these drugs provide some beneficial effects, they neither work in all patients nor arrest the underlying neurodegeneration found in Alzheimer's disease, i.e. they are not disease modifying. This means that there is plenty of opportunity to improve upon the current medicines, particularly if a novel drug slows down or even reverses the progression of the disease.

15.1.2.3 Company Research and Commercial Portfolio

The major biopharmaceutical companies have programmes in a number of therapeutic areas, but dominate in one or two commercial franchises depending on which drugs generate the highest revenues. Alzheimer's disease comes under the central nervous system (CNS) diseases therapeutic area, where companies like Eli Lilly have historically been very active. As a result of this historical (and current) activity, these companies have no problem in marshalling the resources (in-house or contracted out) that are required for a CNS drug discovery programme. Internal lobbying by project champions who support the proposal is necessary to make these resources available from the research and commercial management. Although Alzheimer's disease is chronic and difficult to treat, there is unlikely to be much opposition to attempting at least one drug discovery programme because of the potential to produce a commercial blockbuster. Sometimes, a target or even a drug candidate is produced by a small company or a spin-out from a university, where the academics wish to exploit a laboratory discovery. Since it should be clear from reading this book that no small organization can possibly resource a full drug development programme on its own, some partnering or licensing to larger biopharmaceutical companies is inevitable. The stage at which this happens is partly based on the estimates of risk and the escalating cost of each clinical trial stage. Assuming that the human and financial capital is available to pursue the programme, the next stage is to see whether this can be recovered through drug sales.

15.1.2.4 Return on Investment

The amount of money recovered over the commercial lifetime of the drug obviously depends on the number of patients and the amount that healthcare providers are prepared to pay for each course of treatment. In the case of Alzheimer's, the number of patients worldwide is increasing inexorably as the average lifespan of the general population increases. Although there is an early onset form of the disease affecting those younger than 65, the majority of cases occur in later years. The risk of contracting the disease rises from about 10% between the ages of 65 and 85 to about 45% thereafter.[1] The number of cases in the USA alone is 5 million and rising, so the market size in this most affluent country in the world is substantial. In the (unlikely) event that every one of those patients were to be given the proposed new drug at $10,000 per year, this would produce revenues of $50Bn. Given that the best-selling blockbuster drugs are creating around $10Bn in annual sales, even a fraction of this market would be worth the investment. Another commercial aspect is the willingness of healthcare providers (governments and managed care organizations) to pay for new medicines or to support research and development efforts. In the case of Alzheimer's disease, the costs are truly terrifying; the Alzheimer's Association quotes $172Bn in annual costs to the US economy (http://www.alz.org/alzheimers_disease_facts_figures.asp, Accessed 1 Dec 2010). It has been estimated that delaying the onset of the disease by 5 years could save $50Bn, so it is unsurprising that government funding of research has increased substantially (Mount and Downton 2006). Cost/benefit considerations like this are evaluated by the commercial departments of biopharmaceutical companies and government and academic departments wishing to assess the value for money provided by medicines of this type (see pharmacoeconomics, Chap. 16).

---

[1] I recall hearing a talk in which a graph of prevalence compared with age was extrapolated to 150 years, in which case everyone would have the disease, something that those who want to dramatically extend the human lifespan might wish to ponder.

15.1.2.5 What Type of Drug and How Will It Be Administered?

The next item on the product profile list concerns the type of drug that should be produced and how it should be delivered.

The ideal medicine is an orally bioavailable small molecule that can be administered once or twice a day and be safe for chronic use over many years; furthermore, because Alzheimer's is a CNS disease, the drug must cross the blood brain barrier to get to its target. It is possible that there will be too many obstacles to be overcome in achieving this idealized situation, so alternatives to small molecules may be considered instead. In fact, there are a number of biologicals, including vaccines, which are being evaluated in the clinic, but the small molecule route is used in this hypothetical example.

15.1.3 Discovering and Testing the Drug

The search for drug targets and molecules interfering with their action has been extensively covered in earlier chapters, and the basic principles described there have been applied to this case history.

15.1.3.1 Identifying a Chemically Tractable Drug Target

Although important target discoveries are made in company laboratories, many ideas that stimulate the drug development come from university or hospital research laboratories as part of investigations into basic cell biology and mechanisms of disease. Experimental findings are published in scientific journals and presented at conferences and seminars, often with the conclusion that "such and such may make a good drug target". Company scientists will be in a position to take these speculations to a higher level by judging whether the idea is practical and, if sufficiently enthused by it, may later develop a formal project proposal based on the target.[2] Ideas may even come from non-scientific sources; the example of compounds from Chinese herbal medicines (Chap. 4) came from a newspaper cutting passed on by the author's mother. Alternatively, the target may be the same as that being worked on by a competitor, so the objective of the drug development programme has to produce a compound that is safer and more effective.

A suitable drug target for Alzheimer's can only be discovered through having a basic understanding of the disease. Alois Alzheimer himself was a Munich physician who followed the decline in mental function of a patient over 5 years and then

---

[2] Hence the vision of scientists going into their manager's office brandishing the latest copy of *Science* or *Nature* that might contain a useful idea.

(in 1904) examined her brain *post-mortem* to look for abnormalities. He identified a series of tangles and plaques (translucent areas) in the brain (using histochemical staining, Chap. 6) that appeared to be a hallmark of Alzheimer's, but not other degenerative conditions in the brain. In later years, the chemical nature of the molecules in the tangles and plaques was established, along with an analysis of their effects on the viability of nerve cells. The results of these analyses showed that neurofibrillary tangles consist of a protein (called tau) that kills nerve cells from within. The production of tau, however, is stimulated by β-amyloid peptide (also called Aβ) which is the main component of amyloid plaques. Opinion is divided as to whether tangles or plaques are more important for disease progression; it depends on whether one subscribes to the tau hypothesis (a tauist) or the amyloid hypothesis. In this example, the amyloid hypothesis is used as a guide to the drug target.

Different techniques are employed to provide evidence for the role of Aβ in Alzheimer's. For example, transgenic mice have been engineered to produce human Aβ peptides in their brains, the result being a pathology that is very similar to the human disease. Other evidence comes from epidemiological studies and from genetic evidence in families with early-onset Alzheimer's disease, where mutations in amyloid precursor protein (APP) (see below) have been detected by DNA sequencing. Although these are rare mutations, they at least provide some support for the role of amyloid peptides in the disease.

The next logical step is to ask where the Aβ peptide comes from and how it is formed. Peptides found in biological tissues are often derived from the breakdown of proteins by the action of protease enzymes; this proteolysis is used in the digestion of food as well as in a series of important biological control mechanisms, such as blood clotting and the regulation of blood pressure. In the case of amyloid peptide, the parent protein was identified as a molecule called APP that is expressed on the surface of cells in many parts of the body, including the brain. This identification was achieved by comparing the amino acid sequence of the peptide with the sequences of proteins held in computer databases. The sequence of the Aβ peptide was duly found to be contained within the sequence of the APP protein. With this information, the search for a drug target can then be narrowed down to working out how APP is broken down into the toxic Aβ peptides.

Since protease enzymes cut at a characteristic amino acid "signature", it is possible to guess what type of protease enzyme may be cutting APP to form Aβ by examining the amino acid sequence information. If such a protease can be identified and studied in the laboratory, it would be a potential drug target, since inhibiting it with a small molecule would stop the production of Aβ, prevent the formation of amyloid plaques and slow down the disease progression. Proteases are good targets for small-molecule drugs (e.g. the HIV protease inhibitors for AIDS), which add to the attraction of this target. There are in fact three different proteases (α-, β- and γ-secretases) that cleave APP in different positions to give peptides of different lengths. Current drug company interest has centred on inhibiting β- and γ-secretases.

For the purposes of this case history, the β-secretase enzyme is used as the example target for small-molecule drug discovery. This enzyme is also known as beta-amyloid cleaving enzyme-1 (BACE-1) or memapsin-2, just another example of the curse of biochemical nomenclature.

The enzyme was actually identified by scanning online DNA sequence databases. One sequence in particular looked interesting, as it encoded a protease from the aspartyl protease family (that includes the digestive enzyme pepsin) which had not been seen before. The enzyme was associated with the membranes of cells in the brain, hence the name *mem*brane-anchored *a*spartic *p*rotease of the pep*sin* family (Lin et al. 2000).

The protein was produced in bacteria using genetic engineering technology and shown to cleave APP at the correct site to produce Aβ peptides. At this stage, the drug discovery scientist would want to anticipate any side effects that might occur as a consequence of inhibiting the β-secretase enzyme. One way of doing this is to use transgenic animals where the enzyme has been "knocked out" using genetic engineering. Such animals do exist and show no obvious pathology that would cause concern. The stages leading to the enzyme target, as outlined above, are given in Fig. 15.2.

Once the decision has been made to develop β-secretase inhibitors as drugs, the resources for chemical synthesis and screening are put in place.

15.1.3.2 Finding the Right Compound

The biochemists and screening scientists must now develop an assay that measures the activity of the β-secretase enzyme as it releases Aβ peptide from APP protein. This assay is used to screen for inhibitors of the enzyme using the methods described in Chap. 9. This is not a trivial exercise, as it may take a great deal of work to develop the assay into a form that can be used to screen tens of thousands of compounds or more. Meanwhile, medicinal chemists examine the enzyme-active site, namely, the part of the enzyme that binds the target protein (APP) and breaks a bond between the amino acids to release the peptide (Aβ). The nature of the active site and protein that binds to it provides ideas for creating synthetic inhibitors of the enzyme in the laboratory. As discussed in Chap. 9, there are several approaches that can be taken to this problem, namely, random screening of compound collections and natural products, design of peptide analogues[3] or *in silico* design in the computer. Although one or more of these routes may be followed in practice, chemists have amassed a great deal of experience with particular target classes, so this may influence their starting point. The aspartyl proteases (of which this target is one) are a case in point; past successes, like HIV protease inhibitors, have been achieved using peptide analogues that were later optimized using *in silico* design.

---

[3] Peptide analogues are peptides that are selectively modified in the laboratory. The principle is similar to that used to create histamine analogues as anti-ulcerants (Chap. 4), where the natural histamine molecule is modified to produce drug compounds.

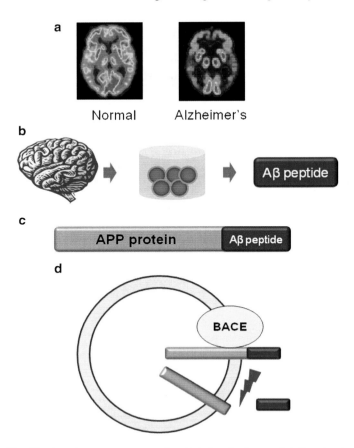

Fig. 15.2 Identification of an enzyme target for Alzheimer's disease. (**a**) Examination of brains from affected and normal individuals. This example is a PET scan on living subjects, but much has been observed using *post-mortem* tissue. The main features are amyloid plaques which are revealed using a contrast agent. (**b**) Biochemical analysis of brain tissue. Tissue is broken up, and its proteins and other molecules dissolved in buffer. The amyloid plaques are shown to consist of the amyloid beta (Aβ) peptide using the standard methods for purifying and characterizing peptides. (**c**) The peptide must be derived from a larger protein. The amyloid precursor protein (APP) is identified in protein databases and shown to include the Aβ peptide in its sequence. (**d**) Cell biology studies indicate that APP is inserted through the cell membrane with the Aβ portion sticking outwards. A protease enzyme (BACE) that clips APP to produce Aβ peptide is identified as a drug target in brain cells

The process of synthesizing compounds and testing them for inhibitory activity in the β-secretase assay (screen) continues in a back and forth way, as medicinal chemists modify the compounds to pass back to the screeners to test for activity and selectivity. The screeners test active compounds against other enzyme targets to ensure that the final candidate for development is as selective for β-secretase as possible. This again is a far-from-trivial exercise as the active sites of related enzymes are very similar to each other. Having achieved the desired potency and selectivity, it is important that the molecular weight is kept below a certain level to ensure that the drug compound is orally bioavailable. Finally, the compound must be sufficiently lipophilic (Chap. 7) to ensure that it can pass across the blood brain barrier.

15.1.3.3 Selection of a Clinical Candidate

Compounds that selectively inhibit the β-secretase enzyme in a test tube assay may look promising, but they must also be shown to work on whole cells and, ideally, in animals. Sometimes, a compound that inhibits the purified enzyme is inactive against the same enzyme present in its normal cellular environment. This is because it is unable to penetrate the outer membrane of human cells and reach its target. It is, therefore, necessary for cell biologists to set up cultures of human nerve cells to measure the release of Aβ *in vitro*. Having established that the compounds do work with whole cells, the next step might be an *in vivo* test to show that the compound inhibits Aβ formation in the brain and possibly even improves cognitive behaviour. Such models exist in the form of the transgenic mice described earlier in Section 15.1.3.1.

Assuming that the compounds pass these tests, the next task is to anticipate any problem with ADMETox that may preclude a full development programme. At the same time, scale-up and formulation studies begin to ensure that sufficient compound is made available in the correct dosage form to support preclinical and clinical trials. A series of preliminary screens are run to assess the metabolism of the compound in cultures of liver microsomes and possibly also a panel of CYP450 enzymes (see Chap. 11). Adsorption and distribution will be measured (using the Caco2 assay or similar), as will protein binding. A preliminary toxicity analysis may take the form of bacterial Ames test to check for mutagenicity. Unless any "show stoppers" occur, a full development programme can then be initiated using animal models in two species for a full pharmacokinetic and toxicology study. Since the drug is intended for the CNS, the pharmacokinetic studies will include animal models to measure the amount of compound that is able to enter the brain. The outcome of the preclinical studies will be an estimation of the dose of β-secretase inhibitor that can be administered to human volunteers in phase I clinical trials.

15.1.3.4 Clinical Trials

Having established a starting dose for phase I clinical trials and approval from the regulatory authorities, the sponsoring company must identify the clinical centres that will conduct all the safety, efficacy and confirmatory studies as detailed in Chaps. 12 and 13. Clinical trials for drugs that slow down the progression of a neurodegenerative disease are particularly challenging, however. Firstly, patients enrolled in efficacy trials must be correctly diagnosed as having Alzheimer's disease in the first place. Although this condition may be present in the majority of enrolled patients, it is quite possible that some people with unrelated dementias will be included in the trials and confound the results. The problem is that a definitive diagnosis is currently available only after the death of the patient. Another problem is the actual measurements that are used to show improvements in mental (cognitive) function. Standardized tests have been devised, such as the Alzheimer's disease Assessment Scale (ADAS), which contains a series of evaluations of memory, speech and other functions considered central to the disease. Another test used in real-life trials involves measuring the level of Aβ peptide in the plasma and cerebrospinal fluid. If a drug that inhibits the breakdown of APP is working correctly, there should be a reduction of Aβ levels compared to those in untreated subjects.

Once the drug has (hopefully) been shown to achieve a statistically significant reduction in disease progression in the pivotal phase III trials lasting at least 18 months, marketing approval is sought from the regulators. If granted, the drug discovery and development programme will be near its end, although not completely, as further safety and efficacy studies may be performed once the drug is marketed. In practice, the whole process from inception of the project to the final approval may have taken 12–15 years. It is, therefore, quite possible that the people who started the project will have long departed the company, rather like the scientists and engineers who design a spacecraft and then have to wait for years before it reaches its destination in space. In fact, the drug discovery business tends to recycle staff through companies of varying size so that experience gained in one is transferred to another. This can have the effect of increasing efficiency through not repeating mistakes made in other organizations, but it can also result in a certain uniformity of approach to discovery projects.

15.1.3.5 Biomarkers and Pharmacogenetics

As discussed in Chap. 14, the search for biomarkers, which can be used for diagnosis and treatment of disease, is becoming a major concern of the drug discovery industry. In a chronic disease, like Alzheimer's, the ideal biomarker should be detectable before the disease symptoms become apparent; otherwise, it may be too late to reverse the neuronal damage in the brain. Furthermore, the cognitive tests, although sophisticated, are not guaranteed to discriminate between Alzheimer's and other dementias. The hypothetical drug discovery programme described here would certainly include a search for biomarkers to guide clinical trials. The term "biomarkers", as well as encompassing the proteins found in blood or CSF, includes the results of imaging, which are particularly relevant to diseases of the brain. MRI and PET scanning can reveal some information about the disease in living subjects; PET scanning, in particular, can locate amyloid plaques that have been stained with specially designed imaging dyes.

The pharmacogenetics of responses to the experimental drug would also be investigated. If it could be shown that a patient's response to secretase inhibitors has a genetic basis, obvious candidates would be the gene coding for the β-secretase enzyme itself, as well as metabolizing enzymes in the CYP450 family. The most studied genetic risk factor in real life is APOE4ε4, a protein involved in the transport of lipoproteins (proteins modified with fatty compounds). Individuals with a double dose of this particular gene have a significantly elevated risk of developing Alzheimer's, so the effects of this particular gene on treatment response would definitely be included in any pharmacogenetic study.[4]

The Situation with Real β-Secretase Inhibitors

The above case history is based on scenarios that are being played out in reality by companies and academic institutions. The amyloid hypothesis is still considered sufficiently compelling that companies are prepared to invest millions of dollars in clinical trials. Different approaches to removing amyloid plaques have been tried, including the following: using small molecules and antibodies to disrupt the aggregation of the Aβ peptide in the brain, producing a vaccine based on the APP protein and creating inhibitors of both the β- and γ-secretase enzymes. None of these approaches have been successful so far, either because of lack of efficacy or because of side effects (as occurred with an otherwise promising vaccine trial). The design of the clinical trial may be part of the problem; some patients may not have been correctly diagnosed with Alzheimer's (through a lack of suitable biomarkers or imaging techniques) or the disease may have progressed too far to be reversible. In the case of β-secretase inhibitors (which have been under investigation for several years), the difficulty lies in producing small molecules that satisfy all the criteria of potency, selectivity, oral bioavailability and ability to penetrate the brain. This is not to say that interest in this target has waned. One inhibitor from Comentis (licensed to Astellas in Japan) has been tested in a phase I study, where it was shown to be well tolerated and capable of reducing Aβ levels in the plasma. Other companies, including Merck, are slowly progressing compounds towards the clinic, having overcome some of the difficulties with pharmacokinetics (Drahl 2010).

The end of this chapter is also the end of the description of drug discovery from a predominantly scientific and technical perspective. The next two chapters cover the commercial side of the drug discovery industry and the roles played by companies, academia and charities.

---

[4] This high risk has meant that some people (like James Watson), who have had their genomes sequenced, have preferred to remain ignorant about their APOE4 status.

References

Drahl C (2010) Beta Testing. Chem Eng News 88:14

Lin X et al (2000) Human aspartic protease memapsin 2 cleaves the β-secretase site of β-amyloid precursor protein. Proc Natl Acad Sci USA 97:1456–1460

Mount C, Downton C (2006) Alzheimer disease: progress or profit? Nat Med 12:780–784

Part IV
The Global Pharmaceuticals Business

Chapter 16
Commercial Aspects of Drug Development

Abstract This chapter moves away from the technical aspects of drug discovery to cover the commercial operations of biopharmaceutical companies. Starting with the global market for prescription medicines, the chapter describes the different types of organizations that conduct pharmaceutical research and development and then covers the customer base, pharmacoeconomics and portfolio management. Lastly, the all-important subjects of intellectual property and generic competition are reviewed in some detail.

16.1 Introduction

This chapter highlights some of the key commercial aspects of the biopharmaceutical industry. These include the market for pharmaceuticals, company structures, intellectual property (IP), generic competition and commercial operations, such as portfolio management.

The pharmaceuticals market is truly global, as the need for medicines has no geographical boundaries; it is, however, strongly biased towards the affluent western-style economies, since the enormous costs of drug development have to be covered by those who have the resources to pay. Of course, this is a rapidly changing business like many others, so specific details about companies and legislation may become outdated relatively quickly. Fortunately, there are numerous sources of market information, including private business intelligence companies, such as IMS Health, along with academic groups, such as the Tufts Center for the Study of Drug Development (TCSDD). In addition, there are a number of printed and online journals and magazines that provide up-to-date information on commercial, scientific, clinical and regulatory developments in the biopharmaceutical industry. Some of these publications are listed in Appendix 1, Further Reading.

E.D. Zanders, The Science and Business of Drug Discovery: Demystifying the Jargon, DOI 10.1007/978-1-4419-9902-3_16, © Springer Science+Business Media, LLC 2011

16.1.1   The Pharmaceuticals Marketplace

Before describing the current marketplace for drug sales, it is useful to describe the actual costs required to bring a single medicine from discovery to the marketplace. A much-quoted figure for the cost is $802M, which is derived from a study of 68 drugs that were manufactured by 10 pharmaceutical companies (DiMasi et al. 2003). This figure includes the cost of failed compounds, as well as the cost of capital required over the many years before the drug can be marketed. This figure has inevitably been used as a political football between the companies that have to recoup this expenditure and those who think that the industry is profiteering from medicines. Interestingly, the results of a 2010 study, using publicly available data on a larger number of companies, suggest that this figure should now be nearer $1Bn (Adams and Brantner 2010). This enormous figure only applies to some of the (relatively small) number of drugs entering the marketplace each year, but it lends some support to the industry's perspective on drug pricing.

16.1.1.1   Global Pharmaceutical Sales

The total market size [2009 figures (IMS Health Press Room Top line industry data 2010)] is estimated to be $808.3Bn. This is broken down by the region in Fig. 16.1.

The USA is the largest market, followed by Europe, Asia/Africa/Australia, Japan and Latin America. The US figures include Canada, the European figures are mainly from the European Union (EU) and the Asia/Africa/Australia figures are dominated by China, South Korea and India. Although the USA has dominated the market for many years, the situation with the rest of the world has changed markedly

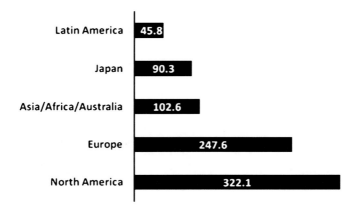

Fig. 16.1 The global pharmaceuticals market. Figures represent estimated 2009 sales in $Bn. Data courtesy of IMS Health (2010) with kind permission

since the end of the twentieth century. In the 1990s, for example, Japan was the second largest market, with other Asian countries much further down the list. Since then, the EU has expanded and Russia has increased its share of the pharmaceuticals market. The most dramatic change has been the emergence of the BRIC economies, namely, Brazil, Russia, India and China, as major consumers of healthcare. These countries, and others like Turkey and South Korea, have been called pharmerging markets (further proof of the resilience of the English language) which have current growth in excess of the mature markets. China alone showed a growth of 26% in 2008 and is set to become the third largest pharmaceuticals market by 2011 (see Table 16.1).

This dramatic growth by the emerging economies contrasts with the much slower growth of the western markets, at around 5%. It is, therefore, unsurprising that the major biopharmaceutical companies have established operations in the BRIC countries to exploit the local markets and to access highly qualified personnel for research and development (R&D) activities. The Swiss pharmaceutical giant Novartis, for example, is planning to invest $1Bn in its Shanghai R&D centre and to increase its staff there from 160 to 1,000 (Cyranoski 2010).

Table 16.1 Projected changes in the global pharmaceuticals marketplace

	2009	2011
1	USA	USA
2	Japan	Japan
3	France	China
4	Germany	Germany
5	China	France
6	Italy	Italy
7	Spain	Spain
8	UK	Brazil
9	Brazil	UK
10	Canada	Canada
11	Russia	Russia
12	Turkey	India
13	India	South Korea
14	Mexico	Venezuela
15	South Korea	Mexico
16	Australia	Australia
17	Greece	Turkey
18	Venezuela	Greece
19	Netherlands	Poland
20	Poland	Netherlands

Japan is the second largest market, if European states are considered individually, and China is following closely. Data taken from Campbell and Chui, IMS Health (2010) with kind permission

Table 16.2 Global sales revenues for top ten selling medicines in 2009

Brand name	Company	Indication	Sales ($Bn)
Lipitor	Pfizer	Cholesterol lowering	13.3
Plavix	Sanofi-Aventis, BMS	Cardiovascular	9.1
Nexium	AstraZeneca	Anti-ulcerant	8.2
Seretide/Advair	GSK	Asthma	8.1
Seroquel	AstraZeneca	Antipsychotic	6.0
Enbrel	Amgen, Wyeth, Takeda	Arthritis, etc.	5.9
Remicade	Johnson and Johnson	Arthritis, etc.	5.4
Crestor	AstraZeneca	Cholesterol lowering	5.38
Zyprexa	Eli Lilly	Antipsychotic	5.35
HUMIRA	Abbott	Arthritis, etc.	5.0

All are small molecules except for the therapeutic proteins which are highlighted in bold. Data from IMS Health (2010) with kind permission

A more detailed discussion of how global economies might change over the next decade is outside the scope of this book (and author's knowledge); nevertheless, the consequences of these changes will be felt by anyone who works in the drug discovery industry or who has dealings with it. It is very likely, for example, that a Chinese company will be among the world's top ten biopharmaceutical companies within this time frame and that the threat to the dominance of North America and Europe in biomedical research will increase.

16.1.1.2   The World's Top-selling Medicines

The state of the pharmaceuticals market at any given time is partly reflected by the top-selling medicines that bring in the major revenues. The top ten best-selling branded prescription medicines in 2009 are shown in Table 16.2.

One of the first things to note (apart from the large revenues) is the presence of different drugs for the same indication. The sales figures would suggest that each product can be clearly differentiated from its competitor; Lipitor® and Crestor® in both for example, are both cholesterol-lowering statins. Another point to note is the presence of three biologicals in the top ten list. This would be unthinkable until quite recently, but the market share of biologicals can only increase, particularly with the emergence of therapeutic antibodies such as Herceptin® and Avastin®.

16.1.2   Drug Discovery Organizations

While drug discovery and development are dominated by the long-established pharmaceutical companies, this is certainly not the whole picture, since major contributions are also made by biotechnology companies, academia, charities and contract research organizations (CROs). Some brief comments about the main drug discovery players are listed below:

Large (big) pharmas

International sites
Multiple therapeutic areas
Large sales and marketing activity
Dependent upon blockbuster sales

Small pharmas

Similar structure to large pharmas, but scaled down
Large proportion of products may be in-licensed from other companies

Large biotechs

Companies with several products, possibly a mix of biological and small molecules
Boundaries with small pharmas may be blurred

Small biotechs

Develop technology and out-license discoveries for other companies to develop
Small number of employees, often ex-university scientists

Not-for-profit organizations

Academia, funded by governments, industrial grants and charities
Medical research charities
Philanthropic research foundations

CROs

Used by all organizations to outsource drug development operations

16.1.2.1 Large Pharmaceutical Companies

The drug discovery industry is dominated by multinational pharmaceutical corporations, such as Pfizer and GlaxoSmithKline. Many of these companies have a long and tortuous history, having grown through mergers and acquisitions. GlaxoSmithKline, for example, was formed in 2001 after a merger between GlaxoWellcome and SmithKline Beecham.[1] These, in turn, were formed by mergers between Glaxo and Wellcome and SmithKlineFrench and Beechams so that two once-famous names disappeared. In my experience, the name Glaxo is so catchy that people instinctively use it to refer to the company, despite the fact that it has merged into a new organization. The name Glaxo was created in 1906 as a trademark for the powdered milk that was exported from New Zealand to England by the company's founder, Joseph Nathan. Meanwhile, Smith Kline and French had developed as a drug store, founded by John Smith in Philadelphia in 1830. Beechams originated as a laxative pill invented by Thomas Beecham in 1842, and the Burroughs Wellcome Company was formed in London in 1880. Each of these companies produced innovative medicines that have had a major impact on the treatment of infectious diseases, asthma, cancer and metabolic diseases.

Although major pharmaceutical companies may be headquartered in one country, they have research, development and manufacturing sites in many parts of the world. While in the past, the research sites may have been mostly confined to Europe and the USA, there is a move towards establishing centres in countries, such as Singapore, China and Japan, where the local market is expanding and there is a good supply of qualified personnel. Large companies have the resources to work in multiple therapeutic areas, thereby spreading the risk and improving the chances of finding the blockbuster products they require for survival. In addition to having to support clinical trials and regulatory affairs, large pharmas must also employ large marketing departments and a trained sales force to maximise the return on their investments. Most large pharmaceutical companies are publicly listed on international stock exchanges and, therefore, have a large shareholder base. The financial performance of these companies is followed carefully by pension fund managers, as the pharmaceuticals sector is conventionally seen as a defensive "safe haven", in contrast to the more volatile biotechnology sector.

16.1.2.2 Small–Medium Pharmaceutical Companies

These organizations may be based on the traditional pharmaceutical company model, or else may have developed from a biotechnology company, such as Amgen Inc, that has grown through commercial success. Since these smaller companies do not have the massive resources of the major pharmas, they develop fewer products

---

[1]A more detailed historical timeline can be found in http://www.gsk.com/about/history.htm, Accessed 3 Dec 2010.

and may specialise in a particular disease area. Examples include Shire plc based in Ireland, which not only markets drugs for attention deficit disorders, but also develops and acquires products for other diseases, including relatively uncommon genetic disorders. In this respect, it is similar to another medium-sized pharma, Genzyme Corporation, whose name is derived from the genetically engineered enzymes it produces as a replacement therapy for treating certain childhood diseases.

16.1.2.3 Large Biotechnology Companies

Sometimes, it is hard to make a clear distinction between a large biotechnology company and a small/medium pharmaceutical operation. This is because the biotechnology revolution that began in the 1970s has developed to the point that it is now part of mainstream drug development. The defining nature of biotechnology, however, has been innovation and the risk that accompanies it. Although traditional pharmaceutical companies have long been innovative in drug development, this has been mostly related to small molecule discovery. As discussed in previous chapters, biotechnology companies have concentrated on large molecule proteins or nucleic acids that, until recently, have been quite alien to many working in big pharma. The commercial success of proteins, such as erythropoietin and therapeutic antibodies, has allowed some biotechs to grow independently to a reasonable size. Others have survived by broadening their portfolios to include small molecule drugs against targets in diseases being pursued by rival pharmaceutical companies or in niche diseases, where they have the field to themselves. Since drug discovery is capital intensive and the biotechnology sector is underfunded and often operating at a loss, companies with promising technologies or products become targets for acquisition by larger pharmaceutical corporations. Examples of successful biotech companies with strong small molecule portfolios include Vertex and Gilead. The former started out as a specialist chemical genomics company with expertise in computer-aided drug design. Gilead was formed on the basis of its antisense nucleic acid technology, but the patent rights to this technology were assigned to Isis over a decade ago. Their success has, in fact, come from small molecule drugs, including Tamiflu®, which was licensed to Roche for the treatment of influenza.

16.1.2.4 Small Biotechnology Companies

These companies are generally formed as spinouts from university departments and may only have a handful of employees. They are strong in innovative technology, but short in capital, and must form collaborations to be viable. Funding for small biotech companies often takes the following route: initial venture capital funding, further rounds of finance and hope that the investment can be recovered at an Initial Public Offering (IPO) on the Stock Exchanges or a sale to a pharmaceutical company. When things go wrong, the company may collapse and have its assets sold off in a fire sale. The biotechnology sector has, in the past, suffered a similar fate to the dotcom companies in that valuations were unrealistically high for businesses that were nowhere near profitability. However, this has not deterred those biotech entrepreneurs who have weathered the investment storm and managed to create small companies; these may not always be profitable, but many do make a very positive contribution to drug discovery.

16.1.2.5 Contract Research Organizations

In principle, CROs can undertake any of the drug development and commercialisation activities that are normally undertaken by employees of major pharmaceutical companies. The financial advantages are obvious, since the company does not have to pay salaries to people who may not be needed at a particular time of the development cycle. On the other hand, projects outsourced to CROs have to be very closely managed by each party to avoid costly mistakes. CROs are particularly useful for biotech companies that wish to bring a drug candidate up to phase I clinical trials or even beyond. The value of the product increases significantly as evidence is gathered to show that it has genuine commercial potential; if this is the case, it can be licensed to larger companies with the expertise and facilities to progress it through to the marketplace. Multinational CROs, such as Covance, offer a range of preclinical, clinical and regulatory activities in the mature pharmaceutical markets as well as in rapidly growing areas, such as Asia and Latin America.

16.1.2.6 Academia

The relationship between academia and industry is not always straightforward, but successful drug discovery and development is dependent upon good interactions between the two. Most of the science and technology behind target identification, small and large molecule discovery and clinical research arises from university and hospital laboratories that have been funded by the taxpayer or medical research charities. The National Institutes of Health (NIH) in the USA receives over $30Bn in taxpayer funding for basic and applied medical research; it is a strong advocate of applying laboratory findings to clinical practice in as short a time as possible (see translational research, Chap. 6). In recent years, the NIH has set up its own small molecule screening activities that are designed to produce chemical probes for use in target validation and small molecule discovery. The NIH has also established, in 2009, the NIH Therapeutics for Rare and Neglected Diseases (TRND) programme to develop drugs for conditions, such as sickle cell disease, schistosomiasis and hookworm. This is a significant departure for a basic medical research body and is part of a new trend for non-pharmaceutical organizations to become involved in drug development. It should be borne in mind, however, that the $24 million assigned to TRND for six conditions is not sufficient to bring a drug all the way to the market without further investment. The Medical Research Council (MRC), the UK's main funding body for biomedical research, has also entered into drug discovery collaborations through the MRC Technology's Centre for Therapeutics Discovery based in London, which offers small molecule design, synthesis and screening.

16.1.2.7 Charities and Philanthropic Foundations

Medical research charities have been around for a long time. Often founded by individuals who have a personal reason for wanting to find cures for particular diseases, these charities depend upon private donations and government tax breaks. Some, like the Wellcome Foundation in London, have large financial assets and can influence the course of medical research through the disposition of their research grants. Britain's large investment in the Human Genome Project, for example, was made possible with Wellcome Trust funding. Similarly, charitable foundations like the Howard Hughes Medical Institute contribute indirectly to the business of drug discovery by supporting some of the best biomedical research to be found anywhere in the world. The Wellcome Foundation was created from the profits gained by the Burroughs Wellcome pharmaceutical company, while more recently, the Bill & Melinda Gates foundation was created from the profits gained by Microsoft Corporation. The latter organization represents a new type of charitable funding called Venture Philanthropy; here, money is carefully targeted at drug development projects using the same business principles of due diligence and accountability that are found with other commercial investments. The current (2010) head of the Gates Foundation's Global Development Program is Tachi Yamada, former research director of GlaxoSmithKline; his appointment is an example of how large pharmaceutical company expertise is being used to oversee the drug development programmes supported by this charity. Since these programmes concentrate on diseases of the developing world, they do not compete directly with the activities of most drug companies who are more interested in "western" diseases like cancer and neurodegeneration; however, this is beginning to change (see next chapter).

Table 16.3 lists representative examples of each of the organizations described above.

Table 16.3 Examples of organizations that are directly involved in drug discovery and development

Category	Organization	2009 Revenues ($M)
Large pharma	GlaxoSmithKline	34,900
Small pharma	Genzyme Corporation	4,500
Large biotech	Vertex	102
Small biotech	Phytopharm	1.35
CRO	Covance	1,867
Academia	National Institutes of Health (NIH)	30,168
Charity	Cancer Research UK	0.774
Private ventures	Bill & Melinda Gates Foundation	2.6[a]

Data were obtained from company annual reports and other public financial data
[a] The last figure represents investment income and donations; the actual operating assets are over $28Bn

Table 16.4   2009 sales for top 15 major pharmaceutical companies

Company	2009 Sales ($Bn)
Pfizer	57.0
Merck & Co	38.9
Novartis	38.5
Sanofi-Aventis	35.5
GlaxoSmithKline	34.9
AstraZeneca	34.4
Roche	32.7
Johnson & Johnson	26.7
Lilly	20.3
Abbott	19.8
Teva	15.9
Bayer	15.7
Boehringer Ingelheim	15.2
Amgen	15.0
Takeda	14.3

Data kindly provided by IMS Health (2010)

There can be no question that large pharmaceutical companies generate by far the greatest revenues and, therefore, always dominate the drug discovery industry.

Table 16.4 illustrates the list of the top 15 pharmaceutical companies in order of 2009 global sales.

While these sales figures are impressive, the companies are vulnerable to patent expiries, so the order is changeable (see later and Chap. 17). It should also be noted that the market share of the largest companies is around 5%, which is low compared with that of similar-sized industries. Aircraft manufacture, for example, is split approximately 50% in market share between Boeing and Airbus while General Motors takes up roughly 20% of the car market.

16.1.3   Commercial Operations

Prescription medicines are, in many ways, like any other branded product; they are marketed to customers with a particular profile of needs and interests. The main difference between promoting drugs and say, consumer electronics lies in the fact that major restrictions have been placed on the biopharmaceutical industry regarding advertising and inducements. This section discusses some of the main areas covered by the commercial arm of a biopharmaceutical company.

16.1.3.1   Customers

While the patient is clearly the end-user of a marketed drug, he or she is rarely the direct customer. The primary customers are the healthcare systems and managed care organizations that buy medicines in bulk and negotiate discounts from manufacturers. The customer categories are listed below.

Individual Patients

With greater medical awareness among the general public comes greater knowledge of the types of drugs that are available to treat particular conditions. This, along with direct-to-consumer advertising, stimulates the demand for specific products that may not be provided by the primary care physician. Countries, such as the USA, which permit such advertising, employ all of the communication media to advertise medicines; this can have a downside, such as excruciating revelations of embarrassing personal medical problems being broadcast on prime time television. Of far more concern is the high cost of innovative drugs which means that patients may not be able to get them through their healthcare system; if they are made aware of these products through direct advertising, they may feel compelled to pay large amounts of money for them out of their own pockets. This situation is not restricted to the USA, but is coming about because of increasing pressure on healthcare budgets (see next chapter).

Physicians and Pharmacists

Physicians, whether primary care- or hospital-based, represent the most important customer group, since they choose which drugs to prescribe to their patients. As a result, biopharmaceutical companies spend a great deal of money on targeting doctors in their offices; they do this by employing sales forces to make face-to-face visits (detailing), running advertisements in medical publications or by sponsoring conferences and training courses. Some doctors are identified as opinion leaders in a given therapeutic area; their views can have a profound influence on the prescribing habits of their colleagues within a medical specialty. It is well known that the relationship between doctors and the drug discovery industry is not without controversy. However, as I have stated in previous chapters, I can only say that the vast majority of my collaborations with physicians have been highly professional, focusing on the research and its potential benefit to patients.

Pharmacists are also major customers since they have the responsibility for dispensing medicines through the primary care practice, hospitals, private retail pharmacies or wholesalers.

Government-Financed Healthcare Services

The relative proportion of social healthcare provision and private/insurance funding varies from country to country. At one extreme, Britain's National Health Service (NHS) provides most of the country's healthcare from taxation. The NHS spends over $15Bn on drugs, which is 10% of its total expenditure (2009 figures from

ABPI 2010). In the USA, Medicaid and Medicare Part D are administered by a government department, namely, the Centers for Medicare and Medicaid Services (CMS). Medicaid is a social welfare system that provides healthcare support for those with low incomes while Medicare is a social insurance system available to older people through both direct taxation and employee contributions. The cost of drugs for Medicare part D is over \$55Bn representing, like the NHS, 10% of total healthcare expenditure. Not surprisingly, these organizations are major customers of the pharmaceutical industry.

Private Healthcare Organizations

These operate alongside state-funded healthcare systems and, in many countries, form the basis of most healthcare provision. The Health Maintenance Organization Act was passed in the USA in 1973 to regulate the private health management organizations (HMOs) that have arisen over the years. Well-known HMOs include CIGNA and Kaiser Permanente. There are different HMO models from companies with dedicated staff and premises to looser affiliations of physicians and hospitals. Since individual HMOs control access to their customers' healthcare, they are in a position to negotiate with pharmaceutical companies for favourable terms on price and exclusivity. Employers use HMOs to manage the healthcare provision for their workforce, but this is expensive. For example, General Motors spends roughly \$5 billion on annual healthcare costs for its 1.1 million employees and former employees; these costs per car sold are actually greater than the cost of the steel used to make it (Johnson 2010).

16.1.3.2   Pricing and Reimbursement

Setting the price of a branded medicine is a difficult process; healthcare markets are under great cost pressures, and yet the industry needs to be able to cover its costs and invest in new products. Reimbursement is the money that the holders of healthcare funding pay the front-line suppliers of that care. In the UK, for example, the pharmacies dealing with primary care are reimbursed by the NHS for the cost of drugs dispensed, but hospitals pay the manufacturers and wholesalers directly. Governments or managed care organizations naturally try to keep prices as low as possible, often using generic products that are substantially cheaper than patented medicines (see later). This cannot provide the whole solution, as new products, such as the biologicals, can have significant medical advantages over existing drugs; in the long term, it may not be cost-effective to use a cheaper option. Comparative effectiveness research has been undertaken by government and private research foundations for many years, but with increased pressures on healthcare funding, the field is being reinvigorated. Organizations which are set up to be independent of industry and government have, or are being, established to objectively evaluate the cost and benefits of new medicines. Their remit is to recommend, or otherwise, the provision of a particular medicine by state-funded healthcare systems. In Britain, the National Institute for Health and Clinical Excellence (NICE) was established in 1999 to provide these recommendations, although not without some controversy, as has been widely reported in the UK press. Despite the severe misgivings of some in the USA who are concerned about the political consequences of healthcare rationing, the 2010 Patient Protection and Affordable Care Act mandates the establishment of a Patient-Centered Outcomes Research Institute (PCORI) with similar aims to those of NICE.

An example of NICE guidance for the anti-cancer drug gefitinib illustrates the actual prices being negotiated and the resulting discounted price (NICE technology appraisal guidance 192 2010). Briefly, the drug gefitinib (trade name Iressa®) developed by AstraZeneca has been approved for use in patients with small cell lung cancer, assuming that they have the appropriate genetic background (see Chap. 14). The manufacturers have agreed a patient access scheme with the Department of Health in which the drug is supplied at a fixed cost of £12,200 per patient, irrespective of the treatment time (a pack of 30 tablets costs £2,167.71). Payment for the first 3 months of treatment is also waivered if the patient discontinues the drug before this time.

Pharmacoeconomics

The discipline of pharmacoeconomics exists to put the cost-benefit analysis of drug pricing on an objective footing (International Society for Pharmacoeconomics and Outcomes Research 2010). It deals with questions such as: is the money spent on an expensive drug treatment offset by the money saved if the patient returns to productive work after an illness? Another important consideration is the cost of hospital care versus treatment at home or at a primary care centre.

A pharmacoeconomic analysis might include a survey of health expenditure by disease category. Table 16.5 illustrates this with data taken from a UK Government report on NHS expenditure in 2005–2006 (UK Department of Health 2007). The top disease category by expenditure is mental health, which includes dementia. A large proportion of this cost is taken up by keeping patients in hospitals or secure accommodation, so new drugs that keep even a small proportion of them out of institutions could, on balance, save a significant amount of money.

16.1.3.3 Portfolio Management

Portfolio management is central to pharmaceutical business strategy; this is because a biopharmaceutical company has to maximise its financial returns to cover the soaring costs of drug development and to return value to its shareholders. By looking at a company's portfolio of products, managers have to make decisions about the balance between novel targets and those for which there are a number of competitor drugs already available. There is also the spectre of patent expiration hanging over

Table 16.5 2005–2006 expenditure on different conditions by the UK National Health Service to illustrate most expensive treatments

Condition	Gross Expenditure (£Bn)
Mental health (includes dementia)	8.5
Circulation problems (cardiovascular disease)	6.4
Cancers and tumours	4.3
Gastrointestinal system problems	3.9
Trauma and injuries (include burns)	3.8
Musculoskeletal system problems	3.7
Respiratory system problems	3.5
Genitourinary system disorders (except infertility)	3.5
Maternity and reproductive health	2.9
Dental problems	2.7
Learning disability problems	2.6
Neurological system problems	2.1
Endocrine, nutritional and metabolic problems (including diabetes)	1.9
Social care needs	1.7
Eye/vision problems	1.4
Skin problems	1.3
Healthy individuals	1.3
Infectious diseases	1.2
Blood disorders	1.0
Neonate conditions	0.8
Poisoning	0.7
Hearing problems	0.3

Figures (rounded to one decimal place) taken from the UK Department of Health report 2007. Information licensed under the Open Government Licence v1.0

any drug development programme, given the long times between initial patent filing and commercial launch (see later). Pharmaceutical portfolio management is designed to make a business case for embarking upon a particular drug development programme or investing in new manufacturing processes. In order to make decisions about projects, there must be a set of Value-Added Indicators (VAIs) that help managers to decide whether it is worth investing in a particular project. One of the most commonly used VAIs is the Net Present Value (NPV) calculation. NPV is the current value of all cash receipts and outgoings during the lifetime of a project. It takes account of the changing value of money over time (discount rate) that may occur, for example, through inflation. Details of the simple formula used for the NPV calculation can be found on financial or business Web sites. The NPV figure is a monetary value which, if positive, means that the project is likely to be worth pursuing. If it is negative, however, then the company will gain nothing by taking the programme any further. The standard NPV formula does not take into account factors, such as the risk of a particular stage of drug development, so the risk-adjusted NPV (rNPV) can be calculated instead. The following table shows a comparison of rNPVs for different therapeutic areas taken from a study of antibiotics development (Projan 2003) Table 16.6.

Table 16.6 Risk-adjusted net present value calculations for different therapeutic or product areas

Disease Area	rNPV $M
Musculoskeletal	1,150
CNS	720
Oncology	300
Vaccines	160
Injectable antibiotic	100
AS-psoriasis	60
Liver transplant	20
Oral contraceptive	10

The larger the figure, the greater the financial incentive to pursue the project. Data are taken from Projan (2003) with kind permission of Elsevier

The market for antibiotics is currently out of favour with the biopharmaceutical industry for a number of reasons, one of which is the low NPV compared with CNS and musculoskeletal diseases, as shown in the table. NPV calculations are also used in negotiations between biotech companies and larger pharmaceutical organizations for placing a value on licensing candidates.

Other VAIs include Internal Rate of Return (IRR) and Return on Investment (ROI) calculations. Positive values for each of these, as with NPVs, give portfolio managers the confidence to initiate a development programme. Financial tools, such as Real Options Analysis, Decision Tree Analysis and Monte Carlo Simulation, are also used in an attempt to make decision making more scientific (actually based on statistical principles) without having to rely upon "gut instinct". It is understandable that this instinct is frowned upon by business schools, particularly with such a complex area as modern drug development. Nevertheless, it is tempting to speculate that few of the great medicines of the past would have seen the light of day if companies had relied totally upon economic forecasting.

16.1.4   Intellectual Property

The statutory protection of inventions by legislation is the foundation stone of commercial R&D. The main elements of IP are patents, copyright, trade secrets, trademarks and bailments. These are summarised briefly, with the exception of patents, which are covered in more depth.

- Copyright
  This often relates to written material or images, where the originator has an automatic right to ownership. From a pharmaceutical R&D perspective, this will most likely apply to materials in technical or commercial publications.

- Trade secrets
  These only last as long as they remain secret, i.e. are not disclosed to others without a prior legal contract, such as a confidentiality or non-disclosure agreement (CDA or NDA).
- Trademarks
  These can be registered in most countries and are used for company logos and related branding material.
- Bailments
  This is a legal term used to describe the property rights of a donor who gives physical materials to a third party. These materials may be biotechnology products, for example, in which there is a great deal of associated know-how that must be protected. A common bailment is the Material Transfer Agreement that occurs between laboratories in academia and industry.

16.1.4.1   Patents

Patents (or letters patent) are legal instruments, which are designed to prevent the exploitation of a particular invention by competitors. The modern system used by the USA and the UK originated in the eighteenth century England in the reign of Queen Anne. From this point in history onwards, the patent had to be submitted to the relevant office as a written document detailing the invention. Each country has its own patent law, but harmonisation through the World Trade Organization encourages individual countries, in particular the newly industrialised ones, to comply with global regulations. The Agreement on Trade-Related Aspects of Intellectual Property Rights (TRIPS) has helped to bring the trade in pharmaceuticals under a global umbrella; this has influenced western investment in China and India because concerns about IP protection in these countries have been, to an extent, alleviated.

Pharmaceutical patents cover Composition of Matter, Process and Secondary Patents as reviewed below.

Composition of Matter Patents

These protect a novel compound or biological on the basis of it having a unique chemical structure. For example, cimetidine and ranitidine are two compounds which bind to the histamine H2 receptor but are protected by composition of matter patents. This is because the patent examiners in these cases felt that the chemical structures of the two compounds and their derivatives were sufficiently different from each other. Patent applications are written in such a way that makes it very difficult for a rival company to mount a legal challenge. This means that many different analogues of the compound must be laboriously documented in large, often heavy-going, documents. The skills required to prepare these applications and to maintain them over the years of the patent mean that many biopharmaceutical companies run dedicated IP departments.

wherein:

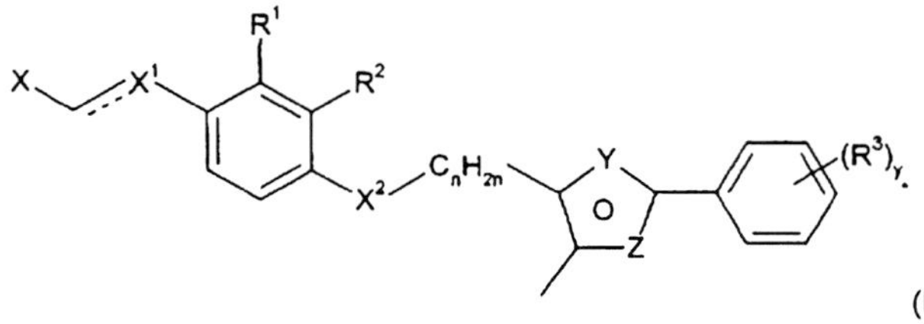

5   X represents a COOH (or a hydrolysable ester thereof) or tetrazole group;
       X^1 represents NH, NCH_3, O, S, a bond (i.e. is absent), CH_2, or CH where the
       dashed line indicates that when X1 is CH the depicted bond is a double bond;
       X^2 represents O or S;
       R^1 and R^2 independently represent H, CH_3, OCH_3, or halogen;
10   n is 1 or 2;
       one of Y and Z is N and the other is S or O:
       y is 0, 1, 2, 3, 4 or 5;
       Each R^3 independently represents CF_3 or halogen.

Fig. 16.2 Portion of typical composition of matter patent taken directly from the Espacenet online patents resource. Reproduced by kind permission of esp@cenet

A hint of the level of detail required for pharmaceutical composition of matter patents is given in Fig. 16.2, which is taken from the Espacenet online patents resource (Esp@cenet 2010).

This figure shows a basic backbone structure consisting of rings joined together by single bonds. The letters (X, Y, Z, R and variants) refer to the possible substitutions to the basic structure, and these are listed in the patent. This is the so-called Markush claim, named after the US chemist who devised a system of notation for chemical structures in patents. An example of this is shown with the benzene ring at the far right of the figure. The line joining $(R^3)_y$ to the benzene is directed at the centre of the structure. This means that the $(R^3)_y$ group can substitute at any point in the ring.

Patenting Genes

One of the most contentious issues in the commercialisation of life sciences has been the patenting of DNA sequences. In the early days of the Human Genome Project, companies such as Celera and Incyte Genomics filed patents for many of the novel gene sequences they identified in their laboratories. The feeling, in academic and other circles, was that this amounted to the patenting of life and should therefore be discouraged. Large pharmaceutical companies were fairly relaxed about using sequences for drug targets that were patented by others, but the situation with diagnostics is more problematical. This is exemplified by the patenting of the BRCA1 gene by Myriad Genetics in the USA. Mutations in this, and the BRCA2 gene, provide strong diagnostic evidence for increased risk of breast or ovarian cancer. Myriad was granted patents on these genes by the US Patent and Trademark Office (PTO) and has a virtual monopoly on this genetic test, which it offers for sale. This monopoly position has been recently challenged in the US courts by various groups, including pathologists and patients, on the basis that the patents were unlawful because they concerned a product of nature. The key issue under consideration by the court is whether the PTO has greater authority than the US Constitution in deciding the legality of patents. At the time of writing, a judgment has been made against Myriad Genetics which states that some of its patents were invalid. If this remains the case after appeal, this could mean that many other gene patents will be invalidated in the USA, something which will have a profound impact on other biotechnology companies.

Process Patents

The chemical and biological processes that lead to patented small molecule and biotech drugs are often an important part of a company's patent estate. Sometimes, companies even attempt to patent manufacturing processes for out-of-patent drugs. Patents for these so-called analogy processes can be granted if genuine inventiveness can be proved. Process patents are important for biotechnology; the humanisation of monoclonal antibodies is a good example, where a highly competitive technology was developed by Greg Winter in Cambridge and patented by the UK's MRC. Any company that wished to develop therapeutic antibodies, with most of the mouse regions replaced by human sequences (see Chap. 8), was obliged to pay royalties to the MRC.

Secondary Patents

These are used to extend the patent life of drugs through reformulation, finding new indications or producing different chemical or physical forms. These topics are covered at the end of the chapter under the heading of Life Cycle Management.

16.1.4.2   Patent Timelines

Once a patent application is filed in a given territory, it has a lifespan of 20 years before the patent expires. This might seem like a long time, but given the years that it takes to develop the drug, the amount of patent protection left once it goes to the market is significantly reduced. Figure 16.3 illustrates this in a comparison of pharmaceuticals with other types of patentable products. In a commentary on this situation, S. Knowles from GSK wryly notes that a novelty umbrella that can be attached to beer bottle has 18 years of patent life compared with 13.5 years of a breast cancer therapy (Knowles 2010).

A question that is often raised during my courses is "why don't companies wait as long as possible before patenting?" This is tempting, but given the fluid nature of

Fig. 16.3 Patent life for medicines compared with other products. All patentable inventions have 20 years of protection after approval, but the time remaining after medicines are marketed is much shorter than the other high-technology products. This is because of the exceptionally long time taken for the development and approval

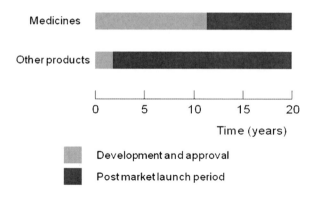

employment in the industry and the general leakiness of information, this would be tantamount to commercial suicide. Risks are sometimes taken, however. I recall a situation in which a novel compound was isolated from a natural product that had been screened against a particular disease target. It was felt that delaying the filing of a patent would not be a problem, since the chance of a competitor finding the same drug was very small. Although it later turned out that the compound could not be turned into a drug, a rival company did actually come up with the same compound from a similar source, completely by chance.

It is normal practice to ensure that all experimental findings are recorded in lab note books; these are countersigned and dated to provide evidence of priority in the case of a dispute. This is a bit of an inconvenience to a working scientist, but much less so than having to provide technical evidence to a court as the result of a patent dispute.

16.1.5   Generic Drugs

Once the patent on a prescription medicine expires, the field is open to the generic drug manufacturers who then sell the product at a much lower price. Not surprisingly, consumers of healthcare encourage the use of generics wherever possible in order to save money. Equally unsurprisingly, the developers of branded medicines wish to recoup the costs of drug discovery and development and to invest in future programmes. There is an inevitable tension between these different parties, assisted by various pressure groups, including those who accuse the biopharmaceutical industry of profiteering from disease. Whatever the pros and cons of the argument, the existence of generic competition is one of the major challenges for the drug discovery industry.

Attempts have been made to encourage the introduction of more generic medicines while at the same time providing a "soft landing" for the patent holder once the term has expired. The key legislation in the USA was introduced in 1984 as the Drug Price Competition and Patent Term Restoration Act, otherwise known as the Hatch-Waxman Act. Approval of a patented medicine requires a New Drug Application,

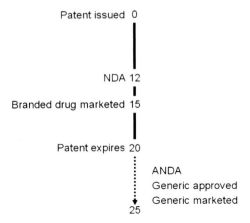

Fig. 16.4 Patent timelines for branded and generic medicines. The original drug has 20 years of patent protection until the point where generic manufacturers can develop their own version. The time frame for the Accelerated New Drug Application (ANDA) approval and launch in the market is comparatively short because requirements for testing bioequivalent compounds are modest. The Hatch-Waxman extension time (*dotted line*) is granted to the original patent holder until the generic is launched

supported by large amounts of data, as outlined in Chap. 13. It was considered that expecting generics manufacturers to go through the entire process themselves for a given compound (biologicals excepted) would be too great a burden. The Hatch-Waxman Act, therefore, specifies an Accelerated New Drug Application (ANDA) that just requires the generics company to demonstrate bioequivalence with the patented drug. In practice, this means testing absorption pharmacokinetics in patients and accepting a difference of 20% or less. In return, the patent holders can receive an extension of patent life up to a maximum of 5 years; this covers the time that the drug was under FDA review prior to marketing. The Act allows patent holders to create legal objections that can delay the introduction of a generic product by a period of 30 months. This has had the unintended consequence of allowing large companies to file a series of legal challenges to a whole range of patents, thereby adding an extra series of 30-month delays for each one, but this loophole in the Act is now being tightened.

A summary of pharmaceutical patent timelines is shown in Fig. 16.4.

16.1.5.1   Generics and Biologicals

This is a very hot area commercially, since a number of high-value protein drugs are coming off patent over the next few years. The situation is more complex than that with small molecule drugs, however, since it is difficult for a generics manufacturer to show that its drug is chemically identical to the patented molecule. This is due to the chemical nature of proteins and particularly to their glycosylation (Chap. 8), where variations occurring in different batches of recombinant protein can have a profound influence on the pharmacokinetics of the drug. Although a highly detailed analysis of glycoprotein structure and purity is possible with mass spectrometry, it is not possible to produce it in a cell line in a totally uniform way. For this reason, generic biologicals, or follow-on biologicals, are commonly known as biosimilars. Generic biologicals with improved pharmacokinetics, or other properties, are called biobetters or biosuperiors by some companies; where will this end – are bioawesomes on the way? The Hatch-Waxman Act did not consider generic biological products, since insulin and growth hormones were the only recombinant proteins available at the time the legislation was drafted. Two competing bills for regulation of biosimilars have been drafted in 2010 (the Waxman and Eshoo bills) and are under consideration in the USA. European legislation for biosimilars has been in place since 2004, but generics manufacturers are required to perform more regulatory studies, but excluding phase III trials, than would be the case for a small molecule. The development of generic proteins is inevitably costlier than that of their small molecule equivalents, but the rewards are likely to be significant. Interestingly, much of the activity in biosimilars is occurring in China and India, but industry attention is focusing on Israel's Teva Pharmaceutical Industries. This major generics company is developing follow-on drugs to compete with therapeutic antibodies from giants, such as Roche, whose European patent for MabThera antibody is due to expire in 2014. Activities like these are expected to cause profound changes in the pharmaceuticals market over the next decade, particularly since biologicals have become a lifeline to the branded manufacturers whose small molecule sales are under threat from patent expiries.

Orphan Drug

This is a term for a branded medicine that has been developed for conditions affecting fewer than 200,000 people (FDA) or 5 in 10,000 (EMA). Since these numbers do not normally interest pharmaceutical companies, orphan drug status provides an incentive to manufacturers by providing several years of market exclusivity. The EU's Orphan Regulation provides 10 years of exclusivity, plus fast access to regulators, unless the drug becomes too profitable, in which case the period is decreased. In the USA, the Orphan Drug Act of 1983 provides 7 years of market exclusivity. Since this Act was introduced, more than 240 drugs have been brought to the market, representing over 200 different diseases, the most common of which is cancer (Braun et al. 2010).

Paediatric Exclusivity

An act passed in the USA in 2002 was designed to encourage companies to conduct studies in children, thus allowing an extra 6 months of patent protection. In practice, this makes for some interesting studies, such as Pfizer's use of sildenafil, to treat pulmonary hypertension in children. Sildenafil is better known as Viagra®, but is also marketed as Revatio® for the treatment of this serious disease.

16.1.6   Life Cycle Management

The life cycle of a branded prescription medicine lasts as long as patent protection can be maintained before generic competition takes over. It is, therefore, in a bio-pharmaceutical company's interest to manage the life cycle in such a way as to maximise profits over the time available. This process of "ever-greening" requires a battle of wits between the company and the patent examiners; the latter must decide whether the relevant secondary patents are admissible. Patent life extension can be achieved through line extensions and secondary medical uses as follows.

16.1.6.1   Line Extensions

These may be reformulations of patented NCEs, or else different chemical or physical forms that may affect the formulation or delivery. For example, raniti-dine, the active ingredient of the anti-ulcer drug Zantac®, was reformulated as ranitidine bismuth citrate and marketed in 1996 as Tritec®. This line extension took advantage of new findings that implicated the bacterium *Helicobacter pylori* in peptic ulcer disease. This bacterium can be killed by bismuth, so the combina-tion of an H2 antagonist and this metal helped Glaxo to maintain sales in the gastrointestinal area for a while longer. The patent for ranitidine was also extended by producing it in a different crystalline (polymorphic) form (Chap. 10). Form 2 ranitidine hydrochloride was patented in 1985 on the basis of it having "favour-able filtration and drying characteristics". As the original (form 1) 1978 patent was due to expire in 1995, the form 2 patent gave Zantac® an extra lease of life up to 2002. Although highly lucrative in terms of sales, this period also saw an exten-sive litigation between Glaxo and Novopharm, a generics drug maker that attempted to market ranitidine itself. Nevertheless, Glaxo's strategy of holding off generic competition by patenting different polymorphs has been eagerly adopted by other companies. Another strategy is to identify different salt forms, or hydrates, of active compounds which may have superior properties to the original drug. These properties may include increased stability in the stomach, or ease of formu-lation. The approach adopted by AstraZeneca involved the separation of chiral (mirror image forms) of its drug to extend patent life. This was achieved with its anti-ulcer drug omeprazole (Losec®) that replaced Zantac® as the treatment of choice for peptic ulcers. Losec® is actually a mixture of two mirror image forms, omeprazole and esomeprazole (Fig. 16.5).The latter binds to the drug target, and the former is inactive. AstraZeneca separated the two forms and then performed clinical trials to show that the esomeprazole was superior to the mixture (racemic

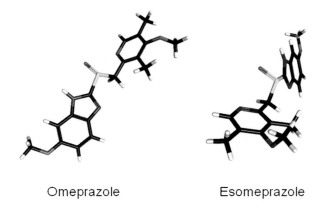

Omeprazole   Esomeprazole

Fig. 16.5 Three-dimensional structures of chiral molecules that comprise the anti-ulcerant Losec®. The esomeprazole has the relevant biological activity and was patented by AstraZeneca as Nexium®, thereby extending the patent life of this molecule. The sulphur atom (in *yellow*) is the centre of symmetry, where the two mirror image forms overlap. Nitrogen atoms are shown in *blue* and oxygen in *red*

mixture, see Chap. 7). This strategy has allowed the company to market esomeprazole as Nexium® and maintain its position in the anti-ulcerants marketplace until 2014, when generic competition will take over.

Finally, it is possible to patent on the basis of new formulations as long as the product is demonstrably better than the original, i.e. it shows an inventive step. An example of this is the anti-inflammatory drug diclofenac produced by Novartis. The original patent on the oral formulation of this drug has expired, but Novartis has produced a line extension by formulating the drug as Voltaren® gel for topical application.

16.1.6.2 Second Medical Use Patents

These are sometimes referred to as use patents; they may be used by companies who want to extend the patent life of their own products, or else by companies that want to patent the use of an unpatented drug for a new indication. There appears to be more resistance to this from the patenting authorities than other line extension strategies, but examples do exist, such as thalidomide. This compound, discussed earlier in the book, gained notoriety through the birth defects it caused after being prescribed to pregnant women for morning sickness. Academic investigators subsequently noticed that the drug was useful in treating leprosy, some AIDS symptoms, and multiple myeloma. Later still, the FDA authorised the use of thalidomide in leprosy, and the drug was marketed by Celgene, under the trade name Thalidomid®.

Summary of Key Points

The cost of developing a new drug can be as much as 1 billion dollars.

The USA is the largest market for prescription medicines, followed by the EU.

The BRIC countries, particularly China, are showing the highest growth.

The top ten medicines in 2009 global sales included three biological products.

Patent life for branded medicines is compromised by the time taken for them to be developed and approved.

The approval process for generic medicines is underpinned by the US Hatch-Waxman Act that provides opportunities for generic manufacturers, while simultaneously protecting patent holders.

Portfolio and life cycle management are key commercial functions within a biopharmaceutical company.

References

2009 figures from ABPI (2010). http://www.abpi.org.uk/industry-info/knowledge-hub/medicines/Pages/nhs-expenditure.aspx#fig1. Accessed 7 June 2011

Adams CP, Brantner VV (2010) Spending on new drug development. Health Econ 19:130–141

Braun MM et al (2010) Emergence of orphan drugs in the United States: a quantitative assessment of the first 25 years. Nat Rev Drug Discov 9:519–522

Campbell D, Chui M (2010) Pharmerging shake-up new imperatives in a redefined world. IMS Health, http://www.imshealth.com/pharmergingreport2010. Accessed 3 Dec 2010

Cyranoski D (2010) Shanghai by the numbers. Nature 466:518

DiMasi JA et al (2003) The price of innovation: new estimates of drug development costs. J Health Econ 22:151–185

Esp@cenet (2010). http://www.espacenet.com/access/index.en.htm. Accessed 3 Dec 2010

IMS Health Press Room Top line industry data (2010). http://www.imshealth.com. Accessed 3 Dec 2010

International Society for Pharmacoeconomics and Outcomes Research (2010). http://www.ispor.org/. Accessed 3 Dec 2010

Johnson T (2010) Healthcare Costs and U.S. Competitiveness. Council on Foreign Relations. http://www.cfr.org/publication/13325/healthcare_costs_and_us_competitiveness.html. Accessed 3 Dec 2010

Knowles SM (2010) Fixing the Legal Framework for Pharmaceutical Research. Science 327:1083–1084

NICE technology appraisal guidance 192 (2010). http://www.nice.org.uk/nicemedia/live/13058/49880/49880.pdf. Accessed 3 Dec 2010

Projan S (2003) Why is big Pharma getting out of antibacterial drug discovery? Curr Opinin Microbiol 6:427–430

UK Department of Health (2007) Departmental Report 2007 of the UK Department of Health. http://www.dh.gov.uk/prod_consum_dh/groups/dh_digitalassets/@dh/@en/documents/digitalasset/dh_074766.pdf. Accessed 3 Dec 2010

Chapter 17
Challenges and Responses

Abstract This chapter examines the state of the biopharmaceutical industry in the early part of the twenty-first century. It highlights the challenges facing the industry such as a fall in productivity despite an increase in R&D investment, pressures from healthcare providers and patients, and loss of patent protection for several major drugs. The second half of the chapter ends on a more positive note, with a description of the responses that companies are making through restructuring, mergers and acquisitions and opening new markets. Finally, some comments are made about the future of drug discovery, including speculations about science, industry structures and new opportunities provided by online social and professional networking.

17.1 Introduction

This chapter concludes the long journey from drug target to marketed product by examining the state of the drug discovery business in the early part of the twenty-first century. Its purpose is to highlight the challenges facing the biopharmaceutical industry and the different responses that are being made to meet those challenges. There are many difficulties to be overcome, as those who have lost their jobs in biopharmaceutical companies will attest. Also, to be frank, there is a pervading sense of doom and gloom about the future of the biopharmaceutical industry. This is partly due to the nature of drug discovery itself, coupled with external pressures from governments, regulators and patients; the global economic downturn that began in 2008 does not help matters either. On a positive note, it is unthinkable that the industry will collapse, since it has immense human and financial resources to help it ride out these present difficulties. Furthermore, human disease will never disappear completely, so there is always the need for a viable drug discovery industry, even one that may have been through a painful period of restructuring.

E.D. Zanders, *The Science and Business of Drug Discovery: Demystifying the Jargon*,   329
DOI 10.1007/978-1-4419-9902-3_17, © Springer Science+Business Media, LLC 2011

17.1.1 Pressures on the Industry

17.1.1.1 Productivity Slowdown

The figures say it all: for every US dollar of revenue lost by the largest pharmaceutical companies between 2007 and 2012, only 26 cents are replaced by revenue from new products (Goodman 2008). This is because there has been a marked slowdown in productivity, defined as the number of new molecular entities (NMEs) entering the marketplace each year.

There must be some explanation for the fact that productivity has decreased at the same time as investment in research and development increased dramatically over the same period (Fig. 17.1). The search for this explanation is exercising the minds of many pharmaceutical executives and industry analysts; there is some urgency to this, as initiatives that are put in place now could take several years to come to fruition.

Rates of Attrition by Development Phase

Since there is no shortage of drug discovery projects, the relatively small number of NME approvals must be due to project failure at different stages of the development process. Table 17.1 is taken from an analysis by CMR International (2010) which shows the average number of compounds required at the beginning of the development pipeline to get a single candidate molecule ready for a marketing submission.

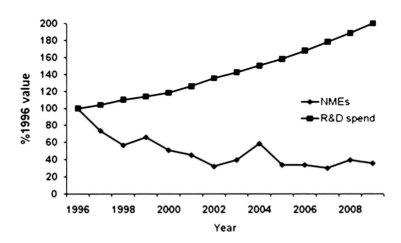

Fig. 17.1 Change in number of FDA approved NMEs since 1996 compared with industry R&D expenditure over the same period. Data plotted as % of 1996 values (53 NMEs and $3.3 billion spend). 2009 values: 19 NMEs and $70.6 billion spend. Data adapted from Hughes (2009)

Table 17.1 Estimate of number of molecules required at each stage of development to submit one drug candidate to the regulatory authorities (CMR International Pharmaceutical Factbook 2010)

Development stage	Molecules required
Preclinical	12
Phase I	9
Phase II	5
Phase III	2
Submission	1

Reasons for Failure

There are several reasons why a drug discovery project may not succeed; one analysis (Schuster et al. 2005) has come up with the following figures:

Efficacy 43%
Toxicity 33%
ADME/other 24%

This is expanded upon in the following sections:

Efficacy

We do not understand enough about complex diseases to be able to identify drug targets in a systematic way. Quite often the target appears to be suitable because of extensive preclinical work and compounds or biologicals may be available with good potency and selectivity towards the target; despite these promising findings, the resulting drug may have no effect on the disease in clinical trials. One example is the search for drugs for treating septic shock, an acute life threatening condition that arises after infection. Septic shock might be started after cutting a hand while gardening; an infectious bacterium or fungus can then enter the body and multiply to a point, where a cytokine storm is produced, with all its unpleasant consequences (see Chap. 12). Any scientist familiar with the biology of inflammation will be able think of a whole range of targets whose inhibition might be expected to control the shock to the body. Unfortunately, none of the inhibitory drugs developed for this condition, even the corticosteroids, have worked in clinical trials. This clearly indicates that the basic knowledge of the pathophysiology of septic shock is inadequate (Rice 2006). Later studies have, however, implicated the blood coagulation system in the organ failure that results from septic shock, thus sending drug development down a more promising path. The end result was Eli Lilly's drotrecogin alfa (Xigris®), a recombinant coagulation protein that is now approved for use in septic shock. This example reveals both the limitations of our basic knowledge about complex diseases and the need to continue basic biomedical research to uncover new mechanisms which may provide new drug targets. The consequences of these limitations are clinical trial failures, which create disappointment for patients and companies alike.

Just occasionally, a seemingly unsuccessful programme can lead to new opportunities. The classic example is Pfizer's discovery of Viagra® (INN name sildenafil), which started life as a drug for treating angina. The original idea was to replicate the clinical effects of nitrates, but without the problems of tachyphylaxis, a pharmacological term used to describe a drug's loss of effectiveness after repeated administration. Nitrates work by relaxing the smooth muscle in the arteries through the production of the gas nitric oxide (NO); this results in an increased blood flow and relief of the angina symptoms. The enzyme phosphodiesterase V (PDEV) was selected as a drug target, since its inhibition would lead to elevated levels of NO in the arteries. Sildenafil was identified as a potent and selective PDE inhibitor (there are over a dozen different PDE enzymes) and, in 1991, was entered for clinical trials after the compound was shown to relax blood vessels and generally perform according to expectations. Early clinical trials in healthy volunteers showed a modest relaxation of blood vessels by sildenafil, but there was an interaction with conventional nitrate medicines. Furthermore, the pharmacokinetics of the drug meant that it would have to be administered at least three times per day; this meant that, by mid 1993, the angina programme was finished. Now, part of drug discovery folklore, the volunteers in the multiple dose study reported an increase in penile erections that could retrospectively be associated with increased NO production. As a result of this, Pfizer initiated a clinical trial of sildenafil in patients with erectile dysfunction (using measuring devices that are best left to the imagination). Viagra® was approved for marketing by the FDA and EMA in 1998, after 21 separate clinical trials (Ghofrani et al. 2006). It rapidly became a blockbuster drug and an example of how a whole new area of drug research could be identified by following up on clinical observations.

ADME-Tox

Even if the target is right, many compounds fail because of poor absorption through the gut, a lack of (or too much) stability in blood, toxicity, or through formulation problems. The rate of failure due to poor pharmacokinetics has fallen over the years as companies improve their preclinical development operations. The problems with toxicity are likely to be more complicated; in any drug development programme, it is important to determine whether the toxicity is mechanism-based, that is, is the target itself related to the side effects. Answers to these questions can be obtained early on in the development programme by investigating the role of the target in preclinical models. If its removal, e.g. through transgenic knockouts or siRNA, eliminates the toxicity, then another target will have to be chosen.

Commercial and Strategic

It is not unusual for commercial priorities to change during the long years of drug development, so programmes can terminate early even if the compounds or biologicals look promising in the clinic. This inevitably leads to tension between the non-scientists involved in financial or commercial management and the scientists or clinicians involved in the technical side of drug development.[1]

17.1.1.2 Healthcare Cost Pressures

Biopharmaceutical companies attempt to maximize their revenues as soon as possible after the launch of a drug; there are several reasons for this: for example, patent life is ticking away, so there is a relatively short period of time available before generic competition sets in. There is also the need to recoup the considerable investment required to produce the drug in the first place; finally, the business must be profitable in order to be able to invest in future research and development. For the reasons just outlined, newly introduced medicines are sold at the highest price that the healthcare provider can bear. Healthcare costs have soared in the developed world and will continue to do so as the average age of the population increases. The situation is, of course, far worse in the developing world, where western branded medicines are mostly unaffordable. This has led to considerable political pressure on companies who have been forced to adopt new pricing models in different markets, particularly for drugs to treat infectious diseases. In the UK, medicine prices are negotiated with government using the Pharmaceutical Price Regulation Scheme (PPRS) which places a cap on the maximum profits that a company can make. The scheme may be replaced in 2014 by Value Based Pricing (VBP) that relates the cost of a medicine to its actual health benefit. This is quite rational from a medical and economic point of view, but it will make companies think much more carefully about the cost of running lengthy clinical trials for a drug that is not perceived by healthcare providers to be significantly better than existing products. Price controls, of the type outlined above, have an effect on the blockbuster model of drug development, in which sales of mass market drugs exceed $1 billion per annum. We have seen previously that personalized medicine is becoming a reality, albeit very slowly. This reality means that markets fragment, as the same drugs cannot be prescribed to everybody with a given illness. VBP clearly impacts upon this, although there is the added complication of taking into account the cost of the companion diagnostic test that accompanies the medicine.

Drug profits may be reduced as a result of the parallel trade that occurs between different countries, for example, the different countries of the EU, or the USA and Canada. This is because the same drugs are priced differently in each country; they can, therefore, be bought in bulk from countries, where they are cheaper to be sold on in other markets at a higher price. Parallel trading is not illegal, and the actual impact on profits is quite small, but counterfeit drugs certainly are illegal. This is becoming more of an issue with the developed world as "lifestyle" drugs, such as

---

[1] For an interesting commentary from an industry insider, see ref. (Cuarecasas 2006).

Viagra® and weight loss treatments, are sold over the Internet. Many counterfeit drugs contain reduced levels of API or none at all. This is not only potentially dangerous for the patient, but it also reduces confidence in the biopharmaceutical industry itself.

17.1.1.3 Product Withdrawals and Litigation

Clinical trials can only go so far when it comes to assessing drug safety. Even large phase III studies do not continue for long enough to be able to pick up long-term safety issues. The medicine will usually have been taken by millions of patients before any problems are brought to the attention of doctors, companies and regulators. One of the most high profile product withdrawals in recent years was Merck's anti-inflammatory drug rofecoxib (Vioxx®), used to treat millions of patients suffering from arthritis. The drug is a small molecule inhibitor of the enzyme cyclooxygenase II (COX II) that is involved in the production of inflammation-causing molecules during infection and disease. This is the same enzyme that is targeted by aspirin, except that the latter also inhibits a related enzyme, COX I, thereby greatly increasing the risk of ulcers. For patients who suffer from chronic pain and inflammation, any drug that controls these symptoms without producing undesirable side effects is to be welcomed. Vioxx® had these properties because it was a selective COXII inhibitor; it was successfully launched in 1999 and taken by millions of patients in over 80 countries until its withdrawal from the market in 2004. The withdrawal occurred after clinical data indicated that patients had a significant risk of developing cardiovascular disease while on Vioxx®. The outcome was bad for Merck because its revenues from a blockbuster drug were eliminated; to add to this, the company was also subjected to litigation from patient groups. From a purely scientific point of view, it is reasonable to speculate that patients with chronic inflammatory conditions, such as arthritis, are also susceptible to other illnesses (comorbidities) that may be exaggerated by certain drugs. This puts greater emphasis on the need for careful planning and execution of phase III trials and post-marketing surveillance (Chap. 13).

Suspicion is hanging over some other high profile medicines, such as Herceptin® and Avandia®, both of which appear to have cardiovascular side effects. The latter drug, which achieved blockbuster sales for GSK as a diabetes treatment, has now been restricted by the FDA and completely withdrawn from sale in the EU. Ironically, recent studies have shown that the active compound rosiglitazone may work through a completely different target to the one originally selected for the original drug discovery programme (Choi et al. 2010); this means that, at least in principle, compounds lacking the cardiovascular side effects of rosiglitazone could be developed to treat diabetes via this new target.

The above examples highlight the negative impact of drug safety concerns on the business and reputation of individual companies. If a medicine causes death and disability in a proportion of patients who take them, the company is generally considered responsible. There are situations, however, where the company has withdrawn a drug from market because of safety concerns, but patient groups then demand that it be reinstated. This has occurred with the therapeutic antibody natalizumab, marketed as Tysabri® for the treatment of multiple sclerosis. It works by blocking an adhesion molecule in blood vessels that allows the migration of inflammatory leukocytes into the brain. In 2005, the drug was voluntarily withdrawn from sale by its manufacturer Biogen Idec after three patients developed a severe brain inflammation called progressive multifocal leukoencephalopathy (PML). Tysabri® was relaunched in 2006 after the FDA had taken evidence from interested parties, including patients with MS who were desperate for the medicine. The relaunch was authorized on the condition that the drug was to be used in the clinic under strict guidelines. This example illustrates the dilemma faced by drug makers and patients; if few treatments exist for a chronic illness other than a drug with potentially serious side effects, should the patient be allowed to make a choice, or will this be denied because of regulation and probable litigation? The Tysabri® case showed that it is possible to follow a path between the two; most companies, however, will become more risk averse, particularly if bad publicity about their drugs is rapidly broadcast through online resources, with little chance of them being able to redress the balance.

17.1.1.4 Falling Off the Patent Cliff

Perhaps the most immediate and dramatic problem for individual biopharmaceutical companies is the loss of patent protection on the best selling medicines that bring them blockbuster profits. This loss of protection, called the patent cliff, is disturbing for the manufacturers of branded medicines since more than $100 billion of revenues will be lost in the period up to 2016. Between 2010 and 2012, for example, the world's best selling drug Lipitor® will come off patent, along with other blockbusters, such as Plavix®, Levaquin® and Zyprexa®. The situation with biologics is more complicated, due to the need to prove that the generic product is biologically equivalent to the patented product. In this case, it is more difficult for generic competition to make an immediate impact on branded sales, but not impossible. Patent expiry on big biological products, such as Remicade® (in 2011) and Herceptin® (in 2014), will open the way for generic companies to produce cheaper versions that satisfy the regulators and change the market (see biosimilars, Chap. 16).

17.1.2 Meeting the Challenges

Having described the scientific and commercial pressures felt by the biopharmaceutical industry, it is now time to conclude the chapter (and book) on a positive note. The problems facing the industry are immense, but essentially solvable, given enough time, resources and political will. Assuming that most people who are involved in the drug discovery industry agree that there is a problem, solutions may emerge quite rapidly over the next few years. Alternatively, with apologies to US readers, the spirit of Winston Churchill's quotation: "One can always trust the United States to do the right thing, once every possible alternative has been exhausted" might be applied to the biopharmaceutical industry. Whatever the future holds, there are a number of emerging trends which will shape it, as discussed below.

17.1.2.1 Mergers and Acquisitions

Merger and acquisition (M&A) activity with the biopharmaceutical industry has increased in response to falling revenues resulting from poor drug pipelines and patent expiries. The purpose of M&A is to either acquire another company's products and marketing infrastructure, or else to buy in technical expertise that is lacking in the parent company. Some examples of M&A activity are shown in Table 17.2.

These acquisitions are not cheap; the takeover of Schering-Plough by Merck cost that company $41 billion, for example. However, as a result of the takeover, Merck has been able to immediately add 19 new clinical candidates to its portfolio (eight in phase II, eight in phase II and three under regulatory review).[2] The above table does not include the acquisitions of small technology based companies, such as those of MedImmune by AstraZeneca and Domantis by GSK. These were prompted by the clinical and commercial success of humanized antibodies and the fact that the larger company could gain access to readymade technology in this area. Current interest in vaccines and stem cells is reflected in similar deals with relevant technology companies. There is, however, a shadow cast over siRNA therapeutics because Roche is abandoning the field altogether as part of its 2011 restructuring plans (citing problems with drug delivery).

The mergers of large independent companies can, of course, lead to considerable disruption of science and business activities and hence productivity. It also means site closures and job losses, which, of course, is of great concern to employees, their families and local communities. Some, but by no means all, are able to find new employment in the industry through bringing their skills and experience to new drug

Table 17.2 Major pharmaceutical M&A activity in the past decade

Activity	Year
Glaxo Wellcome – SmithKline Beecham merger	2000
Sanofi-Synthélabo acquisition of Aventis	2004
Pfizer acquisition of Wyeth	2009
Roche acquisition of Genentech	2009
Merck acquisition of Schering Plough	2009

[2] Based on the SCH compounds listed on Merck's website (Merck pipeline 2010).

discovery companies. Ironically, managers of these start-up organizations often form business alliances with their former companies. There has always been a strong need for large pharma expertise in the biotechnology industry, and there is no longer a shortage of qualified personnel to guide smaller companies through the minefield of drug development.

The acquisition of smaller biotech companies by medium/large pharma can be problematical if the culture that built value in the smaller company is not allowed to continue in the new organization. There is a danger that key personnel will leave and that the large company culture of tight management will dampen creativity. Managers of large companies are well aware of this danger, of course, and are themselves trying to reorganize their own structures to be "leaner and meaner" like the biotechs.

Has all of this actually improved productivity in the form of NMEs? According to a recent analysis, $1 + 1 = 1$, i.e. there is no improvement or reduction in productivity (Munos 2009). However, the same analysis suggests that smaller company acquisitions appear to be more productive, but as the author points out, the figures underlying such statements are complex and incomplete.

17.1.2.2 Restructuring R&D

Large multinational biopharmaceutical companies have the same problems of scale as other major corporations. Although large organizations have strong financial and human resources, the culture of management hierarchies, meetings, committees and fighting for internal resources does not compare well with that of the leaner biotech companies that are attractive to creative people. The business world is changing, however, and companies such as Google or Apple demonstrate that it is possible to sustain a more youthful business culture within a multinational enterprise. Most large companies have restructured their R&D, or are in the process of doing so, in order to emulate the biotech culture; at the same time, they are trying to maintain their expertise and financial muscle for the complex business of bringing a drug to market. Soon after the formation of GSK in 2001, its chief executive Jean Pierre Garnier introduced the Centres of Excellence in Drug Discovery (CEDDs) that were designed to be autonomous within the larger company. The CEDDS were dedicated to individual therapeutic areas, such as respiratory diseases, and are still part of the GSK organization. Changes were made in 2008 by the next CEO, Andrew Witty, who subdivided the CEDDS into smaller discovery performance units (DPUs). These operate very much like a small biotech company in that they are required to write business plans and have the freedom to form external alliances.

Other companies have followed suit by establishing smaller disease-focused units, streamlining their R&D procedures, and being creative in the use of outsourcing. Eli Lilly, for example, has established an external group called *Chorus* that manages the clinical development of a number of compounds by outsourcing and bypassing the internal procedures of the parent company. The result has been a significant reduction in development times and costs (Eli Lilly Chorus 2010).

In addition to reorganizing the composition and remits of research groups, the actual diseases that large companies are working on have come under the spotlight. Pfizer, for example, is now focusing on the chronic diseases of an ageing population, including cancer, Alzheimer's and inflammatory diseases. This list does not include cardiovascular diseases, despite the enormous success of Pfizer's cholesterol lowering drug Lipitor®; this may partly be due to the high costs of clinical trials in this therapeutic area.

Breaking Down Barriers

The profit-driven culture of industry has always sat uneasily with academia, despite many successful collaborations between the two. The current dearth of new drugs and the need for innovation is prompting the large biopharmaceutical companies to fine tune their approach to academic collaborations. One way of doing this is to move into purpose built facilities near a university, an example being the creation of Bayer's US Innovation Center at the University of California in San Francisco (UCSF). Another example is the 5-year collaboration formed by GSK in 2008 with the Immune Disease Institute (IDI) in Boston to research autoimmune and inflammatory diseases. At a cost of $25 million, the collaboration gives the Boston researchers freedom to pursue their own research agenda, while at the same time, giving GSK first refusal on any products or technologies they may develop. The agreement allows scientists from both organizations to physically work alongside each other, thus helping to break down the cultural barriers that exist between academia and industry.

Another way in which companies benefit through collaboration is by establishing consortia that deal with problems of mutual interest. This is in a spirit of cooperation rather than competition, and is a tacit realization that no single company has the necessary resources to address all of the technical problems that arise in modern drug discovery. One of the first collaborations of this type was the SNP consortium which, as its name suggests, was formed to identify the many SNPs scattered throughout the human genome. This information was made freely available to participating companies, and the scientific community at large, who were therefore all given the opportunity to use the data for drug target discovery and pharmacogenetics. More recent collaborations include the Biomarkers Consortium (http://www.biomarkersconsortium.org, Accessed 4 Dec 2010) and the Innovative Medicines Initiative (http://www.imi.europa.eu, Accessed 4 Dec 2010), originating in the US and Europe respectively.

Open Source Drug Discovery

The open source model exists because individuals are prepared to offer products and services for altruistic reasons, or just personal satisfaction. Although there may be an ultimate financial reward for these acts, this is not the primary motivation.

Open source software for computers is one of the best known examples, but this idea is beginning to impact upon drug discovery as well. In one well-publicized example, data from GSK's anti-malarial screening programme have been made available to the entire research community. These data consist of the structures and biological activities of over 13,000 compounds that are active against the malaria parasite; the data can be downloaded from freely accessible online databases (Gamo et al. 2010).

This initiative is a major departure from the conventional practice of keeping proprietary data securely within the walls of a company, unless publicized in a patent or scientific publication. Of course, this way of sharing data is ultimately to the benefit of patients and clinicians if the development of new anti-malarial drugs is accelerated, but does it benefit the pharma company? It certainly does from a public relations point of view, and possibly in tangible commercial benefits; however, it remains to be seen how this will work with highly competitive disease areas like cancer and neurodegeneration.

17.1.2.3 Outsourcing

One way of dealing with the increasing costs of pharmaceutical R&D is to cut operational costs by outsourcing key operations to other companies. These operations cover much of the activity required for preclinical and clinical development, but do not generally include discovery science. Specialist contract research organizations (CROs) which offer their services to the biopharmaceutical sector include such names as Covance and Quintiles. The estimated value of this sector in 2010 is $24 billion, but it is fragmented into over 1,100 companies worldwide (The CRO Market Outlook & Business Insights report 2009). Since R&D costs in China are only 20% of those in the West, it is not surprising that this country tops the list for global outsourcing. Outsourcing of manufacturing is undertaken by Contract Manufacturing Organizations (CMOs) whose value could reach $33.7 billion by 2014 (The CMO Market Outlook: Emerging Markets & Future Trends Business Monitor International 2009). As with CROs, there is increasing activity in Asia, but the main concern in the industry is the need for manufacturing capability for biologicals. This is particularly important, as the market share of these drugs compared with small molecules is increasing in both the branded medicines and biogenerics sectors.

From Company to Network

The historical model of an almost totally self-sufficient fully integrated pharmaceutical company (FIPCO) is being challenged by the fully integrated pharmaceutical network (FIPNET) to use Eli Lilly's terminology. This network is a series of different outsourcing and collaborative activities that further break down the barriers surrounding the traditional large pharma company. These activities include traditional fee-for-service outsourcing, as well as cost and risk sharing with academia and other companies, which may be allowed to retain a large degree of independence in their work.

Drug Discovery for the Developing World

One of the major criticisms of the biopharmaceutical industry has been its neglect of diseases that are more prevalent in the developing world. Although these illnesses affect huge numbers of individuals, the healthcare systems of the most affected countries do not have the resources to pay western prices for medicines. The situation with HIV in these countries is particularly controversial, as the drugs with proven efficacy are freely available to western populations, but are priced at an unaffordable level for other markets. The industry is well aware of the negative impact that this has on its business, so more attention is being paid to the so-called neglected diseases and drug pricing policy. There is no shortage of basic research into diseases like malaria and tuberculosis, but funding for the clinical development of promising medicines is not easy to obtain. This is why product development partnerships (PDPs) have been established between biopharmaceutical companies, governments and non-government organizations (NGOs) to direct money towards focused drug development programmes. These are run on commercial lines, with input from drug discovery experts and include the Global Alliance for TB Drug Development, Medicines for Malaria and the Drugs for Neglected Diseases Initiative (DNDi). Mention has already been made of "open source" drug discovery for malaria, where compound screening data are made freely available to the global scientific community. Some large companies take this commitment a step further by establishing in-house research units that concentrate on R&D for tropical diseases. Novartis, for example, while based in Switzerland, runs the Novartis Institute for Tropical Diseases (NITD) in Singapore as an affiliate business that collaborates with multiple global partners.

One of the more interesting collaborations of recent years has been the 2009 merger of Pfizer's and GSK's HIV drug franchises into a joint venture called ViiV Healthcare. In addition to sponsoring R&D into new HIV treatments, the new company also sells branded anti-HIV drugs at reduced prices to developing countries, either directly at the point of sale, or through licensing agreements with generic drug manufacturers.

Opening New Markets

The reliance of the major drug discovery companies on billion dollar blockbuster sales has created a dependency that is becoming unsustainable. It is generally recognized throughout the industry that the marketplace is becoming fragmented and will become more so when personalized medicine enters the mainstream. As a result, the commercial emphasis is moving towards "nichebuster" rather than blockbuster drugs. Drug development for therapeutic "niches" is now part of the remit of the largest companies as they change their business models to meet the challenges of diminished revenues. Pfizer, for example, established, as part of its Worldwide R&D Division, a Rare Diseases Research Unit with the specific intention of widening its offering of medicines for unmet medical needs. There are over 5,000 rare (orphan) diseases, but fewer than 10% are currently treated. This new approach by large companies, therefore, helps to counter the criticism levelled at the industry that it is ignoring rare diseases. The dynamics of the market will also change as a result of these moves, since companies like Genzyme Corporation, which specialize in treatments for rare diseases, will begin to feel the competition from the pharmaceutical giants.

Another survival strategy for large companies which are exposed to generic competition is to adopt the "if you can't beat them, join them" approach. In other words, the major biopharmaceutical companies have acquired generic drug manufacturers in order to exploit the increasingly lucrative market for off-patent drugs. Novartis, in the form of its Sandoz generics unit, was one of the first to get involved in this and now other major companies have followed suit. This strategy is also being used to penetrate emerging markets, one example being GSK's partnership with South Africa's Aspen Pharmacare. This provides GSK with exposure to the African market through sales of both patented and generic products.

17.1.2.4 The Internet and Drug Discovery

Computers and the Internet are now integral parts of many people's lives; it is, therefore, not surprising that the biopharmaceutical industry is interested in harnessing these electronic resources to increase the efficiency of its scientific and business operations. IT has applications in every stage of drug discovery, from basic science, regulatory procedures and clinical trials, through to direct sales and marketing. The World Wide Web is essentially a networking tool, like earlier communication systems, such as the Victorian postal service or the telephone. The difference, of course, is its speed and global reach; the Internet makes geographical locations and time zones irrelevant. Many articles have been written about the evolution of the World Wide Web, from the static pages of Web 1.0 to the interactivity of Web 2.0, brought about by fast broadband connections and software, such as JavaScript and XML. Tim O'Reilly, who promoted the idea of Web 2.0 (http://www.oreillynet.com/pub/a/oreilly/tim/news/2005/09/30/what-is-web-20.html, Accessed 4 Dec 2010), has described it as "harnessing collective intelligence". The Web's latest manifestation is Web 3.0, or "the semantic Web", in which much of the process of gathering and interpreting information is automated through new software. Another concept that has been widely discussed is that of cloud computing, in which individual computers are just devices for linking to the Internet; all programmes and data files are held on remote servers. The basic idea is to turn networked computing into a utility, just like electricity or water. One of the reasons for thinking along these lines is the vast amount of data that are being generated worldwide for many different activities.

For drug discovery, there are large databases containing the results of biological and chemical experiments that can be "mined" for new insights into diseases, targets and compounds. The amount of electronic information is enormous, and growing all the time; for example, DNA sequencing projects alone will soon begin to accumulate petabytes of data (10^{15} bytes) that must be stored and analyzed.

It has to be admitted that some of these IT initiatives are surrounded by a certain amount of "over enthusiasm", but there can be no doubt those who champion them make things happen and provide genuinely useful tools for work and leisure. Many readers routinely use Google to search for information, and I am grateful for the secure backup of my computer's data (including the manuscript of this book) on remote servers. The following examples illustrate the ways in which modern IT and networking can make an impact on the science and business of drug discovery.

Diseases and Drug Targets

Large amounts of biological and chemical data relating to diseases, drugs and drug targets are available for interrogation by anyone with access to a computer and Internet connection. So long as the user has some idea of how to use the information to create hypotheses about new drug targets, this approach could be extremely productive. The SAGE organization provides an example of how this might work in practice (http://sagebase.org, Accessed 4 Dec 2010). It was founded by former Merck scientists to identify new drug targets, or diagnostics, by analyzing genetic and cell biology data (e.g. from gene expression microarrays). This can be undertaken by bionetwork teams directly associated with SAGE, or be offered to anyone who can extract value from them via the "SAGE Commons". Such a precompetitive approach to drug target discovery is quite different to that normally taken by biopharmaceutical companies, where they try to exclude the competition at this early stage through secrecy and patent protection.

Distributed computing, also known as grid computing, is a key part of "eScience", in which professional computer networks are employed to analyze scientific data from sources like the Large Hadron Collider or astronomical observatories. It is also used in drug discovery to analyze the structures of proteins and their interactions with small molecules. Distributed computing is based on the spare processing capacity of the millions of personal computers used on a daily basis by individuals and organizations. When coordinated by a centralized facility, the result is massive computing power that can be used to tackle problems, ranging from the search for extraterrestrial life (SETI@home initiative), to virtual drug discovery. One of the latter projects, run at the University of Oxford from 2001 to 2007, involved the networking of over 3.5 million PCs in more than 200 countries. Over the period of the project, billions of virtual small molecules were screened *in silico* (see Chap. 9) against a range of protein targets for cancer and other diseases. The fraction of "active" compounds in the computer that actually worked in the laboratory was about 10%, which is significantly higher than the rate found with random screening (http://www.chem.ox.ac.uk/cancer/news.html, Accessed 4 Dec 2010).

Clinical Trials and Pharmacovigilance

Electronic data capture for clinical trial investigators and regulators is an obvious area in which modern IT can play a major role; it eliminates wasteful paperwork and presents data in a form that can be readily analyzed using appropriate software. In 2009, the US government provided $19 billion for healthcare information management, with the objective of computerizing all of the country's medical records within 5 years (Tang and Lee 2009). This creates a massive resource of electronic health records (EHRs) that can be collated by the clinician. There is also an emerging realization that the tools of Internet networking could allow patients to provide their own information. Patient support groups have existed for a long time, but now it is possible to use online resources to reach many more people in similar situations and to receive advice and support from anywhere in the world. Patients and clinicians collaborate to produce personal health records (PHRs) which can then be used for different purposes, including recruitment for clinical trials. The commercial opportunities of kind of healthcare information have not been lost on the IT giants Microsoft and Google, who have launched PHR management systems, called HealthVault and GoogleHealth, respectively.

Social networking is one of the hallmarks of the modern Internet with Facebook, Twitter, YouTube and similar sites creating global connections between individuals on an unprecedented scale. They also provide the means for biopharmaceutical companies, or disease advocacy groups, to identify patients who would be willing to participate in clinical trials. Given the slow pace of conventional drug development, some patient groups sponsor their own clinical trials, knowing that they can easily find the patients they need. One example is the online study of Parkinson's disease genetics sponsored by the personal genetics company 23andme and the co-founder of Google, Sergey Brin (https://www.23andme.com/pd/, Accessed 4 Dec 2010). The idea is to tap into a resource of 10,000 patients who are not restricted to one geographical location and to collect large amounts of personal medical information which can be analyzed using computer search algorithms. These social networking approaches appear to be well suited for pharmacovigilance studies, since patients who experience adverse drug reactions to marketed medicines can easily report this online. This provides a powerful resource for clinicians if other health and lifestyle information is included as well, because they can then analyze the data to identify both high risk and beneficial activities (Boguski et al. 2009).

Finally, the increasing sales of smart phones and tablet computers allow software developers to create "Apps" that can be used for almost anything, including patient recruitment for clinical trials. In a recent example of this (2010), GSK oncology has teamed up with the US company MedTrust Online to provide an iPhone App which allows patients to locate the nearest clinical trials for 12 different cancers. Internet networking undoubtedly reduces bottlenecks in the clinical and regulatory process and also provides tools for marketing drugs to doctors and consumers. The negative side of this revolution is the overload of information, poor quality of much online material and the invasion of personal privacy; but the genie is out of the bottle and cannot be put back.

17.1.3   The Future of Drug Discovery

Predicting the future for anything is fraught with hazards; to use Benjamin Franklin's observation: "In this world nothing can be said to be certain, except death and taxes." However, when it comes to the biopharmaceutical industry and the technicalities of drug discovery, it is possible to make an informed guess about what might happen over the next decade or so because the results of actions taken now may only be felt years later. For example, the impact of genomics and related technologies on the practice of drug discovery is only beginning to make a real impact, almost two decades after its adoption by the industry. One of the most talked about aspects of the biopharmaceutical industry is how declining productivity will affect the major companies. These conversations are along the lines of: "end of the blockbuster model which will lead to the fragmentation of large companies, who may give up discovery research altogether to concentrate on clinical trials and marketing". I can recall these same conversations over 20 years ago, but this fragmentation has yet to happen; in fact, the opposite has occurred with increasing M&A activity. I have always been struck by the fact that certain companies were admired for their research or commercial organization, yet somehow they were never emulated by others; changing the internal culture of a company was extremely difficult and tended to happen only as a result of mergers and acquisitions. Despite this conservatism, large pharma companies are now making significant changes to the way they operate internally and present themselves externally to the world. The futures of all organizations involved in drug discovery and development depend upon advances in science and technology. It is reasonable to expect that many technical obstacles will eventually be overcome or sidelined, and we can expect to see some totally novel drug types being introduced into the clinic in the future.

A possible future scenario for drug discovery and development by the biopharmaceutical industry is summarized below:

17.1.3.1   Industry Structures

The major biopharmaceutical companies still have large financial resources despite the decline in productivity. This ensures that they will remain at the top of the "drug discovery tree", since there is no other organization (private or public) that has the ability or willingness to support major drug development programmes on their own. It is unlikely that large pharma will abandon its internal discovery research completely, but it will continue to augment it by forming partnerships and acquiring technology from small biotech companies. The demographics of the industry will change, as China and other BRIC countries contribute more to innovative R&D and increase their share of the market for prescription medicines. Biotech companies, charities and new entrants into drug development, such as software companies, will contribute innovative ideas, but still be hampered by lack of investment. This can only improve if the huge costs of drug discovery and development can be brought down by introducing more efficient and flexible processes at every stage of the pipeline. Since governments, regulators, industry scientists and patient advocacy groups are all aware of this, changes will surely be forthcoming, albeit slowly, and perhaps painfully.

Social Attitudes

The drug discovery industry is making efforts to repair its image problem by becoming more transparent in its dealings with the medical profession and the public. A long running issue has been the perceived lack of interest by western companies in diseases of the developing world, as well as controversies over the pricing of drugs for these markets. These problems may not disappear completely, but new collaborations and business models will be implemented that allow the costs of drug development to be shared between companies and allow cheaper pricing for certain markets. A more fundamental problem relates to how medicines are perceived by an increasingly risk averse society. The remit of the biopharmaceutical industry is to provide safe and effective medicines, but these can never be 100% safe for every patient. The challenge for drug makers will be to ensure that as much as possible is done to minimize risk, through technology and post-marketing surveillance, while at the same time trying to educate the public about the risk versus benefits in a completely open way. Another problem is the public's perception of the so-called lifestyle drugs being introduced to treat diseases that supposedly do not really exist. It could be argued that drugs are being developed for conditions that could be prevented by simply maintaining a healthy lifestyle.

The future will see the drug discovery industry attempting to overcome its image problems by being much more transparent about its products and procedures by using dedicated Web sites or social media. In addition, the companies increasingly enter into alliances with organizations that promote individual health and well being. This is, in a sense, similar to the situation with electricity companies that promote energy savings measures; it seems counter-intuitive to encourage customers to use less of your product, but this is how the business world is changing in response to its highly vocal customers.

17.1.3.2 Science and Technology

An examination of the very early part of the drug discovery pipeline should provide clues about the sort of products that will enter the clinic several years later. There is no doubt that the market share of biologicals will increase, with a significant number of fully humanized antibodies being launched to treat serious diseases. These products affect drug targets that lie on the surface of cells, or are dissolved in blood; this means that they are actually missing a large number of targets that lie within the cell, so there will still be a need for small molecule drug discovery. New methods of chemical synthesis will be important for increasing chemical space; luckily, new methods are being developed on a regular basis, including methods that won their discoverers the 2010 Nobel Prize in Chemistry. Computer-aided drug design will be another important area of research; the more that is understood about how small molecules bind to proteins, the better the *in silico* design programmes will be at creating active molecules. Direct interference with gene expression will also have an impact on drug discovery, if the problems of delivering siRNAs, or other nucleic acid drugs, into human tissues can be overcome. The first fully approved clinical trial of stem cells is underway at the time of writing, so if the technology can be shown to fulfil its promise, the landscape of drug development could be significantly changed. The time frame for this will not be short, however, as safety and ethical issues, let alone demonstration of efficacy, will add years to these programmes.

There are many more scientific issues in drug discovery, including personalized medicine, which will advance if genetic associations with responses to medicines are properly validated. So far, only a few pharmacogenetic tests have been introduced into clinical practice, but the number will certainly increase over the years.

Over the much longer term, the elusive problem of how human (and other) biology actually works at the finest level of detail may be solved using a combination of experiment and mathematical theory. Maybe one day, it will be possible to predict biological behaviour with the same degree of accuracy as physical behaviour in the natural world and the universe at large. Until then, we must use our imperfect tools the best we can, building on the impressive amount of knowledge that has been gained over the past couple of hundred years and advancing drug discovery through the rest of the twenty-first century.

References

Boguski MS et al (2009) Repurposing with a difference. Science 324:1394–1395

Choi JH et al (2010) Anti-diabetic drugs inhibit obesity-linked phosphorylation of PPARγ by Cdk5. Nature 466:451–456

Executive summary CMR International Pharmaceutical Factbook 2010 (2010). http://science. thomsonreuters.com/m/pdfs/CMR-Factbook_Exec_Sum.pdf. Accessed 4 Dec 2010

Cuarecasas P (2006) Drug discovery in jeopardy. J Clin Investig 116:2837–2842

Eli Lilly Chorus (2010). http://www.choruspharma.com/. Accessed 7 June 2011

Gamo F-J et al (2010) Thousands of chemical starting points for antimalarial lead identification. Nature 465:305–310

Ghofrani HA et al (2006) Sildenafil: from angina to erectile dysfunction to pulmonary hypertension and beyond. Nat Rev Drug Discov 5:689–702

Goodman M (2008) Market watch: pharma industry strategic performance: 2007-2012E. Nat Rev Drug Discov 7:967

Hughes B (2009) 2009 FDA drug approvals. Nat Rev Drug Discov 9:89–92

Merck pipeline (2010). http://www.merck.com/research/pipeline/home.html. Accessed 4 Dec 2010

Munos B (2009) Lessons from 60 years of pharmaceutical innovation. Nat Rev Drug Discov 8:959–968

Rice TW (2006) Treatment of severe sepsis: where next? Current and future treatment approaches after the introduction of drotrecogin alfa. Vasc Health Risk Manage 2:3–18

Schuster D et al (2005) Why drugs fail-a study on side effects in new chemical entities. Curr Pharm Des 11:3545–3559

Tang PC, Lee TH (2009) Your doctor's office or the internet? Two paths to personal health records. N Engl J Med 360:1276–1278

The CMO Market Outlook: Emerging Markets, Key Players and Future Trends Business Monitor International, 2009 (2010). http://store.business-insights.com/Product/the_cmo_market_outlook?productid=BI00025-016. Accessed 4 Dec 2010

The CRO Market Outlook, Business Insights report, 2009 (2010). http://www.globalbusinessinsights.com/content/rbcr0015m.pdf. Accessed 4 Dec 2010

Part V
Professional Interactions with the Drug Discovery Industry

Chapter 18
Technology Transfer Executives

Abstract The next three chapters are written as supplements to the main book, each being written for a defined group of professionals. This chapter focuses on university technology transfer managers and business development executives who offer their products and services to biopharmaceutical companies. Starting with a brief background to technology transfer and pharmaceuticals, the chapter provides a series of suggestions on how to prepare for a meeting with pharmaceutical executives and how to conduct the meeting itself. These suggestions are based on the author's own experiences in dealing with these meetings from both sides of the negotiating table.

18.1 Introduction

The biopharmaceutical industry directly employs hundreds of thousands of people worldwide, but there are also large numbers of people who deal with the industry from the outside. This book has been written as a guide for anyone who is professionally or personally interested in the complex business of drug discovery. The next three chapters are, however, dedicated to the aspects of the biopharmaceutical industry that are relevant to specific groups of professionals, namely, technology transfer managers, recruitment consultants and technical translators or interpreters.

18.1.1 Background to Technology Transfer

The modern era of government-supported science (at least in the USA) was heralded by Vannevar Bush's 1945 report to the US government entitled "Science – The Endless Frontier". His recognition of the importance of science in post-war society encouraged the idea of technology transfer and even spawned the term "basic research" (Pielke 2010). The passing of the University and Small Business

E.D. Zanders, *The Science and Business of Drug Discovery: Demystifying the Jargon*, DOI 10.1007/978-1-4419-9902-3_18, © Springer Science+Business Media, LLC 2011

Patent Procedures Act (Bayh–Dole Act) in the USA in 1980 meant that public research organizations (PROs) were allowed to benefit financially from the patenting of government-funded research. This Act, and the later Federal Technology Transfer Act of 1986 (FTTA), has made technology transfer a key factor in the development of a knowledge-based economy in the USA. The benchmarks for success in technology transfer include the number of licensing deals with companies and the revenues generated for the PROs. The US National Institutes of Health (NIH) for example, generated revenues of $97 million in 2008 and executed 259 licences the same year. It has about 3,500 patents and over 400 of its products have reached the market since 1987, including 25 FDA-approved drugs (Rohrbaugh and Stanton 2009).

The UK has arguably always operated under a Bayh–Dole like system without feeling the need to enshrine this in statute. Universities own IP generated from grant funding because funded scientists are employees of the host institution. In the 1980s, the Thatcher government encouraged public sector research organizations (PSREs) to systematically replace government support with private income, including income from IP.

Other countries have their own laws to cover the patenting of university research, but this is not consistent, and the European Union does not as yet have its own version of the Bayh–Dole Act. Whether the larger number of spinout companies produced by the US universities compared with the rest of the world is a consequence of this legislation is a matter of debate, but it clearly must have made some impact. It is amusing to note, however, that identical complaints about "having plenty of home-grown Nobel Prize winners but none of the commercial benefits" can be heard on both sides of the Atlantic.

The commercialization of university research is generally managed by dedicated offices within the university, or by companies set up for the purpose. In practice, technology transfer groups broker deals with companies to licence IP generated by a university or spinout company. Interestingly, a recent study of the US academics who had formed their own companies concluded that a higher proportion were founded on non-patented knowledge rather than patented IP. This is because much of the company activity is related to non-IP issues, such as consultancy and related activities (Finia et al. 2010).

Some of the pharmaceutical products that have been generated significant royalties for the NIH in 2009 are listed in Table 18.1.

18.1.2   Some Practical Considerations

Some practical tips for dealing with pharmaceutical companies are laid out in the following sections. These are not intended as a guide to the negotiation of licensing terms or to any of the financial and legal activities associated with technology transfer. The only exception to this is to remind readers that when negotiating terms for a pharmaceutical invention, the length of patent protection may be considerably

Table 18.1 List of drugs, diagnostics and procedures that generated significant royalties for the NIH in 2009 (NIH Office of Technology Transfer 2010)

Name	Category
HPV vaccines	Biological
Novel protease inhibitor for treatment of drug-resistant HIV-1	Small molecule
Proteosome inhibitor for treatment of multiple myeloma	–
Paclitaxel as a cancer treatment	–
Serological detection of antibodies to HIV-1	Diagnostic
DNA probe for breast cancer diagnosis	–
Laser capture micro-dissection	Technology
Purified transforming growth factor beta (TGF-beta)	Reagent
Neutrophil chemotactic factor (IL-8)	–

Some of these were discovered many years previously and turned into marketed products by industry before a share of the profits could be returned to the NIH

shorter when compared with other high technology products; this is a consequence of the long development times before a drug reaches the market (Chap. 16).

18.1.2.1   The View from the Client Company

Because large pharmaceutical companies have significant financial resources, there is no shortage of outside visitors who have something to sell to them. These visitors range from representatives of laboratory supply companies to managers from biotech companies and university technology transfer offices. Sometimes, a visitor may be a private individual trying to sell their "discovery" to the company. Some of these visitors can turn out to be quite bizarre. I recall having to test a sample delivered by the son of a Nigerian witch doctor who claimed that it would cure a whole range of unrelated diseases. Quite how this got through the door I do not know, but a herbal mixture dissolved in gin was duly delivered to us in a used bleach bottle for testing in various *in vitro* assays. Not surprisingly, this led nowhere, but it does demonstrate that pharmaceutical company managers have a sense of humour.

Identifying the needs of the client/customer and then satisfying it with products or services is, of course, central to sales and marketing. It is, therefore, logical when approaching a pharmaceutical company to ensure that their way of thinking is understood from the outset. Some companies make this very straightforward by proactively seeking out new products at clearly defined stages of development. These products may be compounds/biologicals for particular diseases areas, or novel technologies in chemistry, biology or IT. This approach ensures that time is not wasted in trying to sell anything outside the core wish list (which might take the form of a printed brochure). In most cases, however, the university or other inventor will have developed something that they feel will interest a drug company and, therefore, approaches will be made to the company on that basis. This is entirely reasonable, but it is important that the questions that will be raised by company scientists are fully anticipated in advance. Many of the key topics are related to material covered in this book and could include the following:

New Compounds or Biologicals

It is assumed that the basic criteria of potency and selectivity will have been established, at least in a relevant *in vitro* test. Has activity been demonstrated in an animal model of the disease? A convincing demonstration of such activity attracts immediate interest, but sometimes this is not possible if the target is different in animals and humans; extra effort, therefore, has to be made to show that the drug has a reasonable chance of working in the clinic. Assuming that the target and disease is of interest to the company (as established by prior research by the visitor), the compounds themselves will come under great scrutiny. A medicinal chemist will identify functional groups within the molecule that are likely to cause problems during development. These problems may include difficulty of synthesis, scale up of the compound itself, poor pharmacokinetics, or potential toxicity. Certain classes of compounds are known to cause specific side effects, so may need to be avoided. If the university or spinout does not have access to medicinal chemistry expertise, it should employ a consultant chemist to check the compounds before attempting to contact a company. If the compound looks really promising, it may be submitted to a contract research organization for some basic metabolism studies and even some preliminary toxicology, such as an Ames test. The problem facing the inventor is that money has to be spent up front to provide these data and improve the chances that the compound will find a buyer. The academic community understandably does not see itself as a drug development company and in any case, it has limited resources. Unfortunately, companies have to apply very stringent criteria for compound selection because of the high failure rate of small molecule drug development. This creates a high hurdle for the university to overcome, so whatever the outcome some serious money will have been spent. The irony is that the pharmaceutical company will spend the money all over again as it repeats each test prior to committing a drug candidate to full clinical development.

The main issues when dealing with biologicals relate to manufacturing and drug delivery. Serious consideration has to be made of the costs involved in producing novel drug types, such as gene expression inhibitors and stem cells. Because these technologies are so new, it will be some time before companies feel able to commit the resources necessary to bring them to market. The adoption of monoclonal antibodies as drugs is a good example of how biological products were viewed by pharmaceutical companies. Once a small number of pioneer companies demonstrated the commercial viability of this technology, momentum built up among the other companies to get involved as well. This was the "herd mentality" in action because nobody wanted to miss out on the potential blockbuster revenues. In the case of nucleic acid drugs and stem cells, the first clinical trials are only just underway. It will, therefore, be several years before pharmaceutical companies will be as comfortable with these drugs as they were with antibodies at the end of the 1990s.

New Processes

Fashions in pharmaceutical technology transfer come and go. One year it may be for clinical development candidates and the next for platform technologies, sometimes it is about 50:50. A few points are made in this section about technologies as opposed to drug molecules.

Technical advances in nanotechnology for drug delivery, or stem cell creation from adult tissues, for example, will be of great interest to companies, but the technology will have limited upfront value. If they become standard techniques with full IP protection, however, their value will be greatly increased because everyone who wants to use them will only be able to do so under licence. This was the case with the patents for antibody humanization held by the Medical Research Council (MRC) in the UK (MRC and therapeutic antibodies 2010). In fact, the MRC has delivered over £500 million in revenues through the sale of equity in spinout companies and licensing revenue, largely due to its pioneering antibody technology.

When it comes to the process of drug development, the biopharmaceutical industry has to reduce the number of clinical trials that fail because the drug candidate lacks efficacy or has problems with ADMET. There may also be problems with manufacturing and formulation, so there are plenty of opportunities for selling improved processes to industry; these could range from chemical synthesis to streamlining clinical development. It is worth noting that the later stages of clinical development are highly regulated and, therefore, less flexible when it comes to the introduction of new technology. Those selling technologies may have more success with products that affect earlier stages of drug development, for example preclinical toxicology, where there is a great need to replace the animal models in current use. The key message for anyone who wishes to provide products and services to the drug discovery industry is that: research moves fast and regulation much more slowly.

18.1.2.2 Getting a Foot in the Door

The following observations on arranging and conducting a meeting with pharmaceutical companies are based on my personal experience from being on "both sides of the table". These may be considered to be highly subjective and a statement of the obvious, but it does no harm to set them out as a reminder. As in all business, personal contacts within the client organization are invaluable. Senior executives often prove to be the best conduits to the part of the company that might be interested in a product or technology. I have often received letters from external organizations that were sent initially to a senior Research Director. The letter would be passed to me and accompanied by a request to "look into the proposal". Given the provenance of the request, this is a guaranteed way to ensure that the work is thoroughly assessed and critically reviewed. Major collaborations with academic groups often emerge from conversations between the relevant professor and a senior company executive. Although it helps to have the buy-in of more junior staff, the final decision to proceed is generally made at the top.

Senior company executives are highly visible even if their personal contact details are not made public (the use of animals in research being part of the reason). There may be situations where it is more appropriate to contact other people within the organization. Many companies have university liaison managers who should circulate proposals around the relevant departments. This generally works well, but there is a danger that the documents will be passed to someone who has neither the time nor the inclination to look at it within a short time frame. Sometimes, negotiations with large companies can appear to move at the speed of the glaciers. The ideal situation is to target an individual or group who is most likely to be interested in the proposal, but this is more easily said than done; where do you start? Large pharmaceutical companies are not homogeneous entities but are made up of hundreds of different groups, each with a different culture relating to the opinions and personalities of the people who work in them. Sometimes, the groups work together harmoniously and at other times are in competition. The recent reorganizations of large pharma companies that were designed to create a more entrepreneurial culture should make it easier to identify the right group to target. Many company scientists publish in scientific journals that are freely searchable on the Internet; failing that, company patents contain the names of individual scientists who have contributed to the work, so online patent searches for companies or topics could pay dividends. Finally, general Internet searches using names or companies may pick up useful leads from online conference agendas or social/business networking sites.

18.1.2.3 Conducting the Meeting

Busy pharmaceutical executives or scientists generally do not like being taken away from their work to listen to outsiders pitching for business. They are also engrained with a large dose of cynicism, brought on by listening to claims that the products are "the greatest thing since sliced bread". Long experience with the realities of drug development has made those who evaluate the proposals more probing with their questioning than might perhaps be the case elsewhere. I had direct experience of this the first time I presented my research to a company research management committee. I had to keep justifying the use of certain biological tests that I used in my experiments, even though these were considered standard procedures in academia.[1] After my initial feeling of annoyance at the relentless questioning, I began to accept that this was not going to go away, so for future presentations I thought carefully about every experiment and interpretation in advance to prepare myself for any

---

[1] Comparisons of the academic and business worlds sometimes feature the stiletto knife that goes silently into the back of the victim so it is not noticed until it is too late. In industry the attack is made from the front, so at least you know exactly who delivered the blow.

awkward questions. If this can happen with a research manager in a large pharma company, it is also likely to occur with a visitor trying to sell/licence a product or service, so rigorous planning is essential. Other things to bear in mind are:

- Getting the company name right
  With all the mergers and acquisitions, the name of the company may have changed since your last visit. Having visitors talk about "Glaxo" when the company is Glaxo Wellcome or GlaxoSmithKline is potentially annoying if you used to work for Wellcome or SmithKline Beecham.

- Do not tell the company that they are doing everything the wrong way
  I have had to deal with combative visitors who are openly aggressive in their criticism of how the company operates. Even if this were true, it does not bode well for any future collaboration. Similarly, getting angry and defensive if your idea is not received enthusiastically does not help. I have been close to a fight after one particularly irate visitor tried to grab the notes of the meeting out of my hands because he was worried about what I might have written down.

- Keep to time
  For better or for worse, scientists and managers in large pharma companies spend a great deal of time in meetings. Most of the scientists who are evaluating a proposal will also have experiments running in their labs and could therefore be keen to leave the meeting at the earliest opportunity. This means that the presentation must be planned to convey the maximum amount of relevant information in the minimum amount of time. This is all part of developing good presentation skills through meticulous preparation and keeping the number of PowerPoint slides (if used) to a minimum. There are also danger points to be noted, for example, when personal reminiscences start to take up too much of the allotted time.

18.1.2.4 The "Not Invented Here" Syndrome

The reluctance of companies to bring in inventions from the outside because of the perceived competition with internal programmes can be a real problem. However, the "not invented here" syndrome is less likely to occur with drug candidates than with technical processes, such as drug design or chemical synthesis. A significant percentage of in-licensed drugs now feed the pipelines of major companies because of their more open attitude towards external providers. Where there is a problem with internal acceptance, the solution is not always easy to find; it depends on the particular technology and the personalities involved in the discussions. Since the company will probably be reluctant to sideline its own research groups, the ideal solution is to establish formal collaborations between external and internal groups to allow a share of the credit for any future success.

References

Finia R et al (2010) Inside or outside the IP system? Business creation in academia. Res Policy 39:1060–1069

MRC and therapeutic antibodies (2010). http://www.mrc.ac.uk/Achievementsimpact/Storiesofimpact/Therapeuticantibodies/index.htm. Accessed 4 Dec 2010

NIH Office of Technology Transfer (2010). http://www.ott.nih.gov/about_nih/FY2009top20.aspx. Accessed 4 Dec 2010

Pielke R (2010) In retrospect: Science – the endless frontier. Nature 466:922–923

Rohrbaugh ML, Stanton BR (2009) Technology transfer at the National Institutes of Health. In: Ganguli P, Khanna R, Prickril B (eds) Technology transfer at the National Institutes of Health, in Technology transfer in biotechnology: a global perspective. Wiley-VCH, Weinheim

Chapter 19
Recruitment Executives

Abstract This short chapter is written for recruitment executives who work with pharmaceutical industry clients. Most of the job descriptions and backgrounds to different areas of work have been covered in the main part of the book. The intention here is to summarize this information as a series of figures which list the job categories and titles as they relate to the drug discovery pipeline.

19.1 Introduction

The sheer number of employees working for the global drug discovery industry means that there is always a need for specialist pharmaceutical recruiting agencies. Many of the large pharmaceutical companies are undergoing major structural changes, due in part, to a significant reduction of revenues generated by their best-selling products as their patent protection comes to an end. The result is a spate of reorganizations and efficiency drives that inevitably lead to job losses; these fuel the labour market with scientists and managers who are moving from job to job (voluntarily or otherwise). The increased globalization of the industry also means that there are large numbers of qualified personnel in China, India and other growing economies; this clearly has an impact upon recruitment in western nations.

Another change in the world of recruitment is the rise of the Internet and online networking. Social and business networking sites in particular are being enthusiastically embraced by recruiters who can advertize their presence to thousands of candidates (and check out their Facebook activities). For example, the group Recruitment Consultants has over 55,000 members on the business network LinkedIn (http://www.linkedin.com/groups?gid=52762, Accessed 20 Jan 2011) and its specialist groups, one of which I manage, has a significant number of pharmaceutical recruiters. The intense competition for clients and candidates, along with the global reach of online

E.D. Zanders, *The Science and Business of Drug Discovery: Demystifying the Jargon*, DOI 10.1007/978-1-4419-9902-3_19, © Springer Science+Business Media, LLC 2011

communication, means that more than ever before, the recruitment agencies need knowledgeable personnel to ensure the success of their business. It is obviously important that their consultants and managers should have a reasonable understanding of the work required for each job specification and the type of individual who would be suitable for the role. The purpose of this chapter is simply to list the job titles and functions that are encountered by pharmaceutical recruiters since it is hoped that this book has already provided enough background information. The titles and job functions are listed next to the various sections of the drug discovery pipeline in Figs. 19.1–19.5.

Fig. 19.1 Some representative examples of senior management roles associated with each part of the drug discovery pipeline. The titles vary according to the terminology followed by a particular company or country, for example, Head of, Director of, VP, etc

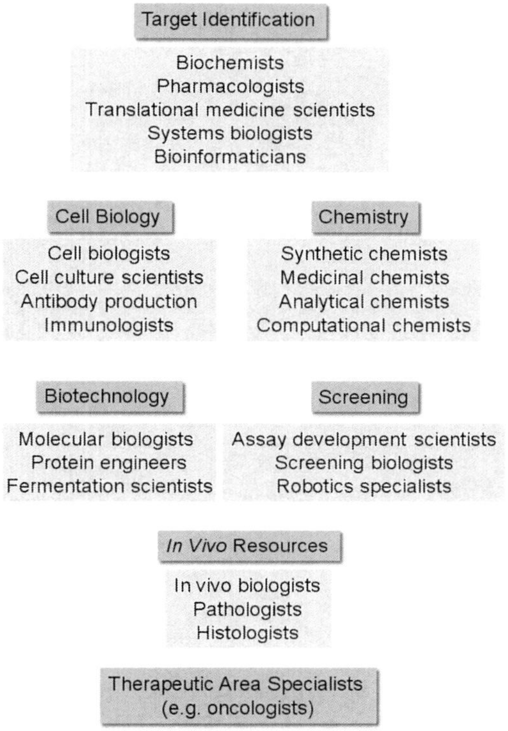

Fig. 19.2 Job roles associated with early drug discovery. This list is not exhaustive because of the wide variety of titles that scientists give themselves (genomics and proteomics are not included, for example). Some of the roles also apply to the later stages of drug development, particularly *in vivo* work

Target Identification

Biochemists
Pharmacologists
Translational medicine scientists
Systems biologists
Bioinformaticians

Cell Biology

Cell biologists
Cell culture scientists
Antibody production
Immunologists

Chemistry

Synthetic chemists
Medicinal chemists
Analytical chemists
Computational chemists

Biotechnology

Molecular biologists
Protein engineers
Fermentation scientists

Screening

Assay development scientists
Screening biologists
Robotics specialists

In Vivo Resources

In vivo biologists
Pathologists
Histologists

Therapeutic Area Specialists
(e.g. oncologists)

Fig. 19.3 Preclinical development job titles. The abbreviation DMPK is "drug metabolism pharmacokinetics"

GLP Assay Development

Quality assurance (QA) managers
Assay development scientists
(biologists, analytical chemists)

Safety Pharmacology & Toxicology

Pharmacologists
Toxicologists
Pathologists
Histologists

Chemical Development

'Qualified person'
Manufacturing chemists
Process chemists

Pharmacokinetics

DMPK scientists

Pharmaceutical Development

Formulation pharmacists
Pharmaceutical chemists

Patents and Trademarks

Patent attorneys

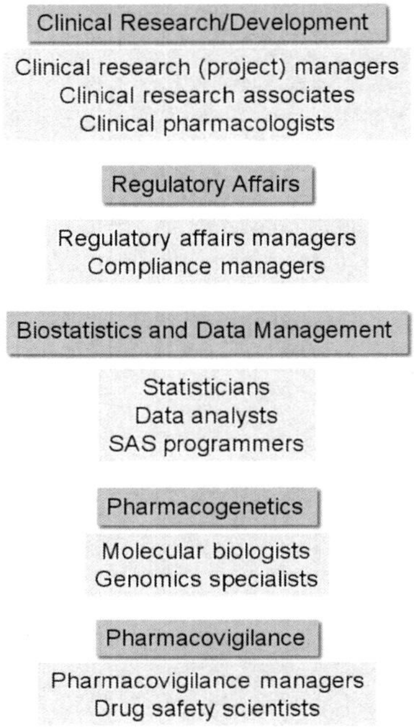

Fig. 19.4 Clinical development job titles. SAS programmers (in the Biostatistics section) use the industry standard statistical software package from the SAS Institute in the USA

Clinical Research/Development

Clinical research (project) managers
Clinical research associates
Clinical pharmacologists

Regulatory Affairs

Regulatory affairs managers
Compliance managers

Biostatistics and Data Management

Statisticians
Data analysts
SAS programmers

Pharmacogenetics

Molecular biologists
Genomics specialists

Pharmacovigilance

Pharmacovigilance managers
Drug safety scientists

Fig. 19.5 Sales and marketing roles

Marketing Communications

Medical affairs manager
Medical writers

Healthcare Economics

Strategic pricing executive
Health economist
Health outcomes executive

Sales Force

Territory Sales Manager
Sales representative

Chapter 20
Pharmaceutical Translators and Interpreters

Abstract The last of the supplementary chapters covers the specific requirements of pharmaceutical translators and interpreters. There are many aspects of drug discovery and development that may require the services of these professionals, but the majority concern regulatory and other documents produced during clinical trials and marketing. After briefly reviewing the types of documents which translators may encounter during the course of their work, the remainder of the chapter deals with the electronic documentation required for the EMA's Summary of Product Characteristics and Patient Information Leaflets. Finally, some links to online resources on terminology are provided to supplement those already given in previous chapters (e.g. on drug nomenclature in Chap. 2).

20.1 Introduction

The global nature of the biopharmaceutical industry, combined with the mountain of paperwork involved at almost every level of drug development, ensures that there is always work for pharmaceutical translators. However, translation of medical and regulatory material carries with it a great responsibility, since any misunderstanding arising from inaccurate translation of a key document could have serious consequences.

Someone once said that the language of science is broken English. Since the USA is the largest market for prescription medicines, it is no surprise that the language of pharmaceuticals is intact US English. Despite the fact that English is still being spoken by a clear majority, the demographics of the USA are changing. Data collected by the US Census Bureau's American Community Survey for 2006–2008 reveal that in a population of 280,564,877 aged 5 years and over, 80.4% spoke only English. The remaining 19.6% was broken down into Spanish or Spanish Creole (12.2%), other Indo-European languages (3.7%), Asian and Pacific Island languages (2.9%) and "other languages" (0.8%). This last figure may be a small proportion of the total, but it still represents nearly two and a quarter million people (US Census Bureau 2010).

E.D. Zanders, *The Science and Business of Drug Discovery: Demystifying the Jargon*,   363
DOI 10.1007/978-1-4419-9902-3_20, © Springer Science+Business Media, LLC 2011

The second largest market is the European Union (EU), which recognizes 23 official languages. Europe has over 60 minority or regional languages, a number that will surely increase as EU membership expands.

Lastly, in the Asia Pacific region, China, India and South Korea are emerging as rivals to Japan in the pharmaceuticals marketplace. This means that the demand for translations from these native languages can only increase.

20.1.1   Translation Challenges

Technical translators are expected to understand the correct terminology displayed in English and to preserve the exact meaning in translation. Unfortunately, there are difficulties from the outset, since clear differences exist between the US English and British English as well as English usage by the UK regulators (MHRA) and the EMA. Some pharmaceutical and medical phraseology is specific to individual languages, but this book covers American or British usage only. Readers who seek to understand how particular terms are used during the drug development process should by now have obtained much of the information they need from the main chapters of this book. The problem for translators lies, however, in the fact that the borderline between correct and colloquial usage of some technical words and phrases is quite blurred. Questions along these lines get raised frequently during the courses that I run for freelance translators and they can give me a few headaches. For example, "what is the difference between a side effect and an adverse drug reaction?" The term "side effect" is a catch-all phrase used to describe a series of negative reactions to a medicine that are known in advance. Adverse drug reactions (ADRs) are any noxious and unintended response associated with the use of a drug in humans. This difference, while not great, is still significant, so the context is important. There may, however, be particular usage guidelines laid down by the originator of the translation, so these obviously have to be followed even if at first sight they might appear to be counter-intuitive.

20.1.2   Types of Documentation

It is impossible to cover all the types of document that a translator is likely to encounter in commissions from the pharmaceutical and biotechnology industries. The nature of the material also depends on the product being manufactured; this could be a branded medicine, a medical device, or a diagnostic test. Like drugs, devices and tests are highly regulated consumer products, where the instructions for their use have to be translated into different languages following European directives.

Figure 20.1 outlines the main types of material that pharmaceutical translators are likely to encounter. The abbreviations are as follows: GLP, GCP, GMP: good laboratory, clinical, manufacturing practice; SOP: standard operating procedure; CMC: chemistry manufacturing and controls; PROs: patient reported outcomes; PIL: patient information leaflet; SPC: summary of product characteristics; EPAR: European Public Assessment Report.

Fig. 20.1 Examples of
different types of
documentation required
throughout the drug
development process.
Although not exhaustive, the
list shows items commonly
encountered by technical
translators. The Research and
Intellectual Property (IP)
section covers the general
themes of biotechnology and
chemical nomenclature, both
of which can occur in many
different documents. Patent
translation, of course, is a
major activity in its own right

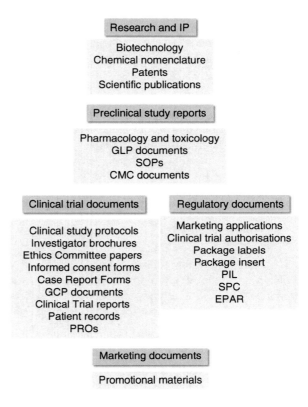

20.1.2.1 Electronic Documents

The key documents required for marketing drugs in the EU are: the SPC or SmPC, labelling information and the PIL. In order to make the process more efficient, the documents are available in electronic form on the EMA Web site and are preformatted in 24 European languages.[1]

How to Find SPCs and PILs for a Particular Medicine

EU-approved SPCs and PILs for a particular medicine can be located on the EMA Web site by accessing the alphabetical list of European Public Assessment Reports for authorized medicinal products for human use (EPARs) using http://www.ema. europa.eu/ema/index.jsp?curl=pages/medicines/landing/epar_search.jsp&murl=menus/ medicines/medicines.jsp&mid=WC0b01ac058001d125. This site is in English only and lists each drug by its trade name. A keyword search button allows searching on Name, INN/Common name/Active substance, Therapeutic indication/Pharmaco

[1] The contribution of Rebekah Fowler to this section is gratefully acknowledged.

Therapeutic Group or ATC Code (Anatomical Therapeutic Chemical Classification System). The SPC and PIL for a given medicine (in various the EU languages) are located by first finding the drug name, using the above link.

Notes

The INN has already been referred to in Chap. 2 in connection with drug nomenclature. A downloadable pdf file from the WHO containing detailed guidelines for using INNs is available from reference (WHO Guidelines for INNs 2011). The Anatomical Therapeutic Chemical (ATC) classification is a WHO-sponsored system that groups drugs in a hierarchy, beginning with the target organ system and then continuing with chemical class, etc. (ATC Classification system 2011). It is used for the statistical analysis of drug use across different territories and for the reporting of ADRs.

Example Search

As an example, a search for the biotherapeutic Herceptin® brings up the EPAR page which links to the EPAR Summary for the public (and at the bottom), to the SPC. Here, the SPC and PIL are available, in several European languages, as sections within the following five annexes from the downloadable pdf document:

Annex I – Summary of Product Characteristics
Annex IIA – Manufacturing Authorization Holder responsible for Batch Release
Annex IIB – Conditions of the Marketing Authorization
Annex IIIA – Labelling
Annex IIIB – Package Leaflet

These documents for specific drugs can be very useful when translating an SPC or PIL for a similar drug or drug type, or more generally to find the correct wording or terminology for a given drug or procedure.

Terminology to be Used in Translating SPCs

For formal pharmaceutical texts, such as the SPC and the PIL, standard product information templates have been prepared by the Quality Review of Documents (QRD) Working Group of the EMA. These set out the required structure of the documents, such as section numbers, headings, fonts and font sizes. They also suggest some standard phrases, such as "Hypersensitivity to the active substance(s) or to any of the excipients <or {residues}>"; extreme care should be taken to follow these templates, even the style or terminology used does not seem to be correct. The only exception would be if the source text deviates significantly from the template in the relevant language. The templates are available in 24 languages and can be downloaded in both English and the working language(s). To access this from the EMA Web site (http://www.ema.europa.eu), follow the links (top or side navigation bar as appropriate) from the Home Page as follows:

Home Page
Regulatory

Human medicines
Product information
Product information templates

The QRD Human Product Information Template v7.3.1 can then be downloaded in the appropriate language. In addition to downloading, the "clean templates" translators can download and use the annotated template and guidance documents that are available in English only.

Standard Terms

It is possible that translators are required to use the "Standard Terms" prescribed in the European Directorate for the Quality of Medicines (EDQM), published by the Council of Europe (Glossary of Standard Terms 2011). This multilingual glossary currently covers 31 languages and is divided into three sections: Pharmaceutical Dosage Forms (including short terms), Routes of Administration and Containers. In general, for any one set of SPC, PIL and labelling for an individual product, only one or two terms are taken from each section.

EU Versus UK Terminology

The UK terminology and style differ somewhat from the EU standards. In general, the British SPCs and PILs follow the same format, but slight differences in terminology and usage may exist. In this case, it is a good idea to cross-check the information available in the EMA templates with any existing SPCs or PILs found at the electronic Medicines Compendium (http://www.medicines.org.uk/emc/). The eMC provides electronic SPCs and PILs, as well as information on thousands of licensed medicines available in the UK.

References

ATC Classification system (2011). http://www.whocc.no/atc/structure_and_principles/. Accessed 7 Jan 2011
Glossary of Standard Terms (2011). http://www.edqm.eu/en/Standard-Terms-590.html. Accessed 21 Jan 2011
US Census Bureau (2010). http://factfinder.census.gov/servlet/STTable?_bm=y&-geo_id=01000US&-qr_name=ACS_2008_3YR_G00_S1601&-ds_name=ACS_2008_3YR_G00_. Accessed 6 Dec 2010
WHO Guidelines for INNs (2011). http://apps.who.int/medicinedocs/pdf/h1806e/h1806e.pdf. Accessed 7 Jan 2011

Appendix 1
Further Reading

Most of the references in the short list at the end of each chapter support a specific item mentioned in the text, rather than a more general theme. This appendix contains a more comprehensive list of printed and online material that will hopefully be of interest to readers, whether they are scientifically trained and want further information about the biopharmaceutical industry, or whether they would like to learn a bit more about the basic science behind drug discovery. It is, of course, possible to access vast amounts of information about drug discovery and development by searching the Internet; there is a great deal of useful material out there and the reader should be able to identify credible work. Unfortunately, when dealing with pharmaceuticals, the incredible can get in the way, particularly with online sources. Authoritative work has generally been scientifically peer reviewed, or at least published by an organization with a good scientific reputation. This does not necessarily mean that every finding is correct, however; science is always moving ahead by overturning pre-existing concepts. A review system that uses the informed opinions of international experts helps to identify errors and to correct them because no one voice (at least in theory) is supposed to dominate the scientific debate.

Accessing the Literature

Literature on the scientific aspects of drug discovery is most easily located by searching PubMed, a freely available database hosted by the US National Library of Medicine (http://www.ncbi.nlm.nih.gov/sites/entrez?db=pubmed).

A search for subjects, authors, journals, etc., brings up a list of abstracts from articles published in scientific and medical journals in printed and/or online formats. The articles can then be downloaded from the Web site of each journal, but most will require a subscription or charge per article. This is obviously not satisfactory for those who are not working for an institution which pays for the journals, but it is possible to find free full-length articles in PubMed. The latter are either made freely available by the journal publisher, or are available from Open Access

E.D. Zanders, *The Science and Business of Drug Discovery: Demystifying the Jargon*, 369
DOI 10.1007/978-1-4419-9902-3, © Springer Science+Business Media, LLC 2011

journals. PubMed Central (listed as PMC in the drop-down list of databases in PubMed) is a collection of scientific and medical articles which are all freely available. Although the PubMed/PMC articles are technical and therefore challenging for non-scientists, it is worth examining how they are structured and how English is used within a scientific context; this is something that could be particularly useful for translators.

There is no shortage of textbooks covering scientific subjects relevant to drug discovery for school or college students; unless the reader is a student of these subjects and therefore issued with appropriate books, it is of course possible to obtain many of them second-hand at bargain prices or to borrow them from a library.

Finally, online video sites, such as YouTube and many educational sites from universities, are extremely helpful in explaining complex science. A search for "polymerase chain reaction", for example, highlights links to animations and even videos of the laboratory procedure, giving non-scientist readers an idea of how these experiments are actually performed in the lab.

References

General Drug Discovery books

This is a series of books that cover (in varying levels of detail for each topic), the main scientific and business aspects of drug discovery and development. Some are aimed at the general reader and others at science students and those studying pharmacy. It is now quite straightforward to browse the contents online to locate information on a topic which may have been highlighted in this book, but not explored in great detail.

Evens R (ed) (2007) Drug and biological development. From molecule to product and beyond. Springer, New York

Chorghade MS (ed) (2006) Drug discovery and development: drug discovery. WileyBlackwell, Hoboken

Chorghade MS (ed) (2007) Drug discovery and development: drug development. WileyBlackwell, Hoboken

Rang HP (2005) Drug discovery and development: technology in transition. Churchill Livingstone, Edinburgh

Bartfal T, Lees G (2006) Drug discovery: from bedside to wall street. Elsevier Academic, Burlington

Ng R (2008) Drugs: from discovery to approval. WileyBlackwell, Burlington

Jacobsen TM, Wertheimer AI (2010) Modern pharmaceutical industry: a primer. Jones & Bartlett Learning, New Delhi

Schacter B (2005) The new medicines: how drugs are created, approved, marketed and sold. Praeger, Westport

Smith CG, O'Donnell JT (eds) (2006) The process of new drug discovery and development, 2nd edn. New York, Informa Healthcare

Campbell JJ (2005) Understanding pharma: a primer on how pharmaceutical companies really work. Pharmaceutical Institute, Raleigh

Case Histories of Drug Discovery

Sneader W (2005) Drug discovery: a history. Wiley, West Sussex
Corey EJ, Czako B, Kurti L (2007) Molecules and medicine. Wiley, Hoboken
Lednicer D (2007) New drug discovery and development. Wiley, Hoboken

Journals and Magazines

The scientific and medical journals with content relating to drug discovery cannot
all be listed here since they are far too numerous. The same applies to pharmaceutical industry magazines and of course the numerous blogs and wikis found online.
The following list contains titles which provide news features and updates on a
regular basis.

Peer Reviewed Journals

Drug Discovery Today
Nature magazine
Nature Reviews Drug Discovery
Proceedings of the National Academy of Sciences (USA)
Science Magazine

Online and Printed Magazines

Biopharm International.
http://digital.findpharma.com/nxtbooks/advanstar/biopharm0910/

Drug Discovery and Development Magazine.
http://www.dddmag.com

Genetic Engineering & Biotechnology News.
http://www.genengnews.com/

in-Pharma Technologist.com.
http://www.in-pharmatechnologist.com/

Inpharm.com.
http://www.inpharm.com/

Pharmtech.com.
http://pharmtech.findpharma.com/pharmtech/

Organizations

Some organizations and regulators, such as the EMA, FDA and ICH, have already been referenced, and there are of course many more throughout the world. The following are repeated here, as they are leading industry sites containing useful facts and figures about the drug discovery business:

The Association of the British Pharmaceutical Industry (ABPI).
http://www.abpi.org.uk/

The Pharmaceutical Research and Manufacturers of America (PhRMA).
http://www.phrma.org/

Chemistry

Royal Society of Chemistry (RSC) Educational resources. The main UK chemistry organization.
http://www.rsc.org/Education/

American Chemical Society (ACS) Education links on main website.
http://www.acs.org

International Union of Pure and Applied Chemistry (IUPAC). Home page
http://www.iupac.org/

Compendium of chemical terminology.
http://old.iupac.org/publications/compendium/A.html

Queen Mary College London compilation.
http://www.chem.qmul.ac.uk/iupac/

Glossary of medicinal chemistry terms.
http://www.chem.qmul.ac.uk/iupac/medchem/

PubChem A US National Library of Medicine database of small molecule structures and links to further information. Use drop down menu to access PubChem compound or PubChem substance.
http://www.ncbi.nlm.nih.gov/sites/entrez?db=pubmed

Chemical Entities of Biological Interest (ChEBI) Small molecule database similar to PubChem.
http://www.ebi.ac.uk/chebi/

Protein structures. RCSB Protein Data Bank educational resources.
http://www.rcsb.org/pdb/static.do?p=education_discussion/educational_resources/index.html

Biotechnology

This heading covers all aspects of biology which are relevant to drug discovery but with an emphasis on modern cell and molecular biology. The references will help fill in details about how proteins are made in the cell using specifications laid down in the genetic code and other technical points that were left out of the main book.

Biotechnology: Textbooks

Lewin B. Genes, vol IX (2007). Jones & Bartlett Learning
Watson JD, Baker TA, Bell SP, Gann A, Levine M, Losick R. Molecular biology of the gene, 6th Edition (2007). Pearson Education
Alberts B, Johnson A, Lewis J, Raff M, Roberts K, Walter P. Molecular biology of the cel, 5th Edition (2008). Garland Science, Taylor and Francis Group

Biotechnology: Online Resources

All about the Human Genome Project. National Human Genome Research Institute (NHGRI).
http://www.genome.gov/10001772

The Sanger Centre. Educational resources.
http://www.yourgenome.org/

Recombinant DNA Factsheet.
http://web.archive.org/web/20070322222148/http://www.unh.edu/ehs/BS/Recombinant-DNA.pdf

Pharmacogenetics/genomics. NHGRI.
http://www.ornl.gov/sci/techresources/Human_Genome/medicine/pharma.shtml

National Institute of General Medical Sciences (NIGMS).
http://publications.nigms.nih.gov/cjs/2007/narr_discover.html

SNPs.
http://www.ornl.gov/sci/techresources/Human_Genome/faq/snps.shtml

Clinical Trials

Applied Clinical Trials.
http://appliedclinicaltrialsonline.findpharma.com/appliedclinicaltrials

Appendix 2
Glossary and External Resources

This appendix is laid out in two sections. The first consists of a small glossary of terms (including some acronyms) derived from all parts of the drug discovery and development process. More terms have been used in the main text and can be located by using the Index.

The second part is designed as a jumping-off point for readers who want to explore online glossaries and lists of abbreviations and acronyms. These are inevitably more comprehensive than anything that could be included in a printed book, and they also have the advantage of being searchable on the computer.

Glossary

ADMET (adsorption, distribution, metabolism, excretion, toxicology) Pharmacokinetic properties of a compound that must be optimized prior to use as a medicine

Agonist A molecule that activates a physiological process by interacting with a target and mimicking the natural ligand

ANDA Accelerated new drug application. Regulatory submission for generic drugs

Antagonist A molecule that blocks a physiological process by interacting with a target and preventing the natural ligand from exerting its effect

API Active pharmaceutical ingredient

Assay The process of testing a chemical sample for activity against a specific target or cellular response

Bioavailability A measurement of the amount of a compound absorbed into the bloodstream

Bioinformatics Bioinformatics is the use of computers to analyze nucleic acid and protein sequence information

Chemoinformatics The use of computers to analyze small chemical molecules

Combinatorial Chemistry The generation of large collections, or "libraries", of compounds by synthesizing all possible combinations of a set of smaller chemical structures or "building blocks"

Cytokines Specialized proteins that allow cells to communicate with each other

DNA (deoxyribonucleic acid) DNA is a chemical compound present in the nucleus of cells. Consists of two strands of polynucleotides entwined in a double helix

Druggable Target These are protein classes that historically have had drugs developed against them. These include cell surface receptors, ion channels and enzymes

EMA European Medicines Agency

Enzyme Complex proteins that are produced by living cells; they catalyze specific biochemical reactions

Excipient Inert product(s) added to APIs to formulate drugs in the correct dosage form

FDA American Food and Drug Administration

Genes The unit of inheritance. Physically present as DNA packaged into 23 pairs of human chromosomes

Genomics The analysis of the full complement of genes in a genome. The human genome contains approximately 23,000 genes

GPCR G protein-coupled receptor

High-Throughput Screening (HTS) Efficient, trial-and-error evaluation of compounds in a target-based assay

Hit Compound A compound that is active in a biological assay, normally a screen. Needs further optimization to become a lead compound

Hormone Messenger molecules that communicate between tissues. Can be small molecules or peptide/proteins

IND Investigational new drug

In Vitro Experiments carried out in cellular systems or on cellular components, such as genes or proteins or sub-cellular fractions

In Vivo Experiments carried out in living organisms

Ion Channels "Holes" in cell membranes that selectively allow transport of charged atoms/molecules (ions)

Lead Compound A compound that exhibits pharmacological or biochemical properties which suggest its value as a starting point for drug development

Ligand A molecule that binds to a receptor. A natural ligand might be a hormone, such as adrenaline

Microplate A standardized plastic tray with 96 (or 384, or 1,536) "wells" or depressions for holding small quantities of material. The 96 wells are uniformly located in 8 rows of 12 wells each

Model Organism/Model System Laboratory grown organism (plant or animal), which is representative of human biology, inexpensive to maintain, and easy to manipulate for the purpose of understanding a complex biological phenomenon

NCE New chemical entity
NDA New drug application
Neurotransmitter Small molecules that transmit signals across nerves
NME New molecular entity

Optimization The process of synthesizing chemical variations, or analogues, of a lead compound, with the goal of creating those compounds with improved pharmacological properties
Orally Active Drugs Drugs that are effective in treating a disease when administered by mouth and absorbed by the digestive system
Organic Molecules Molecules containing the element carbon among the atoms that define its structure

Pathway Very few proteins act in isolation; they usually function by interacting with other molecules along a defined "pathway". These other components of the pathway may be more appropriate for drug discovery
Peptide A molecule composed of two or more amino acids. Larger peptides are generally referred to as polypeptides or proteins
Pharmacogenetics The inherited response to medicines
Pharmacogenomics A genomic approach to pharmacogenetics in which DNA is analyzed to determine sequences which are responsible for individual responses to medicines
Protein A molecule composed of a long chain of amino acids. Proteins are the principal constituents of cellular material. Examples of proteins are enzymes, hormones, structural elements, and antibodies
Protein Therapeutics Protein therapeutics are proteins used as drugs in their own right. They are normally produced artificially using genetic engineering but can be isolated from tissues
Proteomics The equivalent of genomics, but analyzing proteins instead of DNA

Receptor A molecule within a cell or on a cell surface to which a substance (such as a hormone or a drug) selectively binds, causing a change in the activity of the cell

Single Nucleotide Polymorphisms (SNPs) DNA sequences from different individuals show millions of differences of one nucleotide. These polymorphisms can affect protein coding regions and therefore protein structures
Small Molecule A chemical entity having a molecular weight of less than about 700
Specificity Quality of a compound that describes its lack of interaction with targets that are related to the main target of an assay. Compounds with high specificity tend to have fewer side effects

Structure–Activity Relationship (SAR) An analysis which defines the relationship between the structure of a molecule and its ability to affect a biological system

Substrate A molecule on which an enzyme effects a biochemical reaction

Target A target is a protein upon which a drug could act to correct a disease state

Ultra High-Throughput Screening (uHTS) High-throughput screening accelerated to greater than 100,000 tests per day

Validation A demonstration that a protein acts specifically on a cellular or physiological process or pathway that is relevant to human disease

Whole Organism Screens/ *In Vivo* Screens Compounds are screened on animals for their ability to produce measurable responses when the target of interest is affected

Online Glossaries and Lists of Abbreviations

Cambridge Healthtech Institute Pharmaceutical Glossaries & taxonomies A–Z Index.
http://www.genomicglossaries.com/content/gloss_cat.asp

Clinical. Data Interchange Standards Consortium (CDISC) Clinical Research Glossary.
http://www.cdisc.org/stuff/contentmgr/files/0/be650811feb46f381f0af41-ca40ade2e/misc/cdisc_2009_glossary.pdf

ICH E6 R1 Good Clinical Practice. Includes glossary of clinical trial terms.
http://www.ich.org/fileadmin/Public_Web_Site/ICH_Products/Guidelines/Efficacy/E6_R1/Step4/E6_R1__Guideline.pdf

Acronyms and Abbreviations. Applied Clinical Trials online.
http://appliedclinicaltrialsonline.findpharma.com/Acronyms-Abbrvs

Index